United States Air Force Historical Advisory Committee *(As of September 1975)*

Dr. I. B. Holley, Jr.
Duke University

Lt. Gen. James R. Allen
Superintendent, USAF Academy

Dr. Henry F. Graff
Columbia University

Dr. Robert F. Byrnes
Indiana University

Dr. Louis Morton
Dartmouth College

Lt. Gen. Albert P. Clark
USAF (ret.)

Dr. Forest C. Pogue
Director, Dwight D. Eisenhower Institute for Historical Research

Lt. Gen. Raymond B. Furlong
Commander, Air University

Mr. Jack Stempler
General Counsel, USAF

Office of Air Force History

Maj. Gen. John W. Huston
Chief

Stanley L. Falk
Chief Historian

Carl Berger
Chief, Histories Division

Max Rosenberg
Deputy Chief Historian

Lawrence J. Paszek
Senior Editor

Foreword

There has been a tendency to belittle the work of the U.S. Air Service in World War I while singing the praises of heroes like Rickenbacker and Luke. Compared with the bombing of the U.S. Eighth Air Force in World War II or the B–52's in Southeast Asia, the 138 tons of bombs dropped by the U.S. Air Service in France in 1918 may seem almost too insignificant to mention. Any such comparison, however, should not lead to a conclusion that World War I was of little importance in the overall history of the U.S. Air Force.

The U.S. Air Service should be viewed in relationship to its own age. World War I was fought when aviation was still young. The first ace of the U.S. Air Service won his victories in a French plane that had a top speed of about 125 miles per hour and a tendency to shed the fabric of its upper wing in a dive. The American-produced DH–4, used by the 1st Day Bombardment Group, usually carried about 220 pounds of bombs for a mission, which meant a lot of sorties to deliver 138 tons of bombs.

Aviation technology was not always equal to the tasks to be performed. A major goal of the U.S. Air Service, one not attained during the war, was the development of a bomber force capable of hitting strategic objectives in Germany. Targeting for the strategic campaign involved the identification of "a few indispensible targets without which Germany cannot carry on the war"—an idea that would be used years later against Hitler and the Third Reich. Interdiction, close air support, and some other types of missions carried out by the U.S. Army Air Forces in World War II, and by the U.S. Air Force at later times, had already been tried by the U.S. Air Service.

Some documents illustrating various concepts and ideas for the employment of the U.S. Air Service in World War I have been selected for publication in this volume, one of a series being published by the Office of Air Force History.

John W. Huston, Maj. Gen., USAF
Chief, Office of Air Force History

Preface

When the Great War began in Europe in August 1914, aviation in the U.S. Army was a function of the Signal Corps. Its mission was to support infantry and artillery by providing observation services. There were people in the Army and outside who could foresee no other military use for aircraft. Others believed that the airplane should be given a combat role. Some thought that aviation should be a separate combat arm.

As news of aerial operations in the European war drifted across the Atlantic, there was more and more talk of buying fighting planes, battle planes, and bomb-dropping planes for the U.S. Army. Although some faltering steps were taken, little progress was made toward building a fighting air force—or even toward developing observation services for the ground forces—before the United States entered the war in April 1917.

Having joined Great Britain, France, and Italy in war against Germany and Austria, the United States quickly drew plans for an air service to include fighting and bombing airplanes as well as observation planes and balloons. The allies, who had been fighting for two years or more and were much farther advanced in military aviation, provided valuable information to help the United States build up its air service. Allied contributions included not only technical data on new developments in aircraft and other aeronautical equipment but also information on how to use aviation in battle.

One thing borrowed from the allies was the classification of military aviation into three, broad, functional areas labeled "observation," "pursuit," and "bombardment." Another was the concept that aviation had two separate roles, one "tactical," the other "strategical." In addition, the Allies provided ideas, along with detailed information about tactics, techniques, and procedures, that formed the foundation for the employment of the Air Service, American Expeditionary Forces (AEF), in World War I.

The wartime operations of the Air Service, AEF, included visual and photographic reconnaissance, artillery adjustment, infantry liaison, counterair operations, bombing and strafing in close support of ground forces, and interdiction of the enemy's lines of communications. The war ended before U.S. units were ready for strategic air operations, but thinking on strategic air warfare had advanced far enough to raise, and tentatively answer, questions concerning area *versus* precision bombing and day *versus* night operations. Thus, U.S. military aviation in November 1918 was far different from what it had been when the war began four years earlier.

There were wide differences of opinion in the U.S. Army as to how military aviation should be employed. There were those who believed that the sole function of aviation was to assist the ground forces. That point of view was held by Gen. John J. Pershing, Commander in Chief of the AEF, and by many other officers in command and staff positions in the U.S. Army. Others thought that aviation could best be used in a strategic role. While agreeing that some aviation had to be committed to supporting ground forces, they believed that aviation could make its greatest contribution toward winning the war by attacking strategic military and industrial targets behind enemy lines. This was the position taken by Brig. Gen. William Mitchell, the top-ranking air commander in the AEF. Many members of the Air Service, and some from other branches of the Army, held views somewhere between these extremes. The general inclination, even in the Air Service, however, seems to have been toward the view held by Pershing.

The fundamental differences between Pershing's and Mitchell's thinking on aviation can be seen by comparing their ideas on air superiority. Both men believed it essential. Both gave it top priority. But they disagreed on what it was, and how to attain it. Pershing did not want enemy aircraft attacking his troops or otherwise interfering with his operations. The best way to prevent such attacks and interference, he thought, was to keep friendly airplanes over the lines in sufficient strength to command the air and thus prohibit the operation of enemy aircraft in the area. Mitchell, looking to the same goal, believed that the best way to attain it was to hit the enemy's air strength behind the lines, removing the source of the threat by attacking the enemy's airfields and shooting his planes out of the air before they could reach the front.

The principal duty of aviation, in Pershing's opinion, was to support ground forces by protecting them against hostile aircraft and by performing observation services for infantry and artillery. With command of the air over the battle front, his Air Service then might assist ground forces by attacking the enemy's artillery and ground troops. Pershing believed that his Air Service attached too much importance to operations behind the lines to disrupt lines of communication. He approved plans for organizing units for strategic missions but balked at the idea of creating an independent air force for strategic operations.

Mitchell agreed that aviation units should be attached to ground forces, but he insisted that they be under the control of an air service commander. This was necessary, he believed, to permit concentration of air strength when needed, as well as for proper coordination and direction of air operations. Mitchell placed much greater emphasis than Pershing did on close support and interdiction. He and others of this thinking believed that aviation could be used most effectively against strategic targets. For such operations, an air force working independently of ground forces was required.

As indicated earlier, Mitchell did not have a chance to try out his ideas on strategic air warfare during World War I. The air units that fought under American command in World War I were attached to ground forces. Their missions were in more or less direct support of infantry and artillery. Thus the combat experience of the U.S. Air Service in World War I was exclusively in tactical air operations, a fact that was to have a profound influence on U.S. military aviation in the 1920's and later.[1]

Some documents reflecting and illustrating various concepts of the functions of military aviation and ideas concerning the employment of aircraft as an instrument of warfare have been selected for publication in this volume. The period represented is from the creation of the Aviation Section and the beginning of World War I in the summer of 1914 until the end of the fighting in November 1918. The selection of documents for inclusion in this book has been restricted to official materials of American origin available on paper or microfilm in the Albert F. Simpson Historical Research Center of the U.S. Air Force or in the Fairchild Library of Air University; both facilities are located at Maxwell Air Force Base, Alabama. Many documents identified for possible use have been omitted in an effort to avoid repetition so far as possible; others that appeared more appropriate to other volumes in this series have been reserved for later publication. Some items, such as Congressional hearings, Bolling's report, and Gorrell's plan for bombing, have already appeared in print in various places; many are being published here for the first time.

Responsibility for the selection of documents for this book rests with the editor, who worked without the assistance of an

Notes

1. The foregoing summary is based on documents in this volume supplemented by various published works, including the following: John J. Pershing, *My Experiences in the World War* (New York, 1931); William Mitchell, *Memoirs of World War I* (New York, 1960); Alfred J. Hurley, *Billy Mitchell, Crusader for Air Power* (New York, 1964); Thomas H. Greer, USAF Historical Study 89, *The Development of Air Doctrine in the Army Air Arm, 1917–1941* (USAF Hist Div, 1955); I. B. Holley, Jr., *Ideas and Weapons* (New Haven, 1953); and Robert Frank Futrell, *Ideas, Concepts, Doctrine: A History of Basic Thinking in the United States Air Force, 1907–1964* (ASI, AU, 1971).

x

associate editor or an editorial committee. He would like to
claim complete objectivity in making the selection and preparing the documents for publication, but he suspects that he may
be no more successful than most other historians in keeping
his work free of any subjective influence. With a policy of
letting the documents speak for themselves, no attempt has
been made to interpret or explain. Nor have efforts been made
to discover the origins or to point out the factors that helped to
shape the various concepts and ideas. Background information
and notes have been kept to a minimum.

The original text and, so far as possible, the original format
have been followed in preparing the various documents for
publication. As a result, there is some inconsistency, sometimes within a single document, in such things as spelling,
punctuation, and format. For example, "reconnaissance" also
appears as "reconnoissance," and "strafe" often appears as
"straff." The only editorial changes, except for omissions
clearly indicated by ellipsis marks, are those made to correct
confusing punctuation and obvious mistakes, such as slips in
spelling and typing.

The editor is grateful for the administrative support and assist-
ance provided by Mr. Lloyd H. Cornett, Jr., Chief of the Albert F.
Simpson Historical Research Center, Lt. Col. Charles C. Biasi,
Executive, and Mr. Herschel Harvey, Chief of Administration.
Special recognition goes to Mr. Deane J. Allen, Office of Air Force
History, for his help in proofreading the original text, and to Mr.
Lawrence J. Paszek, Senior Editor in the Office of Air Force
History, for his work in photo editing, preparing artwork for this
volume, and maintaining a close liaison with the printer to resolve
the numerous difficulties that arise in the various phases of
production. Mr. Jack Harrison, U.S. Government Printing Office,
deserves credit for the arrangement of typography and design of
this volume. The editor also wants to express his thanks to Mrs.
Linda Copenhaver, Mrs. Mary F. Hanlin, Mrs. Jane Motley, and
especially, Mrs. Lois Wagner for transcribing the documents and typing the manuscript.

Maurer

Contents

List of Illustrations

The U.S. Air Service in World War I

Volume II

**Early Concepts
of Military Aviation**

Part I:

The Aviation Section

1914-1917

When the Great War began in August 1914, military operations with lighter-than-air craft had a history going back well over a century. The airplane, however, was a new and as yet relatively untried instrument of warfare. While European nations had spent considerable sums in recent years in building up air forces of both lighter- and heavier-than-air craft, the United States had lagged far behind.

In the United States, military aviation was under the jurisdiction of the Signal Corps, where the balloon section that had been established in 1892 had been expanded into an Aeronautical Division in 1907 to take in heavier- as well as lighter-than-air activities. In the first part of August 1914 the Army had fewer than 200 officers, enlisted men, and civilians in its aviation establishment. Of the 30 airplanes that had been obtained up to that time, one (the first one, purchased from the Wright Brothers in 1909) was in the Smithsonian Institution, and 21 had been destroyed in accidents or condemned.

Dissatisfaction with lack of progress and with Signal Corps jurisdiction over military aviation had brought on a congressional inquiry and "An Act to Increase the Efficiency of the Aviation Service." Passed by Congress, and approved by the President on 18 July 1914, this act left aviation in the Signal Corps but created a new section to be responsible for aviation matters. Among other things, it also authorized as many as 60 officers and 260 enlisted men for aviation duty.

Meantime, the Chief Signal Officer, Brig. Gen. George P. Scriven, had asked for $1,000,000 for aviation for Fiscal Year 1915, but Secretary of War Lindley M. Garrison had reduced the amount to $300,000, and Congress had cut out another $50,000. Thus the new Aviation Section began business with an annual appropriation of only $250,000, but that was twice as much as had been provided for the previous year.

Early U.S. military aviators:
(left to right) Capt. Paul W. Beck, Lt. Henry H. ("Hap") Arnold, Capt.
Charles D. Chandler, Lt. Thomas D. Milling, and Lt. Roy Kirtland

1. Aeronautics in the Army 1913

Hearings on the "Act to Increase the Efficiency in the Aviation Service" centered on the question of organization. Considerable attention was given, however, to the purpose and function of aviation in the U.S. military establishment. The matter of organization had been taken up early in 1913 by Congressman James Hay (D., Va.), who introduced a bill to take aviation out of the Signal Corps. The bill ran into so much opposition, however, from the War Department and from officers closely associated with aviation that it had to be abandoned. But Hay did not give up. In May 1913 he introduced another bill to create an Aviation Corps which would be directly under the Chief of Staff and would be equal to other branches of the line of the army.

The House Committee on Military Affairs, of which Hay was chairman, held hearings on the new bill from 12 to 16 August 1913. The following were among those who testified: General Scriven; Henry Breckinridge, Assistant Secretary of War; Lt. Col. Samuel Reber, a signal officer and balloon pilot who was slated to become Chief of the Aeronautical Division; Maj. Edgar Russel, Chief of the Aeronautical Division; Capt. William Mitchell, who then was on duty as a signal officer on the General Staff and who had not yet learned to fly; 1st Lt. H. H. Arnold, Russel's assistant; Capt. Paul W. Beck, a pilot and the only officer who appeared before the committee in support of a separate aviation corps; and Riley Scott, a former Army officer who had been experimenting with bomb dropping and who, like Beck, thought that the airplane had a great potential for bombardment. Besides the chairman, the committee members mentioned in the extracts below were Daniel E. Garrett (D., Tex.), J. C. McKenzie (R., Ill.), Frank T. O'Hair, (D., Ill.), Frank L. Greene (R., Vt.), and Maurice Connolly (D., Iowa).

As a result of the hearings of August 1913, the committee struck out everything after the enacting clause and rewrote the bill, which later was enacted (Doc. 3), to provide for an Aviation Section in the Signal Corps. Following are extracts from these hearings in 1913.[1]

. . . .

Gen. Scriven [reading from a memorandum which he had among his papers] . . . Aeronautics and aviation in military affairs are merely an added means of communication, observation, and reconnaissance, and ought to be coordinated with and subordinated to the general service of information, and not be erected into an independent and uncoordinated service.

. . . .

The Chairman. Will you state briefly what are the functions of an Aviation Corps in time of war?

Gen. Scriven. Of course it is all theory. Little has been done offensively with aeroplanes in war, but they have done a great deal in reconnoissance work in maneuvers and the like, especially in France, a little in Italy, and they are trying to do something in Mexico. It seems that the thing divides itself into two different classes of work to be done. One is scouting and reconnoissance work by the fast flying machine, heavier than air.

The Chairman. How does that pertain to the Signal Corps?

Gen. Scriven. The results of reconnoissance work must be reported. The aeroplane is an adjunct to the Cavalry. It makes long reconnoissances and performs distance scouting. The cavalryman outlines his advance position, the aeroplane detects and observes him in the distance, and must send the information back instantly to the commander of the forces, and must do so by wireless.

1. Hearings before the Committee on Military Affairs, House of Representatives, *Aeronautics in the Army*, 63d Cong. 1st sess (1913).

The Chairman. How about the scouts sent out by the Cavalry, they have not to send back information in the same way?

Gen. Scriven. They also have the wireless to some extent; but the aviator must have his wireless man with him, and his observer must be able to manage wireless to be of much use. The aeroplane has also a fighting function, we presume: that is, the bomb dropping. Of this nobody knows much of anything, but we have theories. As to the dirigible, its management is most essentially Signal Corps work, so far as observation and reconnoissance work can be done by balloon. The dirigible is capable of hovering over a city or a command or whatever you like, constantly sending in reports.

Mr. Garrett. You say that both machines will carry wireless equipment?

Gen. Scriven. Yes, sir. The aeroplane probably will carry other means of communication, such as the dropping of dispatches and things of that kind. One of the main services of the aeroplane is that of reconnoissance and the collection of information.

. . . .

Mr. Garrett. In the recent wars, what has been the success of the flying machine?

Gen. Scriven. Well, there has been a little reconnoissance work done, but the reports are not very full, and the fact of the matter is, many of the flyers, of course, are not to be classed as experts, and certainly not as trained military observers. The Turk can not handle an aeroplane—I know that—and the other peoples recently at war probably can not do much with such a machine. Some volunteers, of course, from Europe appeared at the seat of the recent war, but the reports I have read are not very full, not very satisfactory, but an occasional reconnoissance has been made that has proved of value.

Mr. Garrett. The point I have in mind is this: Could any army contend with its opponents if they should have an aviation service?

Gen. Scriven. I do not believe for a moment an army could so contend except at a disadvantage, and the condition in the Philippines is a good illustration of the fact. Consider the island of Corregidor. If an enemy should land, say, at Subig Bay and the defense was provided with aeroplanes, I doubt very much if the attack could get ashore; they must approach with their transports loaded with troops, with their horses and guns exposed in going ashore, and the beach open to anything that might come over it, attack from overhead—an ideal condition for the dirigible and aeroplane, which by dropping nitroplane, which by dropping nitro-gelatin might stop the landing or at least disorganize the enemy's troops. Whatever may be thought regarding the danger of attack to a warship from overhead, there can be no doubt of the tremendous influence of overhead attack upon transports crowded with troops and upon small boats and shore landings. At best this is a time of confusion, or at all events extra hazardous, and when the enemy must be to some extent disorganized and not prepared or capable of resisting to the utmost the approach of aerial war machines, whether dirigibles or aeroplanes.

On the other hand, if the defense had none and the enemy landed and marched to the hills that overlook Corregidor with a few aeroplanes and certainly with a dirigible, it is difficult to see how it would be possible to hold the position if conditions are at all what they may be expected to be in the attack on this position.

The Chairman. Do you mean by that that the science of aviation has advanced to such an extent that any country that is going to war with some other country would be handicapped and at a great disadvantage unless that country had an aviation corps sufficiently experienced to contend with that of the other country?

Gen. Scriven. I believe so, most distinctly. If you look at conditions at the Panama Canal—I have happened to talk with Mr. Scott, well known throughout the world as having conducted some interesting experiments in bomb dropping [Mr. Scott later appeared before the committee], who has informed me that he has dropped 100 pounds of nitrogelatin, and I believe the record shows that 400 pounds have been dropped from an aeroplane. In talking of the Panama Canal, Mr. Scott remarked that he had questioned a flier who the other day passed over the Isthmus in regard to the canal as a target, and especially as to the spillway of Gatun Dam. It appears that the latter makes a very conspicuous target; so, no doubt, do other vulnerable points. Now, the question immediately comes up as to what would be the result of dropping 300 or 400 pounds of nitrogelatin on the lock or spillway. There is probably little difficulty in doing it, and should a foreign fleet anchored beyond the range of the guns of our fortifications, some distance out—say, 15 or 20 miles—aeroplanes may well be sent out and great damage to the canal done. Of course, nobody would expect to see the aeroplanes again, but the probability is that some of them would be effective. Now, if we have nothing to resist the air craft except land guns, it seems more than probable that some damage would be done and the working of the canal interrupted, especially if we have no air craft to resist that sort of attack.

Mr. McKenzie. How would you meet that attack?

Gen. Scriven. By aeroplanes and dirigibles.

The Chairman. Has the Ordnance Department succeeded in getting a gun that could be used on aeroplanes?

Gen. Scriven. The Krupp gun can do it. The Krupps have a gun that can be used against machines. The Ordnance Department has been experimenting, but I do not know that they have yet devised a gun.

. . . .

Mr. Breckinridge. . . . the vast amount of experimental work that has been done and the state of continuous development in which this matter of the service of information has existed during the last 50 years, and now exists, are such that all of the energy and capacity of a separate body, such as the Signal Corps, will be required. I am free to believe that the art of war since the Civil War, if it has

Congressman
James Hay. Chairman.
House Committee on Military
Affairs.

changed at all, has only changed in the service of information, and that the only thing that would make the Battle of Gettysburg different today from what it was 50 years ago would be that the work of each of the armies would be much better coordinated by the work of the Signal Corps, of which aviation would be merely a branch.

The Chairman. Mr. Secretary, may I ask what I asked Gen. Scriven, and that is what function does the Signal Corps perform, or, rather, what functions will the aviation corps perform that pertains to the Signal Corps, which is purely a means of information?

Mr. Breckinridge. This, for instance: the aeroplane goes out under orders, perhaps, of the commander of a screening brigade of cavalry which is protecting the advance of a larger body of mixed troops. Now, the aviator goes and gets his information; he is 20 miles away, and how does he get that information back? You do not transmit that information in the manner in which he came for it. He is 20 miles away, and he will send an instantaneous wireless message. Now, he will send that instantaneous wireless message and that message will be received by what? By another wireless outfit under the command of the Signal Corps, and thus the information reaches the commander of

the screening brigade of cavalry. As I say, that message will be sent back by wireless or wire or through some other agency of the Signal Corps. The transmission of that information from there to the commanding general of the army, who may be 100 miles away, will be through nothing but agencies of the Signal Corps until it gets there. Of course, the Cavalry gets information, but the Cavalry is not under the Signal Corps. The differentiation to be made is the result of experience. It is not a matter of logic. You could say, as a matter of logic, that because the Cavalry gets information the Cavalry should be under the Signal Corps, or you could say, as a matter of logic, that because the Cavalry gets information and is not under the Signal Corps, therefore no branch of the service that gets information should be under the Signal Corps. It is not a matter of logic, but a matter of experience.

The Chairman. What other service is it contemplated that aeroplanes or an Aviation Corps would render in time of war except to get information?

Mr. Breckinridge. At the present time the only established use that is proved for aviation is the expediting of the service of information and the getting of information.

The Chairman. But we are providing legislation not only for the present time but for the future.

Mr. Breckinridge. I would go so far as to say that for the immediate future 99 per cent of the value of aviation will be in the service of information. Now, I do not say that in the development of dirigibles which can carry 5 tons of lyddite or nitroge-latin or any other high explosive, they will not be able to perfect a device which will drop a ton of explosives in a vulnerable place. I can not say that the time will not come when a flock of dirigibles can come to England, if it is unprotected, and may hover in the air for 40 hours, as a dirigible can do, and destroy whole cities; but I do mean to say that, looking at it through the vista of the future with the largest powers of imagination with which we can conceive the probable future growth of aviation, and yet also looking at it from the viewpoint of legislation that is likely to be required, and taking the average development that will be experienced in the next 15 or 20 years in the Army, as far as we can see there ought not to be any separation, because this great development in aviation will not come in that length of time, particularly in this country, because we will follow rather than lead in its development.

The Chairman. We are far behind—

Mr. Breckinridge (interposing). We were the pioneers; we developed it. Wright was the first man to do it, but in the feeling of security that America has always had, and in that she may be somewhat justified, we have

lagged behind other nations which immediately perceived the necessity of this thing from the military standpoint. If the aeroplane is never to be developed another inch, as Gen. Scriven has said, the nation that is without aviation will simply be overwhelmed by the nation that is equally as well prepared in other respects and is better prepared in the matter of aviation, because the question of victory or defeat, where the troops are anywhere near equal, will depend upon the question of information or the lack of information. I think that is all I care to say.

. . . .

Mr. O'Hair. What is the true function of the Aviation Corps?

Col. Reber. It is to receive and transmit information for the tactical commanders. For instance, the commander of a division desires to know what is going on in front of him. He has certain instrumentalities for gathering that information and certain instrumentalities for the transmission of that information. For example, his way of gathering it may be by Cavalry, screened Cavalry patrols, or Infantry patrols. There is a method for getting that information back. That information is transmitted back to the commander and he distributes it as he sees fit.

. . . .

The Chairman. . . . Capt Beck, we will hear you now. I wish you would state what, if any, experience you have had as an aviator, and to what arm of the service you belong.

Capt. Beck. Mr. Chairman and gentlemen of the committee, I am an Infantry officer and was detailed to aviation in January, 1911. My first experience with aviation was in January, 1910, when I was sent by the War Department, as its representative, to a large international meet which took place at Los Angeles. During that Los Angeles meet I had occasion to make a number of flights as passenger with Glenn Curtiss in his machine, which, incidentally, was not a passenger-carrying machine, but it was modified in order to carry me up, and with Capt. B. D. Foulois, who was flying a French Farman machine. During the course of the aviation meet it occurred to me that the aeroplane might be used as an aggressive factor in war, and following that the idea of dropping various and varying weights from the aeroplane to find out, first, whether or not the equilibrium would be changed because of this dropping, and, second, whether or not we could reasonably expect to strike an object on the ground. The largest weight that I dropped at that time was

not in excess of 15 pounds. There was no change in the equilibrium of the machine. I found that the tables which I had roughly gotten up regarding the angle of dropping were totally inaccurate, which led me to perform a good deal of experimentation to bring out the proper tables.

The following November I was detailed by the commanding general of the western division to assist in the organization of a large aero meet at San Francisco. The people behind that meet were the most influential people on the coast, and they wanted to make something exceedingly large on account of the then fight between San

Francisco and New Orleans for the Pan American Exposition. I simply bring that out to show the scope of the meet. I was made secretary on account of the experience I had had at Los Angeles, which, while small, at the same time was greater than anyone else on the coast had at that time. From November until January we worked up the details and the meet was held in January. During that meet I continued the experiments started before at Los Angeles. Lieut. Crissy, of the Coast Artillery, worked with me on the aggressive use of the aeroplane, and devised a bomb-dropping device which was worked from the aeroplane, and he also got up a set of tables which enabled him to determine with considerable accuracy where they would strike the ground at varying altitudes. Those experiments were successful to a height of 1,500 feet, showing conclusively that a weight up to 36 pounds could be dropped within 20 feet from an altitude of 1,500 feet. Understand, we were striving at that time to work out the basic principles. No one ever held for an instant that an aeroplane at 1,-500 feet would be of any military value. We had to creep before we could walk, and we wanted to work out these things in order to arrive at the greater things which lay in the higher altitudes. Since that time ex-Lieut. Scott, of the United States

Army, has devised a bomb-dropping device which has been successful up to altitudes of 5,-000 feet. I can not tell what his accuracy is offhand, but my impression now is that he dropped 14 projectiles from heights varying from 3,500 to 5,000 feet, and his largest miss was something like 30 feet from a given spot. I do not claim this to be absolutely accurate, but that is my impression.

The Chairman. Captain, that leads you to believe—

Capt. Beck. That leads me to believe that there is an aggressive use for the aeroplane.

. . . .

There are four fundamental uses for the aeroplane in war. One is for reconnoissance purposes; two, for fire control of Field Artillery and Coast Artillery; three, the aggressive use, and four, the occasional transportation use. Those things are not experimental; they have all been demonstrated. They have been demonstrated abroad, and if they have not been demonstrated here it is because our people have failed to grasp the situation. We are behind; in five years we have done nothing. . . .

. . . .

Maj. Russel. . . .

One of the best articles on the military value of the aeroplane has recently been written by Jacques Mortane, who as one of the greatest living authorities frequently advises the French military establishment. He brings out with a great clearness the over-

whelming advantage of the aeroplane as an instrument of reconnoissance and report. He admits that its extensive use in offensive warfare by bomb dropping and machine-gun fire is as yet a matter of speculation. In these views he is supported by practically all of the conservative writers in the foreign services. To attempt to organize aviation on a basis of what it may be able to do some time is very unwise and, at any rate, premature.

. . . .

Mr. Green. When the aeroplane begins to be used for bomb throwing and machine-gun work it becomes then an instrument offensive and defensive, and that takes it out of the

range of information transmission for all practical and general purposes, does it not?

Maj. Russel. As I have stated, there is a possibility of development in the offensive warfare utilization. It appears there has not been very much done as yet. No great accomplishment has been reported. It has some promise, but there have been no realizations of it. At present we can rely only on the aeroplane for obtaining and transmitting information.

. . . .

Capt. Mitchell. . . . This aeroplane business is pretty well understood in its relation to the military service; it is well understood by all of the great na-

Lt. Myron S. Crissy devised a bomb-dropping device and dropped the first bomb from a U.S. aircraft on 15 January 1911 at the Tanforan race track near San Francisco. Seated with Crissy is Phillip O. Parmalee, who piloted the Wright aircraft for the experiment.

Charles F. Willard, a Curtiss pilot, flew the Curtiss Pusher Biplane from which Maj. Jacob E. Fickel fired a rifle from an aircraft. The event took place during an air meet held in August 1910, at Sheepshead Bay, N.Y.

At right, Capt. Charles D. Chandler fired the first machine gun from an aircraft in flight on 7 June 1912. Thomas D. Milling was the pilot of the Wright Type "B" aircraft, but Lt. Roy C. Kirtland substituted for him in the pilot's seat.

tions—that is, it is well understood what it is good for. Now, if this thing were not any good at all, if we did not derive any advantage from it, it would not be of any use to do what we are attempting to do; but we all know that there is something in it, and that from the military standpoint it is a necessary and important adjunct to the military organization. We know absolutely that aeroplanes are valuable for reconnoissance service. Now, reconnoissance work means the getting of information in regard to the enemy and bringing it back to the person for whose use the information is intended. Aeroplane reconnoissance means finding out about the enemy; that is, getting information about large units and not little details about small detachments. We have troops for that purpose, but the aeroplane reconnoissance will be used for the purpose of securing information concerning large strategic combinations—the larger tactical movements—or the things useful for the commanding general to know. In other words, they will not be used to secure information respecting small details but of large tactical combinations. Now, the offensive value of this thing has not been proved. It is being experimented with—bomb dropping and machines carrying guns are being experimented with—but there is nothing to it so far except in an experimental way.

Some experimenters in Germany have dropped as much as 300 pounds of explosive from an aeroplane, and all that sort of thing; but, gentlemen, you should bear in mind that if you drop 300 pounds of explosive on one man, while it may tear that one man all to pieces, the effect will be entirely local. On the other hand, it might be used against bridges and it might be used against dockyards and storehouses; but at the present time all that is in the experimental stage. On the other hand, the aeroplane to be safe from fire directed from the ground must be over 4,000 feet altitude. That has been proved in Tripoli and in the Bulgarian war. That is to say, until that altitude is attained it is not safe from hostile fire, from the ground. We have got to be over 4,000 feet to be safe from that hostile fire. Now, gentlemen, with these conditions we know what organization we ought to have with the units of the Army we now have. We know that almost to the extent that we know what a regiment of Cavalry or a regiment of Field Artillery or a regiment of Infantry should be. Reconnoissance with the troops may be divided into two kinds—one strategical reconnaissance—that is, reconnaissance at a distance, to find out what the enemy's plans are away from the field of battle and the other is what we call tactical reconnoissance—that is, reconnaissance on the actual field of battle. We know that when an

aeroplane is sent out alone on a mission it is apt not to get back—that is, the chances are that something is apt to happen to it—so it is the practice in this reconnoissance work to send out two aeroplanes. That would require two for tactical reconnoissance; and then if we have a strategical reconnoissance outfit, we will need two aeroplanes for that purpose. Now, for the purposes of tactical reconnoissance, suppose we are marching in this direction, for instance (indicating); we are reconnoitering the enemy's front for that purpose— that is, for tactical reconnoissance purposes—we need two aeroplanes for that service. At the same time we wish to get a line on the enemy's flank movements, and for that purpose we need two aeroplanes. Obviously, therefore, they ought to run in twos all the time. Therefore, as I said, we need two machines at least for each of these kinds of reconnoissance. We need two at least to reconnoiter ahead of the forces and two to reconnoiter in on a flank or other places for tactical purposes, and we need at least two for strategical reconnoissance, with a given force— say, a division of troops.

There is a third use for them which is very important in France on account of her present deficiency, as they believe, in the matter of artillery materiel. The Germans have recently developed a field howitzer which can probably get next to the

French batteries. Consequently it is very important that they develop their field-artillery fire, and they have definitely worked out a system which is better than anything they had before and that is accomplished by means of aeroplane. That is a very important function—that is, the fire control of field artillery by means of aeroplanes. That is another element of use, and we would need a unit for that purpose. The French in their organization have that. The French, in their organization, have provided aeroplanes for the artillery commander. That is, the commander who handles that artillery has a given force of aeroplanes and they are assigned to each group. They assign machines for the purpose of handling the fire of a particular lot of guns. Their groups correspond to battalions in this country. In starting the organization in this country it seems to me that we have pretty definite things to go on. That organization ought to consist of one unit for strategic reconnoissance, consisting of two machines, and two units for tactical reconnoissance; that is, one unit for the front and one for the sides, or four machines. Then, we ought to have a unit for the field artillery fire control.

Now, in order that we may not overdo this thing, this organization ought to be thoroughly considered. A certain number of aeroplanes have been recommended to constitute this unit, and that number is eight aeroplanes—two for strategical reconnoissance, four for tactical reconnoissance, two in front of the force, two on a flank, and two for field artillery fire control. Each of these aeroplanes must have two officers—one observer and one to do the flying—so that the minimum number in each machine would be two. Then, there should be one officer in command of each one of these forces and another to look after the property, making the number of officers necessary about 20; and of enlisted men in round numbers, 80 would be required for one of these units. Now the unit of Army organization is the division, because that is the smallest complete army in itself; it comprises all of the branches of the service capable of acting together, and, in round numbers, consists of 20,000 men. With the exception of our Civil War and with the exception of the war in the Philippines, where we had 60,000 men, all of our expeditions have been not to exceed that size, in one place. So it seems to me, in so far as our organization in this country is concerned, that our unit to be used with troops should be based on the division, because that is a little army in itself. . . .

. . . .

The Chairman. Do you think in course of time that the military by experience will be able to drop bombs with any accuracy?

Capt. Mitchell. Yes, sir; probably with great accuracy, but the effect would be the same as a high-explosive shell. We do not use that against personnel; we only use it against materiel—houses, buildings, etc.,—because the effect is local. Some of the people in the Russo-Japanese War had a thousand fragments of high-explosive shell taken out of their bodies. Its effect is entirely local. Against personnel we use shrapnel. This may be regarded as a short shot-gun that is thrown in the air and explodes at the proper time and sweeps the ground for about 250 yards by 20 yards with a lot of heavy shot.

The Chairman. How about the machine gun?

Capt. Mitchell. it will probably never be any good for attacking personnel on the ground from aeroplanes; it may from dirigibles. To operate against other aeroplanes and dirigibles it will be used. On the other hand, it is thought in fighting aeroplanes they will try to ram each other as much as they can, and both get smashed up. That is a problem.

The Chairman. We would like to hear what you have to say about the possibility of the dirigible, how much they cost, and whether or not they are so important as to justify our Government in going into them.

Capt. Mitchell. We should keep up with modern methods. The cost of dirigible ballooning is tremendous. We have not the same problems that they have to deal with in Europe, but we should have a few; that is, one or two, and keep them up to date, so we will be capable of developing them if called on to do it. In Germany their idea is that they are the battleships of the air and will be able to carry a great amount of explosives and guns and at the same time reconnoiter. On the other hand, they are very subject to attack from these little hornets of the air—the aeroplanes.

. . . .

Lieut. Arnold. . . . I would like, if I may, to add a few remarks to some of the testimony given by preceding officers. In the first place, I would like to call attention to what has been done by aeroplanes and dirigibles in the Balkan war. Of course the information we receive now is very meager, and most of the information we have gotten is from consuls and considerable from military attaches, no official reports having come over as yet.

However, we do know that there was a naval lieutenant in a hydro-aeroplane—equipped with the bomb-dropping device invented by Mr. Scott, who was here yesterday—who located the Turkish cruiser that was creating so much havoc over in the Dardanelles. He made a cross-country flight of 180 miles out and 180 miles back and was fired on numerous times on that trip, but was not touched. He flew at an altitude of about 6,000 feet. In the Bulgarian Army, at the opening of the war, they had no aviation organization at all. They had four officers in Russia learning to fly and four machines under orders. Outside of that their aviation service did not amount to anything. So when the war broke out they had no experienced pilots whatsoever. But in spite of that fact they determined to organize an aviation corps and hired civilian aviators to enter the service, paying them a large bonus. Four or five of those aviators were crooks and did not develop at all; the others they used to train the officers. Up to about the 1st of December of last year they did not do anything at all, to speak of. At that time the aviation equipment was increased so that they had about 14 aeroplanes in use.

Between December 10 and January 1 it was known that there were a number of reconnoissance flights made and very valuable information turned in to the commanding generals of the different armies. There was a reconnoissance flight of 140 kilometers, at an altitude of between 1,100 and 1,200 meters, flying about opposing troops whose position they were able to reveal. They brought back very valuable information; just what

the nature of that information was we do not know yet, but we know the flight was made and that they turned in a report to the commanding general. On the 11th another aviator flew over Preveza, with a passenger, and flew to a place 47 kilometers away, and brought back very valuable information as to the Turkish position. A short time later a flight was made over Janina to a place 75 kilometers away, at a height of 1,600 meters. This aviator threw down bombs, creating a veritable panic amongst the Turkish troops. Many hostile bullets tore the fabric, but the machine continued its flight unaffected. On the 28th of December a Greek army pilot officer made a flight over the fort of Bisani. He flew at an altitude of 2,300 meters, reporting observations concerning the garrison and the fortifications, which were considered of the highest importance by the Greek commanding officer. It is also known that at Adrianople aeroplanes and dirigibles were both used in going over the city.

Of course, their flight for reconnoissance purposes amounted to practically nothing, but these aeroplanes were equipped with the Scott bomb dropper, and dropped bombs on the city and set fire to it, which caused considerable damage.
. . . .

The Chairman. . . .
Capt. Scott, who has been in the Army and is now a civilian operator, is present, and we will hear him.
. . . .
The Chairman. You were at one time in the Army?

Mr. Scott. Yes, sir.

The Chairman. Did you do any duty as an aviator while in the Army?

Mr. Scott. No, sir. I took up aviation afterwards. I have made a special study of the aeroplane as an offensive weapon.

The Chairman. We would like to hear what your experience has been.

Mr. Scott. About 1908, when Mr. Wright was making his first flights, I came to the conclusion that the aeroplane would eventually become very important as an offensive weapon. The fact that you can get over an object to be destroyed and that you can see it from an aeroplane better than in any other way caused me to come to the conclusion, with proper application of scientific principles, that bombs or explosives could be dropped accurately, and I took up that study specially.

In 1911 a gentleman in France offered a prize for dropping dummy bombs on a target. The prize was 150,000 francs—half of that was available in 1912 and the other half in 1913. I already had an apparatus designed which, through the courtesy of Gen. Allen, I was able to test at College Park. I took the apparatus over to France and was fortunate enough to win the whole series of prizes. The heights from which the projectiles were dropped were 200 meters (about 656 feet) and 800 meters (about half a mile). Fifteen projectiles were dropped on each flight, the time being 50 minutes. The winning machine was able to place 12 out of the 15 projectiles within a radius of 10 meters—that is 33 feet, which would be a little over twice the size of this room—12 out of 15, each weighing 25 pounds.

The second test was at 800 meters—we really flew at 850, over half a mile, and 12 out of 15 projectiles were placed within a radius of 40 meters, 120 feet square, which is a very small portion of the side of this building.

The various tests made—the meet lasted from March until September and included hundreds of flights—and the accuracy attained, convinced me that projectiles could be dropped with a great deal of accuracy on any target from, say, a height of a mile, from 1,000 to 1,500 meters, a mile, or a mile and a quarter. I have been studying considerably the application of such a device, which I believe to be sufficiently accurate at the present time, and I firmly believe that the aeroplane will become a very important destructive weapon, much more so than we realize at the present time. It could be used, among other things, in a siege against a besieged place. There is always some key point like there was at Port Arthur and Adrianople, against which troops are fighting sometimes for days and weeks—against the strongest point—

without any appreciable effort. In such a case, if I were the commanding officer, I would send up as many aeroplanes as were available, 20 or 30, each one carrying 500 pounds of high explosive, and rain that high explosive on this important point that they were trying to attack and just as soon as that was completed, then rush in the troops and storm the fortifications or the strong point, and I believe it would be very effective.

Mr. Connolly. In the event of using the aeroplane as a destructive means in modern warfare and you are up against another power presumably as well fortified with air craft as you are, then does not the warfare actually take place in the air, and would not their air craft protect their fortifications?

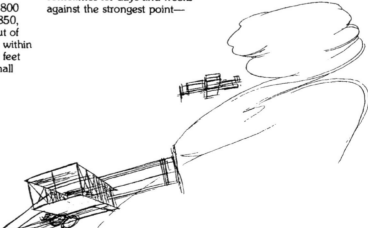

Mr. Scott. When you besiege a place the presumption is they are in more or less desperate straits, and in a case like Adrianople the outside force would have full opportunity to recoup their air force, and in this particular case I think you could presume that you would have the preponderance of aeroplanes, or that the enemy have none at all, but ordinarily the presumption would be that the two powers fighting would have equal forces, in Europe at least.

Another important use, I should think, would be against headquarters. Commanding officers can not be made in a day or a year. From my experience I think that a mile above the earth you can pick out with an eye very readily anything as large as a tent or an automobile, or wagon—anything like that can be seen very clearly on a clear day. I imagine an important use of the aeroplane would be picking out headquarters, the enemy's commanding general and important encampments like that, and by using shrapnel, a large shell weighing 500 pounds with high explosives, and being able to drop it within a square of 120 feet, I think you could make it very uncomfortable for the commanding general. I think that would be an important use of the aeroplanes. Against fortifications—I firmly believe that 500 pounds of nitrogelatin placed near a barbette disappearing gun carriage would put that completely out of service. If dropped

on a mortar battery, I think it would temporarily at least put that out of order, and especially the range-finding system. The accuracy of these guns depends entirely on the range-finding system. These systems are screened as much as possible from the sea in the seacoast fortifications, but they can not be screened from the air, and I think it would be very readily put out of business, and when the range-finding system is put out of business the battery is put out of business, at least until it is repaired.

We have very elaborate fortifications to protect the large cities, especially New York. I can imagine an enemy's fleet of 20 or 30 vessels coming toward New York—our Navy may be in some other part of the seas—they just come outside of the range of the Sandy Hook guns, cruise around and send aloft 20 or 30 aeroplanes at a height of a mile, I do not see any way of bringing down an aeroplane except occasionally by accident—probably by accident one may occasionally be brought down—

but the fleet would cruise out there and the aeroplanes would go over New York with incendiary bombs especially constructed to produce conflagration, probably a few high explosives but mostly incendiary bombs, and drop them over New York and produce such a conflagration that no fire department could cope with—in other words, make New York like San Francisco. I do not think Washington is too far off for a thing like that—Baltimore, Norfolk, Charleston, and Wilmington, the coast cities, would be vulnerable. The same way on the Pacific coast. Those things are in the future, but military people have to look into the future, and the ones who look far into the future are the ones who usually win out in the long run.

My particular hobby, the thing I have been studying about particularly, is the destruction of the Panama Canal. It has cost an immense amount of money. It is a lock canal, and there has been a great deal of discussion as to whether certain parts will hold up. The canal is about 50 miles across, I believe; that is, the center of the canal would be 25 miles from either sea.

Over in Europe, when dropping these bombs in the 800-meter contest, you were allowed to drop any number, one or all of them, at the same time. In the other contests you had to drop one at a time, flying around and going over the target successively, but in the 800-meter contest several of the aviators, two of them to be accurate, just put their eggs all in one basket. One man, a lieutenant in the French Army, who had a light Farman machine, with a 50-horsepower motor, could not carry a passenger, and he dropped the bombs himself. He did not have a particularly scientific way; he just put his eggs all in one basket and dropped them at one time, believing that if he got in the right place he would win out. He did this day after day, and he told me the effect of dropping the bombs was hardly perceptible; that is, the stability of the machine was not affected. Of course it jumped forward and backward and the speed increased after releasing the weight. I have not any doubt that an aeroplane will be built heavy enough to drop from 500 to 1,000 pounds without any trouble whatever.

With the machine I used over there I would not hesitate to drop 500 pounds. I dropped 50 pounds a good many times, and I would have to touch the man on the knee to let him know it. You can build machines, I think, to drop 500 or 1,000 pounds of nitrogelatin, which is a very powerful explosive.

In war the object of the foreign nations is to destroy our

greatest strategic point, which would be the Panama Canal, and they would put all their force against the canal. For some reason our fleet is not there, it has been defeated or it is protecting some other part of the coast—any way, they go there. No matter how strongly the canal is fortified, they do not come within range of the guns; they cruise out 10 or 30 miles. The distance to Gatun Dam or to the locks would be probably half an hour's fly. They send out their aeroplanes loaded with high explosives, say 20 or 30 of them, as many as they can send, hoping that some of them will get back; but in warfare we take chances, and if they destroyed the canal no doubt they would be willing to lose them all. They send them up and they are flying one after another, placing 500 pounds of nitrogelatin first on the spill-way and later up the Culebra Cut, causing slides. I think some of you gentlemen know the effect of an explosive on the earth, causing it to slide. I think the canal would be put out of business, probably in one hour or two hours, by an enemy with aeroplanes. That is, of course, my own personal opinion. We do not know the effect of an explosive dropped from an aeroplane, because it has never been done except in a small way. I firmly believe when the experiments are carried on in that direction that it will be found to be very destructive.

Mr. Connolly. Would it not be difficult to place bombs with precision at an altitude of 5,000 feet on account of the various currents that intervene between the air craft and the target?

Mr. Scott. From my experience, I think the wind does not make a great deal of difference, especially after the first bomb, if it is planed off. In the first place, you usually fly into the teeth of the wind, and at a very high altitude the currents would probably be compensating. I do not believe that the wind would have a great deal of effect if they were up a half a mile. I am speaking from experience.

Mr. McKenzie. You have spoken of danger to the Panama Canal from aeroplanes?

Mr. Scott. Yes, sir.

Mr. McKenzie. What is your idea of the way we should protect the canal, with air craft?

Mr. Scott. I am not able to answer that question at the present time. The only way to fight air craft is with air craft.

Mr. McKenzie. If it is true that the Panama Canal is in danger of being destroyed by the operation of air craft, then, in your judgment, is not the fortification of the Panama Canal a needless expense?

Mr. Scott. If air craft were all the defenders of the Panama Canal were going to contend with, yes; but the fortifications are naturally placed there against the navies at the present time, primarily. I think the authorities should consider the air craft as a menace to the canal and not wait until that menace really develops——take it up now.

Mr. McKenzie. Pardon me, but according to your theory, if I understand you correctly, you would have a fleet of aeroplanes stationed at either end of the Panama Canal, and they would be of greater service in destroying an enemy's fleet than the fortifications?

Mr. Scott. I believe so; yes, sir. The authorities say that 500 pounds of nitrogelatin dropped on the deck of a battleship would have only a local effect.

We do not know; it has never been tried. The proof of the pudding is in the eating and I think it should be done; that some old battleship or monitor should be made a target and that it should be done. A great many authorities say it would have a local effect. I do not believe it.

Mr. McKenzie. I understand one of the older battleships is about ready to go out of commission and that might be a very good experiment.

Mr. Scott. I believe in taking time by the forelock, and at the present time I think the aeroplane is of sufficient importance to warrant very serious consideration.

Mr. Connolly. Do you regard the air craft as a potential force in destroying battleships? From your experiments, it would seem reasonable that you could hit a battleship.

Mr. Scott. I think so. From the height of a mile, I should say 50 per cent of hits. There is a great deal of controversy as to the effect that a high explosive would have on the deck of a battleship, whether it would be local or cause very serious harm. That can only be proven by trying.

The Chairman. We are very much obliged to you, Mr. Scott. (Thereupon the Committee adjourned.)

First serviceman to fly—Lt. Lahm
(art by Richard Green)

1st Aero Squadron, Texas City, Texas, 1913.

2. Four-Squadron Plan

During the hearings of 1913 (Doc. 1), Scriven gave the committee a paper entitled "Suggested Organization for Aeronautical Work in the United States Army,"[1] which explained the basis for the first plan for the organization of units for tactical operations with aircraft. The first such unit, the 1st Aero Squadron, had been formed as a provisional organization at Texas City, Texas, on 5 March 1913 as U.S. Army forces on the border were being strengthened as a result of revolutionary disturbances in Mexico.[2]

. . . this office has convened boards of officers to discuss the necessities which confront us, and these boards, consisting of several experienced officers of the Signal Corps associated with practically all of the aviators on duty, have reported in effect as follows: Our military forces have been apportioned among six divisional commands. Since these are tactical units, and it has been agreed that a large aeronautical organization should be assigned as a part of each main tactical unit, the boards have reported that an organization called an Aeronautical Squadron should be assigned to each of these tactical units to serve therewith as a component part of such units for peace training or for service in war.

On account of the present reduced strength of such divisions, it has been recommended from economical considerations that at present we favor the organization of only 4 of the aeronautical squadrons, subdividing 2 of those so that distribution may be made of these subdivisions among the tactical units requiring them.

The four aero squadrons thus formed are to be placed at appropriate aeronautical centers, each commanded by a field officer and serving incidentally as a center of aeronautical instruction.

The organization and equipment of each of the aeronautical squadrons proposed is as follows:

It is customary to assign for the operation of an aeroplane two officers, who alternate in long cross-country flights as observer and aviator or pilot. It has been found by our experience, and abroad, that at least five enlisted men are required in the care, repair, and handling of an aeroplane. This personnel (two officers and five men) constitute the section necessary for the aeroplane. Two aeroplanes and their sections are proposed as the platoon; two platoons compose the company, and two companies, commanded by a major, constitute the aero squadron, the aero tactical unit proposed to be assigned to a division.

. . . .

1. *Aeronautics in the Army*, pp. 120–122.
2. Maurer Maurer (ed.). *Combat Squadrons of the Air Force, World War II* (Washington, 1969), pp. 4–6.

3. Creation of The Aviation Section, Signal Corps

18 July 1914

. . . there is hereby created, an aviation section, which shall be a part of the Signal Corps of the Army, and which shall be, and is hereby, charged with the duty of operating or supervising the operation of all military aircraft, including balloons and

aeroplanes, all appliances pertaining to said craft, and signaling apparatus of any kind when installed on said craft. . . .[1]

Shortly after the
1st Aero Squadron had been formed as a
provisional squadron, Lts. Thomas D. Milling and
William C. Sherman broke the U.S. duration
and distance record, on 28 March 1913, flying non-stop,
cross-country, from Texas City to San Antonio. On the return
flight, on 31 March, they drew the first aerial map from
an aircraft. The picture was taken upon
landing at Texas City.

4. Field Service Regulations

1914

The position taken by Breckenridge and Scriven in the hearings of 1913 (Doc. 1) with regard to the function of aviation was reflected in the War Department's *Field Service Regulations* of 1914.[1] These regulations made infantry the principal combat arm of the U.S. Army, with artillery and cavalry as the principal supporting arms. Aviation, which was not mentioned in the section concerning the use of combined arms in combat, was given a reconnaissance mission that included strategic and tactical reconnaissance and observation of artillery fire. The only reference to a fighting role for aircraft was a single sentence relating to the use of aircraft in preventing aerial observation by the enemy. Though these regulations were altered in several instances between the time they were issued in 1914 and the end of the war in 19 8, statements concerning the status and mission of aviation remained unchanged. Following are some extracts.

11. Reconnaissance—Reconnaissance is the military term used to designate the work of troops or individuals when gathering information in the field. Reconnaissance begins as soon as the theater of possible operations is entered and continues throughout the campaign. No matter what other sources of information of the enemy may be available, reconnaissance must be depended upon to obtain the information upon which all tactical movements of troops should be based.

12. By Aero Squadron.—In forces of the strength of a division, or larger, the aero squadron will operate in advance of the independent cavalry in order to locate the enemy and to keep track of his movements. Contact with the enemy once gained will be maintained thereafter continuously.

13. By the Cavalry.—Reconnaissance in the theater of operations is best made by the cavalry, which from the beginning of the campaign seeks to determine the enemy's strength and dispositions. It protects its own army against surprise, screens its movements, and insures the safety and success of the troops of other arms. The defeat of the hostile cavalry, and its expulsion from the field are usually the best means to this

end. As the opposing armies draw near each other, the cavalry endeavors to secure control of the ground between and bends every effort to that close and continuous reconnaisance of the enemy's forces that is vital to the success of the entire campaign.

21. During combat the aero squadron will operate around the flanks and over and to the rear of the enemy's position, for the purpose of reporting his dispositions, the approach of reinforcements, or the beginning of his withdrawal from action.

30. Employment of Air Craft.—Military air craft of all kinds will be employed under the direction of the commander of the forces to which they are assigned and the immediate control of the officer commanding the aero organization.

Balloons are classed as free, captive, and dirigible. Free balloons may be used to convey information from besieged places, the return message being sent by radiotelegraphy, carrier pigeons or otherwise. Free balloons are of little use for any other service, and are not very dependable on account of their uncertainty of movement. Cap-

1. War Department, *Field Service Regulations, United States Army, 1914, Corrected to July 31, 1918 (Changes Nos. 1 to 11)* (Washington, 1918). No changes are indicated for the passages printed above.

tive balloons may be used for tactical reconnaissance, for observation of artillery fire, and for signaling. Communication from a captive balloon to the ground should be by telephone.

Large dirigible balloons are of practical value for strategical reconnaissance and to travel great distances; they are also suitable for carrying a number of observers, radio equipment, machine guns, and considerable weight of explosives. Aeroplanes are more dependable for field service with a mobile army than dirigible balloons, as the latter require substantial shelter from winds while on the ground.

31. Reconnaissance by aeroplane includes strategical and tactical reconnaissance and the observation of artillery fire. Aeroplanes are also used to prevent hostile aerial reconnaissance.

Strategical reconnaissance by aeroplane is effective within a radius of 150 miles from the starting point, and is for the purpose of determining the position, strength, and direction of advance of the large elements of an enemy's forces, and also the character of the roads, railroads, streams, and the general military topography of the theater of operations.

Tactical reconnaissance by aeroplane is used both in attack and defense. It is extended in nature and does not involve minute examinations of very small localities or detachments. It is designed to discover turning and enveloping movements, the position and strength of the enemy's general reserve, artillery positions and movements of cavalry; also, from the movement of combat or field trains behind an enemy's position information may be gained as to whether certain parts of the line are being weakened or strengthened, or whether a retreat is contemplated.

For observation of fire of field artillery, aeroplanes are usually assigned to the artillery commander. They are especially useful against targets which are invisible from the position of the artillery officer conducting the fire.

Aeroplanes are safe from hostile fire at altitudes of 4,000 feet or more.

The results of reconnaissance are reported by radiotelegraphy, signals, and the dropping of messages.

Transmission of Information

36. Information is transmitted as follows:

1. By wire (telegraph, buzzer, telephone).

2. By visual signaling (flag, helio, night lamp).

3. By radio telegraph.

4. By messenger (foot, mounted, cycle, motor car, flying machine).

. . . .

Use of the Combined Arms

123. Infantry.—The infantry is the principal and most important arm, which is charged with the main work on the field of battle and decides the final issue of combat. The role of the infantry, whether offensive or defensive, is the role of the entire force, and the utilization of that arm gives the entire battle its character. The success of the infantry is essential to the success of the combined arms.

124. Artillery.—The artillery is the close supporting arm of the infantry and its duties are inseparably connected with those of the infantry. Its targets are those units of the enemy which, from the infantry point of view, are most dangerous to its infantry or that hinder infantry success. The greater the difficulties of the infantry the more powerful must be the artillery support.

125. Cavalry.—The cavalry, preceding contact of the opposing troops of the other arms, is engaged in reconnaissance of the enemy and of the terrain and in accomplishing such mission as may be assigned it. During combat it directs its activities to the support of the other arms and particularly toward insuring the success of the infantry as soon as that arm is fully committed to action.

. . . .

The Burgess-Dunne (above) was used by the Army in 1915. A
tailless pusher, it was propelled by a Salmson engine, and it had
sweepback wings (below).

5. Funds for Aeronautics (Fiscal Year 1916)
December 1914

When it came time to budget for Fiscal Year 1916, General Scriven asked for a little more than $1,000,000 for aviation. Secretary Garrison again imposed a cut, this time to $400,000. On 8 December 1914, Chairman Hay and members of the House Military Affairs Committee (D. R. Anthony, (R-Kan.); William S. Howard, (D-Ga.); Julius Kahn, (R-Calif.); and Kenneth McKellar, (D-Tenn.) questioned the Chief Signal Officer about how the money for 1915 was spent, about the $400,000 requested for 1916, and, among other things, about the use of aviation in the war in Europe. In the end Congress cut the amount to $300,000 (see Appendix A). Following are extracts from the hearings.[1]

. . . .

The Chairman. How many airships, aeroplanes, or biplanes have you on hand?

Gen. Scriven. We have on hand just now 11. Col. Reber is just placing an order for 8 more, and there are 2 training machines, so that we will have a total of 21 machines, and subtracting the cost of these orders that are now placed . . . we [will] have about $40,000 left for fiscal year 1915.

The Chairman. What do you propose to do with that $40,000?

Gen. Scriven. We have six months to run and we have to buy gasoline and oil, and we will have a thousand and one little expenses. An air machine is very much like an automobile. When you buy an automobile, then your expenses begin.

The Chairman. You expect to spend that for the upkeep and repair of the machines?

Gen. Scriven. For upkeep and repairs. Of course, if we have any of that appropriation left, and I hope we will, we will buy some more machines.

The Chairman. You have not a sufficient fund to buy more than the 21 machines you have already provided for?

Gen. Scriven. I have been thinking it over, Mr. Chairman, and I am in hopes that we may be able to squeeze out two or three more machines, making a total, with the 21 on hand, of 23 or 24 machines. If we can create four aero squadrons, like the one represented in that picture, of 8 machines each, that will give us 32 machines, and with that number we are quite well provided for an army of our size—32 machines in first line in commission. Then we should add 50 per cent of spare parts, or what really amounts to other machines, in the warehouses ready to put together, so that we will then have 50 machines, and then we shall be as well off in this respect as we need to be.

The Chairman. You only want to accumulate 32 machines?

Gen. Scriven. We only want to accumulate 32 machines in the first line and a reserve of 50 per cent because we have under the bill 60 aviator officers and we are only allowed 12 enlisted men for instruction in flying. The limit is therefore 72. If we organize 4 squadrons of 8 machines each that is 32 machines—each squadron is supposed to have 20 pilots and observers—4 squadrons would require 80 men, observers and pilots. That would constitute the necessary complement of men. Now we are allowed 60 officers. We will probably get these officers, because they are coming in very fast and they appear to appreciate the work. We should then require 20 enlisted men to make up the full complement of 800 men. If these can not be obtained it will be necessary to cut off some of the 4 officers comprising the commander and staff of each squadron, or an observer need not be sent out with every machine. At all events it will be possible to put 4 squadrons in the field fairly well manned and equipped.

But to the 4 squadrons of 32 machines should be added a reserve of 50 per cent of spare

1. Hearings before the Committee on Military Affairs. House of Representatives. *Army Appropriation Bill. 1916* (1914).

parts, because the machines require this for spare parts all the time. That would add 16 more machines to be purchased, as the spare parts should constitute an entire semblance not put together, so that in case of immediate necessity the spare parts could be assembled and replace broken machines in the field at once.

The Chairman. Of the $400,000 you are asking for, how much do you expect to spend for this purpose?

Gen. Scriven. I think I can give that exactly. We have 21 machines now and $40,000 left. The running expenses from now until July will be, I should say, about $25,000, which will give us $15,000 free and two more machines, which will make 23 machines. To make up the 32 machines we will have 9 macines to buy and to make up the reserve for the 32 machines, 50 per cent, 16, making it necessary to buy in all 25 new machines during the coming year to put the aviation squadrons into fairly good shape.

Mr. Kahn. Gen. Scriven, you stated to the committee that you thought if you could build up a corps of 32 flying machines it would serve your present purpose in proportion to our Army?

Gen. Scriven. I think so.

Mr. Kahn. Can you give the committee any data as to the number of machines that each one of the belligerent nations had at the outbreak of hostilities in Europe?

Gen. Scriven. Yes, sir; I can. I do not know how accurate it is, but it is the most recent thing on the subject I know of. It comes from a publication called the Clash of Nations published by Thomas Nelson & Sons, of New York, 1914. They give the number of aeroplanes for France,

500; dirigibles, 11. Russia, aeroplanes, 500; dirigibles, 4. Great Britain, aeroplanes, 250; dirigibles, 8. Germany, aeroplanes, 500; dirigibles, 20. Austria, aeroplanes, 100; dirigibles, 3. Italy, aeroplanes, 150; dirigibles, 2.

Mr. Kahn. So that your request is an exceedingly modest one in comparison with what they had when war broke out in Europe?

Gen. Scriven. I think it is a very modest one. I would like to go on and explain that a little further. The idea is to have four squadrons, three of them aeroplanes proper and one a squadron of hydro-aeroplanes. It must be understood that we require certainly eight machines (one hydro squadron) to be used in the Philippines, and especially for use in Panama, and also, as I think, in Hawaii.

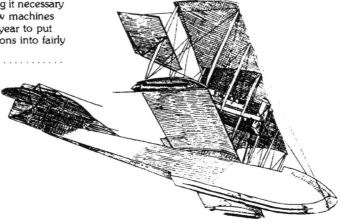

The Chairman. What is your information as to the effect of the aeroplane service in the armies of the countries now at war?

Gen. Scriven. Mr. Chairman, I have pretty pronounced views on that.

The Chairman. I mean, what is your information about that?

Mr. McKellar. Are they doing any real service?

Gen. Scriven. They are the most tremendous implement for reconnoissance and for the gathering of information that modern war has ever seen, I think. I think they have changed, as I said in my annual report, not strategy, but the principles of grand tactics.

Mr. Anthony. It has not developed that they are of any practical value for offensive military purposes?

Gen. Scriven. No, sir; I believe not.

A man to make a cruise of 400 miles, across a course 200 miles each way, has to carry, we will say, 400 pounds of fuel and oil. He can not take an observer with him because that would add too much weight, and he goes alone. The amount of destructive material he can carry in the way of bombs or guns under these conditions must be small, as their weight makes any considerable supply of ammunition prohibitive, but in addition a pilot alone without help can hardly do any effective firing either with bomb or gun; and if 4,000 or 5,000 feet in the air, he can do little more than drop his shots broadcast upon the earth. We have recently tried bomb dropping at San Diego with three types of bombs, one weighing 25 pounds, one weighing 50 pounds, and one weighing 100 pounds. As a matter of fact, we did not use the 100-pound bomb. It has been estimated that our aeroplane carries about 25 to 50 gallons of gasolene for a flight of, say, 350 miles; but this depends upon current winds. At all events, the machine carries enough gasolene to stay in the air about four hours, and carries also an observer and a pilot, besides oil. So loaded it is estimated that one of our aeroplanes has a free lifting capacity of about 120 pounds. With a lifting capacity of 120 pounds and with each bomb weighing not less than 25 pounds—and a 25-pounder is not good for much, so that the bomb should be as large as 50 pounds to do any damage—of what value is the aeroplane as an offensive weapon?

Of course, I do not now refer to attack of aeroplane against aeroplane or aeroplane against dirigible, nor do I wish to be understood as saying that in a few isolated cases bomb dropping may not do harm, but only that as a fighting machine the aeroplane has not justified its existence, except aeroplane against other air craft.

As an implement for reconnaissance and as the far-seeing eye of a commander the aeroplane is superb.

Mr. McKellar. You say they are used for getting information. How can a man in the air, several hundred or several thousand feet above the country, running a machine get any information about what is actually going on down below?

Gen. Scriven. Not the man running the machine, but the observer.

Mr. McKellar. How does he get any information about what is going on down below?

Gen. Scriven. We can not say how he does it, but as a matter of fact we know he does it, because we know what they are doing in Europe. He also gives signals of what he sees.

The Chairman. General, I apprehend that the greatest use of the aeroplane so far in the war in Europe has been that the observer in the aeroplane has been able to signal to his side the position of the enemy.

Gen. Scriven. Yes, sir.

Mr. Kahn. And that supplements the work of the cavalry in that respect?

Gen. Scriven. It supplements cavalry and it leads cavalry. It gives the cavalry the point of objective to get in touch with the enemy.

The Chairman. And it also aids the artillery?

Gen. Scriven. Yes, sir; visual signaling is done in several ways. There is a smoke bomb which is dropped above the point to be indicated, also fragments of tinsel paper, which fall down from the aeroplane and in the sunlight gives a streak of light. From such signals the observer at the guns, who is constantly following the plane gets his range with the glass. This, if well calculated, gives him his range and his direction. I believe, too, that other signals of the wigway type are used. Indeed, the matter is not difficult—a flag thrown to the wind from the aeroplane, a smoke bomb dropped, a sudden rise or dip of the machine perhaps might serve the purpose.

Mr. Howard. The observer ought to be a very competent military officer.

Gen. Scriven. Yes, sir; he must be a trained man.

Mr. Howard. And a strategist?

Gen. Scriven. Yes. At all events, he should be able to interpret the movements of troops that he sees. We have tried, and I think successfully, the wireless with the aeroplanes, and by that means, through ground stations, should keep the commanding general constantly in touch with the movement of troops. If he (pointing) is sending a column over the hills yonder he can see through the aeroplane how far the column has gone and just what its position is. Hence he keeps in touch with the positions of his own moving troops and knows where they actually are, and not merely where they should be according to arranged plans.

In regard to the enemy, his airmen outline the latter's lines, see the movement of his troops, indicate his reinforcements. In fact, the whole game is open to a commander; the cards lie on the table.

Mr. Kahn. Gen. Scriven, I have seen it stated in some of the papers that the aeroplane is largely responsible for the indecisiveness of the battles that have been raging in northern France lately.

Gen. Scriven. I think that must be so.

Mr. McKellar. Has not the use of aeroplanes in the European war now going on been a distinct disappointment to those who believed that air craft would play an important part in warfare?

Gen. Scriven. Well, I think in one direction, that of destruction, such is the case; in another direction, that of information, their usefulness far exceeds the expectations and hopes of anybody. In reconnoissance work they have done more than anybody could have dreamed of. Gen. French's official reports show that. As far as aggressiveness and destruction are concerned, they have fallen far short of what we anticipated at the hearing a year and a half ago.

Mr. McKellar. The only destruction they have accomplished is that of helpless women and children?

Gen. Scriven. There has been no destruction of military importance, absolutely none, so far as I have observed. Their attack has inspired fear, but even that seems quickly to pass away.
. . . .

**Brig. Gen. George P. Scriven,
Chief Signal Officer (1913–1917).**

In a circular on "The Service of Information" in 1915, General Scriven emphasized the importance of aviation as an instrument of reconnaissance and communication. At the same time, however, he recognized that the role of military aviation was expanding as aircraft were used for other kinds of operations in the war in Europe. Following is the section of the circular concerning the employment of aircraft.[1]

Air Craft

The signal corps is intrusted with the air service of the army—undoubtedly the most important, as it is the most recent, auxiliary in the collection and transmission of military information. Air craft are now employed for strategical and tactical reconnaissance and the prevention of reconnaissance by the enemy's air craft; for the direction and control of fire of the field artillery; for the destruction of the enemy's personnel and materiél by explosive and incendiary missiles and other means; and for the rapid transportation of superior commanding officers. The value of air craft and especially of the aeroplane, in the field of reconnaissance has been proved beyond the shadow of a doubt. Whatever may be the opinions of military men as regards the offensive importance of air craft and the present standing of the dirigible there is no longer a question as to the value of the aeroplane in rapid

and long-range reconnaissance work, and of its power to secure and to transmit by radio, visual signal or direct-flight information of the utmost importance to armies in the field. So true is this that it seems probable the aeroplane and, to some smaller degree, all air craft have altered not the principles of strategy, which are immutable, but the theory and application of grand tactics. It now appears that the actual game of war is played openly with cards laid on the table, and opportunity no longer is given for inference as to concealed movements or for surprises, perhaps not even for the exercise of the high military quality of anticipation of the unseen movements of the adversary. It is now recognized that the possibility of brilliant and unexpected blows and surprises by enterprising commanders has been largely eliminated from modern operations of war by the information supplied by the aviators. It is proved that the modern air craft lays open to the field of mental view the whole visible area of the immediate theater of war and that the commander's vision reaches far beyond the limits of the actual sight of his marching troops. The air craft sees and indicates the larger operations of war and points out to the slowly moving men on the ground not only the object to be attacked or defended, but to reconnaissance troops, especially the cavalry,

1. Scriven, *The Service of Information*, Circular No. 8, Office of the Chief Signal Officer (Washington, 1915), pp 21–23.

the objective to be sought, the localities to be searched, and the character of information to be obtained.

By no means does the air craft supersede, nor can it ever supersede, the work of obtaining detailed information which can be acquired only by close observation, by contact, and by development of the enemy's forces and positions. This remains the duty of the troops in the field; but the air craft does indicate to either commander the character, location, and general disposition of opposing forces, and of his own commands. Not only has it been proved that the aeroplane is invaluable in locating the position of the enemy, but it has especial value to a commander in finding his own troops, in keeping him informed when movements are taking place, and of the position of his flanks and center, his outposts, his

cavalry, his artillery, of the positions attained by any detached body—in short, of keeping him constantly in touch with the locations and movements of all the units of his command under the changing conditions of war.

This much is proved, but it does not follow that the air craft curtails the work of reconnaissance of other arms of the service, the infantry, the signal corps, and, more especially, the cavalry. On the contrary, it extends the usefulness and power of all, for if the general field of reconnaissance is outlined, it is obvious that the cavalry or infantry can more readily strike its objective and more quickly and accurately obtain information regarding any particular point than if obliged unseeingly to search the whole field of operations for locations and forces regarding

which an intimate knowledge is desired or contact expected. In other words, by aid of air craft, and more especially of the aeroplane, a reconnaissance by troops moves less in the dark, knows better what to look for and search in detail, and loses less time and effort in accomplishing the object sought. No move of concentration from flank or center, no envelopment of a wing nor reenforcement of a weak position should remain unknown to the adversary in the case where he possesses a thoroughly efficient flying corps. It would seem, therefore, that not only has the power of all reconnaissance troops been increased by the air craft, but also that the need and importance of the cavalry in reconnaissance work have not been lessened, but, on the contrary, have been greatly increased by them.

In addition to the influence exerted by air craft on grand

operations, events now appear to show that their value in more detailed operations is great and may increase in the future to enormous proportions. It is well established that the accuracy, value, and effect in service of field and siege artillery and, indeed, of the heavy guns afloat and ashore have been greatly increased by this agency. It may almost be said that guns are fought by means of the eyes of the aviator. So clearly has this been shown that there now appears a noticeable change in artillery practice. Instead of the old-fashioned system of range finding by trial fire or of observation from the battery or elevations near by, the exact range is now found with the help of aeroplanes, by signaling positions and noting the fall or burst of the shrapnel, and there can be no doubt that artillery-fire direction has been enormously increased in accuracy by the aeroplane, especially when the shrapnel burst can not be seen from below. Infantry fire has been largely improved in efficiency by the same means.

Besides influence of this character the aeroplane has undoubted use in the finding of concealed positions, in locating hidden howitzers or mortars, and in pursuit and rear-guard actions. It will be useful in the location of ships at sea or at anchor within defenses, possibly in the detection of submarines and submarine mines, and certainly in the enormous increased efficiency given to seacoast gun fire, and especially to the coast defense, the coast guard, and many other details of observation.

But the useful, approved, and most important work of air craft is to be found chiefly in reconnaissance and the collection and transmission of information in the theater of military operations. For this reason aviation must be reckoned as a vastly important branch of the signal corps of the army.

The use of the aeroplane as a defense against aeroplane attack and for the rapid transmission of commanding officers or important personages to destinations sought is, of course, obvious.

Signal Corps'
Burgess-Wright seaplane at Corregidor
Island in the Philippines, November 1913, Lt. Herbert A.
Dargue in the cockpit.

The section on aircraft in Scriven's *The Service of Information* (Doc. 6) was also used as an introduction to a chapter on aviation in the Chief Signal Officer's annual report for Fiscal Year 1915, extracts from which are printed below.[1] Reviewing events of the past year and noting the situation that existed in mid-1915, Scriven looked toward the future to an expansion of the aviation service to perhaps as many as 18 squadrons. At that time there was only one, the 1st Aero Squadron, which was made up of two companies, each with four airplanes for reconnaissance work. Developments in Europe, however, had indicated that squadron organization needed to be changed.

. . . hereafter aeroplane squadrons should be composed of 3 companies, with a total of 12 machines to the squadron. Two companies should have 8 reconnoissance machines (4 to each company), and the third company should be made up of 2 rapid-flying machines for chase or transport purposes and 2 machines of the bomb-carrying or offensive type. Such are the conclusions reached from experience abroad.

The organization and instruction of the personnel of the First Aero Squadron were completed during the year (at North Island) and the squadron sent to Fort Sill, Okla., for duty in connection with the problems of fire control and direction of the field artillery.

The War Department has directed the maintenance of an aviation school and a squadron for land flying in this country, the stationing of an aero company at each of the following places: Corregidor, P.I.; Fort Kamehameha, Hawaii; Canal Zone, and when this has been accomplished, an increase of the force at Corregidor to a squadron.

Under this program the Signal Corps Aviation School will continue at North Island, in San Diego Bay, until a permanent site has been obtained. The First Squadron, now at Fort Sill, will proceed to San Antonio, Tex., in the early part of December, when it is expected that the buildings now being erected for

its use on the old target range at Fort Sam Houston will have been completed. The personnel for the company designated for Corregidor is now at the Aviation School and its equipment is being purchased. It will leave for Manila at the close of the typhoon season of the present year. Steps are being taken to obtain and train the personnel for the companies intended for Hawaii and Canal Zone, and such of their equipment as is practicable to purchase from the appropriation for the current fiscal year will be procured. Sufficient funds have not been provided for in the current year's appropriation to purchase complete equipment for these companies. It is expected to send a company to Hawaii by next April and one to the Canal Zone when funds are available for the equipment of the organization destined for that station.

The estimate for the ensuing fiscal year has been prepared on the basis of the program prescribed by the War Department for utilizing the personnel authorized by the act approved July 18, 1914.[2] The total of this estimate is $1,358,000.

The recent war in Europe has emphasized the absolute necessity for an adequate aviation service, has illustrated in a most forceful way the dangers resulting from an inadequate supply of personnel and materiel, has

1. *Report of the Chief Signal Officer, United States Army, to the Secretary of War, 1915* (Washington, 1915).
2. The act which created the Aviation Section (Doc. 3).

shown that aeroplanes are invaluable for reconnoissance purposes, and that their absence from a combatant force has resulted in most serious disasters. Aeroplanes have proved their value in the direction and control of artillery fire, in preventing the operation of the aeroplanes of an enemy, and have been used with great effect against both personnel and materiel. The difficulties surrounding the creation of an adequate aeronautical service after the outbreak of hostilities have been vividly illustrated during the past year, and the great inconveniences and dangers resulting from the lack of adequate aeronautical personnal and materiel have been so forcibly demonstrated that comment is unnecessary.

The greater need at such a time, however, will be for trained men as pilots and observers. . . . The inadequacy of facilities for building aeroplanes and the manufacturing of their accessories has to a large extent been removed in this country. At the present time it is known that something more than 100 flying machines per month can be produced. While this supply might meet the needs of a small army, it would be totally inadequate in a great war. However, there can be no doubt that American manufacturers would arise to the occasion with a sufficiently large output. The training of men,

therefore, is the crying need of the present time.

The number of officers and men now authorized by law is inadequate to the needs of the Army as it is at present organized. With one aero squadron per division, the present organization of the Army calls for five aero squadrons. The commissioned personnel provided by law allows a sufficient number of officers for three aero squadrons, as at present organized, while the enlisted strength is insufficient; and if the number of officers and men allowed by law should be organized into three aero squadrons there would be no personnel left for the conduct of the Aviation School.

The present war in Europe has developed three separate types of aeroplanes—the reconnoissance and fire control machines, the combat machine, and the pursuit machine. The aviation section possesses a satisfactory type of reconnoissance and fire-control machine and has taken up the question of the development of both the combat and pursuit types. For this purpose an item of $50,000 has been included for experimental machines in this year's estimates.

The organization of the aviation units in the foreign armies suggests a squadron of 12 machines as the basis for our organization, 8 of these machines to be of the reconnoissance type and 2 each of the pursuit and

combat types. Our aero squadron as at present organized has sufficient commissioned personnel for this increase in the number of machines, but the enlisted personnel is deficient by 24 men to provide crews for the additional machines and drivers for the additional autotrucks. In case the Army remains at its present authorized strength, the personnel of the aviation section should be increased by 46 officers and 410 men to give sufficient personnel to supply five aero squadrons, one for each of the five tactical divisions at present organized in the Army, and to maintain the Aviation School. It is to be pointed out that there is need for at least one squadron for reconnoissance work in each of the three Coast Artillery districts in this country, and that a sufficient number of aeroplanes should be provided for fire direction and control for the Field Artillery on the basis of one aeroplane per battery, with one in reserve, or, in round numbers, six aero squadrons for this arm. This calls for the addition of nine squadrons to those above mentioned.

If the plan for the reorganization of the Army by the War Department, which calls for seven tactical divisions and five Cavalry brigades, be approved by Congress, provision should be made for 1 aero squadron for Corregidor, 1 for Hawaii, 1 for Canal Zone, 1 for each of the three Coast Artillery districts in the United States, 1 for each of the tactical divisions, and 5 for the Field Artillery, giving in all 18 squadrons, with a total strength of 368 officers and 2,360 enlisted men.

The total cost of the equipment necessary for these organizations will be $4,284,000.

. . . .

Proposed organization of the aviation section for service with an Army of 180,000 men.

	Brigadier general	Colonel	Lieutenant Colonel	Majors	Captains	First lieutenants	Master signal electricians	First-class sergeants	Sergeants	Corporals	Cooks	First-class privates	Privates	Total enlisted
Mobile Army: 18 aero sqs				18	171	171	90	144	270	594	72	792	324	2,286
Service of the interior: Administration		1	1											
Aviation school detachment				1	3	2		6	12	18	2	24	12	74
Total		1	1	19	174	173	90	150	282	612	74	816	336	2,360

A captive balloon inflated at Ft. Myer, Virginia, summer of 1908.

8. War College Division: A Proper Military Policy
1915

In March 1915 the Chief of Staff directed the War College Division of the General Staff to make a full study of "a proper military policy for the United States." In the report submitted to the Chief of Staff on 11 September 1915, the War College Division recommended a mobile army of 1,000,000 men prepared to take the field immediately on the outbreak of war. Of these, half should be fully trained, and the other half should have enough training to enable them to be brought to full combat readiness within three months. The 500,000 fully-trained troops were divided between regular army and reserve. For the regular army, the War College Division recommended 65 infantry regiments, 25 cavalry regiments, 21 field artillery regiments, 289 coast artillery companies, and, among other units, 8 aero squadrons. Five of the squadrons were for duty with five tactical divisions recommended for service in the United States; the other three were to be stationed in the Philippines, Hawaii, and the Canal Zone.[1] The report of the War College Division was supplemented by a series of special studies which were published a little later. One of the studies was on military aviation, which is printed below.[2]

Military Aviation

I. Introduction.

1. Relation of Aviation to The Military Service

In this paper it is proposed to consider various aeronautical appliances in regard to their practical value in campaign, as shown by such data as are now available from the theater of war in Europe.

In its relation to the military service, aviation to-day may be regarded as embracing all aerial appliances, such as heavier-than-air craft, dirigibles lighter-than-air craft, and nondirigibles or captive lighter-than-air balloons, together with the personnel necessary for their operation and management.

2. Use of Aircraft on Our Coast and With Our Mobile Land Forces.

In considering this subject account should be taken, first, of the use of aircraft of various types along and beyond the coasts and frontiers of the United States upon the outbreak of war; second, the use of aircraft in the Army by the mobile forces; third, the use of aircraft by our over-sea garrisons.

In addition to the battle fleet and units of the Navy designed to take the offensive on the high seas, the waters contiguous to the coast line of the United States are organized into naval defense districts. These cover certain sections of the coast line and contain patrol vessels, both surface and subsurface, and aircraft for reconnoissance purposes. These are essentially for the purpose of finding out and locating hostile vessels which are approaching the coast and of determining their strength, dispositions, and probable intentions.

Added to the strictly naval formations included in the naval defense districts, in time of war the United States Coast Guard (in peace under the Treasury Department) passes to the control of the Navy.

The Coast Guard, in addition to its boats and revenue cutters which will be utilized as patrol vessels, embraces the Life-Saving Service. The latter has stations more or less regularly distributed along the coasts which are connected by telephone lines. They are also equipped with visual signaling appliances to communicate from shore to ships. The Navy maintains a chain of radio stations along our coasts and over-sea possessions.

The naval defense districts become of great importance in case that the main battle fleets are defeated or in case they are operating at a great distance.

Notes

1. War College Division, *Statement of a Proper Military Policy for the United States* (Washington, 1915), p. 13.

2. War College Division, *Military Aviation* (Washington, 1916).

Therefore, when an enemy expedition breaks through the naval defense and approaches the coast with a view to forcing a landing the resistance to such an expedition becomes primarily a function of the Army.

The defensive formations of the Army consist of the harbor defenses and accessories and the mobile units. The harbor defenses consist of fixed and mobile gun defenses and mine defenses; also obstacles both on land and in the waters. The aircraft required in connection with the harbor defenses should consist of machines used for one or more of the following purposes:

(a) For reconnaissance—that is, to determine the strength, dispositions, and probable intentions of the enemy.

(b) For preventing hostile aerial reconnaissance.

(c) For destroying hostile aircraft and for offensive work against enemy submarines and other vessels, including the interruption of enemy mining or countermining operations.

(d) For aiding in spotting the fire of Coast Artillery, both against ships and against any invading force that may invest the seacoast fortifications.

The number and character of the aircraft required depends on the locality, number of harbor defenses, their organization, strength, and positions. Each harbor-defense area, therefore, needs to be studied with this specific end in view, and should

have radio apparatus not only for communicating with the Navy but also for communicating with its aircraft and with the units of our mobile forces.

In addition to the aircraft required with the harbor defenses themselves, aircraft are required with modern movable coast-defense armament employed as an auxiliary element of the mobile forces in defending the intervals between our fortified harbors and with units of the mobile forces.

The use of aircraft with the mobile units is a definite matter; each division requires one squadron of 12 aeroplanes. These are divided into three companies of four aeroplanes each, two companies having re-

Wright Model D Scout purchased by the Signal Corps in 1913. It was a single-seat pusher type aircraft propelled by a 6-cylinder. 60 hp. Wright Field engine.

connaissance and artillery observation machines and one company having two high-speed machines especially constructed for long-distance reconnaissance and for combating the enemy's aerial craft; two battle machines for the purpose of bomb dropping and offensive work against enemy material of all sorts. This is in keeping with the best practice that has been developed in the European war.

3. Use of Aircraft At Over-Sea Stations

The use of aircraft with the Army in the over-sea possessions analogous to that mentioned above with the harbor defenses; and in addition, wherever mobile units of the Army happen to be, they must be provided with suitable aircraft. The defense of over-sea possessions constitutes a problem in itself, and these garrisons must be equipped not only with machines capable of reconnaissance over land but also with those capable of operations over water, with the power to alight in water—that is, hydroaeroplanes.

The type of machine to be

used necessarily depends on the locality; for instance, in Hawaii practically all of the military machines would need to be hydroaeroplanes; in the Philippines and Panama a great proportion of them. To the Coast Artillery troops in the United States proper and in the districts around the Great Lakes the same considerations apply. It is believed that the main principles enunciated above should be followed, and that an estimate of actual machines and material, both heavier and lighter than air, should be made for all places.

II. General Types of Aircraft.

4. Captive Balloons.

For over a century captive balloons have been used by the armies of all the leading military nations. Their function has been one of observation; that is, to see what those on the ground were unable to see. They have therefore proved a useful means of observing and reporting the effects of artillery fire. Electrical means of communication greatly

enhanced the utility of captive balloons, as it made communication instantaneous from car to ground instead of by the older way of raising and lowering written messages by ropes. In clear weather and on favorable terrain captive balloons are able to distinguish different branches of the service at a distance of 16,000 yards or about 9 miles. With the best glasses at the present time the field of observation is said to extend to 20,000 yards. In general, captive balloons of the "Sausage" or "Drachen" type are used by all the armies of the great nations. Along the French-German front in northern France these balloons are used in great numbers all along the lines. Their function is to observe the fire of artillery and keep watch of all movements of hostile parties within their field of view. They are connected with telephone directly with the batteries whose fire they are observing and with the headquarters to which they are attached. In many cases the captive balloons work in conjunction with aeroplanes. The aeroplanes by flying over the terrain where the hostile targets are located find out the exact position of those which the captive balloons have been unable to locate by themselves. When by means of signals the locations of the targets have been indicated to the observer in the captive balloon, the aeroplanes proceed to other duty. Aside from the use of the captive balloons in conjunction with aeroplanes,

A Caquot or "sausage" balloon, a type of captive observation
balloon widely used during World War I.

their duties are practically the same as they have been for many years or were in our own Civil War. Free balloons such as were used from Paris, for instance, in 1870 are now a thing of the past, their place having been taken by the aeroplane or the dirigible airship. All military captive balloons are now so constructed that their undersurface acts like a kite, thereby making them steady in a strong wind. To keep the envelope distended properly in the face of the wind, a wind sail is provided so as to transmit pressure to the rear part of the envelope by means of the wind itself. Captive balloons are used not only with the field forces, but also are especially useful in fortress warfare. The organizations which handle these balloons consist ordinarily of some 4 officers, 72 men for each balloon section.

5. Dirigibles.

The term dirigible, as applied to aeronautical appliances, signifies a lighter-than-air craft, which is equipped with engines and propellers capable of moving it from place to place. Dirigibles may be roughly divided into three classes: Non-rigid, or those whose envelope can be entirely packed into a small space when deflated, and that have no rigid framework of any kind; semirigid, or those that have a stiffening for a part of their length in order to enable the envelopes to maintain their shape to better advantage than the nonrigid; the

rigid, which have a framework for the whole envelope that maintains itself continuously. All have been tried for the last 15 years. The nonrigid types have not given very good results, as they are too much dependent on the weather, due to distortion of the envelopes; the semirigid have given some satisfaction and have been largely employed. The advantage of the semirigid types is that they may be packed for shipment and reassembled much more easily than the rigid types; they can be deflated quickly and, consequently, are not so subject to complete destruction as the rigid types when anchored to the earth. On the other hand, they are not able to develop the speed that the rigid types, such as the "Zeppelin," are capable of.

Dirigibles and aeroplanes are frequently compared with each other as to their utility in general. As a matter of fact, they are two entirely different military accessories and are as different in many ways as is a captive balloon from an aeroplane. Dirigibles are able to stay in the air at any height for long periods of time. They are capable of running at reduced speed, can

hover over localities for minute observation and to take photographs. They are able to carry several tons weight in addition to their passengers and crew. From the fact that they are able to remain stationary over a given place they are able to launch their projectiles with greater accuracy. Dirigibles in present war have been used both over land and sea. At sea they have carried out reconnaissance, have acted offensively against hostile submarines, have accompanied transports in order to observe the approach of hostile craft, have been used in mine laying, stopping and examining hostile merchant vessels at sea, and for bombarding hostile localities. The airships which have made the longest trips and developed the greatest efficiency thus far are the German "Zeppelin" rigid-frame type. These have repeatedly flown over England at a distance of at least 300 miles from their base, and have nearly always returned in safety. Some have been lost, however. Aeroplanes appear to be unable to cope with them at night. While dirigibles have not proved themselves to be a determining factor in combat, either on land or sea, they are being developed to the greatest extent possible, especially by the Germans, who have dirigibles of very great size. The principal features of this type are a rigid framework of aluminum, a number of drum-shaped gas

Signal Corps dirigible,
Baldwin Airship #1, in flight at Ft. Myer,
Virginia, summer 1908.

At right, *Baldwin's* motor.

bags, and a thin outer cover. Although the details of construction are not definitely known up to date, their length is about 485 feet, their volume about 900,-000 cubic feet, their total lift over 20 tons, and their useful lift about 5 tons. They are driven by four motors of a total horsepower of about 800, which is applied to four propellers. Their speed is from 50 to 60 or more miles per hour and a full-speed endurance of over 100 hours, or more than 4 days. It is therefore evident that in good weather these airships have a radius of action of from 5,000 to 6,000 miles. Moreover, they are being constantly improved, and are probably capable of crossing the Atlantic Ocean. Crews of from 10 to 20 men are required for their operation; they are armed with bombs of various sorts, light guns, and are equipped with searchlights. They carry very efficient radio apparati, which have equipments for determining the directions from which radio impulses are being sent. In this way they are able to locate themselves at night or in foggy weather when the ground is invisible. They require very large and expensive hangars, gas plants, and equipments for their operation. When forced to make landings outside of their hangars, on account of their bulk, they are very difficult to handle in hard winds, and are liable to destruction thereby.

The best of the nonrigid and semirigid airships have a capacity of more than 800,000 cubic

feet, a maximum speed of 50 miles per hour or less, and a full speed endurance of about 24 hours. As mentioned above, their great asset is extreme portability and cheapness as compared with the rigid type.

6. **Aeroplanes.**

Heavier-than-air craft made their appearance as military agencies in 1908, when the Wright brothers demonstrated thoroughly the possibilities in this respect. While many of the salient features of heavier-than-air machines had been worked out years before, it remained for the internal-combustion engine to really make mechanical flight possible. The military possibilities of aircraft of this description were appreciated immediately by the great nations. Large appropriations were made at once, notably by France and Germany for their development. At first England was slow to take up the matter, but in 1912 had gone at it thoroughly and was spending large amounts of money for their development. Italy, Russia, Japan, and the smaller nations of Europe and South America made liberal appropriations for obtaining the material and developing the personnel. Aeroplanes were used in a small way during the Italian campaign in Africa during the Balkan-Turkish War, and during the Balkan War. These nations had very little equipment and very few

trained flyers. Wherever the aeroplanes were given the opportunity under average conditions they rendered efficient service in reconnaissance.

7. **Types of Aeroplanes.**

We now find aeroplanes consisting of three principal classes: (a) Scout or speed machines; (b) reconnaissance aeroplanes; (c) battle machines. The first are used for distant reconnaissance and combating the enemy's aircraft, the second for ordinary reconnaissance and the observation of fire of artillery, and the third for the destruction of enemy's material, personnel, or equipment.

8. **Requirements of Various Types of Machines.**

Great advances have been made since the war began in all these machines, all the details of which are not yet available. The following table, which appeared in the London Times of February 19, 1914, gives the approximate requirements of each type of machine at the beginning of the war. These general characteristics are still desired, but the radius of action and the speed have been considerably increased.

9. **Aeroplane Engines.**

As to material, the most important consideration in aeroplane construction has been the engine. Without excellent engines the best aeroplanes otherwise are of no service; in fact, may be a source of danger. In the countries where aeroplane development has made the most progress large prizes have been given for the development of suitable engines. At the same time, research and experimentation have gone on along this line at Government plants. Engines require frequent replacement. In fact, it is reported that after 100 hours in the air engines are "scrapped" and new ones installed. The plan found to give excellent results for the development of material is for the Government to have stations where experimentation along all lines is carried on. On the data furnished by these establishments specifications are made up for the construction of aircraft by private individuals and civil manufactories. If any parts, such as the engines mentioned above, need additional development, prizes are offered to stimulate construction and progress.

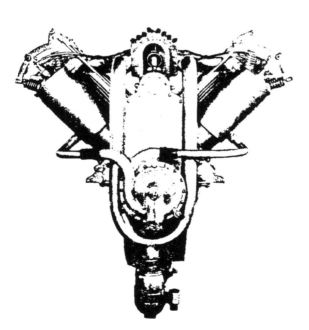

III. **Functions of Aircraft.**

10. **Height At Which Aeroplanes Must Fly.**

It was soon found out that to escape the fire of small arms, a height of about 4,000 feet above the ground had to be maintained. As soon as balloon guns were created this height had to be increased to 6,000 feet, at which height it is now necessary to fly in order to be reasonably safe from being hit by hostile projectiles sufficient to bring the machine down. At this height, 6,000 feet, small details of the terrain and small detachments of troops or material are very difficult to distinguish. On the other hand, large columns of troops, trains, railways, bridges, artillery firing, and sometimes in position, defensive positions of large extent, and things of that nature can be readily distinguished. Whenever it becomes necessary for the aircraft to fly at a lower altitude than 6,000 feet the chance of destruction by gunfire must be considered.

11. **Strategical Reconnaissance.**

Reconnaissance of this kind is strategical in its nature, the tactical reconnaissance of particular localities is still carried out by troops or captive balloons. In fact, it may be said that all strategical reconnaissance is now carried on by aircraft. The reconnaissance is carried out by an officer who requires considerable experience in order to be able to

Performances required from various military types.

	Light scout.	Reconnaissance aeroplane. (a)	Reconnaissance aeroplane. (b)	Fighting aeroplane. (a)	Fighting aeroplane. (b)
Tankage to give an endurance of.	300 miles	300 miles	200 miles	200 miles	300 miles.
To carry	Pilot only	Pilot and observer plus 80 pounds for wireless equipment.	Pilot and observer plus 80 pounds for wireless equipment.	Pilot and gunner plus 300 pounds for gun and ammunition.	Pilot and gunner plus 100 pounds.
Range of speed	50 to 85 miles per hour	45 to 75 miles per hour	35 to 60 miles per hour	45 to 65 miles per hour	45 to 75 miles per hour.
To climb 3,500 feet in	5 minutes	7 minutes	10 minutes	10 minutes	8 minutes.
Miscellaneous qualities	Capable of being started by the pilot single-handed.		To land over a 30-foot vertical obstacle and pull up within a distance of 100 yards from that obstacle, the wind not being more than 15 miles per hour. A very good view essential.	A clear field of fire in every direction up to 30° from the line of flight.	A clear field of fire in every direction up to 30° from the line of flight.

distinguish objects on the earth and assign to them their true military value. The pilot is either an officer or noncommissioned officer. The observer is always a trained tactical officer, because in reconnaissance of this nature an untrained person can not interpret the military significance of what he sees.

12. Photography From Aeroplanes.

Photography is utilized to the greatest extent possible in aerial reconnaissance. The devices are so arranged that they are capable of taking one or a series of views of a particular locality. The plates or films thus made are rapidly developed and are thrown on a screen by means of a stereopticon, when all details are magnified to any extent desired and details invisible to the naked eye are brought out plainly. These details are then entered on the maps of the officers concerned. As the height at which an aeroplane is flying can be taken from the barograph, and as the focal angle of the lens of the camera is known, a scale can easily be worked out and the views form good maps of the terrain photographed.

13. Aeroplanes and Artillery.

In addition to reconnaissance in general, aeroplanes have taken their place as a fixture for observing the fire of artillery. Due to the degree of concealment which artillery is now given, it is impossible to determine its location from the ground. The aeroplanes first pick up the targets, report their location to the field artillery, and then observe the fire of the batteries. By means of prearranged visual signals or radiotelegraphy the aeroplanes are able to indicate to the artillery where their fire is making itself felt. If artillery is insufficiently provided with aeroplanes, it is well established that an enemy so provided has an overwhelming advantage.

14. Control of The Air.

For this reason, among others, attempts to gain "control of the air" are made by belligerents at the inception of hostilities. This takes the form of offensive action by aeroplane against aeroplane. For this purpose machines known as "speed scouts" and "battle aeroplanes" have been developed. All the great European nations are now equipped with them. The only way in which enemy aeroplanes can be effectively dealt with is by aeroplanes, because they are difficult targets for gunfire from the ground. To gain control of the air a great preponderance in number and efficiency of aircraft is necessary. So far in the European war, unless one side had a greatly preponderating number and quality of aeroplanes, they have been unable to obtain and keep control of the air. An excellent instance of obtaining control of the air seems to be furnished by the Austro-Germans when they initiated the campaign against the Russians in May, 1915. In this instance complete control of the air appears to have been obtained. The results to the Russians were disastrous because the Austro-Germans were able to fly at will wherever they wanted to, could pick up the location of the Russian masses, and make their movements accordingly, entirely unobserved by the Russians. In the fire of their artillery they had the advantage of being able to locate the Russian guns and observe their own fire while the Russians were powerless to do so.

In an article on "Recent progress in military aeronautics," published in the Journal of the Franklin Institute for October, 1915, Lieut. Col. Samuel Reber, Signal Corps, United States Army, sums up the question of machines for control of the air as follows:

Experience has developed three types of aeroplanes for military purposes. The first, the speed scout, for strategical reconnaissance, a one seater, with a speed up to 85 miles per hour and radius of action of 300 miles and a fast climber, about 700 feet per minute; the second for general reconnaissance purposes with the same radius of action, carrying both pilot and observer and equipped with radiotelegraphy, slower in speed, about 70 miles per hour, and climbing about 500 feet per minute, and in some cases protected by armor; the third, or fighting craft, armored, and carries in addition to the pilot a rapid fire gun and ammunition and so arranged as to have a clear field of view and fire in either direction up to 30 degrees from the line of flight, the speed to run from 45 to 65 miles per hour, and the machine to climb about 350 feet per minute.

15. Surprise Movements.

It is often said that due to the use of aeroplanes surprises are no longer possible. Generally speaking, this is so, providing both sides are equally well equipped with machines and weather conditions are favorable. If, however, complete "command of the air" is obtained by one side, the chances of surprising the enemy are greater than they have ever been before.

16. Bomb Dropping.

In addition to their functions of reconnaissance, the observation of the fire of artillery, and the combat of hostile machines, both heavier and lighter than air, much time, thought, and ingenuity have been given to the subject of dropping projectiles. Bombs of various sorts weighing from a couple of pounds to 50 pounds have been tried. The most common ones weigh from 15 to 35 pounds. At the height at which aeroplanes are required to fly it is extremely difficult to hit an object with any certainty. Various devices have been used and tried for this purpose. The factors of height, speed, and wind, are almost impossible to compensate for entirely, up to the present time, so that consequently bomb dropping in general or the launching of projectiles of all kinds from aeroplanes has not attained great results in so far as the actual destruction of material or personnel is concerned. Advances along this line are constantly being made, however, but progress is slow. A special type of aeroplane has been developed for dropping

bombs and battle purposes. For bomb attacks on any locality these machines are sent in flotillas of from 30 to 60 machines, each of which is provided with from 5 to 10 bombs. They go to the locality and circle over it, dropping their projectiles. Against railways, roads, bridges, and hostile parks of various kinds, this method of attack has given considerable success.

IV. Organization of Aeroplane Units

17. Tactics of Aeroplanes.

As to tactical use aeroplanes seem to be approaching methods similar to those used by a navy. That is, first the speed machines reconnoiter to the front; they are followed by the battle machines, which in their turn clear the way for the reconnaissance aeroplanes; those assigned to the artillery stay right with their guns. Fortresses, harbor-defense works, and naval formations require special organizations of aeroplanes, some or all of which may be operated from the water. The organization, kind, and number of the machines and personnel required for this particular service depend on the special locality and mission of whatever formation the aircraft are to be attached to.

18. Development During European War.

The use of aeroplanes is gradually being developed from experience in the European war. Organization has been found to be one of the most important considerations; in general the organization has been into squadrons. The squadron is a tactical and administrative unit. It has a personnel consisting of pilots, observers, bomb droppers, mechanicians, chauffeurs, and drivers. Flying personnel has to be developed in the military service. Unlike chauffeurs, for instance, there are few in the civil population who can be drawn on. The few who fly are demonstrators, exhibition flyers, or sportsmen. They are very few in number and scarcely a military asset. In France the squadrons usually have six machines and two spares. They have the same organization of depots of resupply that other units of the armies possess. The squadrons usually consist of complete units of one kind of machine; that is, speed, reconnaissance, or fighting. These squadrons are usually assigned to an army, or more if the machines and personnel are available.

In general an aeroplane requires for its operation a personnel of 1 pilot, 1 observer, and 2 enlisted men, mechanicians, chauffeurs, etc.

In England 12 machines of different classes are assigned to a squadron.

19. Assignment of Aeroplanes to Artillery.

Many are of the opinion that machines with the personnel to operate them should be assigned permanently to artillery regiments so that they would be immediately available whenever action is required by the artillery. If they have to be obtained from a higher headquarters valuable time is often lost. It is believed that before long aeroplanes will be assigned permanently to regiments of artillery.

V. Development of Aeronautic Personnel.

20. General Line of Development in Europe.

In the development of their aeronautical personnel all nations have worked more or less along similar lines. At first these detachments were attached to the engineers. All the pilots and observers were officers, while the mechanicians and others were enlisted men. As the science developed and more and more machines became necessary the importance of this branch constantly increased until eventually it formed a separate arm of the service.

Instead of officers only being employed in the flying of the machines noncommissioned officers began to be used as the pilots.

21. Officer-Observers and Noncommissioned Officer Pilots.

The observers were either trained staff officers or officers of particular branches when the reconnaissance being made especially concerned a certain branch. For instance, in the observation of artillery fire an artil-

lery officer, for the inspection of a demolished bridge over a great river an engineer officer, or for the observation of the tactical or strategical dispositions of an enemy's troops a staff officer. Noncommissioned officers are now very generally used as pilots. All countries now at war have found that they have places for all the trained pilots they can possibly obtain. In general the units are commanded by officers and a certain number of the pilots are officers, but the bulk of the piloting is done by enlisted men while the officers are carried as observers.

On 27 May 1913 the War Department established the Military Aviator Certificate. Officers of the Army qualifying under rules approved by the Secretary of War received the certificate, and an insignia (at right) to wear on their uniforms.

22. Losses to Aero Personnel in War.

The losses to the flying personnel in war, when equipped with proper machines, seems to be less than that of infantry, cavalry, and artillery in the order named.

23. Development of Aeronautic Personnel in the United States.

In the United States the development has been along similar lines to those employed in Europe, with the difference that here a branch of the service existed that did not formerly exist in European armies. It was a development of the Civil War, i.e., the Signal Corps. This corps is charged with the transmission of information between the various units of an army; the captive balloons had formerly been assigned to it, and when the aeroplanes made their appearance they naturally fitted in. In this way all the agencies for the transmission of information are kept under one head, which should give not only the maximum amount of efficiency in such transmission but also obviate the necessity of creating a new arm of the service. The development of aero units in the United States has been slow for various reasons: First, on account of the fact that very little money has been appropriated compared to the sums appropriated in Europe. Second, the selection of the flying personnel has been limited to lieutenants of the Regular Army, unmarried, and below 30 years of age. This reduces the number of eligibles to a very small compass and does not give the results that are necessary. In the development of a flying personnel it is thought that, in addition to a certain number of officers obtained from the Regular Army as now provided for by law, pilots should be obtained both from among the enlisted men and from suitable civilians who enlist for that purpose. When they have proved their ability to be efficient pilots they should be placed in a special grade to be designated by a suitable name, such as "aero pilot, Signal Corps," for instance. This grade should be analogous to the grade of warrant officer in the Navy. When such men leave the service for any cause which does not interfere with the performance of the duties of pilot, arrangements should be made to obtain their services at once at the outbreak of war. The observers should be tactical officers who have received training. The present organization authorized for the aero squadrons in the United States provides that each one have 12 aeroplanes—8 of the reconnaissance type, 2 of the speed type, and 2 of the battle type. The personnel numbers 20 officers, 18 of whom are pilots. It is intended that staff and Artillery officers be used as observers. The United States squadron appears to be a well-balanced unit for work in this country, judging by the experiences obtained in Europe. It should be perfected as soon as possible and every effort made to give our Army the aircraft of all types needed for its use. Lieut. Col Reber, in this connection, says:

We who in the beginning started the movement are now at the tail of the procession. We have no dirigibles, but very few trained men, and fewer machines. The manufacturing industry is moribund from the lack of business, and there is no future for it. We have no aerodynamical laboratories in which to study the problems, and no engineering courses, except one, in which to develop our constructors. The Government has not stimulated any advance in the design of machines or motors by competition for substantial reward. We have no national league, as in France and Germany, to assist the Government by private subscription and by public demand for the development of air power. The interest of our people in aeronautics at large is dead, and has been perhaps so lulled by a sense of false security and the belief that war will not come to such a vast and powerful Nation as ours; that it will not heed an oft-quoted maxim of the Father of our Country, "In time of peace prepare for war." In no particular is it more impossible to make up deficiencies after the outbreak of hostilities than in aeronautics. What is to be done?

Evidently a strong appeal should be made to Congress for suitable legislation.

24. Scope of Needed Legislation.

What is needed is legislation that will give means of obtaining a sufficient personnel of pilots, enough money to buy suitable machines including excellent engines, and the training of a suitable number of officer-observers. Provision should be made for the creation of captive-balloon units, and dirigibles of various types should be developed.

The Martin TT
was a training plane used in 1915 at North
Island, San Diego, California. The extra front wheels were added
to keep the plane from nosing over.

9. To Increase the Efficiency of The Military Establishment
1916

On 1 May 1915, during the time the War College Division was formulating a military policy (Doc. 8), the American merchantman *Gulflight* was torpedoed by a German submarine. A week later, on 7 May, the *Lusitania* was sunk. Despite repeated protests from President Wilson, the sinkings continued; and as they continued, the need for U.S. military preparedness became more and more evident.

On 18 January 1916, the Chief Signal Officer, General Scriven, again appeared before Hay's Committee on Military Affairs, the subject being another bill "To Increase the Efficiency of the Military Establishment." The following extracts from the hearings are concerned mainly with Scriven's testimony in behalf of an expansion of the Aviation Section and his response to a question from Congressman Kahn about bombing operations in Europe.[1]

The Chairman. You are asking for 73 additional aviation officers. I wish you would state the reason for that.

Gen. Scriven. In order to explain it thoroughly, I think it might be well for me to state to the committee the scope, as I understand it, of the aviation service which is needed at the present time. I will do that briefly, sir, and give you the figures in regard to that.

The organization of the aviation units in the foreign armies suggests a squadron of 12 machines as the basis for our organization, 8 of these machines to be of the reconnaissance type and two each of the pursuit and combat type. In case the Army remains at its present authorized strength the personnel of the aviation section should be increased to give the sufficient personnel to supply seven aero squadrons, one for each of the four tactical divisions organized for duty in the United States, three for over-seas garrisons, and a detachment for duty at the aviation school.

It is to be pointed out that there is additional need for at least one squadron for reconnaissance work in each of the three Coast Artillery districts in this country, and that a sufficient number of aeroplanes should be provided for fire direction and control of the Field Artillery on the basis of one aeroplane per battery with one in reserve, or, in round numbers, six aero squadrons for this arm. This calls for the addition of nine squadrons to those above mentioned.

While the above-mentioned force will give a personnel for a flying establishment in time of peace, a much greater number of officers and men will be required in time of actual hostilities. As a step toward getting the flying men necessary to meet war conditions, an aviation reserve corps should be created including citizen aviators, mechanics, and constructors of air craft. . . .

. . . .

I have said that the organization of the aviation units in foreign armies suggests a squadron of 12 machines as the basis of the present organization. We have heretofore had eight machines, which we have called squadrons. They have been scout machines. It seems desirable, in accordance with the present practice, to add a third company of four machines, two of which shall be what we call pursuit machines, capable of pursuing dirigibles or attacking aeroplanes, and two of them heavy

1. Hearings before the Committee on Military Affairs, House of Representatives, *To Increase the Efficiency of the Military Establishment of the United States,* 64th Cong, 1st sess, vol 1 (1916).

A formation of JN–3 aircraft, which were modified JN–2's used
by the 1st Aero Squadron (late 1915 early 1916) at Fort Sill,
Okla., and San Antonio, Tex.

carrying machines, which would be capable of carrying a considerable amount of ammunition in the shape of bombs, and which could be used for combat or destructive purposes. That makes the squadron as at present proposed 12 instead of 8.

Now, it is also, I think, to be accepted that an aeroplane is an expendable article. It is like ammunition used with the gun. It is subject to destruction, and therefore we must have 12 machines for replacement, and also a reserve of 12, so that a squadron consists of 36 machines. . . .

. . . .

As I have said, if the reorganization plan of the Army by the War Department, which calls for seven tactical divisions and five cavalry brigades, should be approved by Congress, provisions should be made for one aero squadron for Corregidor, one for Hawaii, one for the Canal Zone, one for each of the three Coast Artillery districts in the United States, one for each of the tactical divisions and five for the Field Artillery, giving in all 18 squadrons, with a total strength of 368 officers, counting 20 officers to a squadron and 6 officers for the school, with a total strength of 368 officers and 2,360 enlisted men.

. . . .

Mr. Kahn. Well, I have in my office here in this building a picture that was issued by the British Government calling for volunteers, with a legend on it that this was the damage done by a German dirigible; and according to that picture the wreckage was something terrific. Now, does the bomb dropped by an aeroplane accomplish the destruction that those heavier missiles accomplish? As I understand it, the dirigible can carry much heavier missiles.

Gen. Scriven. Oh, yes. Of course, the bomb dropped by the aeroplane is a very small matter; that is to say, it has very slight destructive power, because, so far as we know, they have not had the power to carry free weight enough to make it worth while. They can carry a bomb or two, but it is not much.

. . . .

The Chairman. There seem to be no further questions.

Gen. Scriven. May I say just one word before you go? In regard the first question you asked me, in connection with the Signal Corps at large, I have endeavored in this pamphlet here submitted to point out the need of a corps of information in modern armies, and I have endeavored to show how absolutely inadequate the strength of the Signal Corps is to meet those requirements. . . .

. . . .

Sen. George E.
Chamberlain, Chairman,
Senate Committee on Military
Affairs, 1916.

10. Preparedness for National Defense
1916

Early in 1916 the Senate Committee on Military Affairs was holding hearings on bills for reorganizing the Army and for creating a reserve. The Chief Signal Officer, General Scriven, and the Chief of the Aviation Section, Colonel Reber, testified on 28 January. They were questioned by Chairman George E. Chamberlain (D–Ore.), and Sen. Thomas Benton Catron (R–N.M.) .[1]

. . . .

Gen. Scriven. In the first place, I would like to emphasize, as far as I can, the growing importance of the service of information. I have endeavored to do this in a little pamphlet before me, which I think has come to the committee room. But the service of information has become so obviously important and of such paramount value in military operations, especially in the light of events abroad, that I think it is well to emphasize it as strongly as possible. The general officer or the commanding general of any force or any expedition who has not a service of information, as compared with the man who has, is like a blind man fighting one who can see, one who has all the information on current happenings and changing events before him upon which to base his actions.

The service of information is performed in these days, first, largely, in broad scope, by the aeroplane, which gives the general survey of the field, but must be supported by the other means of transmitting information now employed, such as, of course, the telegraph, telephone, what we call the buzzer, visual apparatus of various kinds, and largely, as is now pretty well recognized, by wireless telegraphy, or radio telegraphy, as it is now known. . . .

. . . .

The needs of the aviation section were gone into quite fully in the hearing before the House committee, and I understand that it will not be necessary for me to repeat what appears in the report of that hearing. I do, however, wish it to be fully understood that the aviation organization which is called for in the preceding table—that is, seven aero squadrons and a school detachment, has been reluctantly offered as absolute minimum in case the Army remains at its present strength.

The Chairman. You went into that in the House committee?

Gen. Scriven. Yes, sir. I asked there for 18 aero squadrons.

Senator Catron. What constitutes a squadron?

Gen. Scriven. A squadron as we had it consisted of two companies of four aeroplanes each—that is, of eight aeroplanes, all of which were intended for scouting purposes.

Senator Catron. How many men to a company?

Gen. Scriven. Under the old plan it was 90 to the squadron, but now it has been proved by events abroad that to these two companies of scout machines for general outlook over the country must be added a third company of four aeroplanes, two of which shall be rapid-pursuit machines to counterattack any enemy's air craft, and two heavy weight-carrying machines, armed with machine or other types of guns and capable of carrying a considerable weight of ammunition used for destructive purposes. So that a squadron properly organized now consists of 12 aeroplanes in the first line, 129 men and 20 officers.

Senator Catron. You mean 129 men in a squadron, or in each company?

Gen. Scriven. In the whole squadron. There are 20 officers and 129 men to the squadron, 6 officers to each company, which make 18, one squadron commander, who should be a major, and one adjutant and supply officer. But a squadron of 12 machines, in my opinion, is not enough. The organization is good as a fighting unit, but I think that for each machine you should count three—that is, one machine that is actually in use,

1. Hearings before the Committee on Military Affairs, United States Senate, *Preparedness for National Defense*, 64th Cong, 1st sess, pt 12 (1916).

one replacement, so that when the first is broken up or out of commission it can be at once replaced and a third aeroplane be kept as a reserve, not necessarily assembled, but ready to be used. As I see it, we should have one squadron in the Philippines, one in Hawaii, one in the Canal Zone, seven for use with the field armies—that is, one at the headquarters of each division and three squadrons for the use of the Coast Artillery—that is, one squadron for the North Atlantic, a squadron for the South Atlantic, and a squadron for the Pacific. To these 13 squadrons there should be added one aeroplane, with its replacement, for each battery of Field Artillery.

The Chairman. How many would that mean?

Gen. Scriven. That means 18 squadrons.

The Chairman. Of 129 men each?

Gen. Scriven. Eighteen squadrons of 129 men.

The Chairman. And 20 officers?

Gen. Scriven. Yes. . . .

. . . .

The Chairman. How many squadrons have you now?

Gen. Scriven. We have to-day, I think, 23 aeroplanes. Call it two squadrons. As a matter of fact, we have a squadron at San Antonio and we have the aviation school at San Diego, and then we have a company on its way to the Philippines.

The Chairman. That is three.

Gen. Scriven. I could hardly call it three.

The Chairman. Not three squadrons?

Gen. Scriven. No. Two squadrons by number; but bet-ter, one squadron and one company, and a school detachment.

The Chairman. You have not three, then?

Gen. Scriven. No, sir; not of the approved squadron organization. We have 46 officers and 243 men.

The Chairman. How many machines have you now?

Gen. Scriven. Twenty-three, and two awaiting acceptance tests.

The Chairman. How many do you need for 18 squadrons?

Gen. Scriven. I think we need 36 machines to a squadron. But, as a matter of fact, perhaps we will say 24 machines to a squadron would be well enough, though each unit in service should have a support of two machines, rather than of one replacement.

Officers of the U.S. Signal Corps Aviation School, North Island, San Diego, California, 1916. Thirteen of the 28 officers in the photo attained a general officer rank in later years.

The Chairman. You need 432, and you have 23?

Gen. Scriven. Yes; reckoning 24 to the squadron; or if you reckon 36 machines to the squadron, the total number of machines we should have is 18 by 36, or 648. The machines should be considered as expendable, for they are easily placed out of commission.

The Chairman. There must be a great number in reserve with the European armies?

Gen. Scriven. It is no doubt tremendous.

The Chairman. What does a machine cost?

Gen. Scriven. I think, roughly, $10,000, with the instruments, and so on.

The Chairman. I should think it would be almost as perishable as ammunition.

Gen. Scriven. No doubt, and should be so reckoned.

Abroad they are getting tremendously powerful machines, and will undoubtedly be able to carry guns and missiles in sufficient quantity to do a great deal of destruction.

The Chairman. What do these Zeppelins carry?

Gen. Scriven. They carry several tons. The new ones I do not know about, but the old ones had a capacity of something like 4 or 5 tons free weight.

The Chairman. That is what the Germans are using for bombs?

Gen. Scriven. Yes.

Senator Catron. Can they drop their bombs with any accuracy?

Gen. Scriven. No, sir; they can not. They have small chance to hit what they are aiming at. They simply drop the bombs when and where they can.

Senator Catron. And they have to get up about how high to be at a safe distance?

Gen. Scriven. Now, to be beyond the range of the powerful anti-aircraft guns, they must rise to at least 13,000 feet. This is probably beyond the ability of the dirigible.

Senator Catron. If they drop them while they are moving and their machine is not entirely steady, they would have all kinds of trouble about where their shots would go?

Gen. Scriven. They would.

Senator Catron. What are you doing in regard to improving your machines, or whatever you call them? Have you adopted any machine that is a standard machine, or are you open to getting better ones?

Lieut. Col. Reber. We are keeping abreast of the practice as developed at home and abroad, and every time any improvement is made we endeavor to put that in our machines. . . .

. . . .

Senator Catron. What machines are you using?

Lieut. Col Reber. Aeroplanes.

Senator Catron. What kind of aeroplanes are you using?

Lieut. Col. Reber. We are using a biplane tractor, two-seated scout machine.

Senator Catron. Any particular make, designated by the name of any particular person?

Lieut. Col. Reber. We have those machines made both by the Curtiss Co. and by the Martin Co.

Senator Catron. I suppose you have in them the advantage of every machine there is in the country?

Lieut. Col Reber. We try to get them.

Senator Catron. What is the greatest speed you can get out of one of those?

Lieut. Col. Reber. Do you mean the ones we have?

Senator Catron. Yes.

Lieut. Col Reber. I think about 80 miles an hour.

Senator Catron. It seems to me that over in Europe they have gotten more speed than that out of them.

Lieut. Col. Reber. But not out of the same type of machine we have.

Senator Catron. Do we need another type of machine?

Lieut. Col. Reber. We do, and the only reason we haven't it is because we haven't enough money to buy it.

Senator Catron. That was what my first question was addressed to, whether you were keeping abreast of the times, getting machines as efficient as those now being used in Europe, that would be efficient for and beneficial to the Army in its operations. You now say you have not got as rapid a flying machine as they have?

Lieut. Col. Reber. I might say this, that the average scout machine abroad, of the same type we have, has approximately the same speed as ours has. They have a faster type machine they have developed that we have not as yet been able to buy, as it has not been developed in this country, although American manufacturers now are planning to build it, and they have offered to build some types which we expect to have tried out in the next two or three months. As a specific case, the Curtiss people are building and will have for exhibition and trial within about a month a fast machine, which will probably make 110 miles an hour.

Senator Catron. The paper stated some machines over there are making 110 miles an hour.

Lieut. Col Reber. That is a fact.

Senator Catron. Is that the greatest speed any of them has reached?

Lieut. Col Reber. No, sir. I think the fastest speed on record is a little over 126 miles an hour; but that is not a military machine. That was a racing machine.

Senator Catron. Where was that?

Lieut. Col. Reber. That was in France. In a Duperdussin mono-plane, Prevost made a speed of 126.59 miles per hour.

Senator Catron. As I understand, Gen Scriven, you claim you ought to have some additional machines, and particularly these very fast machines?

Gen. Scriven. Yes, sir; I think it is pretty well developed

that if the aeroplane is actually used in war, there must be means of counterattack by aeroplane. An aero attack must be met by a counterattack, and a Zeppelin attack should be met probably by the fast aeroplanes.

Senator Catron. What is the speed of the Zeppelin?

Gen. Scriven. I do not recall anything higher than about 65 miles, whereas the aeroplanes have gotten up as high as about 125 miles an hour.

Senator Catron. What would be the particular benefit of the exceedingly fast machine in connection with the others?

Gen. Scriven. Like a blackbird attacking a crow. He can fly all around his enemy, get above him, fire projectiles at him, and has the advantage of always being able to manuever for position. Like a fast ship, he can keep out of the way of the other's guns, and make his own attack.

Senator Catron. Have these machines proven a success as scout machines?

Gen. Scriven. Our machines are very successful as scout machines.

Senator Catron. How do these machines inform the Army where a battery that may be firing against the troops is located?

Gen. Scriven. They do it by visual signaling, by dropping or displaying objects of various shapes and colors, by directional

flying, by smoke bombs, signals from a Very pistol, and by wireless apparatus.

Senator Catron. You stated a while ago that they could wire out, but they could not receive a message.

Gen. Scriven. No; they can not hear. The aeroplane makes so much noise.

The Chairman. How accurate is photography from those machines?

Gen. Scriven. It has been very excellent.

The Chairman. At what elevation?

Lieut. Col. Reber. They have taken photographs from 12,000 and 13,000 feet.

Gen. Scriven. It is very good work. In making signals they have sometimes used little scintillations of silver paper.

The Chairman. They have a code?

Gen. Scriven. They have a conventional code.

The Chairman. Is there anything else you want to discuss, General?

Gen. Scriven. I have been thinking of the best means for obtaining a reserve of men who would be required in war for signal work, and also in regard to aviators regarding which I have made a suggestion, but that is in the House hearing. The question of a reserve of men and officers is going to be the most serious matter we have to face.

The Chairman. It all looks serious to me, General.

Gen. Scriven. I know. . . .

Woodrow Wilson, President of the United States during the
formative years of military aviation.

The hearings in the House and Senate early in 1916 (Docs. 9 and 10) were steps toward the enactment of the National Defense Act of 1916. With the War College Division's study on military policy (Doc. 8) in hand, Secretary Garrison proposed a plan that included the creation of a Continental Army of 400,000 volunteers under federal control. The idea was approved by President Wilson and found support in the Senate. The House, however, favored a plan based on a large national guard. The President changed sides, Garrison resigned, and Newton D. Baker became Secretary of War. With some help from Pancho Villa, who raided Columbus, N.M., in March 1916, the preparedness measure finally cleared Congress and was approved by the President on 3 June 1916.[1] It provided for an increase in the regular army over a five-year period, quadrupled the national guard, established officer and enlisted reserve corps, and provided for a volunteer army to be raised in time of war. The regular army, after expansion over a period of five years, was to include 64 regiments of infantry, 25 regiments of cavalry, and 21 regiments of field artillery, which is what the War College Division had recommended except that the law provided one less regiment of infantry.

1. 39 Stat 166 (1916).

Each infantry regiment was to have 12 infantry companies (103 men each) organized into 3 battalions, plus 1 machine gun company, 1 supply company, and 1 headquarters company. Organization of brigades, divisions, and corps was authorized when needed.

The National Security Act of 1916 did not specify the number of aero squadrons to be formed or give any indications as to their organization and functions, but it did state that squadrons could be formed as the need arose. Further, it tied the aviation establishment to the division organization of the ground forces.

. . . .

SEC. 3. Composition of Brigades, Divisions, and So Forth.

The mobile troops of the Regular Army of the United States shall be organized, as far as practicable, into brigades and divisions. The President is authorized, in time of actual or threatened hostilities, or when in his opinion the interests of the public service demand it, to organize the brigades and divisions into such army corps or armies as may be necessary. The typical Infantry brigade shall consist of a headquarters and three regiments of Infantry. The typical Cavalry brigade shall consist of a headquarters and three regiments of Cavalry. The typical Field Artillery brigade shall consist of a headquarters and three regiments of Field Artillery. The typical Infantry division shall

consist of a headquarters, three Infantry brigades, one regiment of Cavalry, one Field Artillery brigade, one regiment of Engineers, one field signal battalion, one aero squadron, one ammunition train, one supply train, one engineer train, and one sanitary train. The typical Cavalry division shall consist of a headquarters, three Cavalry brigades, one regiment of Field Artillery (horse), one battalion of mounted Engineers, one field signal battalion (mounted), one aero squadron, one ammunition train, one supply train, one engineer train, and one sanitary train. The typical army corps shall consist of a headquarters, two or more Infantry divisions, one or more Cavalry brigades or a Cavalry division, one Field Artillery brigade, one telegraph battalion, and one field signal battalion, and such ammunition, supply, engineer, and sanitary trains as the President may deem necessary. . . .

. . . .

SEC. 13. The Signal Corps.

. . . .

. . . Authority is hereby given the President to organize, in his discretion, such part of the commissioned and enlisted personnel of the Signal Corps into such number of companies, battalions, and aero squadrons as the necessities of the service may demand.

. . . .

Pancho Villa,
Mexican bandit and
revolutionary, raided American
territory in March 1916. His actions
led to Pershing's Punitive
Expedition into Mexico, during
which U.S. aviation gained the
opportunity for field testing.

In October 1915 General Scriven requested $3,768,743 for aviation for Fiscal Year 1917. Since the estimate had been based in part on the plan for a Continental Army, which by April 1916 appeared to be doomed, Secretary Baker reduced the amount to $1,222,100. When Baker, accompanied by Capt. Charles S. Wallace, appeared before the House Committee on Military Affairs on 8 April 1916 for hearings on the 1917 budget, the questioning related more to the Punitive Expedition than to events in Europe. After Pancho Villa's raid on Columbus, N.M., the previous month, the 1st Aero Squadron had been sent to Columbus to join the Punitive Expedition headed by Brig. Gen. John J. Pershing. An emergency appropriation of $500,000 had been made, at Baker's request, on 31 March to purchase airplanes and other aeronautical equipment. In the hearings in April the committee wanted to know about the 1st Aero Squadron's activities and about the performance of the Curtiss JN–3 planes with which the squadron was operating.

Following are some extracts from Secretary Baker's testimony under questioning by Chairman Hay and members of his committee.[1] Between the time Baker appeared before the committee and the time the appropriation was passed in August, growing concern over the state of preparedness resulted in a huge increase in funds for aviation. The amount appropriated for 1917 was $13,881,666.

. . . .

The Chairman. Out of the $1,222,100 for the Aviation Section how many machines is it proposed to purchase?

Secretary Baker. The intended expenditures include the cost of supplying one and two-thirds squadrons at $233,400 each, to furnish sufficient equipment for the present authorized strength, making an aggregate of $389,000; then that also includes one additional aero squadron at $233,400, making a total for new material for the Aviation Section of $622,400.

An aero squadron consists of 12 machines, and this price is arrived at in this way. The 12 machines with 50 per cent of spare parts it is estimated would cost $144,000. The actual fact about the price of an aeroplane is that it is pretty widely variant, of course. It depends a good deal upon the type of machine and a good deal upon the manufacture.

The machines we have most recently bought for use in Mexico we are paying about $7,500. That is just for the machine. There is one manufacturer who claims to have the latest type of machine, and they cost $12,500 apiece. So that shows there is a somewhat wide variation in the price.

The object of the aviation section is to continue to develop a reconnoissance machine until we have an adequate reconnoissance machine, and then to undertake to add to the equipment some of the so-called war machines, which means slightly armored machines, machines with larger carrying capacity.

The intention is to have two squadrons of 12 machines with 50 per cent of spare parts, and the machines are estimated at $12,000 each, including the spare parts. Then there is an estimate to be added, in addition, for certain trucks, motorcycles, supply trucks, tank trucks, carrier trucks, machine-shop trucks, making up the entire equipment of an aero squadron, with 12 aeroplanes, and all the attendant and accessory trucks and parts, the total cost of one squadron being $233,400.

The Chairman. What are you going to do with the $800,000 that remains?

Secretary Baker. Of the amount that remains, Mr. Chairman, $288,500 is made up in this way: For replacing existing machines, $75,000; for maintenance, $50,000; for salaries of the civilian force, $27,500; for experimental machines, $50,-000; that is an experiment item for developing a better type. It has been recommended by the aviation section, and I think has the approval of such members of the General Staff as have considered it, that we ought to have in War Department a specific sum of $50,000 available for experimenting on aviation matters. The weak point in American aviation has been the motor, and it has been thought that the War Department could, after a competition in the development of an adequate aviation motor, perhaps, develop a type that would be satisfactory.

The Chairman. Then it is proposed only to buy 12 machines during the coming fiscal year?

Secretary Baker. No. The first figure I gave you was to supply one and two-thirds squadrons, which, with the squadrons on hand now—that is, one and one-third squadrons—would bring that up to three squadrons. That figure for supplying the one and two-thirds squadrons is $389,000. That would buy the one and two-thirds additional squadrons, and an additional squadron besides that is estimated for at a cost of $233,400, so that the intention would be to buy 32 machines.

The remainder of the $288,-500 to which I was referring a moment ago is to be used in the following way: For experimental machines, $50,000; for motor competition, $50,000; for instru-

ments and incidentals, $10,000; for one rescue sea sled, $8,000; for four motor trucks, $16,000; and for maintenance of transportation, $2,000. That makes a total of $288,500.

The Chairman. How many machines have you on hand?

Secretary Baker. I have a complete history here, Mr. Chairman, of all that has happened in the department in the way of buying aeroplanes, where they are, and what has become of those that are no longer anywhere. I do not want to take your time to go into details in regard to that history, but it seems to me to be rather interesting.

The Chairman. We are anxious to have a full statement in reference to that matter.

. . . .

Secretary Baker. The first machine the Army ever had was an original Wright, which was acquired in 1908. It is now in the Smithsonian Institution.

In 1911 we bought seven machines, three Curtiss, three Wrights, and one Burgess. The first Curtiss and the first Wright were condemned for further use in February, 1914, having lasted practically three years. The next Wright was destroyed by an accident in September, 1912, very shortly after its purchase. The Burgess machine was con-

demned in February, 1914, and the next Curtiss machine was also condemned in February, 1914. The next Wright was destroyed by accident in August, 1913, and the last of the Curtiss machines was condemned in June, 1914.

That was almost the initial year of real experimentation with heavier-than-air machines, and all of the defects that at first appeared were, of course, inherent in our machines, and they were finally condemned and destroyed.

In 1912 we bought 12 machines. All of them have either since been condemned or destroyed by accident. Of the latter class 9 were destroyed by accident in 1913 and 1914, of the machines bought in 1912. The others were condemned in June, 1914.

In 1913 we bought eight machines, adhering to the types originally purchased, the Curtiss, the Wright, the Burgess, and the Burgess-Dunne, and of those eight machines one is now in commission; one Burgess-Dunne. That was the new type of that year. The others have either been condemned or are out of repair. One of them is marked "out of repair," which means probably that it can be put into service with some spare parts added.

In 1914 we bought 11 machines. One of them is out of repair, five of them have been condemned, and five are now in commission. That year we had an experiment in a new type of machine, known as the Martin machine. I comment on that only to show that new makers are coming into the art and the department is keeping up with them by experimenting with their types.

In 1915 we bought 20 machines—the Burgess, the Curtiss, and the Martin machines. The preponderating number bought that year was the Martin type. Of those, 2 have been condemned—2 Curtiss machines. The rest are substantially all in commission, making a total aggregate number purchased from the beginning of our experimenting in the art, of 59 machines and they are distributed as follows: One in the Smithsonian Institution, 32 have been destroyed or condemned, 3 are out of repair, and 23 are now in service as follows:

Four hydroplanes at Manila, 2 flying boats and 9 training machines at San Diego, and 8 machines with the expedition in Mexico, making a total of 23 machines. That does not account for the 8 machines bought this year which are now in process of delivery and experimental trial at Newport News.

. . . .

Mr. Anthony. What did we pay for the 20 machines we purchased last year?

Capt Wallace. Those machines cost from $7,000 to $10,000 each.

The Chairman. Heretofore it has been stated by the representatives of the Signal Corps that they were buying the best type of machine, and they told us they cost $10,000 apiece, and we appropriated in accordance with what they said they wanted. In other words, we practically gave them all they asked for for their aviation section.

A great deal of criticism has appeared in the newspapers in regard to the kind of machines now in use not being machines that ought to be used, and we would like to know whether or not those machines that were bought in 1915 were the kind of machines that ought to have been bought for use in the Army?

Secretary Baker. Mr. Chairman, I have given as much personal attention to that subject as was possible to give it in the limited time I have been in contact with the matter, and I want to say I am satisfied that the Army has bought as good machines as were made each time it has bought, but that in an infant art, undergoing very rapid development, the Army would hardly have a machine before some new development would be made that would antequate its machines.

Perhaps the best illustration of that is what took place with Curtiss machine at the time we

bought a number of machines known as the CURTISS J. N. 2. They turned out to be exceedingly dangerous machines. Nobody knew it beforehand; but there was some improper calculation of the wing area in those machines. Our men experimented with them and unhappily some of them lost their lives, not, probably because of the defect in the machine so much as because of the men's. I do not like to say lack of skill, but lack of experience of the men dealing with experimental machines, which increased the possibility of accident.

The net result of that was that our men very quickly put their finger on the defect, increased the wing area, and made what is known as the CURTISS J. N. 3, which, in the hands of competent aviators is regarded as good reconnoissance machine as there is. In other words, the makers have been experimenting, our Aviation Corps have been experimenting, and the combined experience of both has now been very lately increased by the experiences in Europe, so that we are approaching a development of a more stable type and model of aeroplane. I think the Army has always bought as good machines as there were to be had.

The Chairman. Mr. Secretary, are the eight machines in operation in connection with the expedition in Mexico being operated successfully?

At the time
of Secretary Baker's testimony
before the House Committee on Military
Affairs, powered flight itself was scarcely
more than a decade old. In 1900 Wright
brothers were still experimenting with kite
gliders (top). In 1902 they were soaring on
the Wright Glider at Kitty Hawk, N.C.,
(center), one year before their first successful
powered flight. Five years later, the Army
purchased from the Wrights the first military
aircraft, Wright Type A, which Orville Wright
flew in acceptance tests at Ft. Myer, Va., on
9 September 1908 (bottom).

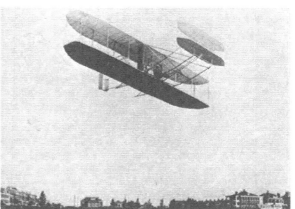

The Wrights taught others to fly. Orville taught students at
Montgomery, Ala., in 1910 (top). Army pilots, in turn, learned to
fly from Wrights' students. Lt. Benjamin D. Foulois received
instruction from Phil Parmalee (at the controls) in operating a
new Wright Type B aircraft at Ft. Sam Houston, Tex., in
February 1911 (center). Lt. Frank M. Kennedy, at the controls of
a Curtiss Trainer at College Park, Md., 1911, learned to fly from
Army pilots at the new Army aviation school (bottom).

Secretary Baker. They are being operated successfully, Mr. Chairman. That needs a word of explanation. The first aeroplanes that were made had the propellers behind the aviator, and when any accident took place, in the way of the machine stalling in going along, so much of the power would be used to secure added elevation that the machine would lose its forward motion and come to a standstill, except that it would be attempting to rise. The loss of the forward motion deprived it of the sustaining friction with the air, and the machine would stall and plunge head first down to the ground.

When that happened the great weight of the motor and of the propeller and the gear behind the aviator crushed him.

That led to the novel suggestion that the motor and propeller should be put in front. That is the so-called tractor type. All of the heavy machinery is in front of the aviator, and he is protected from the rushing air by a mica cage. That seems to have solved the problem to a great extent, and since that time there have been few fatal accidents, although there have been a number of falls. Apparently that machine is much more stable.

The young men in charge of it now say they are perfectly willing to take it up and turn over two or three times as long as they are 500 feet above the ground.

The Chairman. Is that the type which is now being used in Mexico?

Secretary Baker. That is the exclusive type. Those machines require a good landing place. One of the highly desirable qualities to develop in aeroplanes is that which will enable a machine to slow down very gradually so that the aviator can pick his landing place and land in a relatively small level field. In Mexico their landing difficulties are very great. The country is mountainous, and the landing is very difficult. For that reason when the eight machines went down there they met with a series of minor accidents, and at one time only two of them were in actual operation. At the present time six out of the eight are in operation.

Mr. McKellar. Mr. Secretary, is any real good being accomplished by them?

Secretary Baker. We are relying on them entirely for communication with the front.

. . . .

Mr. McKellar. Would you mind, if you are not prepared to give the information about it now, looking up the question of the separation of the aerial force from the Signal Corps?

Secretary Baker. I would be glad to do that.

Mr. McKellar. And give us the information about it?

Secretary Baker. Yes.

. . . .

Mr. Greene. I remember at the hearings when they instituted the Aviation Section, it was suggested that the Aviation Section has to work also in connection with the combatants, because they give back directions for firing, and all that sort of thing.

Secretary Baker. I think the most serious addition to your discussion is the fact that they are now devising a battle aeroplane which is in itself an offensive arm and that places a new phase on the whole thing.

Mr. Greene. That was suggested at the time.

. . . .

Secretary Baker. All the aeroplanes we now have and are proposing to buy are reconnoissance machines, and the machines in Mexico are doing what would be done by the wireless telegraph if the static conditions were not so bad.

Mr. Shallenberger. What is the length of life of an aeroplane in war, the average length of life?

Secretary Baker. Ten days, I am told; certainly a short time.

Mr. Shallenberger. If the machines in Mexico are now doing good service, it shows what they can do under war conditions, does it not?

Secretary Baker. They are hardly under war conditions. There are no antiaircraft guns in Mexico.

. . . .

Aircraft #43, landing in Mexico during the Punitive Expedition,
was one of the JN–2's converted to JN–3 by expanding the top
wingspan and otherwise stabilizing the aircraft.

Brig. Gen. John J. Pershing and Maj. John J. Ryan, the Chief
Intelligence Officer on his staff, in Mexico, 1916.

13. Foulois: The 1st Aero Squadron in Mexico 1916

When Secretary Baker testified on 8 April 1916 (Doc. 12), he spoke well of the Curtiss JN–3, which the 1st Aero Squadron was using on the Punitive Expedition. There had been some minor accidents, he said, but six of the squadron's eight planes were now in commission. The Secretary's information, however, was out of date. Two planes had been wrecked on 20 March and another on 5 April. And by the 19th of the month only two would be left, and they would not be in serviceable condition.

The story of the difficulties the 1st Aero Squadron had in Mexico were recorded by the squadron commander, Capt. Benjamin D. Foulois, in a report completed at Columbus on 28 August 1916. The report is interesting and significant for what it has to say about the capabilities and employment of U.S. military aviation just a year before the United States entered the war. The major part of the report is printed below.[1]

Report of Operations of the First Aero Squadron, Signal Corps, with Punitive Expedition, U.S.A. for Period March 15 to August 15, 1916.

In compliance with Par. 1, S.O. No. 61, Southern Department, March 12, 1916, the 1st Aero Squadron, left Fort Sam Houston, Texas, on March 13, 1916 en route to Columbus, N.M., with the following personnel and equipment.

Personnel—Captains B. D. Foulois, T. F. Dodd, Lieuts. C. G. Chapman, J. E. Carberry, H. A. Dargue, T. S. Bowen, R. H. Willis, W. G. Kilner, E. S. Gorrell, A. R. Christie, I. A. Rader, 82 enlisted men, and 1 civilian mechanician. 2 Hospital Corps men, attached.

Equipment—8 aeroplanes, 10 trucks, 1 automobile.

Upon arrival in El Paso, March 14th, 1st Lieut. S. S. Warren, M. R. C., and one Hospital Corps enlisted man joined Squadron. Two additional trucks were also received from the Depot Quartermaster, El Paso, giving the Squadron, about 50% of its necessary motor transportation.

The Squadron arrived at Columbus, N.M., March 15, 1916, and started immediately to assemble aeroplane equipment. . . .

Aeroplane #44, Capt. Dodd, pilot, Capt. Foulois, observer, made the first reconnaissance flight into Mexico on March 16, 1916.

. . . .

March 19, 1916

Telegraphic orders were received from the Division Commander at Nuevas Casas Grandes, Mexico, for the Squadron to proceed at once to Casas Grandes, Mexico, for immediate service.

. . . .

All aeroplanes of the Squadron, eight in number, were started in flight, from Columbus, at 5:10 p.m. One aeroplane was compelled to return to Columbus due to motor trouble.

Four aeroplanes landed at Las Ascencion, Mexico, on account of darkness. The other three became separated from the Squadron, in the darkness. One landed at Ojo Caliente, Mexico, one at Janos, Mexico, and another near Pearson, Mexico. This latter machine was wrecked upon landing.

1. The copy used is one bearing Foulois' name stamped in the signature block at the end of the report. It is a carbon copy that was acquired by Lt. Col. Ernest L. Jones and is now part of the Jones Collection in the Albert F. Simpson Historical Research Center, 168.65011-7A. The same folder also contains another version, more in the form of a narrative account than a formal report. This second version, which presumably was also written by Foulois, was printed, with five paragraphs (numbers 2–6) deleted, as Appendix B to Col. Frank Tompkins, *Chasing Villa* (Harrisburg, 1934).

Officers of the 1st Aero Squadron, San Antonio, Tex., prior to departure for the Punitive Expedition (l. to r., above): Lts. T. S. Bowen, J. E. Carberry, and C. G. Chapman; Capt. B. D. Foulois; and Lts. T. D. Milling and I. A. Rader.

Capts. B. D. Foulois (left) and T. F. Dodd stand next to the squadron's auto at San Antonio (bottom).

March 20, 1916

The four pilots who had landed at Las Ascencion proceeded south to Casas Grandes and reported for duty. The pilot, who had been compelled to return to Columbus, and the one who had landed at Janos arrived at Casas Grandes at approximately the same hour, this date. The pilot who had landed at Ojo Caliente reported in to Casas Grandes, several days later, having incurred slight damage to his aeroplane, which had to be repaired.

The aeroplane which had been landed near Pearson, was so badly damaged that the pilot abandoned it, and returned to Casas Grandes on foot.

Upon reporting to the Division Commander at Casas Grandes, instructions were received, to make an aero reconnaissance south toward Cumbre Pass, in the heart of the Sierra Madre Mountains, for the purpose of locating troops moving southward toward Lake Babicora. Aeroplane #44, Capt. T. F. Dodd, pilot, and Capt. B. D. Foulois, observer, proceeded south at noon, March 20. Proceeded about twenty-five miles, from Casas Grandes, but were unable to rise over the foothills of the Sierra Madre Mountains,

due to constantly encountering whirlwinds and terrific vertical currents of air, which, on account of the low power of the aeroplane, effectually prevented the aeroplane rising to an altitude sufficiently high to allow of crossing the mountains, which at this particular locality, rise to a height of over 10,000 feet above sea level.

On this same date aeroplane #48, Lieut. T. S. Bowen, pilot, while making a landing was caught in a whirlwind, which completely wrecked the aeroplane. Lieut. Bowen, escaped with a broken nose, and minor injuries.

March 21, 1916

Orders received to locate troops under Colonel Irwin in the Galeana Valley. Aeroplane #44, Capt. T. F. Dodd, pilot, and Capt. B. D. Foulois, observer, located these troops at Galera Lopena, landed, and reported to Colonel Irwin. Returned to Dublan, with report from Colonel Irwin. As a result of this reconnaissance and report from Colonel Irwin, six trucks of this Squadron, loaded with supplies, were sent to Colonel Irwin's column.

March 22, 1916

Orders received to communicate with troops moving south on the Mexican North-Western Railroad, and Colonel G. A. Dodd's command in the Galeana Valley.

Aeroplane #42, Lieut. W. G. Kilner, pilot, Lieut. I. A. Rader, observer, and aeroplane #45, Lieut. J. E. Carberry, pilot, flew to the Galeana Valley, located Colonel Dodd's troops, landed and reported to Colonel Dodd. Returned to Dublan, with reports from Colonel Dodd, to Division Commander. Aeroplane #44, Capt. T. F. Dodd, pilot, Lieut. A. R. Christie, observer, and aeroplane #53, Lieut. C. G. Chapman, pilot, flew south into the Sierra Madre Mountains, in an endeavor to locate the troops, moving south on the Mexican North-Western Railroad. These aeroplanes were driven into the heart of the Sierra Madre Mountains, as far as the northern end of the Cumbre Pass tunnel, but due to terrific vertical air currents and whirlwinds, which at times drove the aeroplanes within twenty feet of the tree tops, the pilots were unable to cross the Sierra Madre Mountains, and were compelled to return to Dublan.

As a result of this failure to accomplish the reconnaissance as directed the Squadron Commander submitted the following memorandum to the Division Commander:

22 Mch. 16.

Memo for the Commanding
General Punitive Expedition,
U.S. Army at Casas Grandes,
Mexico.

1. In view of the fact that the
present aeroplane equipment of
the First Aero Squadron is not
capable of meeting the present
military service conditions, it is
urgently requested that the following number of aeroplanes,
motors, and spare parts be purchased, if they can possibly be
secured in the United States. It is
further requested that this order
be placed by telegraph and immediate delivery of all equipment, by express, be specified.

2. Aeroplanes—

(a) Two (2) Martin aero-
planes, Model S, with army
standard landing gear, Hall-Scott
125 h.p. 6 cyl. motors.

(b) Two (2) Curtiss aero-
planes, Model R2, Curtiss 160
h.p. steel cylinder motors.

(c) Two Sturtevant aero-
planes, 140 h.p. Sturtevant motors.

(d) Two (2) Thomas aero-
planes, 135 h.p. Thomas motors.

(e) Two (2) Sloane aero-
planes, 125 h.p. Hall-Scott 6 cyl.
motors.

All of the aeroplanes above to
be completely equipped, and
ready for immediate use.

3. The manufacturer to furnish
one (1) spare motor for each
two (2) machines purchased,
and in addition the following
aeroplane and motor spares:

Two (2) spare propellers.
One set lower wings, complete,
with fittings and wires.
One landing gear complete.
One set tail control surfaces,
complete, with fittings and wires.
Three (3) spare radiators.
Three (3) spare magnetos.

B. D. Foulois
Captain, Signal Corps,
Comdg. First Aero Squadron.

On this same date, a detachment was sent to salvage such
parts of aeroplane #41, which
was wrecked near Pearson on
the evening of March 19, as
were serviceable. This detachment returned same date, and
reported that it had been fired
upon, by Mexicans, in the vicinity of Pearson.

March 23, 1916

Received orders to communicate with Colonel G. A. Dodd's
troops in the Galeana Valley.

Aeroplane #44, Lieut. A. R.
Christie, pilot, aeroplane #45,
Lieut. J. E. Carberry, pilot, and
aeroplane #53, Lieut. C. G.
Chapman, pilot, flew to El Valle,
landed and reported to Colonel
Dodd. These aeroplanes and pilots, were unable to return to
Dublan, until March 25, due to
high winds, dust storms, and
snow storms. Detachment from
Squadron proceeded to Pearson, Mexico, this date, and returned to Dublan, with such
parts of aeroplane #41, as could
be considerable serviceable.

The Squadron Commander
submitted the following plan to
the Division Commander, which
contemplated the establishment
of aeroplane and fuel bases in
advance of Division Headquarters.

The JN-2
(converted to JN-3) in
which Dodd and Foulois made the
first reconnaissance flight into
Mexico, 16 March 1916. Pershing's
staff cars parked in rear.

Headquarters, 1st Aero Squadron, Signal Corps, Colonia Dublan, Mexico, Mar 30/16.

Memorandum for Chief of Staff, Punitive Expedition, U.S. Army.

1. Plans are herewith submitted for the most effective use of the 1st Aero Squadron, with its present equipment of six low powered aeroplanes.

Also other data in reference to same.

Plan I

Object: To maintain aero communication between Columbus, N.M.—Casas Grandes—El Valle and Namiquipa.

(a) Two aeroplanes, with sufficient commissioned and enlisted personnel and supplies to take station at El Valle. One aeroplane to fly from El Valle to Namiquipa every morning, returning the following morning to El Valle.

(b) Two aeroplanes to be assigned to maintain aero communication between Casas Grandes and Columbus, as follows: One aeroplane to leave Casas Grandes every morning, flying to Columbus without stop, and returning the following morning without stop.

(c) Two aeroplanes to be assigned to maintain aero communication between Casas Grandes and Namiquipa, as follows: One aeroplane to leave Casas Grandes every morning, flying to Namiquipa without stop, return-ing the following morning without stop.

The foregoing plan contemplates the *maximum use* of *all aviators* and *all aeroplanes*, for maintaining aero communication between Columbus—Casas Grandes—El Valle and Namiquipa only, and does not contemplate the use of aeroplanes for communication, south, east, or west of Namiquipa.

Plan II

Object: To maintain aero communication between Casas Grandes—El Valle—Namiquipa—and points south of Namiquipa (communication between Casas Grandes [and Columbus] to be maintained by radio-telegraph, motorcycles, and road transportation).

(a) Transfer entire Squadron of six aeroplanes to Namiquipa, maintaining fuel bases only, at Casas Grandes, El Valle, and an advanced fuel base south of Namiquipa, to be determined later.

(b) Upon transfer of Squadron to Namiquipa, the following assignment of aeroplanes to be made—(1) Two aeroplanes to maintain daily communication between Namiquipa and Casas Grandes—(2) Two aeroplanes to maintain daily aero communication between Namiquipa and El Valle—(3) Two aeroplanes to maintain daily aero communication between Namiquipa and points south, within effective radius of aeroplanes.

Plan III

(a) Upon establishment of effective radio-telegraph communication between Namiquipa and Casas Grandes, the following is recommended—(1) Discontinue the use of aeroplanes between Namiquipa and Casas Grandes except in emergencies—(2) Continue the aero communication between Namiquipa and El Valle, if radio-telegraph, motor cycles, or other means fail—(3) Concentrate all available aeroplanes at Namiquipa for daily communication between Namiquipa and advanced troops—(4) If communication between Namiquipa and El Valle is of secondary importance only and can be maintained by radio-telegraph, motorcycles, or other means of communication, the use of aeroplanes between these two points should also be discontinued, and every available aeroplane concentrated at Namiquipa for the purpose of maintaining communication south of Namiquipa.

Plan IV

(a) In the event that contact is gained with the enemy, it is recommended that every available aeroplane be concentrated at the front for observation and reconnaissance of the enemy, as far as practicable.

2. In connection with the foregoing plans, for *effective use* of the aeroplanes of this organization, the following is furnished.

The six aeroplanes now in use, have been subjected, for nearly ten months, to severe weather conditions, in Oklahoma and Texas, exposed to rain, high winds, and severe cold weather conditions.

As a result of these months of field service, all aeroplanes have been subjected to severe wear and tear. With the present extreme field service conditions every machine is liable, at any day, to be placed out of commission as unfit and too dangerous for further field service.

3. Further information is furnished to the effect that these aeroplanes are not capable of meeting the present military needs, incident to this expedition. Their low power motors and limited climbing ability with the necessary military load makes it impossible to safely operate any one of these machines,

in the vicinity of the mountains which cover the present theatre of operations. These same limitations as to power, climbing ability, and weight carrying ability limit these machines to safe operations for a few hours each day, chiefly on account of the altitude and extremely severe atmospheric conditions encountered every day in the present theatre of operations.

4. The entire commissioned and enlisted personnel of this organization are exerting every effort to maintain all aeroplanes in the best possible condition for further field service, but even the united efforts of the entire technical ability in this command can not make these aeroplanes suitable for to meet the present military needs.

5. An urgent appeal is therefore made, that this organization be supplied, at the earliest possible moment, with at least ten of the highest powered, highest climbing and best weight carrying aeroplanes that can be secured and purchased in the United States.

With this new equipment, the present commissioned and enlisted personnel of this organization, will be able, under the present service conditions, to increase its effectiveness to this expedition at least five hundred percent.

B. D. Foulois
Captain, Signal Corps,
Commanding
1st Aero Squadron.

Plan III of the foregoing was approved and ordered put into effect, April 1.

Nine flights were made this date between Dublan, Galera Lopena, and El Valle, carrying mail and despatches.

March 27, 1916

Seven flights were made this date between Columbus, N.M., Dublan, and El Valle, carrying mail and despatches.

March 28, 1916

Reconnaissance flights made as follows—Aeroplane #43, Lieut. H. A. Dargue, pilot, from Dublan to Bachineva, Bachineva to Namiquipa, Namiquipa to Santa Ana, and return to Namiquipa. Aeroplane #53, Lieut. Chapman, pilot, from El Valle, east and south, for a distance of 110 miles returning to El Valle.

March 29, 1916

Six flights made this date by five aeroplanes, between Columbus, N.M., Dublan, El Valle, and Namiquipa, carrying mail and despatches.

March 30, 1916

Three flights made this date, with three aeroplanes, between Columbus, N.M., Dublan and El Valle, carrying mail and despatches . . .

March 31, 1916

Nine flights were made this date by four aeroplanes between Dublan, El Valle, Namiquipa, and San Geronimo, carrying mail and despatches. Severe rain, hail, and snow storms were encountered this date, causing several forced landings, away from the base at Dublan, until the storms had passed.

April 1, 1916

Nineteen flights made this date, by six aeroplanes, between Columbus, N.M., Dublan, Espindeleno, El Valle, Cruces, Namiquipa, San Geronimo, and Santa Ana, carrying mail and despatches.

Rain, hail, and snow storms were encountered on this date, causing several forced landings, until storms had passed.

April 2, 1916

Fourteen flights made this date by five aeroplanes, between Dublan, El Valle, Cruces, Namiquipa, San Geronimo, and Bachineva, carrying mail and despatches.

April 3, 1916

Six flights made this date, by four aeroplanes, between Dublan, El Valle, Namiquipa, and San Geronimo, carrying mail and despatches.

April 4, 1916

Four flights made this date by two aeroplanes, between El Valle, Namiquipa, and San Geronimo, carrying mail and despatches.

April 5, 1916

Seven flights made this date by four aeroplanes, between Dublan, El Valle, Namiquipa, and San Geronimo, carrying mail and despatches.

Aero Squadron headquarters changed to San Geronimo.

Orders received this date to locate Colonel W. C. Brown's column, reported in the vicinity of San Antonio. Aeroplane #43, Lieut. H. A. Dargue, pilot, Capt. B. D. Foulois, observer, left San Geronimo on this reconnaissance. Flew to San Antonio and located a pack train of Colonel Brown's column, returning toward San Geronimo. Landed aeroplane and received information that troops were proceeding toward Cusihuirachic. Flew to Cusihuirachic Canyon, and located troops entering Canyon. Landed and reported to Colonel Brown. Flew back to San Geronimo, with report from Colonel Brown to Division Commander.

April 6, 1916

Four flights made this date by three aeroplanes, between Namiquipa, San Geronimo, and Cusihuirachic, carrying despatches to troops. Aeroplane #44, badly damaged on landing at San Geronimo. All serviceable parts salvaged, remainder of aeroplane condemned and destroyed.

April 7, 1916

Aeroplane #43, Lieut. H. A. Dargue, pilot, and Capt. B. D. Foulois, observer, from San Geronimo to Chihuahua City with despatches for Mr. Marion H. Letcher, American Consul. Aeroplane #45, Lieut. J. E. Carberry, pilot, and Capt. T. F. Dodd, observer, from San Geronimo to Chihuahua City, carrying duplicate despatches to American Consul. Both aeroplanes arrived at Chihuahua City at same time, causing considerable excitement. By pre-arrangement aeroplane #43 was landed on south side of city, aeroplane #45 on the north side. Lieut. Dargue, in aeroplane #43, was directed to fly his machine to the north side of town in order to join #45. As he started off, four mounted rurales opened fire on the machine, at a distance of about one half mile. Capt. Foulois, having started into town, heard the firing, proceeded in the direction of the rurales and stopped their firing. Capt. Foulois was then arrested by the rurales and taken by them to the city jail, followed by a mob of several hundred men and boys. Enroute to the jail Capt. Foulois succeeded in getting word to an American bystander, requesting that he notify the American Consul of his arrival in the city and that the Consul take the necessary steps for the protec-

Lt. Herbert A. Dargue,
posing by his aircraft on 7 April 1916.
The picture was taken just after Dargue and his plane were
stoned at Chihuahua City. He kept the photographer posing him
as long as possible to avoid further violence from the mob.

tion of all aviators and machines that had arrived in the city.

Upon arrival at the city jail and after considerable delay, Capt. Foulois succeeded in getting in touch with Colonel Miranda, Chief of Staff to General Gutierrez, Military Governor of Chihuahua. Colonel Miranda then took Capt. Foulois to see General Gutierrez, who soon ordered Capt. Foulois' release. Capt. Foulois, then requested that a guard be placed over the two aeroplanes, which request having been granted, Capt. Foulois, in company with Colonel Miranda, then proceeded to the north side of the city to locate the other three aviators and aeroplanes. Upon arrival at the landing place, only Lieut. Dargue, with aeroplane #43, was found. Lieut. Dargue reported that he had landed alongside of aeroplane #45; that Capt. Dodd had then proceeded into Chihuahua City to locate the American Consul and deliver his duplicate despatches; that after Capt. Dodd had left, a large crowd of natives, Carranzista soldiers, and officers, had collected and proceeded to crowd around the machine, making insulting remarks; that several natives burned holes with cigarettes in the wings of aeroplane #43; that others have slashed the cloth with knives, in several places, and extracted bolts and nuts on both machines. The two pilots left with the machines, Lieuts. Dargue and Carberry, felt that the mob would ultimately wreck the ma-

chines and decided to fly the machines to the smelters of the American Smelter and Refining Company, located about six miles from Chihuahua City. Lieut. Carberry got away safely without encountering any further difficulties. Lieut. Dargue, in aeroplane #43, got away in the midst of a shower of stones, thrown at him by the mob. He had only flown a short distance when the top section of the fuselage flew off and damaged the stabilizer, causing him to make immediate landing which he accomplished safely. He then stood off the crowd without further damage to the aeroplane or to himself until the arrival of the guard. Captains Foulois and Dodd spent the remainder of the day with the American Consul in arranging for supplies to be sent to the advance troops by railroad. Lieuts. Dargue and Carberry spent the remainder of the day repairing the damage done by the mob on the two aeroplanes.

April 8, 1916

Aeroplane #43, Lieut. Dargue, pilot, Capt. B. D. Foulois, observer, and aeroplane #45, Lieut. Carberry, pilot, and Capt. T. F. Dodd, observer, from Chihuahua City to San Geronimo with despatches from American Consul to Division Commander.

Orders received to move Aero Squadron base to San Antonio, Mexico.

April 9, 1916

Ten flights made this date, by five aeroplanes, between Namiquipa, San Geronimo and San Antonio.

April 10, 1916

Orders received this date to locate troops in vicinity of San Borja, Mexico.

Aeroplane #43, Lieut. H. A. Dargue, pilot, Capt. B D. Foulois, observer, reconnoitered the area from San Antonio to Ojo Azules—Ojo Caliente—San Borja—Santa Maria—Tres Hermanos—Satevo—Carretas and return to San Antonio. No troops discovered within this area.

Aeroplane #45, Lieut. J. E. Carberry, pilot, and Capt T. F. Dodd, observer, reconnoitered the area from San Antonio—Ojo Azules—Ojo Caliente—Santa Maria—Satevo—San Lucas—Santa Cruz—Manula—Santa Ysabel and return to San Antonio. No troops discovered within this area.

Orders received this date to move Aero Squadron base to Satevo.

April 11, 1916

Ten flights were made this date, by five aeroplanes, between Satevo—Santa Rosalia—San Lucas—San Antonio—Namiquipa—Dublan and Columbus, N.M.

Aeroplane #43, Lieut. H. A. Dargue, pilot, and Lieut. E. S. Gorrell, observer, flew from San Antonio, Mexico, to Columbus, N.M., making one stop at Dublan. Total distance 315 miles.

Aeroplane #53, Lieut. C. G. Chapman, pilot, on reconnaissance trip to Santa Rosalia (south of Chihuahua City, on Mexican Central Railway.) Upon landing at Santa Rosalia, Lieut. Chapman was taken by Carranza troops, to the Commanding Officer of the Carranza garrison. During his absence from the aeroplane, his field glasses, goggles, and considerable ammunition were stolen from the aeroplane by Carranza soldiers. . . .

April 12, 1916

Six flights made this date, by three aeroplanes, between Satevo—San Geronimo—Namiquipa and south toward Parral.

Aeroplane #53 Lieut. C. G. Chapman, pilot on reconnaissance flight south toward Parral, for the purpose of locating troops moving in direction of Parral.

April 13, 1916

Aeroplane #42, Lieut. I. A. Rader, pilot on reconnaissance flight south toward Parral, for the purpose of locating troops in direction of Parral. No troops located.

Four other flights this date, by three aeroplanes, between Satevo—Chihuahua City—and San Andreas.

Aeroplane #45, Lieut. J. E. Carberry, pilot, Capt. B. D. Foulois, observer, to Chihuahua City with despatches for the American Consul. Received first information regarding flight at Parral.

April 14, 1916

Aeroplane #43, Lieut. H. A. Dargue, pilot, Lieut. E. S. Gorrell, observer, on reconnaissance flight from Columbus, N.M. to Boca Grande—Pulpit Pass—Oaxaca Pass—Carretas—Janos—Ascencion and return to Columbus, N.M. Reconnaissance made for the purpose of locating a large Carranzista force, reported to be moving east toward our line of communications. No hostile troops were located within the area covered. Distance of flight 315 miles. American aeroplane record for non-stop flight with two men.

Aeroplane #52, Lieut. I. A. Rader, on reconnaissance flight south from Satevo, toward Parral, to locate troops in vicinity of Parral. Located Major Robert L. Howze's command in vicinity of Ojito, near Durango State line. Pilot was compelled to land on very rough ground, and damaged aeroplane.

Being in a hostile country, 100 miles from the nearest base, and unable to make necessary repairs, the aeroplane was abandoned, and the pilot proceeded with Major Howze's column.

Aeroplane #45, Lieut. J. E. Carberry, pilot, Capt. B. D. Foulois, observer, from Chihuahua City to Satevo with despatches from Mr. Marion H. Letcher, American Consul, and despatches from General Gutierrez, Military Governor of Chihuahua.

Capt. B. D. Foulois and 14 enlisted men, 1st Aero Squadron, from Satevo to Chihuahua City, in automobile and truck, with despatches for American Consul, and General Gutierrez, Military Governor.

Due to intense feeling in Chihuahua City over the clash between the American troops and troops at Parral, the Detachment of enlisted men was placed in concealment in the outskirts of the city. Capt. Foulois, accompanied by Cpl. Arthur Westermark (chauffeur) proceeded to the American Consulate, delivered the despatches for the American Consul and Military Governor, and left the City without difficulty. Returned to Division Headquarters, at Satevo, same date.

Lts. Herbert A. Dargue and Edgar S. Gorrell pose next to
"Aeroplane #43" between reconnaissance flights in
Mexico, 1916.

April 15, 1916

Aeroplane #43, Lieut. H. A. Dargue, pilot, Lieut. E. S. Gorrell, observer, on reconnaissance from Columbus, N.M., to Boca Grande—Pulpit Pass—Dublan—from Dublan to Namiquipa—from Namiquipa to Satevo. Total distance 415 miles, with two stops.

Three other flights made this date, between Satevo—San Antonio—and Namiquipa, carrying mail and despatches.

Aeroplane #42, dismantled, condemned and destroyed. Lower wings of this aeroplane placed on aeroplane #45, to replace wings damaged in flight to Chihuahua City.

April 16, 1916

Two flights made this date, between Satevo, San Antonio and Namiquipa, carrying mail and despatches. Division Headquarters moved to Namiquipa.

April 17, 1916

Two flights made this date from Satevo to San Antonio and Namiquipa. Squadron Headquarters moved to Namiquipa.

April 18, 1916

Two flights this date between Namiquipa and San Antonio, carrying mail and despatches.

April 19, 1916

Aeroplane #43, Lieut. H. A. Dargue, pilot, Capt. R. E. Willis, observer, on reconnaissance flight from San Antonio to Chihuahua City, for the purpose of taking photographs and reconnoitering all roads and approaches to Chihuahua City. Roads in vicinity of Chihuahua City were reconnoitered and several photographs were taken. While reconnoitering roads in the hills west of Chihuahua City, the aeroplane motor failed, causing a forced landing in the hills. The aeroplane was completely wrecked. Lieut. Dargue escaped uninjured, Capt. Willis was pinned under the wreckage, sustained a severe scalp wound and considerably bruised about the legs and ankles. As the aeroplane was completely wrecked, it was burned up, on the spot. The two aviators, with their personal equipment, started to walk to San Antonio, their nearest base, a distance of about 65 miles. After constant suffering and hardship, due to lack of food and water, they reached San Antonio, on April 21st. Stayed at San Antonio until April 23, when they proceeded by automobile to Namiquipa, and reported the results of their reconnaissance to the Division Commander.

April 20, 1916

Orders received for the Squadron to return to Columbus, N.M., to secure new aeroplanes. Of the eight aeroplanes taken into Mexico on March 19, 1916, but two were still in commission on this date. These two aeroplanes (nos. 45 and 53) were in such condition as to be unsafe for further field service.

They were therefore flown to Columbus, this date, and ultimately condemned and destroyed.

The Squadron personnel and transportation arrived at Columbus, N.M., April 22, 1916.

Upon arrival at Columbus, the Squadron received four new aeroplanes, which had been purchased from the Curtiss Aeroplane Company.

From April 23 to April 29, the Squadron was employed in testing these four new aeroplanes. Practical tests in flight with these machines demonstrated their unsuitability for Mexican field service, and they were declared unsuitable for such service.

On May 1, 1916, two Curtiss aeroplanes (R—2 type 160 horsepower) were received. By May 25, twelve of this type had arrived.

During the months of May, June, and July, constant troubles and difficulties were encountered with defective propellers, defective construction in aeroplanes and defective motor parts.

. . . .

Total number of flights made from March 15, 1916 to August 15, 1916:—540.

Total number of miles flown, from March 15, 1916 to August 15, 1916:—19,553.

Total duration of flights, from March 15, 1916 to August 15, 1916:—345 hours, 43 minutes.

. . . .

The Squadron Commander invites attention to the fact that the 1st Aero Squadron, S.C., is the first organization of its kind that has ever been used in active field service in the history of the United States Army. This command took the field with aeroplanes of very low military efficiency, and with less than 50% of its authorized allowance of truck transportation. Due to lack of aeroplanes with greater carrying capacity, all flying officers were continuously called upon to take risks in every reconnaissance flight made while on duty in Mexico. All officers, thoroughly appreciated the fact that the failure of their aeroplane motors, while flying through mountainous canyons and over rugged mountains, would invariably result in death. They also appreciated the fact that in a forced landing even if safely made, there was every possible risk of being taken prisoner by an enemy, whose ideas of the Laws of War are on a par with an uncivilized race of savages.

All officers, pilots, on duty with command, during its active service in Mexico, were constantly being exposed to personal risk and physical suffering. Due to inadequate weight carrying capacity of all aeroplanes, it was impossible to even carry sufficient food, water or clothing, on many of the reconnaissance flights. Pilots, in flight, were frequently caught in snow, rain and hail storms which, due to inadequate clothing, invariably caused excessive suffering.

In several instances, pilots were compelled to make forced landings in desert and hostile country, fifty to seventy miles from the nearest troops. In nearly every case, the aeroplanes were abandoned or destroyed and the pilots, after experiencing all possible suffering due to lack of food and water, would finally work their way on foot, through alkali deserts and mountains, to friendly troops, usually arriving thoroughly exhausted as a result of these hardships.

The earnest and willing spirit, shown by every officer in the command, in performing this new and perilous service, with inadequate equipment, and under very severe conditions, is deserving of the highest commendation. Foreign Governments have decorated their flying officers for far less perilous flying. The officers of this command considered their hardships and their service with the Punitive Expedition as part of the day's work, and simply in line of duty.

The experience gained by the commissioned and enlisted personnel of this command while on active duty with the Punitive Expedition has been of the greatest value, and it is believed that the knowledge gained by all concerned should result in more rapid and efficient development of the aviation service in the United States Army.

Lt. Dargue,
Capt. Foulois, and Lt.
Gorrell plan a reconnaissance
mission to locate Villa's troops
during the Punitive
Expedition.

With the first increments provided by the National Defense Act of 1916, the Aviation Section had personnel authorizations for 77 officers and 1,978 enlisted men effective 1 July 1916. In his annual report, dated 3 October 1916, General Scriven outlined plans for using these people to expand the tactical organization of the Aviation Section.[1]

. . . .

It is proposed to organize this force into . . . 2 aero squadrons, 2 aero companies; and a school detachment for duty at the Signal Corps Aviation School at San Diego, California. There were organized at the end of this fiscal year . . . 1 aero squadron; 1 aero company. . . . These organizations will be expanded into the units proposed.[2]

. . . .

Two of the aero squadrons will be organized and stationed in the Southern Department; one aero company will be assigned to the Philippine Islands and one to the Canal Zone.

. . . .

An aero squadron is required for service with each division, or when divisions are operating as parts of a field army corps the squadrons may be detached from divisions and grouped under the immediate control of the field Army commander. The recommendation in my last report that aero squadrons of 12 machines be the basis of our organization has been approved, and existing Tables of Organization provide for three companies of four machines each for a squadron. A major will be in command of the squadron, with a first lieutenant as squadron adjutant and quartermaster; 2 master signal electricians; 2 sergeants, first class, 6 corporals; and 2 privates, first class, for duty with the headquarters and supply detachments. Each aero company has an authorized strength of 1 captain; 5 first lieutenants; 1 master signal electrician; 2 sergeants, first class; 5 sergeants; 9 corporals; 2 cooks; 14 privates, first class; and 6 privates.

1. *Report of the Chief Signal Officer, United States Army, to the Secretary of War, 1916* (Washington 1916).
2. The company was the 1st Company, 2d Aero Squadron, which was organized at San Diego on 1 December 1915 and sailed for the Philippines early in January 1916. Maurer, *Combat Squadrons*, pp. 15–16.

15. Funds for Fiscal Year 1918

January 1917

When General Scriven appeared for budget hearings early in 1917, his days as Chief Signal Officer were numbered. There had been dissension within the Aviation Section between the flyers and the non-flyers. There had been charges that non-flying officers had been drawing flight pay. Scriven had openly accused aviation officers of insubordination and disloyalty. In hearings the previous April (Doc. 12), Baker had informed the committee that Scriven would be replaced and the Aviation Section reorganized. To take Col. Samuel Reber's place as Chief of the Aviation Section, Baker had brought Lt. Col. George O. Squier back from London, where he had been military attache. Squier had taken charge of the section in May 1916, but that was just a temporary arrangement. He was slated to become Chief Signal Officer upon Scriven's retirement in February 1917. The committee was interested in what Squier, who accompanied Scriven to the hearing, had learned from conversations with British officials and from personal observation of aircraft in action on the battle front in Europe.

Wilson, re-elected President on 7 November 1916 on a peace platform, was having no success in bringing the war to an end. Rather, the nation seemed to be moving inevitably toward a war for which it was ill prepared. The performance of the 1st Aero Squadron in Mexico, when contrasted with events in Europe, had helped to reveal how far the United States had fallen behind in the development of military aviation.

For Fiscal Year 1918 the Signal Corps had requested $16,600,000, which was $2,300,000 more than it had received for 1917. When asked about the cause of the increase, Scriven explained that the amount for the "Signal Corps proper" was only $1,000,000, which was $100 less than the previous year. The remaining $15,600,000 was for aviation.

S. Hubert Dent, Jr. (D., Ala.), had become committee chairman following Hay's resignation to accept a judicial appointment. Congressmen Greene, Kahn, McKellar, and McKenzie were still members of the committee, which also included William Gordon (D., Ohio) and John Tilson (R., Conn.). In addition to Scriven and Squier, Maj. William Mitchell and Maj. Charles S. Wallace were present at the hearing on 5 January 1917.[1]

Mr. Kahn. Have you been using any aircraft in connection with fire control?

Gen. Scriven. No, Mr. Kahn; I do not think I can say we have. There has been no general organized work in that direction, but there has been a little experimental work at Fort Sill with the Field Artillery, observations in the Philippines in connection with the coast defenses, and at San Diego some experiments looking to the detection of submarine obstacles.

Mr. Kahn. They are using aircraft for fire control very extensively on the European battlefields, as I understand it.

Gen. Scriven. It is absolutely essential, and we must come to it as soon as we can.

Mr. Kahn. How does it happen we have not done any of that?

Gen. Scriven. It is because we have not had the machines or the personnel.

Mr. Kahn. When you have the machines, do you expect to operate them in connection with the Coast Artillery, too?

Gen. Scriven. I have just recently submitted a memorandum to the General Staff, asking them to decide, in connection with the military policy of the United States, the locations of various aviation centers, schools, aerodromes, etc., according to the needs of the service, and

1. Hearings before the Committee on Military Affairs, House of Representatives, *Army Appropriation Bill, 1918*, 64th Cong, 2d sess (1917).

also the locations of airplane centers, in connection with the Coast Artillery defenses.

Of course you know we have just purchased a very large tract of land near Fort Monroe, costing $290,000, where there is to be established one of these centers and schools, and the Navy is coming in on that to some extent, temporarily. That will undoubtedly be an aviation center for the defenses of Chesapeake Bay. What the policy will be in regard to the locations for other squadrons of aeroplanes, so far as the Coast Artillery is concerned, I do not know. We plan the placing of squadrons in the Philippines, in Hawaii, and in the Canal Zone. They will be very largely used in connection with the Coast Artillery for defense.

Mr. Kahn. Do you expect to operate those aeroplanes?

Gen. Scriven. We must; yes, sir. The men we are training must operate them.

Mr. Kahn. You do not intend, as far as you know, to turn over any of your aeroplanes to the Coast Artillery, to be operated by the Coast Artillery?

Gen. Scriven. That is a question of policy for the future. . . .

. . . .

Mr. Kahn. How many machines have you purchased with the appropriation of last year, and how many have you obligated the department to purchase?

Gen. Scriven. I have the data in regard to that.

Mr. Kahn. Will you put that in the hearings?

Gen. Scriven. The total number of aeroplanes purchased or under order is 423. There have been 21 machines destroyed and condemned, and there are 27 out of commission. Of those in service 4 are in Manila, 30 at San Diego, 18 at Mineola, 7 at San Antonio, and 14 at Columbus and on the border, making a total of 73 in service. There are 302 machines under order but not delivered.

. . . .

Mr. Kahn. Have you had any occasion to revise your opinion which you gave last year as to the life of an aeroplane? I think you said the life of a machine in time of peace is about 10 months and in time of war about 7 days.

Gen. Scriven. No, sir. I think the use of an aeroplane is just like the use of so much ammunition. A machine goes up and comes down and may be smashed. If the machine goes along without an accident, I suppose anywhere from 6 to 10 months is about as long as you can expect it to last. It depends on the conditions under which it is used or maintained, climate, weather, service, and the like. They are very fragile, and it is very difficult to estimate their life exactly.

Mr. Kahn. Of course, the committee, I take it, is anxious to let the country know that, while we are willing to appropriate money for this purpose, the country ought also to know that the life of these machines is exceedingly short.

Gen. Scriven. It is very short. Take, for instance, the conditions as they exist on the border. An aeroplane goes up, meets with some unfavorable conditions, and comes down perhaps 30 or 40 miles away from any place where it can get any assistance. That is the end of the machine. On the contrary, if the machine came down at a place where repairs could be made, the broken parts may be replaced without difficulty.

Mr. Kahn. What do you mean when you say that is the end of the machine? Do you have to abandon it?

Gen. Scriven. We may have to abandon it if you can not get any of the parts you need. That would be especially true in case the machine came down in an enemy's country.

Mr. Kahn. How many of our machines have met with such a fate recently?

Gen. Scriven. There have been a good many of them which met such a fate down in Mexico. All of the first lot we sent down there suffered that fate.

Mr. Kahn. There was some question about those machines being fitted for the work you expected them to do, was there not?

Gen. Scriven. They were picked up and taken down there because they were all we had. They were taken down from Fort Sill and San Diego, where the conditions were different; but it was absolutely necessary to send them out as the days were those of war. They were low-power machines—90-horse-power Curtiss machines—and for that allotment the committee only gave us $300,000, which, as a matter of fact, extended over some 14 months.

Mr. Kahn. What is the average price of one of these flying machines?

Gen. Scriven. The machines which are proving very satisfactory now with the border troops at Columbus, communicating with Gen. Pershing, are 160-horsepower Curtiss machines.

Maj. Mitchell. The average cost is $12,000; $20,000 with the spare parts.

. . . .

Mr. McKenzie. Since we have done our flying with the aeroplane, what is your judgment about the practicability of the use of balloons?

Gen. Scriven. I think the captive balloon is very valuable. Of course, we know they have been using them on the Belgian coast and on the coast of France for observation purposes and very largely on the fighting fronts. Of course, they are limited in the altitude which they can reach. The free balloon is of no special value, as its use is exceedingly limited. As to the dirigible, I have never been much of a believer in it. The dirigible is six or seven hundred feet long, of enormous diameter, has powerful searchlights, guns, bomb-dropping devices, the ability to hover over a certain selected point, but it is vulnerable to attack from the aeroplane or from the ground and susceptible to weather conditions, and I can not see where the dirigible has ever done anything commensurate with its cost, or fulfilled the expectations of the people who believe in them. In fact, I do not believe in them at all. Of course, there may be times when such a machine as the dirigible might be of some service, but those times are so infrequent, and the chances of success are so remote, I do not believe they are worth having at their present cost.

Mr. McKenzie. Would you advise striking out the work "balloon" in the appropriation bill?

Gen. Scriven. Oh, no. Balloons are very important. Captive and kite balloons are absolutely necessary. The captive balloon is much more valuable than most people recognize. When I was military attache of the United States in Italy I saw a captive balloon being carried along with the cavalry at a trot. It makes a very fine observation station.

Mr. Kahn. Germany is the only country which uses the Zeppelin type of dirigible, is it not?

Gen. Scriven. Yes, sir. I believe the English have tried the dirigible. Col. Squier is rather more in favor of the dirigible than I am. As far as I can see, the longer this war continues, the less the Zeppelin is proving its value; but, of course, that is an individual opinion.

. . . .

The Chairman. How are the aeroplanes armed?

Gen. Scriven. That is another question that is very difficult of solution. They are carrying now merely the service rifle and pistol. Some men think that a short riot gun, a shot gun, should be used; others think that a gun of the Lewis type or some other such type may be well used.

The Chairman. You have not equipped them with the machine gun at all?

Gen. Scriven. Oh, yes; experimentally, we have tried some. We have used the Lewis gun, but they are not mounted. The Lewis gun weighs only 27 pounds, and can be used from the shoulder. It is a very good gun.

Mr. Kahn. Are they all armed with Lewis guns?

Gen. Scriven. There are some down there; 14, I think.

Mr. Kahn. Have you ever used any other machine gun, except the Lewis gun?

Gen. Scriven. The Benet-Mercier gun was used. We tried it out. I think there are some down there now. We have tried them all out thoroughly.

. . . .

Mr. McKellar. The first item is on page 7 of the bill, "Signal Service of the Army," a very comprehensive item. Will you explain to the committee, in general, exactly what you are doing in carrying out the provisions of that item?

Col. Squier. Yes, sir. Last year you remember that we had $300,000 as the appropriation, and then you gave us an emergency fund of $500,000 in March or April, on account of the Mexican situation; and then it was suddenly increased from those small amounts until, on the 28th of August, the Army appropriation act was signed, and we got under that act $13,281,666. In other words, gentlemen, beginning the year with the small amount of $300,000, we suddenly got a large amount of money with which to carry on the development of the Aviation Service.

. . . .

Lt. Col. George O. Squier,
Officer in Charge of the Aviation
Section, Signal Corps (1916–1917). Later (1917–1923) in the
rank of first brigadier and then major general,
he served as Chief Signal Officer.

Col. Squier. . . . The equipment we are getting now is as good, I am sure, as this country can produce, and it is improving very rapidly. We are having very few accidents, and there are very few forced landings. Our troubles are now disappearing, because we have better equipment. I think I may say with considerable satisfaction that we have very few accidents of any sort at our schools now. The figures with regard to that are really astonishing.

Mr. Kahn. If it is not too much trouble, will you put them in the record of this hearing?

Col. Squier. I will be glad to do so. . . .

. . . .

Flying Record, Army Air Service, Signal Corps Aviation School, San Diego, Cal., Jan. 1 to Dec. 26, 1916.

Total number of flights . .7,087
Total time in air (hours and
  minutes) 3,356.56
Distance tranveled
  (miles) 251,775
Fatalities . . . . None.

Col. Squier (continuing). We have been confronted by the fact that there has been no buying market for aeroplanes in this country, and, of course, without a buying market, you can not develop an engine or an equipment. Consequently, we were

_ very much behind Europe, which, under the spur of the war, has gone forward in a marvelous way along these lines. The flying movement abroad is simply prodigious; and any questions you may wish to ask me about that I will be very glad to answer, provided my answers are not to go into the record or to become public. I have had unusual opportunities to follow the flying movement abroad, because I have been the military attache to London for the past four years, and I have been privileged to see a good deal at the front. Naturally, I must be very circumspect in anything that I may say here in regard to the present war.

The Chairman. Do you mean that you do not want to speak of that unless we go into executive session?

Col. Squier. Certainly, because whatever I have seen has been under diplomatic privileges.

The Chairman. All right. . . .

. . . .

Col. Squier. . . . . . We hope to have seven squadrons for the Regular Army developed, or nearly so, with materiel and personnel by the end of the year. Of those seven squadrons four will be for the four departments; three will be for over-sea service—in the Canal Zone, Hawaii, and the Philippines.

Mr. Kahn. For the sake of the record, will you state again how many machines are in a squadron in the aviation service?

Col. Squier. The unit of this service is the squadron, which consists of three flights of four aeroplanes each, or a total of 12 aeroplanes in a unit. It will perhaps clear the atmosphere a bit if we bear in mind two ideas which will help us to make a proper estimate about this whole subject; and I will tell you the way it appealed to me from the beginning and the method that I used.

Before leaving England I made inquiry on two points: Very generally I made inquiry as to how many aeroplanes should be assigned to each mobile unit or division of an army. I considered that if I knew that it would be a great help. Second, I made inquiry as to what was the cost of one aeroplane maintained in the air per year.

So I made it my business to inquire of the Government officials and others and tried to get an answer to those two questions, because they are fundamental questions.

I found that the allowance of aeroplanes per division of the mobile army is one squadron of active aeroplanes in the air whenever the commanding officer wants them. That does not mean that each division of a large army would have its own squadron, by any means; it means that the average would be according to that formula. If, then, any mobile army has six divisions, we know just how many squadrons we ought to provide.

The other important consideration is the price of keeping aeroplanes in the air for a year. I found in Europe, or in England, from separate sources, as near as they could guess it—of course, it is more or less guesswork, because you may have a series of accidents in a day that will wipe out whole squadrons—that the figure is about $50,000 a year, or £10,000 a year, to keep an aeroplane in the air. So that 12 aeroplanes in a squadron would cost $600,000 a year for maintenance.

Mr. McKellar. Have you given the original cost of the aeroplanes?

Col. Squier. I am coming to that. So that the unit squadron, which will produce 12 flying aeroplanes in war, wears out an aeroplane, on the average, every three months; and 4 aeroplanes are therefore required to keep 1 aeroplane in the air all of the time; so that you would have 48 aeroplanes in a squadron used up in war per year. In peace it is less, of course, but not so much less as you would imagine, because an aeroplane is a fragile thing, and it wears out very quickly. The life of an engine is only about 300 hours, roughly,

and you would have to have several engines for each aeroplane, and the engine is an expensive part of the aeroplane, costing about $50 per horsepower.

So that I can say that the basis we are now working on is that the original cost of a squadron for a division, with all its equipment, which includes this book (indicating) full of accessories, the number of which would surprise you, is $800,000, roughly; and to maintain that after you got it is $600,000 per year, which is $50,000 per machine per year in the air.

. . . .

I have said, then, that with the appropriation you have given us, we propose to equip, as far as we can, seven squadrons for the Regular Army, and we will probably have pretty well under way six reserve squadrons which will be used temporarily, at least, in connection with coast defenses, in such manner as the War Department may decide. These machines have already been ordered for coast defense, bids have been called for, and if the committee desires to see them, the specifications are here (indicating).

There will be 6 of these squadrons, in addition to the 7; for the Regular Army that would be 13 in all. And for the next fiscal year we propose to maintain those 13, and add 4 more at a cost of $800,000 each, maintaining those 13 at $600,000 each. Those figures I gave you

before. If you will bear those figures in mind, it will be easy to get a general idea of what we are doing. We feel very much encouraged as to the personnel also, and have inaugurated—

Mr. Greene (interposing). $800,000 you say is the original cost?

Col. Squier. Yes, sir; for the unit, the squadron.

At present the President has authorized for the aviation section for the present year 1,800 men; he has authority to do that. . . .

. . . .

There has been authorized by the War Department for the next year no less than 3,200 men; the personnel for the squadrons for the Canal Zone and for Hawaii, and for the completion of the squadron at Manila—the officers to command them have already been selected, and the supply officers have already been designated, and the men themselves who are to go have been selected, very largely, with the view of keeping the two elements of personnel and equipment side by side. There are something like 200 of these men at the San Diego School; 50 of them will be sent to Panama and 50 to Hawaii.

. . . .

I have given you then, Mr. Chairman, our hopes for this year, namely, seven squadrons for the Regular Army, four of which are to be in this country and three for the over-sea possessions; and six reserve squadrons for the Coast Defense; those six squadrons would be, speaking generally, two near the city of New York, say, one in Chesapeake Bay, one near Boston for instance, one near San Francisco, and one in the Seattle district.

The machines are all bought, or under contract; the personnel is largely in hand for those; and two of the new squadrons for the Regular Army will be formed at San Antonio; all four of the Regular Army squadrons will be in the Southern Department at present, because there is the active border duty. Later some may be assigned to other departments. But the urgent base for us now is San Antonio, Tex.; and as one squadron is completed and ready, it goes out, and another one is formed.

The Chairman. Let me ask you this question in that connection: The squadrons that you will use for the posts will be under the jurisdiction of the Signal Corps, will they?

Col. Squier. Yes, sir; it is all under one head.

The Chairman. And the use that they may be devoted to in directing fire will be under the Signal Corps?

Col. Squier. Yes, sir. I may say, Mr. Chairman, that we regard the air service as being designed and provided for the whole of the Army; and in my judgment that is very wise at present, because you can look at the whole problem and spend the money with the greatest economy in that way. There may come a time afterwards when you may want to segregate the bookkeeping part of it. I have an open mind upon the subject—if there is to be any question of authority between committees of Congress.

Mr. Kahn. Is that done largely in Europe in the belligerent countries? Is it one service?

Col. Squier. Yes, sir; the air service in Europe is one central service. It is then assigned to any service that they may wish; for instance, to "spot" artillery fire. The way they use the aeroplane is that certain aeroplanes will be assigned to certain batteries; and they do it by numbers, and you can see them go to those batteries and perform that service for that day, and then return to their stations with their squadrons.

Mr. Kahn. They are sent out by the Signal Corps?

Col. Squier. Yes, sir; by the aviation service.

Mr. Kahn. And they report to a certain battery commander?

Col. Squier. Yes, sir. Of course, they are all under the general.

Mr. Kahn. Yes; I understand.

Col. Squier. It is like you send a doctor to a general, and he is under the general's command, but is in a separate service for technical training and equipment.

. . . .

Mr. McKellar. Here is a subject as to which I think you could tell us a good many things we would like to know. As I understand it, when you went down on the border, all the machines that you had failed to come up to what was required of them; in other words, you could not fly over mountains?

Col. Squier. Yes, sir; that is correct.

Mr. McKellar. And you have to abandon those. Now, in the purchase of these 306 that are contracted for, have you secured by these contracts such machines as can fly over mountains, or can fly to almost any height? Will you just state how that is?

Col. Squier. My answer is that the present squadron with the punitive expedition is fully equipped with suitable reconnoissance machines, which I am satisfied are the best that this country can produce now; and with every auxiliary part that is needed for its service, including automatic Lewis machine guns, rifles, automatic cameras, incendiary bombs, demolition bombs, wireless, etc. There is a base at Columbus, N. Mex., capable of repairing anything that happens, within reason, and it is self-supporting, so that we do not have to devote any attention practically to it at this end of the line. We have a propeller factory right there, and they make their own propellers there to suit the dry climate and the heat.

. . . .

Mr. Kahn. These [aerial] battles are all fought with machine guns?

Col. Squier. Absolutely. On that point I might add the angle of view of the machine gun as it appears to our Aviation Section. If you will eliminate the demolitions, for instance, where you drop bombs, or the incendiary bomb, and take the pure case of a fight between aeroplane and aeroplane, it would appear that what we want is not a large gun with a few number of rounds, but a small-caliber gun with a large number of rounds, for the following reason: You get the upper berth and come at the opponent by gravity, shooting through the propeller, and you only have a very short time in which to shoot. You then go by

him at the rate of a hundred miles an hour, and you come back again, if you are faster than he is. So that if you had a large gun with only one shot and did not hit him at all, your shot would do no good; but if you had the same weight of lead in a hundred shot you would be more apt to hit him; and the aeroplane is so vulnerable at present, that he would be disabled as much by that small shot as by the large one.

Mr. Kahn. And do they ordinarily aim through the propeller?

Col. Squier. They ordinarily aim right through the propeller and the pilot sits right back of the propeller, they aim the whole machine; they do not aim the gun; they just pull a string to fire and aim the machine itself. The point is this, that you can only have a certain weight of lead on the aeroplane.

Mr. Kahn. Yes; I understand.

Col. Squier. And you can have that in one big shot, or a lot of little shots; and you can not carry an extra man, because he weighs so much; you must fix it so that this same man must do it; you can not take up an extra man just to shoot a machine gun, because the extra weight would be so much. And you would be going by the other machine at perhaps 120 miles an hour, and you want to hit him with one of those shots, and not to miss him. So you want a multiple machine gun, or something by which you will not be likely to miss him as you pass;

you do not have much time to fire; then you go by and begin maneuvering again and repeat the operation.

So that, as a general thing, we are against larger guns for aeroplanes; but I am speaking now about a machine that goes up and fires in the air at another aeroplane.

Mr. Kahn. Are there many American aviators using those machines in the various armies in Europe?

Col. Squier. There are in France a considerable number, as you know.

Mr. Kahn. Yes.

Col. Squier. They are known as the "American legion" or something of the kind.

Mr. McKellar. Are you an aviator yourself?

Col. Squier. No, sir. I have ridden as a passenger frequently, but I am not a driver. It is not the policy; in fact, I am too old to drive. The driver is, in war, a man under 30 years old, usually; it is a young man's job; there is no question about that.

Mr. Kahn. That is true also of the mobile army, the infantrymen?

Col. Squier. Well, it is particularly true in this. In fact, I can tell you that, in a residence of several months with an army in war, I have never found a single actual flier that was over 24 years of age at that time. Well, the only point I want to make is that it is distinctly a young man's job.

The Chairman. How close do these machines come to each other in a fight?

Col. Squier. They have actually rammed each other. It is a most thrilling thing to watch them; in fact, there is no use reading novels any more; real life is more interesting; it is simply wonderful to see them.

Mr. Greene. Col. Squier, I understand that the theory of this combat in the air is to gain control of that territory, for the other purposes for which the aeroplanes are subsequently to be used in it?

Col. Squier. Yes, sir.

Mr. Greene. The fighting itself has no particular military object?

Mr. Gordon. Well, it is to kill the other man.

Mr. Greene. Well, to kill him, but it is in order to get control of the air zone?

Col. Squier. Yes, sir.

Mr. Tilson. Reconnaissance and fire control is what you are looking for?

Col. Squier. Yes, sir. In fact, the only way they know now about the maze of trenches along that line, which any human being could not go over, is by taking photographs of each zone from aeroplanes and matching them together each day. Without that they could not tell the new pieces of trench dug during the previous night.

Mr. Kahn. Control over the air is just as important as control over the sea?

Col. Squier. And after this war the armies, in general, will disband or shrink, but the air service is going to stay where it is and go on. They realize it is an asset that is going to remain, and not shrink or disband. All we learn in this war about aerial navigation will be applied to the uses of civilization in the peace which follows. It is one point of permanent gain, at any rate, and that is why this country is safe in putting money into it.

(Thereupon, at 1:30 o'clock p.m., the committee adjourned. . . .)

. . . .

When Germany resumed unrestricted submarine warfare at the beginning of February 1917, the United States broke off diplomatic relations. Then came the Zimmermann note, the arming of American merchantmen, the sinking of American ships, a call for a special session of Congress, and, finally, on 6 April 1917, the declaration of war against Germany.

Meanwhile, on 5 February 1917, the Signal Corps was asked to estimate requirements for an army made up of the regulars, the national guard, and 500,000 volunteers. The estimate submitted on 16 February included $48,666,666 for aviation proportioned to the rest of the army. On 21 March Secretary Baker called for another estimate, this time with 1,000,000 volunteers. Using the same formula, the Signal Corps came up with $54,250,000 for aviation. During this time estimates for aircraft production had mounted to 3,700 a year. In such exercises, the major concern apparently was production, with little attention being given to how the planes were to be used. The aircraft industry of the United States was not then geared up to any such production, even if the government had known what kinds of planes it needed for combat service.

For several years officials of the War Department, the Signal Corps, and the Aviation Section had lamented the secrecy that prevented them from learning about the latest technical developments in aircraft production in Europe. There was plenty of information available, however, to indicate that the major belligerent powers had made great progress in developing not only aircraft but also doctrine and tactics for the employment of their

growing airpower. Britain, France, and Germany had recognized the importance of air superiority and were using their aircraft for counter-air operations, bombardment of strategic and, more often, interdiction targets, close support of ground forces by bombing and strafing, strategic and tactical reconnaissance, both visual and photographic, adjustment of artillery fire, and for informing infantry commanders of the location and movements of their troops.

Although there was some awareness in the United States of these developments in the use of airpower, aviation in the U.S. Army was still regarded as being principally a service of reconnaissance, with plans for expansion of tactical strength being based on the addition of one squadron for each additional Army division. On 6 April 1917, however, the Aviation Section was ill prepared to carry out even the limited function it had been assigned for field service in time of war.

When the United States went to war in April 1917, the aviation service of the U.S. Army consisted of the 1st Aero Squadron, which had been formed in 1913 and had served with Pershing in Mexico; the 1st Company, 2d Aero Squadron, which had been formed in December 1915 and sent to the Philippines the following January; the 7th Aero Squadron, formed in February 1917 for duty in the Canal Zone; and the 6th Aero Squadron, organized in Hawaii in March 1917. Three other squadrons, part of a seven-squadron program, were in various stages of formation in the United States.

For these units, and for administration, training, and other activities, the Aviation Section had about 130 officers (flyers and non-flyers, airplane and balloon pilots,

reservists and retired officers on active duty as well as regulars) and a little over 1,000 enlisted men. No one seems to know for sure how many airplanes the Aviation Section had (about 200? less than 300?), but all sources seem to agree that not one of the planes was suitable for combat service, not even reconnaissance.

Thus the United States went to war without an air force worthy of the name, and without any well formulated ideas, much less plans, for building and employing such a force in battle.[1]

1. The history of the U.S. Army's air service in the period prior to America's entry into the war is traced in considerable detail in USAF Historical Study 98, *The United States Army Air Arm, April 1861 to April 1917* (USAF Hist Div, 1958).

Part II:
Plans and Programs
April 1917 — February 1918

In the days immediately following America's entry into the war, much effort was devoted to plans for the development of an air force for wartime service. In Washington the concern was with production, construction, and training, with little attention being given to how airpower would be used in battle. As events developed, planning for the employment of U.S. airpower in Europe was left largely to General Pershing, his staff, and his Air Service, which was a separate service and not part of the Signal Corps of the AEF.

Gen. Pershing with his World War I staff: First row (l. to r.): Brig. Gen. Harold B. Fiske, Maj. Gen. James W. McAndrew, Gen. John J. Pershing, Brig. Gen. Fox Conner, Brig. Gen. George V. H. Moseley; second row: Brig. Gen. Avery D. Andrews, Brig. Gen. LeRoy Eltinge, Brig. Gen. Dennis E. Nolan, and Brig. Gen. Robert C. Davis.

The production program
involved the assembly of American-
made planes in France. French women participated in
this task at the Air Service Production Center
#2, Romorantin.

16. 12,000 Plane Program

29 May 1917

The development of an aviation program in Washington was given a new direction and greater impetus by a cable received on 24 May 1917 from Premier Alexandre Ribot of France. Ribot proposed that the United States form a flying corps of 4,500 planes, with personnel and material, for service in France in 1918. The cable was based on a French study for a U.S. air force of 60 groups for strategical operations. Half of the groups were to be pursuit and half bombardment, with each group being made up of 6 squadrons of 12 planes each [Docs. 7 and 23]. Since the cable did not specify pursuit and bombardment, officials in Washington assumed that the number covered all aviation and made plans accordingly.[1]

The Joint Army-Navy Technical Aircraft Board quickly translated Ribot's proposal into the following plan.[2] With provisions for replacement and reserve craft, the plan called for the production of 12,000 airplanes during the first half of 1918 for service in France. To this were added more than 5,000 training planes. The plan was to concentrate on the production of training and reconnaissance planes in the United States and obtain fighting and bombing planes from the allies. Funding for production was included in $640,000,000 appropriated by Congress in an act signed by the President on 24 July 1917 for a large expansion of the Aviation Section.

Washington, D.C.
May 29, 1917.

From: Joint Army and Navy
Technical Aircraft Board

To: Secretary of War.
Secretary of the Navy.

Subject: Report of Board

1. The Board met at 10:15 A.M. at the call of its president.
2. Present: All the members.
3. The French Government, on May 24, 1917, requested the United States Government to cooperate with the French Aeronautics, and form a flying corps of 4,500 airplanes, personnel and material; such flying corps to be available for active service in France during the spring campaign of 1918.

To meet the foregoing request, the needs of the United States Army for service airplanes and engines, to be used in Europe, are as indicated [see table below]:

In order that the United States Government may meet the request of the French Government, immediate steps should be taken to start the manufacture, in the United States, of the above airplanes and engines.

B. D. Foulois
Major, Signal
Corps, U.S.A.

V. E. Clark
Captain,
U.S.A.

A. K. Atkins
Lieutenant,
U.S.N.

J. G. Hunsaker
Asst. Naval
Constructor,
U.S.N.

J. H. Towers
Lieutenant,
U.S.N.

E. S. Gorrell
Captain, Signal
Corps,
U.S.A.

Approved:
Newton D.
Baker
Secretary of
War.

Josephus Daniels

Secretary of
the Navy.

1. The statements concerning the Ribot cable and its interpretation follow I. B. Holley, Jr., *Ideas and Weapons* (New Haven, 1958), pp 41–46, supplemented by Ministere de la Guerre, *Les Armees Francaises dans la Grande Guerre*, Tome V, Vol 2 (Paris, 1937), pp 48–51.
2. In Gorrell's History, A–1, pp 11–12.

Service Airplanes and Engines (Latest Types)
(To be produced between January 1, 1918, and June 30, 1918).

Types	Airplanes		Engines		Cost
	Fighting line	Reserve	Fighting line	Reserve	
Reconnaissance & artillery control	3,000	1,000	6,000	2,000	
Fighting	5,000	1,667	10,000	3,334	
Bombing	1,000	333	2,000	666	
Total	9,000	3,000	18,000	6,000	
Grand Total		12,000		24,000	

Brig. Gen. Edgar Russel (at the time a colonel) was
Chief Signal Officer, AEF, and president of a Board of
Officers appointed in June 1918 to make recommendations on aviation
matters in France. (sketch by Joseph Cummings Chase)

17. Mitchell: Air Policy

13 June 1917

Two days after the Ribot cable, Pershing assumed command of the AEF in Washington. Sailing for Europe on 28 May, he stopped in England before going on to France. When he arrived in Paris on 13 June 1917, one of the people on hand to greet him when he got off the train at the Gare du Nord was Lt. Col. William Mitchell, Aviation Section, Signal Corps, U.S. Army. Mitchell, who had left Washington on 17 March, had been sent to Europe as a military observer with orders to investigate the status of French aeronautics. His first stop in Europe had been Spain, where he heard the news that the United States had declared war. He had set out immediately for Paris, and during the following weeks he had talked with French officials, visited French factories and aeronautical schools, toured the French front, flown over enemy lines with a French pilot, visited Royal Flying Corps units in France, talked with their commander, Maj. Gen. Hugh Trenchard, and, among

other things, had set up an office for the U.S. Air Service at 25 Avenue Montaigne in Paris. That office, he informed Pershing's Chief of Staff, Lt. Col. James G. Harbord, in a memorandum dated 13 June, was "ready to go ahead with any project determined upon by the Commanding General."[1]

Mitchell also had prepared for the Chief of Staff two papers dealing with American air policy and organization. Harbord referred them to a Board of Officers appointed on 19 June to make recommendations on various aviation matters. The board was made up of Col. Edgar Russel, Chief Signal Officer, AEF, president of the board; Mitchell, the senior aviation member; Maj. Townsend F. Dodd, Aviation Officer, AEF; Maj. Marlborough Churchill,

Field Artillery; Maj. Frank Parker, Cavalry; and Capt. Joseph E. Carberry, Aviation Section, Signal Corps. Churchill and Parker were members of a U.S. Military Mission, headed by Lt. Col. James A. Logan, that had been in France for some time. Carberry, who served as recorder for the board, had arrived in France only a short time earlier for flight training. Mitchell's papers on policy and organization were received by the board at its third meeting, on 26 June 1917.[2]

1. Exhibit C (Duty Performed by Major Wm. Mitchell, Aviation Section, Signal Corps, dated 13 Jun 17) to Mitchell, Memo for C/S, AEF, subj: Aeronautical Organization in France, 13 June 1917, in Gorrell's History, A–23.

2. The proceedings of the board are in Gorrell's History, A–23.

Memorandum for the Chief of Staff, U.S. Expeditionary Forces.[3] *From: Major*[4] *Wm. Mitchell, Aviation Section, Signal Corps*

1. Now that the United States Military participation in France is assured, it seems to be an opportune moment to consider what policy should be adopted with respect to the aeronautical service.

2. The opinion is advanced that, if a sound policy is adopted to begin with, results will follow quickly and surely. If, on the other hand, a halting policy is adopted, the air service will fall far short of what it is absolutely required to do in modern war. The decisive value of this service is difficult to appreciate at a distance from the field of military operations. It should be an independent arm as artillery or infantry.

3. Aeronautical functions divide themselves into strategical and tactical phases:

a) The tactical function, basically, is to insure observation for the fire and control of our own artillery. To accomplish this, airplanes and balloons observe the fire while others fight off hostile aircraft which attempt to stop it.

This kind of air work has been done now for three years and is well understood. There is attached hereto a copy of the note of General Trenchard (commanding British aviation in France) on this subject, which was written in September 1916, and is as sound today as it was then (Appendix "A").[5]

b) The strategical phase (which has received a very limited application, but which is being seriously considered by all belligerents and is not dealt with in General Trenchard's note) applies to the air attack of enemy material of all kinds behind his lines. To be successful, large combatant groups of airplanes must be organized, separate from those directly attached to army units.

It is with this class of aviation (strategical) that the United States may aid in the greatest way and which, it is believed if properly applied will have a greater influence on the ultimate decision of the war than any other one arm.

4. There is attached hereto the French General Staff's request for what may be termed strategical aviation units (Exhibit B).[6] The first thing to be determined is whether it is to be adopted or modified.

. . . .

(Signed) Wm. Mitchell.

3. In Gorrell's History, A–23.

4. Mitchell had been promoted to lieutenant colonel effective 15 May 1917.

5. This appendix has been omitted. The document was published in Mitchell, *Memoirs of World War I* (New York, 1960), pp 105–109. An extract appeared in Andrew Boyle, *Trenchard* (London, 1962), pp 186–188.

6. This exhibit, which has been omitted, was dated 6 May 1917. It is an extract from the document on which the Ribot cable was based. (See Doc. 23 for further reference.)

Maj. Gen. Sir Hugh Montague Trenchard, General Officer
Commanding Royal Flying Corps in the Field when the United
States entered World War I. (from a drawing by Francis Dodd)

"Billy Mitchell."

18. Mitchell: Aeronautical Organization

13 June 1917

Memorandum for the Chief of Staff, U.S. Expeditionary Force.[1] From: Major Mitchell, Aviation Section, Signal Corps.

1. United States aeronautical participation in France naturally divides itself into two classes:

A. The air squadrons with the American units themselves, such as the divisions, army corps or armies, in accordance with the manner in which the army is organized and employed. The aeronautical units for this service will be attached directly to the troops in the same way, for instance, as the field and heavy artillery are. They always will comprise divisional air squadrons and balloon companies, and may consist of pursuit and bombardment squadrons in addition. Their entire object is to facilitate the work of the division, corps or army. They should be organized progressively.

B. Based on the theory that no decision can be reached on the ground before a decision has been gained in the air, the French General Staff has requested, that in addition to the Aviation Units which form a part of the American troops coming to France, there be organized a number of large aeronautical groups for strategic operations against enemy aircraft and enemy material, at a distance from the actual line. These units would be bombardment and pursuit formations and would have an independent mission, very much as independent cavalry used to have, as distinguished from divisional cavalry. They would be used to carry the war well into the enemy's country.

. . . .

(Signed): Wm. Mitchell

---

1. In Gorrell's History, A–23.

Maj. Townsend F. Dodd (taken while he was captain).

19. Dodd: Aviation Work

18 June 1917

Maj. Townsend F. Dodd, who had served with Pershing in Mexico, accompanied Pershing to Europe as Aviation Officer of the AEF. Enroute to Paris he spent several days in London, talking with the U.S. Military Attache, Col. William Lassiter, and with various British officials. His report on those conversations, submitted to the Chief of Staff, AEF on 20 June 1917, included a note outlining what needed to be done.[1] The Chief of Staff sent Dodd's report to the Board of Officers, where it was received at the first meeting, on 21 June 1917.

Aviation Work Necessary for the Successful Prosecution of the War

The following is a brief synopsis of the most important details of aviation work necessary for the successful prosecution of the war.

I. The first thing to be determined is the results that the American Air Service, in connection with the Allied Air Service and the Allied Armies, is to accomplish.

The results called for by paragraph I are briefly as follows:

a) The unchallenged supremacy of the air on the different fronts, the major consideration being given to the Western Front.

b) The development and maintenance of an aerial offensive force that will be able to carry the war two hundred or more miles behind the German lines. This force, when first available might properly be considered for use strictly for the attack upon military features, such as arsenals, factories, railways, etc. but should also be sufficient to act as a reprisal agent of such destructiveness that the Germans would be forced to stop their raids upon Allied cities.

c) This offensive arm would, of course, be of great value on and immediately behind the German lines in connection with land warfare.

. . . .

Notes
1. In Gorrell's History, A–23.

21 June 1917

At the first meeting of the Board of Officers on 21 June 1917, Churchill submitted two memoranda, one dealing with liaison with the artillery, and the other concerned with air superiority as it affected artillery.[1]

Aerial Observation in Liaison with Artillery.

Informal notes for the Board of Officers convened by Par. 4, S.O. 11, Hqrs. A.E.F.., June 19, 1917.

I. *GENERAL PRINCIPLES.*

The basic idea in connection with aerial observation in liaison with artillery concerns the fact that artillery is today partially blind and partially impotent without efficient aerial observation.

Such being the case, it is evident that connection between the artillery and the air service cannot be too close and that there must be established a complete professional and moral liaison between the two arms. The aerial observer must be an artillery officer, trained in principles governing the conduct of fire, and perfectly familiar with the capabilities of his own arm; but he must live and work with his comrades in the Air Service.

. . . .

---

1. In Gorrell's History, A–23.

Maj. Marlborough Churchill, a Field Artillery
officer, served on the Board of Officers
appointed by Gen. Harbord to advise on
aviation matters.

21. Churchill: Air Superiority

21 June 1917

Notes to Justify the Statement that Military Success Depends Upon Superiority in the Air.[1]

1. If the enemy is master of the air, the artillery cannot conquer the ground which the infantry is to occupy.

2. Even though the ground be conquered, if the enemy regains mastery of the air at the time of the attack, the progress of the infantry advance cannot be known or controlled. In this case liaison is lost and success becomes a matter of chance.

3. To conquer the ground, the artillery must:

a) Know, by means of aerial reconnaissance and photography:

x) the exact nature and location of the enemy's batteries and works;

y) the exact amount of success attained at each period of the preparation;

z) The moment at which the artillery preparation is finished.

b) Be able to adjust its fire upon targets by means of accurate information furnished by well-trained aerial observers.

4. To follow and direct an infantry attack, a general must maintain liaison by means of low flying airplanes.

5. Without air superiority, the artillery is both blind and impotent so far as counter-battery and destruction fire are concerned.

6. The accuracy and efficiency of artillery fire depend upon proper identification of targets and accurate adjustment. In modern war both these are impossible if the mastery of the air is not assured.

7. If the enemy has the mastery of the air his artillery fire, known as "counter-battery" and "counter-preparation", will make even the launching of an attack impossible.

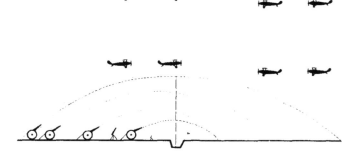

1. In Gorrell's History, A–23.

Maj. Frank Parker, a Cavalry officer,
also served on the Board of Officers
to advise on aviation matters
in France.

22. Parker: The Role of Aviation

2 July 1917

The minutes of the fourth meeting of the Board of Officers, held on 29 June 1917, state that "Major Parker was directed to submit a report on the tactical role of aviation." Born in South Carolina in 1872, Parker was a graduate of the U.S. Military Academy in the Class of 1894. He was commissioned in the Infantry but soon transferred to the Cavalry. He had served as military attache in Latin America, cavalry instructor in Cuba, and member of the U.S. Cavalry Board, and had attended service schools in France on three occasions before being sent to France as a member of the U.S. Military Mission in 1916. In April 1917 he became U.S. liaison officer at French General Headquarters. Later he would command a brigade and then a division in battle in France, and eventually he would retire as a major general.

Parker's wife, Katherine, was the daughter of Frank S. Lahm, the American aviation enthusiast who had resided in Paris for many years, and the sister of Frank P. Lahm, a U.S. cavalry officer who had won the James Gordon Bennett International Balloon Race in 1906, and had been the first U.S. Army officer to fly in a Wright airplane. At the beginning of July 1917, Frank P. Lahm was a major in charge of the Aviation Section's balloon school at Omaha, Nebraska.

The proceedings of the Board of Officers state that, "A report was read by Major Parker on the role and distribution of tactical units . . .," at the fifth meeting, on 2 July 1917. Parker's report,[1] which became Exhibit N to the board's proceedings, and which is printed below, is interesting not only for its ideas on the role of airpower but also because its authorship generally has been attributed to another officer. With a new title, "General Principles Underlying the Use of the Air Service in the Zone of Advance, A.E.F.," and with only a few minor changes in the text, the report submitted by Parker was published in a *Bulletin of the Information Section, Air Service, A.E.F.*, with a preface attributed to "Wm. Mitchell, Lt. Col., A.S., S.C., A.C.A."[2] (see Doc. 35). Thus Parker's report became Mitchell's "General Principles."[3]

The Role and Tactical and Strategical Employment of Aeronautics in an Army.

ROLE.

Military Aeronautics comprise all means of aerial activity which an Army employs to assist it in obtaining victory.

Military Aeronautics are divided into:

A. Aviation, or heavier than air formations.

B. Aerostation, or lighter than air formations.

A. AVIATION.

Aviation is divided into two general classes:

I. *TACTICAL AVIATION*, or that acting in the immediate vicinity or directly attached to organizations of troops of all arms.

II. *STRATEGICAL AVIATION*, or that acting far from troops of other arms and having an independent mission.

---

1. In Gorrell's History, A–23.
2. A.C.A. was the abbreviation for Air Commander, Advance.
3. Primary and secondary sources seen by the editor do not indicate what contributions, if any, were made by Mitchell or others in the preparation of the report assigned to, and submitted by, Parker.

I. Tactical Aviation.

The object of *tactical aviation* is to assist troops in combat. All aviation elements themselves must be ready to fight to accomplish their mission.

Tactical aviation consists of:

A. *Observation aviation*

B. *Pursuit aviation*

C. *Tactical bombardment aviation.*

A. *OBSERVATION AVIATION* is carried on essentially by division squadrons.[4]

OBSERVATION AVIATION consists in:

1. Reconnaissance by eye and by photograph of the enemy's positions and works of all sorts, and the results of all attacks against them.

2. The adjustment of artillery fire.

3. Keeping superior command in liaison with the infantry during attacks by means of wireless, optical signals and horn.[5]

B. *PURSUIT AVIATION* is carried out by pursuit squadrons whose primary object is offensive combat. The mastery of the air is obtained by air battles.

PURSUIT AVIATION consists in:

1. Destruction of enemy aeronautical materiel and personnel by combat in the air.

2. Creating diversions by attacking enemy personnel and material on the ground.

These operate to prevent observation on the part of enemy aeronautical elements, to prevent hostile air incursions into friendly territory and to create a diversion against hostile elements.

C. *TACTICAL BOMBARD-MENT AVIATION* is carried out within about 25,000 yards of the line or roughly within the extreme zone of long-range artillery.

Its object is:

1. To assist in the destruction of enemy materiel of all sorts;

2. To attack hostile personnel both during the day and night, so as to undermine their morale.

3. To attack hostile aerodromes so as to force hostile airplanes to arise and accept combat.

II. Strategical Aviation.

The mission of *strategical aviation* is independent.

Strategical aviation consists in attacking enemy elements, whatever their nature, at a distance usually more than 25,000 yards from friendly troops.

The object is to attack the supply of an enemy army,[6] thereby preventing it from employing all its means of combat. This may be accomplished by:

1. Destroying enemy aircrafts, air depots and defensive air organization.

2. Destroying enemy depots, factories, lines of communications and personnel.

The organization for this purpose whose role is entirely offensive and whose radius of action extends beyond that of tactical aviation, should be:[7]

1. Pursuit squadrons for fighting enemy aircraft.

2. Day-bombardment squadrons for bombing enemy aerodromes to make hostile airplanes rise and accept combat, and to carry out long-distance reconnaissances.[8]

3. Night-bombardment squadrons for destroying enemy elements and lines of communications.[9]

---

4. The Bulletin (Vol. III, No. 132, 30 April 1918) says: ". . . by observation squadrons."
5. Bulletin: . . . by means of electrical and physical means.
6. Bulletin: The object of strategical aviation is to destroy the means of supply of an enemy army. . . .
7. Bulletin: The organizations for this purpose . . . are: . . .

8. Bulletin: . . . accept combat, to carry out long-distance reconnaissance, and to attack personnel and material on the ground by gun-fire.
9. In the Bulletin was inserted an additional unnumbered paragraph: Bombing is carried on in the day-time primarily for reconnaissance. It is carried on at night for destruction.

B. AEROSTATION.

AERONAUTIC UNITS consist of:

1. Observation balloons.

2. Dirigible balloons (these are not being considered at present in connection with U.S. Aeronautics in France).

3. Observation balloons, from[10] an elevated fixed station from which powerful glasses may be used and constant communication maintained by telephone with the earth.

They are used for:

1. Adjustment of fire of artillery.

2. Observation of combats.

3. Observation of elements in and behind hostile lines.

Airplanes and balloons have closely related missions and are therefore placed under one direction.

TACTICAL EMPLOYMENT.

The method of operation and tactical handling of air forces with divisions,[11] army corps, armies and groups of armies is prescribed from time to time in orders,[12] for instance see Annex II, Regulations concerning a General Offensive, dated December 16, 1916 (French).

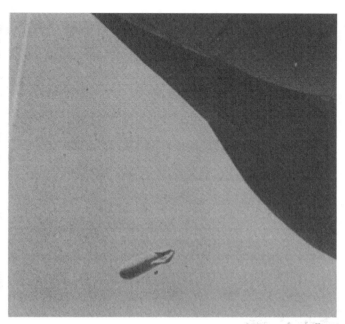

Observation balloon.

10. There may have been a typographical error in the original or in the copy included in Gorrell's History. In the Bulletin the word is "form."

11. In the Bulletin, "divisions" was omitted.

12. In the Bulletin, the remainder of the sentence was omitted.

Capt. Joseph E. Carberry
served as the recorder
for the Board of
Officers.

23. Board of Officers: Recommendations

4 July 1917

A draft of the proceedings of the Board of Officers was presented at the sixth meeting, on 3 July, for revision. The following day a revision was approved, and the board adjourned, *sine die*.

Recommendations[1]

The Board believes that it is now a cardinal principle in warfare that *a decision in the air must be sought and obtained before a decision on the ground can be reached.* Absolute and unchallenged superiority in the air can perhaps never be attained although possibly it may be attained for short periods of time; but experience of three years' war has amply shown that the side which can at critical times dominate the enemy in the air has taken the first, if not the vital, step toward victory.

As a preliminary to the study of the specific recommendations which follow, the board recommends most strongly a careful study of Exhibit N,[2] a memorandum outlining the role of aviation in modern war, with specific reference to the problem now awaiting solution in France.

Proceeding to the specific recommendations required, the Board was ordered to report on the following, which it will discuss in order, concluding the entire proceedings with a series of proposed steps on which action is most strongly urged, to the end that the recommendations herein contained may receive prompt attention:

The board was required to make recommendations on the following:

(a) A complete aviation project for the U.S. Army in France.

(b) The complete organization of the air service, including the manufacture and supply of equipment.

(c) The establishment of depots, repair shops and parks.

(d) The establishment of schools.

(e) The distribution of tactical units and their duties.

An aviation project will embrace two phases of air development, strategical and tactical (See exhibit N).

STRATEGICAL AVIATION.

Based on the letter of the French Commander-in-Chief to the Minister of War, May 6, 1917 (See Exhibit H)[3] which states that the United States should aim to furnish 30 groups of 6 squadrons (pursuit), and 30 groups of 6 squadrons (bombardment).

The estimated number of officers and men required for this project is 20,000 Officers and 110,000 Men.

TACTICAL AVIATION.

The tactical development will follow the development of the American land forces in Europe, and the personnel required to carry out this program can be calculated from the proposed tables of organization (Exhibit I).[4]

For each Army Corps there should be 141 officers and 1340 men.

On the basis of 10 Army Corps, this means

    1,410 Officers
    13,400 Men

The total air personnel will approximate 23,000 Officers and 125,000 Men. . . . .

---

1. In Gorrell's History, A–23.
2. Exhibit N was Parker's report on the role of aviation (see Doc. 22).
3. Omitted.
4. Omitted.

Chaumont, France,
site of Pershing's Headquarters, AEF, during
World War I. (sketch by J. Andre Smith)

24. Duties of the Chief of Air Service

5 July 1917

On 30 June Mitchell replaced Dodd as Aviation Officer. The duties of the position, which were to be changed to Chief of Air Service, were set forth in a general order assigning duties to the various staff officers of Headquarters AEF. The Headquarters had two major divisions, the General Staff, and the Administrative and Technical Staff, with the Chief of Air Service being in the latter.

Headquarters, A.E.F.
France, July 5, 1917.

General Orders,
No. 8.

The tables hereto attached show the present distribution of staff duties of the Headquarters of the American Expeditionary Forces. . . .

The distribution of staff duties in the headquarters of divisions, army corps and other commands subordinate to these headquarters will conform in principle to the distribution of duties shown in these tables.

. . . .

By command of
Major General Pershing:

James G. Harbord,
Lieut. Col. General Staff,
Chief of Staff

Table IV.

Technical and Administrative Services

(Air Service)

Aviation and aero station.

Enlisted and commissioned personnel of aviation units.

Material.

Organization.

Instruction.

Aerial reconnaissance observation and photography.

Aerial combat and bombing.

Etc., etc.[1]

---

1. The second, fifth, and eighth items were dropped and a new one—Airplanes and balloons—was added at the beginning when the duties were revised in G.O. 31, 16 February 1918, at the time Services of Supply was established with jurisdiction over the administrative and technical services of the AEF.

25. 59-Squadron Plan
10 July 1917

On 10 July 1917 Pershing forwarded to Washington a plan for the tactical organization of the AEF.[1] Known as the General Organization Project (GOP), this plan had been developed jointly by the Operations Section of his headquarters and a board of officers, headed by Col. Chauncey Baker, sent to France by the War Department to look into matters relating to the organization, armament, and equipment of troops. In the GOP, which was based on an army of about 1,000,000 men, aviation units were assigned to the army and to each of the army's corps but not to divisions.[2] The total number of aero squadrons in the GOP was 59, of which 39 were observation, 15 pursuit, and 5 bombardment (see Appendix B). Following are extracts from the GOP.[3]

Headquarters American Expeditionary Forces, Office of the Chief of Staff, Operations Section

July 10, 1917.

REPORT ON ORGANIZATION

(Modifications resulting from general conference included herein.)[5]

1. BASIS OF STUDY

In preparing the attached tables of organizations the Operations Section has considered the provisional organization prescribed for the first division ordered to France, definite projects presented by the French Army, Headquarters and British Army Headquarters in France, and has taken as the basis of the study a total force of about 1,000,000 men in France. This force includes not only the combat elements, but also those necessary to main these combat forces.

. . . .

F. C.
H. A. D.
A. B. B.[4]

A force consisting of about one million men has been taken as a basis for the following reasons:

(a) A thorough study of the subject of organization could not be made without considering a balanced force, complete in all the weapons and services essential to modern war.

(b) An Army is the smallest unit fulfilling the conditions included in -a-.

(c) The operations of the American forces in France must, for many reasons not discussed herein, include offensive action on a large scale. To carry this

---

1. The transmittal was dated 10 July, but the memorandum by which Pershing formally approved the project was dated 11 July.

2. In the AEF the infantry was organized into platoons of 58 men (commanded by a lieutenant), with 4 platoons to a company (captain), 4 companies to a battalion (major), 3 battalions and a machinegun company to a regiment (colonel), and 2 regiments and a machinegun battalion to a brigade (brigadier general), the other arms being organized in a similar fashion. Two brigades of infantry and one of field artillery, plus engineer, signal, and other troops, constituted a division (major general). In the GOP the army was organized into five corps (major general), each with four divisions (major general).

3. In Gorrell's History, A–23, also A–7.

4. The staff committee on organization consisted of Lt. Col. Fox Conner, Maj. Hugh A. Drum, and Maj. Alvin B. Barber.

5. This was a conference of members of Headquarters AEF and members of the Baker Board.

action out on a front sufficient to produce results commensurate with the endeavor, there must be available 20 combat divisions for the operations.

(d) With 20 combat divisions as a basis, the Corps and Army troops and necessary Line of Communications troops were determined.

It is evident that a force of about one million is the smallest unit which in modern war will be a complete, well balanced, and independent fighting organization. However, it must be equally clear that the adoption of this size force as a basis of study should not be construed as representing the maximum force which should be sent to, or which will be needed in France. It is taken as the force which may be expected to reach France in time for an offensive in 1918 and as a unit and basis of organization. *Plans for the future should be based, especially in*

reference to the manufacture etc. of artillery, aviation and other material, on three times this force, i.e. at least three million men. Such a program of construction should be completed within two years.

Table III
A Corps (4 Combat and 2 Replacement Divisions.)

	Approximate Strength
Headquarters	350
Combat Divisions	100,000
Replacement Divisions	44,528
Corps Troops	

. . . .

Aviation Troops:	
1 Comdr. & Staff	15
2 Squadrons (Pursuit)	350
3 Squadrons (Art. Service)	500
1 Section, Photographic	150
1 Section Meteorologic	150
1 Aviation Park Co.	104
3 Balloon Cos.	468

. . . .

Table IV.
Army Headquarters and Army Troops.

		Approximate Strength
Headquarters	Commander, Staff and Hq. Details to be subject to future study.	150
Aviation	1 Commander and Staff 5 Squadrons—pursuit 5 Squadrons—Bombardment.	1,600
	24 Balloon Cos. Service with heavy 24 Squadrons Artillery of Army	
	2 Sections, meteorological 3 Sections, photographic	300
	16 Park companies	1,000

. . . .

Maj. Raynal C. Bolling

Maj. Raynal C. Bolling, a New York corporation lawyer who had organized the first aero squadron in the National Guard, was sent to Europe by the War Department in June 1917 with a group of military and civilian engineers and technicians to gather information for the production of airplanes and other aeronautical equipment. His report, like that of the Board of Officers, advocated an air force of fighting and bombing planes over and beyond the aviation that would be assigned to the various elements of the ground forces. In bombardment, Bolling distinguished between operations conducted during the day and those carried out at night, as is indicated in the following extract from his report.[1]

45, Avenue Montaigne, Paris, France.

August 15, 1917.

FROM: Major R. C. Bolling, S.O.R.C.

TO: Chief Signal Officer of the Army, Washington, D.C.

SUBJECT: Report of Aeronautical Commission.

1. The Aeronautical Commission under my charge left New York on the steamship "Adriatic" June 17, 1917, landed at Liverpool June 26, 1917, proceeded to London, remained there about a week, proceeded to France and to Paris, remained there about two weeks, proceeded thence to Italy, remained there about ten days, returned to Paris and remained there about ten days. Thereafter the party was divided according to new instructions and duties. . . .

. . . .

C. American Production Program.

There is general agreement here in the opinion we have formed concerning the governing principle for our American production program. That opinion is as follows:

First:—The United States must provide itself with all airplanes and engines required for training purposes in America.

Second. The United States must next provide the airplanes and engines necessary for use strictly in connection with the operation of American Forces in the Field. . . .

Third. After these first two considerations comes the American program of putting into the field next year air forces in excess of the tactical requirements of its Army in France. It is greatly desired that the United States shall do this. Such air forces should consist of fighting airplanes and bombers. The fighting airplanes are divided into two classes:

(a) Airplanes with fixed engines.

(b) Airplanes with rotary engines.

Both types appear to be essential. We all hold the opinion that the rotary engine is much less reliable and has much less length of service than the stationary engine; but for certain purposes it appears to be indispensable. The bombing airplanes may be divided into day and night bombers.

Day bombing presents much greater difficulties than night bombing because it cannot be conducted successfully by slow

1. In Gorrell's History, I–1, pp 80–88.

machines with great bomb carrying capacity, if the enemy have
in the air any number of fast
fighting machines or have great
numbers of anti-aircraft guns effective at great altitudes. If it
should be possible to drive from
the air practically all the enemy
fighting machines, day-bombing
would become much more effective. Night bombing permits
to [?] use large airplanes without
great speeds but with great
bomb-carrying capacity. There is
practically no effective means of
preventing night-bombing.
Therefore, its possibilities appear
to depend almost entirely on the
number of suitable airplanes
which can be provided. From
the military standpoint these
possibilities are very great and
extremely important. Could
night bombing be conducted on
a sufficiently great scale and kept
up continuously for a sufficient
time, there seems good reason
to believe that it might determine
the whole outcome of military

operations. Up to the present time, the trouble seems to have been that all bombing has been carried on intermittently and sporadically because of the lack of attention to the subject and provision for large enough numbers of the right kind of airplanes. In this connection, it may be well to compare the situation with artillery bombardment. While I speak with some diffidence on such a subject, all I have been able to learn indicates that intermittent and sporadic artillery bombardment produces but small results notwithstanding the great size and accuracy of modern bombardment artillery.

When definite and important results are desired, artillery bombardment must be made systematic and continuous and tremendous quantities of high explosives must be used on the selected objectives. This seems to be exactly the situation which exists with respect to airplane bombardment. There seems every reason to believe that it can be made of vital importance if very great numbers of airplanes carrying great size and numbers of bombs can be provided and used continuously and systematically.

To determine the proportion of airplanes of different types for United States production we have recommended the following rough method of calculation which seems to give results that check up pretty well with the views over here: First deduct from the total number of airplanes it is considered possible to produce the number required for use in direct connection with the military forces. That number can only be determined where it is known what will be the size of the military forces at any given time and that number varies only in proportion to the size of the forces. By this deduction having obtained the number of airplanes within your capacity of production which can be used independently of United States military forces, we recommend that this number be apportioned as follows: About thirty seven and a half percent should be fighting airplanes divided equally between fixed and rotary engine fighters. About twenty five percent should be day bombers and about thirty seven and a half percent should be night bombers. Of course, it is impossible to establish any proportions which are likely to be entirely correct because it is impossible to tell what will be the air conditions at any given portion of the front at any given time. For example, the enemy may have a larger or smaller number of fast fighting machines requiring that we have a larger or smaller number of these machines and permitting our use of a smaller number of day bombing machines.
. . . .

Although the GOP (Doc. 25) included troops for the Service of the Rear (later, Line of Communications, still later, Services of Supply),[1] it did not indicate what kinds of troops would be needed or how they were to be organized. These details were provided in September 1917 by the Service of the Rear Project (SORP). Headquarters AEF used the SORP to add 201 aero squadrons for strategic aviation, which had been omitted from the GOP. This was done to bring AEF planning more into line with production plans made in the United States following the receipt of the Ribot cable (see Doc. 16). With the addition of 201 squadrons to the 59 in the GOP, the total went up to 260: 120 pursuit, 80 observation, and 60 bom-

bardment. Extracts from the SORP, approved by Pershing on 18 September 1917, are printed below.[2]

L.R.E.
S.H.
A.B.B.[3]

Headquarters American Expeditionary Forces, Office of the Chief of Staff, Operations Section
September 6, 1917.

MEMORANDUM FOR
  Chief of Staff
Subject: Services of the Rear and Lines of Communication.

1. The Commander in Chief's letter, dated July 10, 1917, transmitting to the War Department the A.E.F. General Organization Project (G.O.P.) states, in paragraph 3, "Recommendations as to Lines of Communication troops will be submitted later."

. . . .

4. The basis of the projects submitted herewith is identical with that of the G.O.P., i.e., a force of 20 fighting and 10 replacement (base and training) divisions with Corps, Army,

G.H.Q., and L. of C. troops. The total estimated strength of this force, including service of the rear and L. of C. troops, was given in Table 2, G.O.P., as about 1,100,000 men. It is now found that the following modifications in this estimate must be made:

(a) The forward services are to be increased by 55,590 men, of which 6,560 signal troops are to be added to the total strength of the 30 infantry divisions, 1,038 ordnance personnel are to be added to the army troops and 47,992 aviation personnel are to be added to the Army troops. The increase in the divisional signal troops is necessary on account of the adopted signal corps personnel for infantry regiments. The increased ordnance personnel is due to the inadequacy in the G.O.P. estimate. The addition to the aviation personnel consists of strategical units, all of which are not strictly necessary for the American

---

1. These designations apparently are correct although an "s" often was added to "Service" in SOR and to "Line" in LOC and dropped from "Service" in SOS.
2. In Gorrell's history, A 23, also A 12.
3. Col. Le Roy Eltinge, Lt. Col. Stuart Heintzelman, and Lt. Col. Alvin B. Barber.

forces herein considered, but are to be used on the fronts occupied by our Allies as well as on our own. It is necessary, however, to consider them in preparing a project for the service of the rear and in formulating a shipping program. With the

Totals for Aeronautics.

Front—Tactical

	Total Personnel
5 Corps	8,255
Army	15,123
Total Tactical—all recommended by A.E.F. organization Project of July 11, 1917, except 13 Park Cos. of strength of 1352	23,378

Front—Strategical.

41 Observation Squadrons	7,093
105 Pursuit Squadrons	18,165
55 Bombardment Squadrons	10,670
15 Balloon Companies	3,120
73 Park Companies	7,592
Total Personnel	46,640

Rear

Hq. Air Service L. of C.	50
Research, Finance, Purchase, Inspection and Provision of Personnel	295
Training and Replacement	24,066
Repair and Salvage	10,400
Housing of Material and Personnel	2,600
Reserve of Mechanics, etc.	12,272
Supply and Assembly	5,200
3 Port Depots × 104	312
3 Port Balloon Companies × 208	624
	55,819

Recapitulation

Total Strength—Tactical	23,378
Total Strength—Strategical	46,640
Total Strength—Service of Rear	55,819
Grand Total	125,837
Total Service Planes—exclusive of Training and Replacement Planes	4,680
Total Balloons—exclusive of Training and Replacement Balloons	57 in service 87 spare.

above additions the total of divisional, corps, army and G.H.Q. troops, including base and training divisions, amounts to 998,-795 men. This figure includes the noncombatant organizations pertaining to divisions, corps and armies.

. . . .

Kirby Walker
Lt. Col. Cav.,
Acting Chief of Section

Brig. Gen. William L. Kenly, Chief of Air Service, AEF (August–November 1917), inspects gondola.

28. Command in the Zone of Advance
10 October 1917

In August 1917 the activities of the Air Service, AEF were divided between the Zone of Interior, where Col. R. C. Bolling was placed in charge, and the Zone of Advance, where Col. William Mitchell was placed in command. About the same time, Brig. Gen. William L. Kenly was named Chief of Air Service, AEF. Mitchell's authority was outlined in the following order.

Headquarters, A.E.F. France, October 10, 1917.

General Orders No. 46.

. . . .

II. 1. Under the direction of the Chief of Air Service, all Air Service units and personnel serving in the Zone of Advance are placed under the command of the Air Commander, Zone of Advance, who is charged with their proper administration, instruction, discipline and employment.

2. Command of the Air Service, Zone of the Advance, includes:

Tactical Air Units, assigned to armies and corps.

(a) Formation and equipment of units formed in the Zone of the Advance.

(b) Technical supervision and inspection.

(c) Supervision of tactical employment.

(d) Supervision of instruction in the Zone of the Advance.

Strategical Air Units not assigned to armies and corps but attached directly to these headquarters.

(a) Formation and equipment of units formed in the Zone of the Advance.

(b) Tactical employment.

(c) Technical inspection.

(d) Instruction in the Zone of the Advance.

Air Depots and Parks in Zone of the Advance.

(a) Technical supervision and inspection.

Air Schools in Zone of the Advance.

(a) Supervision of instruction.

Liaison With the Air Services of Allied Armies.

This liaison is to be maintained under the direction of the Chief of Air Service by means of liaison officers detailed at the request of the Commander in Chief.

. . . .

By command of General Pershing:

James G. Harbord. Brigadier General, Chief of Staff.

On behalf of the British Government, Gen. Sir D. Henderson,
K.C.B., decorates Col. Edgar S. Gorrell with the "Companion of
the Distinguished Service Order."

When Maj. Edgar S. Gorrell[1] became Chief of the Technical Section, Air Service, AEF, on 15 August 1917, he became responsible for initiating purchases for all kinds of equipment and supplies that the Air Service would need during the following year. Investigating and attempting to anticipate requirements of materiel for bombing operations, he made a study of the bombardment situation and from that formulated a bombardment plan for the Air Service, AEF. That plan, printed below,[2] was to be characterized many years later by Maj. Gen. Laurence S. Kuter of the U.S. Army Air Forces as the "earliest, clearest and least known statement of the American conception of the employment of air power.[3]

Brig. Gen. Benjamin D. Foulois, who became Chief of Air Service, AEF on 27 November, not only approved the plan but made Gorrell, who had been promoted to lieutenant colonel, the head of Strategical Aviation, Zone of Advance, AEF. As events developed, however, Gorrell's bombardment plan could not be carried out. Gorrell explained why in the "Early History of the Strategical Section" which he wrote in January 1919 as part of the "History of the Air Service, AEF."[4] Extracts from the history of the section are presented below as a sequel to the plan.

A. Plan

I. Introduction.

(a) Three and a half years of War finds us in a position in which movement either by land or by sea is rendered vastly difficult and expensive. On the sea the Allies' superiority keeps the Central Power's above-water ships inactive, while on land, where Allied and enemy trench systems face each other from sea to boundary on the western front, movement can only be obtained over short distances by vast concentration of artillery, without which the infantry cannot advance. The speed with which the infantry can advance is determined by the speed of movement of the artillery, and even a minor operation demands a heavy toll of life and material.

If the conduct of the War is to be seriously affected in the near future, a new policy of attacking the enemy must be adopted.

(b) Apparently both the Allies and the Germans have begun at the same time to conceive of the immense importance of aerial bombing, and we find in all countries, both Allied and German, the conception of the immensity of such a problem and the beginning of a preparation for a bombing campaign. Judging from our own knowledge of what the Allied countries are doing and from the report of Allied spies in the German territory, the Allies are far behind the Germans at the present moment in preparation for next year's bombing campaign. We constantly receive reports from our spies and agents in the German territory, indicating an increase in the size of many German factories—to be specific, indicating that about 25 German airplane factories have extended and increased facilities for output and increased number of employees—and our information even goes to show that portions of the Zeppelin Works have been prepared to build bombing airplanes. It is certain that Germany is concentrating on the manufacture of the Gotha airplane, to be

---

1. For biographical data see the Introduction to the first volume in this series.
2. In Gorrell's History, B–6, pp 373–390.
3. Kuter, "Air Power—The American Concept," [c. 1943,] photostat of typewritten copy in AFSHRC 167.6–50.

4. The history of the Strategical Section is in Gorrell's History, B–6, pp 371–401.

Germany's Gotha bomber.

supplemented by pursuit airplanes. The recent activities of the German forces in bomb-dropping, especially by night, have been an indication of her probable use of these bomb-dropping airplanes next year; and the bombs which she is now using have also been an indication of the type of bomb she will attempt to drop upon the Allied forces.

(c) The German Lines are so situated that bomb-dropping is a very easy problem for the German forces, compared with bomb-dropping for the Allied forces; and judging by the character of the airplanes Germany is building for bomb-dropping, together with the realization both

sides have apparently come to—namely that to affect the armies in the fields it is necessary to affect the manufacturing output of the countries—we can readily see that next spring and next summer the Allies will be visited by bomb-dropping airplanes, both by day and by night and will be confronted with the enemy's superiority in the air and with a bomb-dropping campaign against them that will tend to wreck their commercial centers, to say nothing of the moral effect of such bomb-dropping against the inhabitants of the Allied countries.

(d) This scheme which Germany is apparently talking of inflicting upon the Allies is the same as the Allies have recently been talking of inflicting upon Germany; but the difference be-

tween the two is simply that the German words are being rapidly turned to deeds, while the words of the Allies lack deeds to back them. Therefore, it becomes of paramount importance that we adopt at once a bombing project to be immediately put into force and carried out with all vigor at the quickest possible moment, in order that we may not only wreck Germany's manufacturing centers but wreck them more completely than she will wreck ours next year.

(e) German shells are being fired at Allied troops and positions over a large area of the Front; but the manufacture of these shells is dependent upon the output of a few specific, well-known factories turning out the chemicals for them, so we can readily see that if the chemical factories can be blown up, the shell output will cease, to a greater or lesser degree dependent upon the damage done these chemical plants. The same is true of airplane output; the large Mercedes engine plants and the Bosch magneto factories are located in the same city, and if bombing airplanes raid this city of Stuttgart and can inflict damage on one or both of these plants, the output of German airplanes will cease in proportion to the damage done.

(f) Many of these points could be gone into at length, but it is not necessary here for the advantages of bombing manufacturing centers is recognized without debate.

II. Division of bomb-dropping.

(a) Aerial bomb-dropping is divided essentially into two classes, tactical and strategical.

(b) Tactical bomb-dropping is becoming better known every day as the War goes on; and the results obtained by the Handley-Page squadrons in the vicinity of Dunkerque, as well as the bombardment against Dunkerque by the Germans, have more than indicated that wonderful results could be accomplished along tactical lines, should aerial bomb-dropping be really carried out in a manner which some of its ardent advocates have urged for a long time. The necessity for tactical bomb-dropping is evident and will come about as

such a matter of course that it is not treated in this paper since the idea of this paper is solely that of strategical bombing against commercial centers and lines of communications, with a view to causing the cessation of supplies to the German Front.

(c) By strategical bomb-dropping is meant, in the larger sense of the word, bomb-dropping against the commercial centers of Germany. An army may be compared to a drill. The point of the drill must be strong and must stand up and bear the brunt of the much hard work with which it comes into contact; but unless the shank of the drill is strong and continually reinforcing the point, the drill will break. So with the nation in a war of these days, the army is like the point of the drill and must bear the brunt of constant conflict with foreign obstacles; but unless the nation—which represents the shank of the drill—constantly stands behind and supplies the necessary aid to the point, the drill will break and the nation will fall. The object of strategical bombing is to drop aerial bombs upon the commercial centers and the lines of communications in such quantities as will wreck the points aimed at and cut off the necessary supplies without which the armies in the field cannot exist.

(d) When we come to analyze the targets, we find that there are a few certain indispensable targets without which Germany cannot carry on the war.

III. German targets to be attacked.

(a) The first question to consider in an air offensive against German industrial towns is the question of objectives, and these can be divided into four main groups, following the general division made by English experts on this same subject.

(b) The first, or Northerly group, comprises such towns as Dusseldorf, Crefeld, Elberfeld, Essen, and other German towns grouped in their vicinity. For short this may be called the *Dusseldorf group.*

(c) The second group is a collection of objectives, the center of which may be taken as Cologne. This we will call the *Cologne group.*

(d) The third and most important group comprises Mannheim and Ludwigshafen and also the manufacturing industries in the vicinity of Frankfurt, such as the Meister-Luciuc Works at Hoechst, and the Casella Works on the far side of Frankfurt. This we will call the *Mannheim group.*

(e) With the forces which the Allies will have available during the spring and summer of 1918, it is not wise to operate further south along the Rhine than the Mannheim group, except to make feints and infrequent raids against Karlsruhe and Rastadt.

(f) A fourth group of targets enter as a part of a logical scheme for destroying German

British Handley-Page bomber

ammunition works and these have special value for the reason that on days, such as often occur, when weather conditions prevent the airplanes from reaching targets in the Rhine Valley, bomb-dropping raids can nevertheless be made against targets in this fourth group. We will call this fourth group the *Saar Valley group*, which comprises the numerous steel works of this Valley.

IV. Base of operation

(a) Having chosen, as generally outlined above, the German objectives it becomes necessary to consider from what bases they are to be attacked. Two large bases have been used in the past; one from the Ostende region, the other from the region in the vicinity of Toul. These two may be compared as follows:

(b) If the Ostende region is to be taken as a base or center of our operations, the following disadvantages will have to be considered. These disadvantages are inherent in the terrain and cannot be removed. Although it is true that the first two groups— namely the Dusseldorf and the Cologne groups—may be attacked from the Ostende base nearly as easily as from the Toul base, yet the other groups will be entirely out of the question. Furthermore, the Germans will be entirely aware of these facts and therefore, for the purpose of defense, they will know the limitations of the chosen objectives of each and every one of the raids that we may attempt to

make; whereas in operating from the Verdun-Toul base, the Germans will never know for what particular objective the raid is intended and hence must be proportionately extravagent of airplanes for defensive purposes. Furthermore, such concentration of airplanes as Germany effects for defensive purposes against our strategical bomb-dropping raids, means the subtraction of this number from her airplanes in tactical use over our Front. The following figures roughly show the distances involved and the advantages of choosing a base:

(c) There is another disadvantage against the Ostende base, and that is the disadvantage inherent in weather conditions. Past records show that there are only a certain number of days, very far apart, on which it is possible to raid at the distances which are involved in reaching

the first three groups of targets mentioned: British estimates show that these good days do not number more than four or five per month and that only during the summer months. There will, however, be a large percentage of days when short raids can very easily be made. From the Ostende base there are practically no targets against which short raids can be made to injure Germany's manufacturing centers; while from the Verdun-Toul base, the Saar Valley with its enormous steel works offers exactly the type of target which the Allies urgently desire to destroy; and therefore on days when raiding at long distances on Germany's Rhine Valley targets is impossible, short raids against the Saar Valley are feasible and sometimes several raids per day can easily be made.

		Distance	Go and Return	Extra mileage in excess of shortest mileage
From **Ostende District**	Dusseldorf straight	186	372	:32
	Dusseldorf by Maastritt	206	412	:72
	Cologne straight	185	370	:70
	Cologne by Maastritt	192	384	:84
	Mannheim	280	560	:360
From **Souilly**	Dusseldorf straight	170	340	
	Cologne	150	300	
	Mannheim	150	300	:40
	Frankfort	170	340	:20
From **Toul**	Dusseldorf	190	380	:40
	Cologne	170	340	:40
	Mannheim	130	260	
	Frankfort	160	320	

(d) It has sometimes been advocated that raiding might be done across the northern border of Belgium, in order to permit pilots who fail because of engine failure to land in Holland. But such an agrument is a myth rather than a reality. If the Allies are constantly performing raids from the Ostende base across Holland, we might find ourselves in a rather awkward diplomatic situation, and therefore any scheme to deliberately violate the neutrality of Holland is untenable. If neutrality laws be not violated, raiding from the Ostende base against German targets becomes extremely difficult because of the increased length of flight necessary.

(e) Apparently there is only one base from which operations should first be begun, and that is the base which we may call, for the purpose of reference, the *Verdun-Toul base.* It is suggested that we begin operations against the German targets with our airplanes operating from this Verdun-Toul base, and, as the number of airplanes in commission increases, that we spread out from this base as a center on either side, as conditions may indicate best, until, as a climax, airplanes may be used from all portions of the Allied lines to concentrate against the German targets which it is hoped to destroy:—the Rhine Valley targets being the targets for clear day operations and those at hand

being attacked on days when it is impossible to reach the Rhine Valley.

(f) In this base known as the Verdun-Toul base, there are really two bases: one roughly on a quadrilateral bounded by Pont St. Vincent, Toul, Void, and Vezelise. This for short we will call the *Toul group*; and its railheads will be Pont St. Vincent and Toul, with main depot and park at Toul. The second group will be in the district whose center is Souilly, and the rail-head, park and depot will have to be chosen in accordance with details to be taken up later on.

(g) The first concentration of airplanes is suggested for the Toul base, and those to be used next for the Souilly base. As the number airplanes increases, they can be divided proportionately between these two bases until such time as we have a sufficient number to extend in either direction from these bases and to use airdromes along other portions of the line. In the location of airdromes it is to be kept in mind that any German concentration against our airdromes would deplete our aerial forces, and, therefore, our aerial squadrons must be scattered about the country in the most advantageous manner to prevent their depletion by bomb-dropping

raids on the part of the Germans. Furthermore, the existence of numerous airdromes about the bases hereinbefore indicated will increase the difficulties of German intelligence and, therefore, will render less difficult the protection of our airdromes from German aerial raiding.

V. Choice of systems or raiding.

(a) There are two large systems of aerial bomb-dropping. One is what is known as daylight bombing; the other is night-time bombardment. There are many arguments both in favor of and against each kind of bomb-dropping, but it goes without saying that our efforts should be directed against the German objectives both by day and by night, giving the Germans no rest from our aerial activities and no time to repair the damage inflicted. In this project it is proposed to commence this bomb-dropping with day-light bombardment solely because of the question of availability, since deliveries on our daylight bombardment airplanes will take place prior to deliveries on our large night bomb-dropping airplanes of Caproni and Handley-Page types. This will lend itself readily to our final project of both day and night bombardment, since our pilots will be receiving training in aerial navigation over Germany during the day, while we are waiting for the arrival of our night-time airplanes.

VI. Difficulties to be encountered which necessitate immediate preparation.

(a) There will be considerable difficulty in instructing the pilots in the art of navigation when going very long distances, and course of instruction must be immediately established in the flying schools for obviating this difficulty.

(b) The ordinary map of Germany in existence is not sufficient to permit green pilots to find their way across Germany and home again in safety, and therefore the preparation of a special map of Germany must be begun at once, following the indications which the Army Air Service is prepared to submit to the Topographical Section of the Intelligence Division of the Army. This special map was that contemplated in a letter to the Chief, Intelligence Division, A. E. F., dated November 12, 1917, subject "Aviation Maps for the American Army", signed by Brigadier-General Kenly, requesting the preparation of such a map.

(c) Weather conditions along the Rhine Valley permit of raiding only during special times of year—these being mainly in the late spring, the summer, and the early autumn—and therefore if bomb-dropping against German commercial centers is to be fea-

sible during the year 1918, preparations must be begun at once in order that we may be ready in time to take advantage of the weather.

(d) As indicated above, our advices show that Germany is already preparing a large bomb-dropping against the Allies. The existing program of Allied production of airplanes is on too small a scale to manufacture a sufficiently large number in time for 1918, and therefore a decision should be made immediately to undertake this bomb-dropping campaign in order that the necessary impetus may be given to the production of airplanes to permit their receipt in time for such a campaign.

(e) Assuming that each effective machine in commission performs four raids per week—which, considering the short distance from our chosen bases to the Saar Valley targets, is not too optimistic—the total output of bombs heretofore contemplated for next year on a basis of past aviation, when bomb-dropping was not seriously considered, must be increased to meet the demands of next year. This increase can be easily effected if a decision is made, and made now, to consider such a bomb-dropping campaign. Hence the necessity of an immediate decision for strategical bomb-dropping next year, in order that bombs may be ready when weather conditions permit the commencement of such a campaign.

(f) Considering the 50-pound bomb as a standard for calculation purposes, we find that two bombs will pack into a case about 2'6" × 1'3" × 2'9"; or, about 120 cases of bombs may be placed on a railroad truck. In the quantities contemplated, the bombs will have to be dumped into ammunition dumps in the open and provision should be made as soon as possible to provide underground bomb dumps in order that we may not have the regrettable experience of seeing our bomb dumps blown up as recently was the case at Dunkerque, where the Germans instead of attacking airdromes attacked the bomb dumps and rendered the bombing airplanes useless because of having destroyed their bombs. Furthermore, in this question of bombs, the technical sections of the Allies must design water-tight plugs, so that such bombs as are kept in the open or in underground dumps may be protected from weather conditions, thus necessitating keeping only the fuses and detonators in covered water-proof magazines. When handling such a large output of bombs as will be necessary for next year, we must consider that the following operations will be necessary: detonators and fuses must be put into the bomb, the fins must be screwed on, the bombs must be transported to the airplanes, and must then be loaded upon the airplanes. Working with such large quantities it is clearly necessary to commence immediately to train special armament personnel in the loading and handling of bombs. This is not a difficult question, but needs to be undertaken at the earliest moment. Another point in the bomb question is the transportation of the bombs by rail from the seaboard to the point desired, and, when we consider that only about 240 bombs can be transported on an ordinary, average, flat-car we see that the transportation of sufficient bombs for a strategical campaign in earnest against the German targets becomes a large problem and one which the railroad authorities must take immediate steps to meet. This problem is not insurmountable nor difficult if steps are taken now and without delay.

(g) The next question of difficulty is that of sheltering the airplanes. During certain parts of the year, with luck, our airplanes should last roughly three months when kept in the open; but during the other portions of the year, as, for example, the rainy season, experience in Mexico shows that airplanes last only about two weeks; while French advices received about two weeks ago show that airplanes kept in the Toul region in the open, in the fall, or in other bad seasons, last only about 8 days. It becomes at once apparent,

therefore, that every attempt must be made to shelter the airplanes; otherwise the replacement of airplanes due to lack of shelter becomes an enormous problem. For this purpose the United States is making provision to ship hangars to Europe with the various squadrons. Assuming the hangars arrived at the seaboard, the question of transporting them to the bases in the vicinity of Toul (or to wherever else the airplanes may be when they are at the Front) in sufficient numbers becomes rather difficult. Two thousand daylight bombarding airplanes of the DH 4 type would require about 500 Bessonneau hangars. Since about 10 railroad trucks are required to transport four Bessonneau hangars, we see at once that for even as small a number of airplanes as 2,000 we should require 1,250 railroad freight cars to transport these hangars. America is planning to adopt individual tent hangars, but the problem of transportation remains roughly the same as in the consideration of the Bessonneau hangars.

(h) Since the bases are chosen in the vicinity of Toul and are in the country where it becomes rather cold in the winter time, it will be necessary to provide shelter for the personnel. This amount of shelter will depend upon the size of the force involved. Due to the population of the country we cannot safely count upon billeting more than approximately one-third of our aviation personnel, and there-

fore the remaining two-thirds must be provided for, say, perhaps in standard French barracks which, under conditions prescribed by regulations, will accomodate 90 men per barrack. The question of figuring the housing necessary becomes one of mathematics, as the force increases in size, but it is necessary to commence now, owing to the scarcity of material for building purposes, in order to obtain sufficient barracks or sufficient housing facilities by the time that the airplanes are ready for the bomb-dropping campaign next year.

(i) Having chosen our first bases from which the airplanes will commence operation, it is necessary to choose landing fields, after the Italian system of one about every ten miles, from the point of assembly of American airplanes to our probable positions at the Front; to indicate on each landing field the portions where airplanes may land without smashing; and to erect wind-vanes to indicate the direction of the wind. These will be easy to keep up after they have once been established; but the labor of locating these fields and marking them should be undertaken immediately, since it is one of the small points which is essential for success next year.

(j) There are very few places in the vicinity of the entire Verdun-Toul bases where one can land, and therefore details should be out at the present moment choosing these landing places and marking them so that they may be used either as airdromes or as landing places for machines in distress.

(k) The weather in the Rhine Valley does not by any means follow the weather on the French side of the Vosges mountains, and experience has shown that it is not satisfactory to rely upon existing weather reports as they are today predicted. Meteorological officers should, therefore, be sent out at once to study weather conditions in the Rhine Valley between now and next spring and summer, and reports should be received from our agents in Germany to assist in the calculations of probable weather conditions.

(1) Our Intelligence Section of the Army Air Service will have considerable work to do in the preparation of the necessary data for such a strategical bombing campaign as herein contemplated, in order that fully up-to-date information may be had on all targets and in order that proper maps may be prepared and proper instructions given to the various commanding officers and even to the individual pilots and observers.

(m) Any system of raiding such as contemplated herein means carefully prepared and timed plans, and in order that they may be carried out without defects, telephonic communications must be established between the various headquarters

of groups and squadrons. This is a matter which must be done as soon as the airdromes are chosen, and work should be commenced thereon immediately.

(n) The question of rail-heads and transports must be considered, since it will be necessary to install at various points railroad sidings; and, in the case of large night bombarding airplanes, it may be found necessary to run special narrow-gauge railroad tracks into the airdromes themselves. The difficulty of transporting spares of large night bombarding airplanes like the Handley-Page must be overcome at once by choosing the routes which permit of transportation of the spares, since on account of the large chord of the wings of these airplanes it is not possible to transport them over every road in France, because they will not pass under all bridges. This means that special routes for transportation must be chosen.

(o) The question of transportation between the various groups becomes difficult, since in some places the ground is marshy and chalky and since under certain conditions the Germans may command some of the roads by shelling if they desire; and it will, therefore, be necessary to choose specific roads for the use of the transport interconnecting bomb-dropping

routes, in order to supplement such transportation as takes place by railroad and the limited amount which can take place by air.

(p) The question of the actual choice of position of each individual airdrome is one which must be considered immediately; and it should be remembered that these should not be chosen too close to the German lines, as has actually been the case today with certain of the airdromes in that vicinity. A proper location of our airdromes will facilitate their defense against enemy raids.

(q) Since bomb-dropping over a distance of 150 to 200 miles necessitates a special knowledge on the part of pilots and observers far beyond any instruction now being given in any of the Allied schools, navigation becomes not the only problem, since a very large problem is that of teaching the pilots to know the country over which they are to fly. This means months of training in these particular maps of Germany, and pilots trained simply in the art of map-reading as it is taught today can never hope to accomplish their missions and return to their own lines in safety. French relief maps along existing lines should be made up of German terrain, and their formation together with the natural features of the terrain should be indelibly impressed on the minds of pilots and observers during their scholastic training.

Our own experience in the United States and in Mexico, and Allied experience in Europe, has shown that it is very easy for one or more machines or squadrons to start out to reach a certain point and to return to their base, each believing that he has reached the proper point, when probably all, or nearly all, have reached unconnected points and not the target for which they originally started to fly. Therefore, a knowledge of Germany must be taught to the pilots and observers in their instruction period, and provision must be made at the Front to keep up this instruction.

(r) From both the morale point of view and also that of material damage, concentration of our aerial forces against single targets on the same day is of vital importance since it tends to hamper the defense and also to complete in a thorough manner the work which the bombardment is intended to perform. Therefore, it is suggested that often all available airdromes should concentrate upon a single objective in a single day. For example, suppose 100 squadrons are available and that it is desired to attack Mannheim and the Ludwigshafen Works. Assuming a time-table of three minutes between squadrons, this means a bombardment of about five continuous hours. If immediately afterwards, on the next possible day, Frankfurt were at-

tacked in a similar way, judging from the press reports of what has already occurred in Germany, it is quite possible that Cologne would create such trouble that the German Government might be forced to suggest terms if that town were so attacked. Furthermore, after such a bombardment, the manufacturing works would be wrecked and the morale of the workmen would be shattered. It is also to be remembered that in chemical works of this nature a fire once started will spread and that with such a bombardment going on throughout such a length of time the organization of the fire brigade and fire protection, in the already undermanned German villages, would be broken down and therefore the results would be out of proportion to the immediate effects of the bombs. Germany has shown by her attempts to wreck havoc with the morale of the Allied nations, in such cases as the bombardment of London, that her own human nature lends itself to having havoc wrecked with it in a similar manner, and the press reports taken from German papers indicate that this conclusion is correct.

(s) It cannot be pointed out that the scheme suggested herein is possible now; but it will

be possible in the future only by taking the matter in hand immediately and working at extreme pressure from now on till operations are able to commence next year. Therefore, it becomes immediately essential to decide in favor of such an operation for next year and to take the necessary steps to organize and to put into operation such a campaign as that proposed herein. Neither can it be said that an operation such as this is impossible. All of us well remember the huge cry of "Impossible!" that went up when it was proposed to concentrate enormous artillery attacks on the German lines such, for example, as the British have concentrated during the months of August and September against the German Front. Every one of us can now see that what looked impossible in the past has become a reality accomplished with ease in the present. So, with this bomb-dropping campaign, while the difficulties look large at present they will become feasible realities if we only start immediately to prepare.

VII. Future Operations.

(a) After starting the campaign as indicated herein, the difficulties connected with the commencement become negligible; but those connected with transportation and supply of both personnel and material become larger as the campaign increases in size, and it will therefore be necessary for railroad and materiel facilities to increase proportionately with the increase in size of the campaign, until we work up to a climax where our airplanes are dropping bombs on targets in the same proportion as when the artillery shells a target. Statistics will show very easily that, given a fixed amount of explosives to destroy a target, aerial bomb-dropping will reach and destroy this target with less explosive, fewer shells, and less expenditure of money than is required for the artillery and infantry to destroy a target of similar importance to the final issue of the campaign. For practically three years the artillery has constantly shelled German positions and the infantry has sacrificed an enormous number of human lives, only to gain an insignificant number of miles along the Front. With a similar expenditure in aerial bomb-dropping of money, material, and human beings, the transportation in the rear of the German lines and the supplies of all sorts of material to the German troops could long ago have been cut off.

VIII. Cooperation of the Allies.

(a) The targets chosen in this program to be attacked, and the bases from which it is expected to deliver our attacks, are the same as those contemplated by the British in their proposal to wreck the manufacturing centers of Germany and by the French in such programs as they are proposing. The British are seri-

ously considering such a bomb-dropping campaign, but have not started in earnest on the necessary preparation for such a campaign. The French production program for both airplanes and bombs, as well as for personnel, does not lend itself to an attack on the large scale proposed, during 1918, on the manufacturing centers of Germany. The money appropriated by the American Congress was appropriated with the idea in view of dropping the maximum tonnage of bombs on German manufacturing centers and means of transportation, and the American public as well as American industries and financial purse-string lend themselves to this idea and have so lent themselves since the beginning of the War. We find America today building an aerial program with the sole idea of such a campaign against Germany as that outlined herein, and therefore American backing of this program is certain. British participation in this campaign is also certain. French willingness to participate in such a campaign is certain, although her materiel, especially, and her personnel, to a minor degree, do not lend themselves to such a large scale operation as either the Americans or the British are prepared to undertake. Therefore, since all three nations will be desirous of participating in such a campaign as this and to participate against the same targets and from, roughly, the same bases, it is suggested that there be coordination of the efforts of

all the Allied land armies. Therefore, in view of the concentration mentioned herein, as well as other vital considerations, it is suggested as the proper part of America, especially in view of her aerial production, to take the initiative in bringing about such a coordination.

IX. Necessity for immediate action.

(a) Since a bomb-dropping campaign does not mean the mere supplying of airplanes and bombs, and since many other features, as hereinbefore indicated, enter into a project such as that contemplated herein, it is suggested that unless a decision is made to commence this campaign and to commence it immediately, we cannot hope to operate during 1918. Therefore, it is requested that approval of this project be given immediately and that the necessary authority to carry it out be granted in order that it may be started without loss of time and in order that it may be under way in the spring or summer of 1918. If it is not begun at that time, it must go over until 1919. It is not too late yet to commence this campaign; but the time when its commencement is possible with success is drawing to a close, hence the urgency of immediate approval of this scheme.

B. Sequel

After adopting the program for operations it next became necessary to decide upon the staff for Officer in Charge of Strategical Aviation, Z. of A., A.E.F. It was decided that the staff should be comprised of the following officers:

(a) Executive Officer.
(b) Adjutant
(c) Intelligence Officer.
(d) Meteorological Officer.
(e) Armament Officer.
(f) Engineering Officer.
(g) Supply Officer.
(h) Photographic Officer.
(i) Telephone Officer.
(j) Wireless Officer.
(k) Medical Officer.
(l) Transportation Officer.
(m) Officer In Charge of Pursuit and Observation Forces.
(n) Interpreter.

Steps were taken to obtain a few of these officers to start the work of this force.

On December 22, 1917, a conference was held at French G.H.Q., at Compiegne, wherein the following representatives participated,—

British:—Major General Sir Hugh Trenchard, General Officer Commanding the Royal Flying Corps, in the Field.

French:—General Duvall,[5] Commanding the French Air Service, in the Field.

United States:—Lieutenant-Colonel E. S. Gorrell, Officer in Charge of Strategical Aviation, Z of A., A.E.F.

5. Maurice Duvall.

At this meeting General Trenchard told that he had been ordered by his Government to establish a force of bombardment aviation in the vicinity of Nancy for the purpose of bombarding the industrial centers of Germany, that whether or not the Allies intended to join with him in this work did not affect whether or not he continued such work, and that he intended to increase the size of his force and to push this work to its maximum extent in compliance with the orders of his Government on this subject. The French said that, in their opinion, it did not pay to heterogeneously bombard enemy industrial centers and that the Allies must remember bombardment of Allied towns by the enemy was a much easier task than bombardment of enemy towns by the Allies, and therefore not only from the point of view of the fact that the materiel was unavailable for this purpose but also from the point of view of the fact that the use of bombardment aviation as contemplated by the British did not agree with French tactical plans and that the French did not expect to join in this operation. The American representative stated that it was the intention of the United States to also undertake this work along the lines now being commenced by the British but that he could not pledge the United States or the A.E.F. to such a procedure for the reason that decision on that subject lay with G.H.Q., A.E.F.

During the Christmas Holidays, 1917, the Chief of Air Service, accompanied by Lieut-Colonel Gorrell visited Headquarters of the Royal Flying Corps in the Field, for the purpose of discussing this question with General Trenchard, the General Officer Commanding the R.F.C., in the Field. At this meeting General Trenchard proposed that, since he had already begun to operate from the Nancy District, and since the Americans had yet to make their first beginning in this work, that the Americans profit by such experience as he may have gained and such installation as he may have established and place their first few squadrons with his forces in order to train the Americans and to allow them to profit by what experience the British may have already obtained. If the Americans had one squadron it would be General Trenchard's intention to place this squadron in an airdrome with several other British squadrons, the combination of squadrons being commanded by a British officer. When the Americans had several squadrons they would occupy an airdrome by themselves, being commanded by an American officer, to report to the British Commander in that District. When the Americans placed a larger force in the field than the British had there, General Trenchard proposed to turn over the command in that district, at such time as Americans should thus begin to secure predominance in the combinations, to the Americans and to allow the British to serve under an American Commander in that region. These propositions, because they offered both training and maintenance facilities to the American Air Service, both of which were lacking and both of which promised to be difficult to be obtained, were accepted by the Chief of Air Service. However, it may here be said, that shortly after this conference General Trenchard was recalled to England and General Salmond[6] took his place in the field.

Later, approximately the summer of 1918, the British Bombardment Forces in the vicinity of Nancy were separated from the Royal Air Force in the Field and placed under the command of General Trenchard, who would honor the orders of no one except the British Air Ministry. General Trenchard received no orders and would acknowledge no superior in the Field, not even Marshal Foch, who we supposed to command the Allied forces on the Western Front. This turn of affairs necessitated a change in the American attitude towards the problems then confronting them. The Americans had recognized and loyally supported Marshal Foch as the Allied Commander-in-Chief and therefore could not assist the

British Independent Air Force in its efforts. It was therefore decided on June 18, 1918, by the Chief of Staff, A.E.F., that while cooperating in every possible way with air forces of our Allies, the Air Bombardment Force must remain an actual integral part of the American Expeditionary Forces. The Chief of Staff on this same date uttered the fundamental principles of the Bombardment Force when he said every one must be impressed with the importance of the principle of the concentration of the effort of each arm, and of all coordination and all effort to a common tactical end. He then said that all must be warned against any idea of independence and all must know from the beginning that every force must be closely coalescent with those of the remainder of the Air Service and with those of the Ground Army. He further stated that in making of arrangements with the British it must be thoroughly understood that, when the aerial forces reached a certain importance, the regions to be bombed would be designated by G.H.Q., A.E.F. and that the selection of the targets would depend solely upon their importance with respect to the operation which the A.E.F. contemplated for its Ground Army.[7]

The Office of the Strategical Aviation, Z. of A., A.E.F. was being utilized for duties other than those belonging purely to

this office and it was proposed to also place him as Assistant to the Supply Officer of the Air Service. With this in mind, this officer wrote the following memorandum for the Chief of Air Service, which is quoted herein solely for the purpose of setting forth some of the problems which presented themselves as of January 1, 1918.

American Expeditionary Forces
Paris, January 2, 1918.
Memorandum for
Chief of Air Service.

1. It is of the maximum importance possible at the present time that the officer detailed for charge of bombing should take up the reins if he is to bring an efficient, well-trained team to the front at the speed at which deliveries are to take place. Not only that this officer take up his own duties forthwith, but he must collect his technical staff around him without delay, and fight the thousand and one duties in the all-too-short time at his disposal.

2. The fact that the United States is only now entering into the contest makes it almost impossible to obtain the number of specialist officers required, and the men chosen for these duties must be allocated to the best centers for their own instruction.

---

6. John Maitland Salmond.
7. See Doc. 38.

The British and French after three and a half years of experience have decided on the personnel, spares and materiel required for their units, and the closest liaison is necessary for the officer commanding American bombing to reap the full advantage of their experience. It is probable that the original American bombing units will work under British command, and it is necessary to study the British organization with a view to blending in with it efficiently. The O.C.'s decision is required, after consultation with the British, as to the most important position from which to operate with a view to the preparation of various sites, and to determine the methods of supply of those sites. He must inspect the bombing units in order to become himself *au fait* with work in the field and to obtain a close understanding of the operations undertaken. He should inspect the English training schools for bombing, choose the commanding officers for the orignal units, and see that they are competent, efficient and well-trained and organize many other details.

3. Accurate bombing on a large scale is a new science and requires the entire time and study of the man who is to shoulder the responsibility for success or failure during the coming year.

4. The following points must be immediately considered and decided upon, and time will be required to do this in accordance with the estimate set forth hereinafter.

	Time
Decision should be made with regard to having the same organization of units as the British have, and the necessary study is required to harmonize our organization and the British since not even the British have yet decided on a part of their organization.	2 weeks
Obtain staff and send them to learn their duties, since strategical aviation is the most unknown part of aeronautics.	4 days to pick staff 3 to 4 months instruction for them.
Obtain office rooms and clerks.	2 days
Establish well-informed intelligence.	at least 4 months.
Lay down detailed program to be followed in 1918 and prepare this to exchange with British and French in accordance with agreement Dec. 22.	2 weeks
Work out monthly tonnage for railroads and give them estimate of requirements. Indicate where railheads and railroad installations are necessary.	2 weeks.
Obtain accurate list of deliveries from every source. See if sufficient supplies of every kind have been ordered for strategical aviation. Place requisitions for what has not yet been ordered.	1 week.
Decide on commanders of first units; dispatch them for training.	3 days pick commanders, 2 to 3 months for training.
Obtain necessary specialists from England as a loan for two months during winter inaction. Consult with and learn from them principles taught by their experience.	at least 2 weeks.
Choose aerodromes for squadrons that will be ready by end of June. Choose parks and depots. Get these approved and preparation under way, even if only with a very few workmen.	2 weeks search; 2 weeks survey; 2 to 3 weeks for approval. Time for work depends upon number of men used.
Choose dummy aerodromes.	2 weeks choice; 2 weeks connected with their preparation.
Choose concentration aerodromes.	2 weeks.
Choose hopping-off aerodromes.	2 weeks.
Give to Instruction Department our requirements of pilots and observers showing number and date. Follow progress.	1 day, plus variable time following progress.
Give to Personnel Department and Instruction Department list showing different trades which will be required in organization.	3 days.
Have prepared satisfactory map of Germany, since none exists now.	2 weeks work. 2½ months supervision.
Obtain schedule of bombing training school in England and follow progress made in that school.	1 week.
Visit English and American bombing schools.	3 weeks.
Inspect bombing units in the field now and learn the work myself.	at least 1 month.
Inspect aerodromes allocated for bombing work.	2 weeks.
Obtain schedule of navigation training in England; get mariners into U.S. schools; work with Training Department towards perfection of course.	1 week.

Consultation re organization meterological service as it affects bombing at long range.	3 days.
Obtain information on progress of wireless telegraph for navigation; initiate improvements.	3 days.
Check petrol arrangements.	3 days.
Personnel force keep track all our men working on Strategical Aviation on British Force.	Continuous after March.
Contact with Allies learning from them, keeping up with them, and coordinating our plans with them.	1 month.
Laying out equipment depots, parks, etc.	1 month.

5. The above schedule shows that some 14 months would be necessary in order to be prepared to carry on this work if one person were to attempt to do it himself. With an efficient staff things can be divided into classes and separated, and the work can be started by June, but not before. The person who is to be responsibile for the success or failure must be on hand at all times to handle the staff and make the necessary decisions.

6. This is the class of work which we have promised our Congress, our Country and our Allies that we would do, and it is of utmost importance that we are prepared to carry out wholeheartedly, efficiently and without delay.

*Respectfully submitted,
(signed) E.S. Gorrell
Lt-Colonel, A.S.S.C.*

An effort was made to set upon an American organization for the Bombardment units of the Strategical Aviation of the A.E.F., similar to the organization adopted by the British because of the fact that the British had had experience in this capacity while the Americans had had no such experience, because the British were already engaged upon this work, and because it was essential that the organizations be similar in order to allow the commanding officer and any Allied officers engaged upon the work to realize the extent of the striking force under his command.

Thus at this date, December, 1917, American plans based their organization upon the "Group" to be the smallest self-contained bombardment tactical unit. The Americans had no expectation of bombing by squadrons but to bombard by groups and perhaps by various combinations of groups whenever the target to be attacked should be worthy of it.

Just after the middle of January, 1918, the Chief of Air Service was ordered by G.H.Q. to detail an Air Service officer for duty in the Operations Section (G—3), on the General Staff. Lieut-Colonel Gorrell was relieved from duty as Officer in Charge of Strategical Aviation, Z of A., A.E.F. and by Par 7, S.O. 21, H.A.E.F., dated January, 21,

1918, was detailed to report to the Chief of Staff, A.E.F., on February 5, 1918, for this duty.

During the first part of February 1918, the office of the Chief of Air Service was moved from G.H.Q. to Tours and Colonel R. O. Van Horn, Air Service, who had been detailed by the Chief of Air Service as Operations Officer in the Air Service (which designation of Air Service was later ordered, by the Chief of Staff, A.E.F., to be discontinued, for the reason that no such office existed within the Air Service) moved to Colombey-les-Belles with his office force. The Chief of Air Service appointed Colonel A. Monell,[8] Air Service, in the Office of Colonel Van Horn and to command the Strategical Aviation, Z. of A., A.E.F. Colonel Monell was assisted by Major Fowler,[9] Air Service, and Wing Commander Spencer Grey,[10] R.N.A.S. The work previously started was carried on by Colonel Monell for a month or so. In the meantime Major Fowler was relieved from duty with this work and sent to command the American Air Forces with the B.E.F. in the Field. Wing Commander Spencer Grey, R.N.A.S., be-

8. Ambrose Monell, who had resigned the presidency of the International Nickel Company to accept a commission in the U.S. Army.

9. Harold Fowler, who had served with the Royal Flying Corps and had transferred to the U.S. Air Service in 1917.

10. While in charge of the Strategical Section, Gorrell had arranged for Grey to serve on his staff. Grey, he said, "was considered at that time as the world's greatest authority on questions dealing with aerial bombardment." (Early History of the Strategical Section, in Gorrell's History, B–6, p 372).

coming discouraged over the failures of the American Production Program and realizing in detail what would be necessary before America could begin a Strategical Bombardment campaign of any size, left the American Air Service and returned to the Air Service of his own Government. Later on Wing Commander Grey was attached to the Air Service of the U.S. Naval Forces, operating in Europe for the purpose of bombarding enemy submarine bases.

Colonel Monell after having selected an airdrome at Latrecey, several bombardment airdromes on the Toul Sector, and an airdrome near St. Blin, and having seen that construction work was begun on each of these, realized that the larger problems that faced the strategical aviation operations of the Air Service were industrial. He also realized that the pursuit operation of strategical aviation would not and could not become a reality for several years, due to the failure of the Allies to deliver pursuit planes to the American Air Service in accordance with their promises made in the Fall of 1917, and due to the fact that no pursuit machines, because of such promises, were being constructed in the United States.

Therefore, there remained only one possible future for the Strategical Aviation—that was aerial bombardment. The D.H. airplane was being handled satisfactorily at Romorantin[11] insofar as its assembly was concerned. However the assembly of the Handley-Page airplane presented a more difficult situation and thereafter Colonel Monell concentrated his attention upon the question of the night bombardment program.

The use of the words "Strategical Aviation" had led many persons, in and out of the Air Service, to believe that this operation of the Air Service was something independent from the rest of the Air Service and not dependent at all upon the rest of the Army. In order to eliminate such an idea and to cause a realization of the fact that the Strategical Air Service was employed as an integral part of the Air Service, A.E.F. and therefore of the entire A.E.F. and in order to force a realization of the fact that American Bombardment Aviation should and would be used as a combat arm upon missions synchronizing with and coordinated with the missions of the entire A.E.F., the name Strategical Aviation was changed in the Summer of 1918 to "G.H.Q. Air Service Reserve." This change had the desired effect and brought home the realization of the fact that this bom-

bardment aviation was a combat portion of the Army designed for use upon missions coordinated with the entire use of the A.E.F. in Europe.

Plans were made in G-3, G.H.Q., A.E.F. for the future use of the Bombardment Aviation when it should arrive at the size consistent with its being used as G.H.Q. Air Service Reserve. It was contemplated that any bombardment units in existence prior to the time when this reserve had reached a growth sufficient to justify its creation as a G.H.Q. Air Service Reserve would be used as a part of the Army Air Service of the various American Armies in the Field or in some specific cases units might probably be placed with the British Independent Air Force, later known as the Inter-Allied Air Force, for the purpose of receiving training in long distance bombardment. It being understood by the nations concerned that our bombardment forces must remain an actual integral part of the American Expeditionary Forces.

11. Air Service Production Center No. 2.

Looking at this Section previously known as the Strategical Aviation, Z. of A., A.E.F. and gazing upon it with a hind-sight view of one year, in January, 1918, the time when the plans hereinbefore quoted were originally made, there are two great faults which are easily seen.

(a) Entirely too much optimism was felt for the American Production Program.

(b) The Air Service failed to secure the approval of the General Staff of its plans for the employment of this aviation and consequently suffered from the fact that its plans for the use of the Strategical Air Service were not synchronized properly, especially from a mental point of view of its employment, with the ideas of the G.H.Q.

These of course are hindsight view points.

The second point is inexcusable only upon the grounds of inexperience but the first point presents the same facts as affected the entire Air Service, namely, a program far too large to be realized in the length of time allowed for its production. There is no one to be blamed for this program for it had the approval and encouragement of the highest authorities in Europe and it was only cold matter of fact experience which proved to the world the fact that money and men could not make an air program over night and that the time to prepare for war was not after war had been declared but as quoted from the first President of the United States: "In time of peace let us prepare for war."

Assembly of a Handley-Page bomber.

30. Foulois:
Recommendations for Air Service
1 December 1917

Soon after becoming Chief of Air Service, Foulois made a number of recommendations to Pershing's Chief of Staff. His memorandum was devoted mainly to organizational and logistical problems, but one item had to do with aerial operations. The following is an extract from an account written by Foulois in 1919.[1]

. . . .

X—26. Under my orders from the War Department, I proceeded to General Headquarters A.E.F. and reported for duty to the Commander in Chief, on November 16, 1917.

I was directed to make an inspection and report upon the Air Service activities as they existed at that time. While upon this inspection trip, I was assigned to duty as Chief of Air Service, A.E.F. (November 27, 1917), relieving Brigadier General Kenly.

X—27. Upon completion of my inspection trip, and pursuant to my assignment as Chief of Air Service, effective November 27, 1917, the following memoranda for the Chief of Staff, A.E.F. were submitted.

Memorandum for The Chief of Staff:

December 1, 1917

Subject: Recommendations for Air Service.

The following recommendations for the Air Service are submitted for consideration:

. . . .

8. That a comprehensive plan of air operations (including bombing) be authorized at once, and that authority for the necessary construction and material be given, in order that fighting and bombing operations in cooperation with the French and British Flying Corps may be carried on at the earliest practicable date. (General plans now being prepared will be submitted as soon as ready.)

B.D. Foulois,
Brigadier General, S.C.

1. In AFSHRC 168.68–5.

Brig. Gen. Benjamin D. Foulois, Chief of Air Service, AEF
(November 1917–May 1918).

31. Foulois: Report on Air Service Problems

23 December 1917

In a memorandum to Pershing's Chief of Staff on 23 December 1917, Foulois devoted considerable space to what he had recently learned about bombing. His recommendations included support for Gorrell's bombing plan (Doc. 29) and for cooperation with the British and French in strategical operations.[1]

Memorandum for the Chief of Staff.

Subject. Report on Air Service problems, A.E.F., and recommendations re same.

The undersigned reported for duty at G. H. Q. November 16th, 1917, was assigned to duty as Chief of Air Service per G.O. 66 H.A.E.F., November 27, 1917.

From November 16 to November 25, I visited and conferred with Major General Trenchard, Royal Flying Corps, Commanding the R.F.C., in France; visited and conferred with General Petain, and Colonel Duval, in charge of French aviation on General Petain's Staff.

. . . .

From the date of assignment as C.A.S., November 27, up to the present date, I have also had a conference in Paris with Lord Northcliffe, representative of Lord Rothermere, the President of the British Air Board; numerous conferences with our own Air Service Officers in Paris, and have just returned from a four days conference in London with the British Air Ministry and members of the British War Cabinet.

As a result of these conferences and investigations into our own needs as heretofore tentatively outlined by the Air Service, A.E.F., the following general summary of our air problems is submitted, also general air information and data as obtained from official French and British Military and Civil sources.

. . . .

11. Each and every high official, military and civilian, with whom I have conferred has frankly stated that under the existing conditions of ship tonnage, the most swift and effective assistance which the United States can give during the Summer and Fall of 1918, is through its air forces.

The war policy of Great Britain for 1918 places (1) Tonnage; (2) Air Service; (3) Army personnel, in the foregoing order of priority. This information I received officially from one of the most prominent members of the British War Cabinet.

12. The foregoing opinion of English and French military and civil officials as regards the comparative effectiveness, during 1918, of troops on the ground as compared with air troops and airplanes in the air is concurred in or was concurred in, two months ago, by the Congress of the United States, a great portion of U.S. Army and by the American public.

The English, French and American military and civil officials heretofore mentioned fully believe that the air campaign of 1918 will be the most severe

1. In Gorrell's History, A-1, pp 131–136.

and critical insofar as its effect on the morale of the English and French civil population is concerned.

The effect, of air raids, on England during the past few months, has absolutely reversed the British war policy which existed four months ago, as regards reprisals on Germany. Today the cry is "Bomb the Huns."

During my visit last week in London I saw two small air raids and saw four civilians killed by a shell within one hundred yards from where I was standing. I also saw hundreds of poor people sleeping on the station platforms of the underground railway stations, because they were too frightened to go to their homes. So far, the air raids on London and the coast of England have been carried out by German squadrons in very small numbers, and on this particular raid only about 40 bombs were dropped. The morale effect, however, on the British people, of this small number of bombs was very great in proportion to the physical damage (10 killed, 70 wounded—4 small fires and several houses wrecked).

Upon investigation, the morning after this raid, I learned that from the time the first warning is sent out until the "all clear" signal was given, practically all work ceases in factories and other industries. This particular raid which I witnessed, kept the anti-aircraft batteries surrounding London, busy for nearly four hours, putting up a barrage about the city.

When one computes the man-hours lost, in a city the size of London, it is readily understood why the British War policy is being directed to taking active offensive measures against the air menace of the Germans.

There were approximately 20 airplanes estimated to have been engaged in this raid, and I could not learn that there had ever been a larger number engaged in any single raid on England.

The British Secret Service, however, have informed us that Germany is exerting every effort to produce a great number of bombing squadrons for offensive use during 1918.

Such being the case, we should most seriously and most promptly consider the probable morale effect on the French and English civil populations, in the event that the Germans attain air supremacy in night bombing in 1918.

From a strictly tactical viewpoint, if Germany secures air supremacy in night bombing in 1918, the first military objective of the German Air Service will be the Allies Airdromes and their squadrons, in order to prevent counter-offensive on the part of the Allies.

At the present time there is no effective method of combating night bombing raids, and the only answer to the problem is to build more night bombing squadrons than the enemy and carry on a greater offensive bombing campaign against him.

13. The Air Service, A.E.F. has collected a great amount of information, maps and data, on the most vital military industrial centers in Germany, where submarine essentials, munitions, chemicals, iron, steel, engines and airplanes are manufactured all of which are within bombing distance of the Verdun-Toul region.

The British and French authorities have fully appreciated the importance of a strategic air offensive against German industrial centers and lines of communications, but they have never during the present war, been able to provide enough personnel and airplanes to take care of the tactical air units with troops, and also provide additional units for strategical offensive operations.

Our entry into the war with large resources of personnel and aircraft materials, if promptly taken advantage of, will allow the Allies and ourselves to take the strategical offensive next Summer, against the German industrial centers, German airdromes and German lines of communications.

14. The British Air Ministry and the British War Cabinet are now preparing a communication to be referred to the Commander-in-Chief, A.E.F. recommending that the British, French and American Air Services take the necessary steps toward inaugurating a combined strategic offensive against German industrial centers without further delay. This communication should reach these headquarters within a few days.

Recommendations in Air Service Policy A.E.F.

15. In view of the foregoing statement of the needs of the Air Service, A.E.F. and the trend of our efforts toward a co-ordinated air policy with our Allies, it is recommended:

First: Provide the necessary air personnel and material for tactical operations with troops.

Second: Take immediate steps in co-operation with the British and French authorities for a combined strategical fighting and bombing campaign in 1918 against German industrial centers, German airdromes, German aero squadrons and German lines of communications.

Third: Settle as quickly as possible, the question as to priority of Aviation personnel and material over other personnel and material.

Fourth: Determine, as quickly as possible, the amount of tonnage per month which should be set aside for aviation peronnel and material.

Fifth: Obtain official approval of the air program A.E.F. with the least possible delay, in order that the C.A.S. may take immediate steps to carry it into effect, without further loss of time.

Sixth: Designate three members of the General Staff to work with the Air Service, in drawing up, in detail, a complete and co-ordinated air schedule to include all questions regarding instruction, training, organization, transportation and supply.

B. D. Foulois,
Brig. Gen'l S.C.
C.A.S.

Maj. Gen. Hunter Liggett (taken as Brig. Gen.), commander of
I Corps, was one of the few air-minded U.S. infantry generals of
World War I.

32. Command of
The Air Service, AEF
24 December 1917

As plans were made in December 1917 to organize an army corps in the AEF, orders concerning command of aviation units were revised. When I Corps was formed in January under the command of Maj. Gen. Hunter Liggett in January 1918, Mitchell became Chief of Air Service, I Corps and Corps Air Service Commander.

Headquarters, A.E.F.
France, December 24, 1917.

General Orders,
No. 80

I. 1. The Chief of the Air Service will exercise general supervision over all elements of the Air Service and personnel assigned thereto, and will control directly all Air Service units and other personnel not assigned to tactical commands or to the L. of C.

. . . .

3. The Air Service units in each army will be under the general supervision of the Army Air Commander, who will control directly all air units and other Air Service personnel on duty with that army and not assigned to Army Corps or other subordinate commands. The Air Service units of each Army Corps will be under the direct control of the Corps Air Commander.

4. Sec II, G.O. 46, c. s., these headquarters, is revoked.

. . . .

By command of
General Pershing:

James G. Harbord,
Brigadier General,
Chief of Staff.

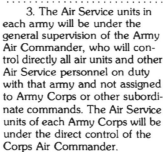

Maj. Gen. (then Brig. Gen.) James G. Harbord served as Gen.
Pershing's Chief of Staff at Headquarters, AEF. (Sketch by
Joseph Cummings Chase).

33. 100-Squadron Schedule

1 January 1918

Following recommendations made by Foulois on 10 December 1917 and again on 23 December (Docs. 30 and 31), a three-man committee was appointed to review Air Service policies, priorities, and schedules. Taking into consideration production, construction, and other problems, the committee concluded that 60 service squadrons ready for combat by the end of June 1918, and 100 by the end of the year, would be the most that could be attained. Following are the report of the committee[1] and a memorandum indicating Pershing's qualified approval.[2]

January 1, 1918.

Memorandum for the C. of S.

Subject: Air Service Program.

1. In accordance with memorandum dated December 21st and your subsequent verbal instructions, the following report is submitted:

2. The committee consulted British Staff Officers. Their opinion appears to be that infantry divisions with corresponding aviation units were most necessary for the immediate future—that no additional aviation should be brought over until an army (including its aviation) was on hand or the situation considered safe. It was, however, admitted that the total number of divisions might be reduced by one by August, 1918, in order to bring over its equivalent tonnage in extra aviation. The principal reasons advanced were probable German superiority on this front, that the British infantry was much worn from fighting and deficient in strength.

3. The Committee also consulted the French Staff. In a general way their discussion may be summarized as follows: They believe an increase of aviation, especially pursuit and bombardment units, will be the most important reinforcement that the Allies will need, stating as a reason for this, that to obtain control of the air will go far toward rendering a German offensive ineffective.

4. The ability of the U.S. to help the Allies this Spring and Summer will not be great either in trained divisions or in aviation units. The number of the latter will be limited also by production of planes, instruction of pilots and other factors.

5. In order to permit the Air Service to be developed within its limiting factors such priority should be given to extra air units as will not unduly delay the formation of a balanced army (including its aviation). With the foregoing in mind it is believed that the weight of the extra aviation should be directed toward, 1st, pursuit, and 2nd, bombardment squadrons.

6. Based on the best estimate obtainable in which allowance has been made for delays in production, preparation of grounds, etc., the Committee believes the following to be about the probable maximum attainment. The program for December 31, 1918, is of course, less accurate and should be considered as subject to later revision, when circumstances warrant it. Program for 1919 to be considered as soon as developments this Spring permit it to be taken up:

1. In Gorrell's History, A–1, pp 136–138.
2. AFSHRC 168.68–5

Type of Unit	To be in service June 30, 1918.	To be in service December 31. 1918.
Service Squadrons	60	100
School Squadrons	40	50
Park Squadrons (incl. supply & repair)	70	100
Construction Squadrons	20	20
Total Squadrons	190	270
Total men	28,500	40,500

The above includes personnel now in England and France. Balance to arrive progressively in England and France by April 1st

The plans devised late in 1917 called for a number of Park Squadrons to assemble and repair aircraft. Top left photo shows wing assembly in progress; bottom left shows the interior of an engine repair shop. Aviation mechanics for these tasks displayed a badge on the left breast of the uniform, above other decorations. It was a large four-bladed propeller within a white embroidered circle (above).

and October 1st, respectively. The probable ratio of service squadrons to be: Pursuit 6, Observation 2, Bombardment 1. Material to be supplied from U.S. for above service squadrons to arrive progressively by June 30, 1918, and December 31, 1918, respectively.

7. The committee recommends adoption of the above program.

8. A separate report will be submitted regarding the balloon program.

Signed: W. B. Burtt,[3]
Col., Aviation Sec., Sig. Corps
H. A. Drum,
Lt. Col., G. S.
A. B. Barber,
Lt. Col., G. S., A.E.F.

January 5, 1918.

Memorandum for:
Chief of Air Service

Subject:
Air Service Program.

1. The Commander-in-Chief approves the attached report dated January 1, 1918, subject Air Service Program, with the understanding that it represents the maximum the Air Service can attain. He desires no change for the present in the schedule for shipment of aviation troops but desires that you submit before February 10th, a careful estimate of Air Service possibilities for the latter part of this year so that the schedule for the period following the 1st of April may be again considered.

2. There is returned to you, herewith, your report on Air Service program, A.E.F.; it is desired that you take up with the proper sections of the General Staff and supply departments and various detail questions presented in your report so that the Commander-in-Chief's decision may be carried out promptly.

By direction:
W. D. Connor,
Acting Chief of Staff.

3. Burtt was Assistant Chief of Air Service for Policy; Drum and Barber, who had worked on the GOP, represented the Operations and Administrative Sections, respectively.

34. 120-Squadron Schedule

6 February 1918

In giving tentative approval to the work of the Burtt committee on 5 January 1918, Pershing asked for a review of the schedule for the last half of 1918. As a result of that review, Foulois raised the number of service squadrons to be ready by 31 December 1918.[1]

February 6, 1918.

Memorandum:
For Chief of Staff
(Administration Section)
(Operations Section)

Subject: Estimate Air Service possibilities latter part 1918.

The following program of the Air Service is submitted as being the probable increase in the project already authorized for the latter part of 1918.

2. The project for the latter part of 1918 calls for the following:

Service at the Front	100
Schools	50
Park (Repair Supply etc.)	100
Construction	20
TOTAL ---------------	270

3. An agreement entered into with the British Air Ministry accounts for approximately 100 squadrons to be trained in England. An additional agreement calls for the training of 30 bombing squadrons in England, of which about 12 were considered as included in the 100 squadrons mentioned in the approved project.

4. The construction of airdromes and other necessary installations we estimate may use about 100 squadrons of either Service or Construction type, of which, 20 are included in the original project. These squadrons can be exchanged for part of the 100 squadrons in England, obtaining trained men for untrained.

5. The project recommended for approval for the latter part of 1918, would be as follows:

Service at the Front	120
Schools	60
Park (Supply & Repair)	120
Construction	100
TOTAL --------------	400

6. The increase of 130 squadrons is accounted for as follows:

In service for the front	20	(bombing)
Schools	10	
Park (Repair etc.)	20	
Construction	80	(work)
TOTAL	130	

7. Referring now to cable request for squadrons in November, which called for 30 service and 20 park for 7 months, plus those already here or enroute, a total of 393 was contemplated. It should be borne in mind that the agreements with England contemplate a total of about 130 squadrons there for training, so that the actual increase herein, is to provide for those agreements, which furnish a pool, from which we can draw, trained men supplying untrained men from here in exchange for them.

8. The equipment required from the United States will not be increased over that for the original project for 270 squadrons, because the men in England will need no squadron or plane equipment.

B. D. Foulois
Brigadier General, A. S., S. C.
Chief of Air Service.

---

1. AFSHRC 168.68–5.

Part III: Combat

February-November 1918

The United States had been at war for more than 10 months before any U.S. aviation unit began active operations in France. The first U.S. aero squadron to enter combat was the 103d, a pursuit unit. Manned by pilots who formerly had fought with the French in the Lafayette Escadrille, the 103d began operations with the French Fourth Army on 18 February 1918. Later that same month the 2d Balloon Company joined the 1st Division in the line in the sector north of Toul. The Toul Sector, where the Germans were relatively inactive on the ground and in the air, was the area to which U.S. aviation units were sent in the spring of 1918 for their initial operations.

"Billy Mitchell."
(art by Linda Mikkelson)

35. Mitchell: General Principles

30 April 1918

In April 1918, after pursuit and observation squadrons had begun operations in the Toul Sector, the Information Section of the Air Service, AEF published Maj. Frank Parker's 10-month-old report on aviation (Doc. 22), to which was added the following preface by Mitchell, Air Commander, Advance.[1]

General Principles Underlying the Use of the Air Service in the Zone of the Advance, A.E.F.

These principles will be held in mind by all personnel in this Service in the execution of their duty.

Wm. Mitchell.
Lt.-Col., A.S., S.C., A.C.A.

PREFACE

1. The issue of war depends primarily on the destruction of an enemy's military forces in the field. To bring this about all elements of a nation's military power are employed to bring about a decision on the field of battle in the shortest time possible.

2. An army is composed of various arms and services whose complete interdependence and working together is necessary for efficiency. No one arm alone can bring about complete victory.

3. The efficiency of an army is measured by its ability to carry destruction to the enemy's forces.

4. The efficiency of any arm is dependent on its military training, experience and direction.

5. The Air Service of an army is one of its offensive arms. Alone it cannot bring about a decision. It therefore helps the other arms in their appointed mission. The measure of this help is its efficiency in its mission.

1. *Bulletin of the Information Section, Air Service, A.E.F.*, Vol III, No 132, 30 Apr 18.

Lts. Follet Bradley and Henry H. ("Hap") Arnold are seated in the aircraft equipped with the "wireless" outfit they used for artillery adjustment from airplanes in tests at Ft. Riley, Kansas, 2 November 1912 (above). Lts. Arnold and Joseph O. Mauborgne make adjustments in the radio set during the tests (below).

Artillery adjustments by observers in airplanes had become part of the work of the U.S. air service after the first such adjustment was made by Lieutenants H. H. Arnold and Follett Bradley at Ft. Riley, Kansas, late in 1912. When U.S. units went into combat in France in 1918, however, they followed procedures derived from French "Instructions on the Employment of Aerial Observation in Liaison with Artillery." Following are extracts from revised instructions based on the French edition of 29 December 1917 and published by GHQ AEF in May 1918.[1]

Aerial Observation for Artillery.

Chapter 1. When Used

Airplane.

1. Under favorable atmospheric conditions, the airplane affords rapid, accurate and, if necessary, vertical observation, even on distant objectives*. It can determine the sense[2] and also the deviation of shots**.

2. The airplane signals to the ground by means of radio (3), projector, dropped messages, or by signal light. The observer can thus report his presence, designate objectives, report the results of fire, and transmit information in regard to both friendly and hostile troops. This information is received by ground stations.

3. The receiving stations can, by means of white cloth panels, radio***, or projectors, answer the observer's questions and give a certain number of simple indications concerning the conduct of fire.

4. Radio.—Radio has greatly enhanced the importance of aerial observation for artillery. Because of the delicate construction of the radio apparatus and the large number of airplanes which of necessity must operate in a restricted zone, careful organization and strict discipline are essential in order to avoid confusion.

Airplanes sending simultaneously may be distinguished by:

a) Call signals for receiving stations.

b) Differences in the wavelength used.

c) Varying the tone of the emission.

d) The use, in certain cases, of watches with colored dials, by which neighboring airplanes send at alternate specified intervals and thus avoid confusion.

This device interferes with the continuity of observation and should be used only when necessary.

Certain airplanes (for command and for high power guns), use radio sets with sustained or undamped waves*.[3]

Airplanes should remain strictly in their own zones. They should not approach closer than two kilometers to their receiving stations, except for very important messages. Messages sent from immediately above the receiving station interfere seriously with other messages. With proper organization in sending, five airplanes can operate on a kilometer of front.

Technical details concerning the use of radio are prescribed in each army, army corps and division by the Signal Officer.

5. Projectors.—When the number of airplanes is too great to permit all to use radio, the congestion may be relieved by the use of projectors carried by the airplanes. By day, the method is applicable only up to a limited distance from the receiving station.

Projectors on neighboring airplanes can be distinguished by pointing the beam of light carefully, and by the use of call signals.

Notes

1. In Gorrell's History, J-3, beginning p 123.

2. Position of burst (deflection and/or range) with reference to the target.

3. Undamped waves, requiring more elaborate equipment, give a more stable signal and are received more easily and clearly than damped waves.

---

*Under particularly favorable conditions, airplane observation can be used at night.

**The deviation of a shot is its distance from the objective.

***Some times by radio telephone.

---

*Ordinarily, airplanes use damped waves.

Following the
Kansas tests, a major
development in transmitting radio-
telegraph messages took place at
the Signal Corps Air Station, San
Diego, in the summer-fall of 1916,
when messages were sent and
received from ground to planes,
planes to ground, and between
planes, for the first time in aviation
history. The Glenn L. Martin #50
(above) was equipped for the
experiments with sending and
receiving sets (below).

The radio sets in
the airplanes were powered by a small fan-
driven generator mounted below the leading edge of
the lower wing (above). An aerial of braided wire trailed the
aircraft, and a reel attached at the left of the
front cockpit was used
to reel it into the
plane (below).

6. Dropped messages.—This method is useful in transmitting information concerning objectives or firing. The message is placed in a container provided with a streamer. It should be dropped from a height not exceeding 300 meters, and as close to the receiving station as possible.

7. Signal lights.—Generally, these are used only for communication with the infantry. During the artillery preparation, their use with the artillery may be authorized by proper authority. A conventional code must be prearranged, and only a few simple messages can be sent.

8. Receiving stations.—Each regiment, group, or battalion, and sometimes each battery, has a radio receiving station.

The artillery radio officer transmits the message received to the unit concerned. The station must have exclusive and continuous communication with each battery dependent on it. Within a regiment, communication must be arranged so as to provide alternate stations in case of damage to particular stations.

If the airplane is equipped with receiving apparatus, the radio officer handles all messages from the ground station.

9. Telephone communication is covered by Liaison for All Arms.[4]

10. Each receiving station has an identification panel enabling it to be recognized by an airplane.

The personnel of a receiving station consists of the radio and panel operators supervised by the radio officer. All are specialists and must be carefully trained. Suitable replacements should be provided for.

11. The functions of receiving stations depend on the tactical unit to which they pertain. The following general classification may be made:

a) The receiving station of a battalion or battery acts principally as an *adjusting station*. It receives the reports of the airplane observing fire.

b) The receiving station of a sub-group acts as a *command post*. The airplane calls on it for fire on objectives found in the zone of the sub-group. It transmits the sub-group commander's decision in regard to each objective. In certain cases of this kind, such as battalions and batteries having a special mission, and prearranged adjustments, the airplane calls directly on the adjusting station.

The receiving station of a sub-group sometimes replaces an adjusting station which is out of action.

c) The receiving station of a regiment or group acts as an *information station*. It follows the work of the airplanes with the battalions or batteries of the regiment, and also the observation airplane and that accompanying the infantry operating in the zone of the regiment. All useful

information is thus collected.

d) In each army corps, supervising receiving stations are established near the command post of the corps artillery. They receive from all corps airplanes, or at least those having general functions (general observation, infantry accompaniment, command). The corresponding commands are thus in a position to exploit promptly all information received.

e) Each landing field has a receiving station for testing the radio equipment of airplanes leaving, for following the work of airplanes at the front, and for providing relief for airplanes about to land.

12. Listening service.—In each division, army corps, and army, the artillery commander, in cooperation with the Air Service and the Signal Corps, decides what portion of the receiving personnel shall be used for listening duty.

At times, particularly during an action or in open warfare, the artillery commander so organizes the listening service that one station at least in each regiment or group will be in a position to receive calls from all airplanes calling the regiment or group, without other previous arrangement. Communication between such stations and the units to which they pertain must be carefully planned. Whatever be the kind of communication used, the radio officer is responsible for its proper operation.

4. See Doc. 40.

Balloon.

13. Balloon observation depends on:

    a) The altitude of the balloon.
    b) The range.
    c) The atmospheric conditions.
    d) The terrain.

14. Altitude.—Altitude is an essential condition for good observation. A balloon can ascend to about 1200 meters with two observers, and to 1600 or 1800 meters with one observer.

15. Range.—The balloon should be pushed as far foward as possible while actually observing, but should be withdrawn at once when it ceases to observe and while descending.

It has been found by experience that, on a well established front, the balloon can be maneuvered up to within about 9 or 10 kilometers of the front line. Points of ascension can be within 6 or 7 kilometers of the front line. These distances are determined by the position of the friendly and hostile artillery. They can be reduced when, during preparation for an attack, the hostile artillery is clearly dominated.

16. Atmospheric conditions.—Fog, strong wind, rain, and low clouds ordinarily prevent successful balloon observation.

For the present balloons, the limiting wind velocity is about 18 meters, or 20 meters during an attack.

17. Terrain.—Even when the balloon is at its maximum altitude, there is generally a portion of the terrain hidden from view. The balloon commander prepares a visibility sketch for each point of ascension, and transmits it to the command and the artillery commander.

18. Communication.—Telephone.—The telephone assures constant and reciprocal communication between the balloon and the command and the artillery. It is the normal means. It should be established so as to permit direct communication between the balloon and the battery whose fire is being observed.

Radio.—Balloon companies are provided with radio equipment for use when telephone communication fails.

Visual communication.—In addition the observer has various means of communication for use with the infantry which may, with prearranged signals, be used in connection with observation of artillery fire.

Chapter 2. Functions.

19. The functions of aerial observation for artillery are:

    a) Information.
    b) General observation.
    c) Liaison with the other arms.
    d) Observation of fire.

20. Information.—This includes the study of the hostile positions to locate objectives, such as command posts, machine gun emplacements, battery positions, communication trenches, etc.

The best means of obtaining information is by photography for the interpretation of aerial photographs affords information which would not be noted by an observer during a reconnaissance.

21. All aerial observers, during flights or ascensions, cooperate in obtaining information. This information is collected in each air unit by the intelligence officer attached, who communicates it at once to the Intelligence Section and the artillery information officer.

Similarly the intelligence officer attached to an observation unit is given such information from other sources as will assist him in his work.

Objectives are designated by coordinates. An Objective Card is made out for each objective, particularly batteries, giving all available information. . . .

Aerial photographs are the basis for rough sketches in the air unit, provisional interpretation in the army corps, and subsequent incorporation in the battle maps. The *destruction maps* are also made up from them.

During active periods, the rapid distribution of such sketches and interpretations is of prime importance, in order to locate new objectives promptly and permit destruction fire.

22. General observation.— This includes watching for hostile batteries in action and determining the objectives on which they are firing, reporting hostile troops which can be fired upon, and sometimes observing the movements of our own troops.

23. Constant observation is very difficult for airplane squadrons. They have no other means than sight, since all sounds are drowned by the motor. They should be used for such observation only for areas hidden to balloon or terrestrial observation. Such observation is particularly the function of the balloon, in areas which are visible to it.

24. General observation requires:

Of the aerial observer, a prompt call for fire, when deemed appropriate.

Of the command, prompt exploitation of the information obtained.

When practicable, the receiving station informs the aerial observer which battery is to fire.

25. Liaison with other arms.— See Liaison for All Arms.

26. Observation of fire.—This includes fire for adjustment, precision fire for effect, and verification during precision fire for effect, zone fire, and systematic fire.

The observer can determine not only the sense but also the deviation, if each salvo or volley is fired at his signal.

In fire for adjustment or verification and for precision fire for effect, the method fulfills this condition, and airplane observation is very advantageous. It saves ammunition and increases the efficacy of the fire.

For zone and systematic fire, in which the volleys are fired without notifying the observer, airplane observation is uncertain and only fairly effective.

27. An airplane can observe for but three hours at a time. Observation may be interrupted at any time by atmospheric conditions or incidents of combat. The fire should therefore be delivered as rapidly as possible, without sacrificing accuracy of laying.

28. The balloon can observe the sense and sometimes the deviation of shots with respect to numerous objectives. It should be used for the observation of all firing on these objectives, including precision fire, when terrestrial observation is impossible.

For objectives hidden from balloon observation, the balloon can still be used for a rough adjustment to be completed by airplane observation, or for the observation of fire for effect begun with airplane observation.

29. The assignment of the available aerial observation is based on the orders of the command and of the artillery and on the reports rendered by the Air Service.

30. Coordination of balloons and airplanes.—Close coordination of balloons and airplanes and a careful assignment of duties to each are essential for successful aerial observation. For this reason both are placed under the Air Service commander of the army corps or army.

The general assignment of duties is made by the artillery commander as follows:

a) To balloons, the general observation and observation of fire for objectives which they can see, except those for which terrestrial observation can also be used;

b) To balloons, the rough adjustment on objectives wherever possible, to be subsequently completed by airplane observation.

c) To airplanes, the observation of fire only in cases for which balloon or terrestrial observation is impossible.

The Air Service commander makes the detailed assignment of duties to airplanes and balloons, in accordance with the general assignments of the artillery commander and conditions at the time. He makes the necessary arrangements for the successive use of the two methods on the same objective, when this is appropriate.

31. Division of duties among airplanes.—When an airplane can be assigned to each regiment or group of artillery in a restricted zone where the artillery preparation is well advanced, the observer should be given a definite task. He is then charged with general observation and the observation of fire.

In order to avoid errors, it is desirable that the observer who reports an objective should also observe the fire upon it.

In some cases however it is better to assign one airplane to general observation and the verification of fire over a larger zone, and to others, the observation of fire for adjustment and precision fire for effect.

32. The relative importance of the various aerial functions varies with the phases and character of an action. This is covered in orders by the command.

In an *offensive against a fortified position*, the duties of artillery airplanes and balloons are generally as follows:

a) Information and general observation accurately to locate batteries and other objectives.

b) Observation of fire for adjustment on datum points and the principal objectives.

c) Observation of precision fire for effect for the destruction of batteries and other hostile positions.

d) At the same time, reconnaissance and photography, to determine the effect produced.

e) The verification of fire, beginning as early as possible on the day of the attack.

f) During the action, the observation of neutralizing or destruction fire on the hostile artillery, in the form of fire for effect based on previous adjustments and on shifting fire on new objectives. Even, at this time, adjustments on important objectives may be necessary. These are assigned to special airplanes.

33. During movements, each large unit, generally the division, is assigned a route of march and a zone of action. Airplanes re-

connoiter this zone and transmit information by projectors, signal lights, dropped messages, or radio, to *information centers*. These are established successively along the route so as to secure continuous reception.

Information centers are in communication with the landing field of the airplanes by visual signals, telephone, radio, carrier pigeons, airplanes, or automobiles. An officer of the Air Service of the army corps or division reconnoiters if possible a suitable landing field near the information center. The necessary sentinels are assigned to it and communications organized.

The division commander generally has his artillery commander with him, and moves successively from one information center to another as the movement continues.

The division artillery commander requests of the squadron commander, through the nearest information center, the airplanes which are needed by him. He states the assignment intended if possible.

The airplanes designated for such duty report at the information center of the division, either from the air or by landing, in order to ascertain the battalion with which they are to work and the objectives. The battalion puts out its identification panel near the receiving station.

34. The division artillery commander establishes a radio receiving station with panels at the information center nearest to him. Each battalion commander installs his radio receiving station as soon as he occupies a position, even if he has good terrestrial observation posts. For this purpose the radio transportation must be pushed forward with the reconnaissance.

35. The designation of objectives and assignment of duties to airplanes is very important. For this reason, an auxiliary landing field near the division information center is desirable, and is the more so when the communications between the latter and the regular landing field of the squadron are not reliable. The division artillery commander sends instructions as to the various assignments to the auxiliary landing field. This is facilitated if he keeps available several artillery aerial observers, who can be given instructions in advance and sent to the landing field to meet the airplane as it lands.

36. But in no case should the lack of an auxiliary landing field or good communications be allowed to interrupt the successful execution of aerial observation.

37. Balloons.—Balloons move with the unit to which they are assigned. The functions remain unchanged. They are charged with general observation and the observation of fire. Communication is by radio, projector or folding cylinder. Telephone communication is established as soon as possible.

A balloon observer is permanently attached to the artillery staff.

When the advance is rapid, the balloon is deflated.

As the attack develops, the organization tends to take the form of that for the attack of an organized position.

. . . .

Chapter 4.
Methods of Fire, Field, Heavy, and High Power Artillery.

Airplane

49. Airplane observation of fire has the following advantages.

a) The accurate location of objectives.

b) Determination of deviations.

c) The observation of a salvo or volley as a whole and the determination of the estimated position of the center.

It has the following disadvantages:

a) Unreliable communication between the observer and the battery commander.

b) Short period of observation possible.

c) Airplane moving at high speed, with difficulties due to clouds, wind, sun, obstruction of view by the wings of the airplane, limited radius of action of the radio, and incidents of aerial combat. These render the observation intermittent.

The following points are thus important:

a) A previous complete understanding between the observer and the battalion or battery commander with whom he is to work.

b) Use of *simple methods*, carefully prearranged, in order to avoid *dialogues*.

c) Short, well conducted firing; to save time.

. . . .

Night Airplane Observation.

91. Night airplane observation requires the following:

a) Specially clear nights* without mist over the ground.

b) Airplanes of certain models.

c) Very well-defined objectives.

d) A thorough familiarity with the ground on the part of the observer.

e) Strict fire discipline**.

---

*Airplane observation has been successfully used on moonless nights.
**The flashes of the bursts are extremely fleeting, and the close attention required of the observer is very trying.

92. Night observation should be as nearly vertical as possible, as it is easier to catch the flashes in this manner.

Communication from the ground to the airplane is by radio when the airplane has a receiving apparatus, or by searchlight.

If searchlights are used, two are needed, pointed in the direction of the objective and elevated to about 15°. One fixes the line of fire, and the other is used for signalling.

. . . .

94. The sense of shots can be determined at night, but not the deviations.

Night observation is safer for the airplane, which must operate well inside the enemy lines. The methods can be used advantageously for harassing and interdiction fire on distant objectives*, effectively protected in the daytime by the antiaircraft defense, such as depots, railroad stations, camps, or points of obligatory passage. It is not suitable for destruction fire on batteries that are difficult to distinguish at night.

Balloon.

95. Methods of fire.—The special signals prescribed in the case of airplane observation are not necessary for balloon observation, because of the continuous and reciprocal communication between the observer and the battery by telephone. Balloon observation imposes no special restriction in regard to the conduct of fire.

The following should be noted however:

a) Only percussion fire can be accurately observed. Time fire should be used only to locate the approximate point of shots which are being lost.

b) In firing by salvos, the interval between shots should be 5 seconds at least, so as to permit observation of the individual shots.

c) To lessen the strain on the observer, he should be warned as to the departure of shots in the following manner:

Battery: "Ready to fire".
Observer: "Ready".
Battery: "On the way".

d) Firing by balloon observation should be followed by firing on a witness point. . . .[5]

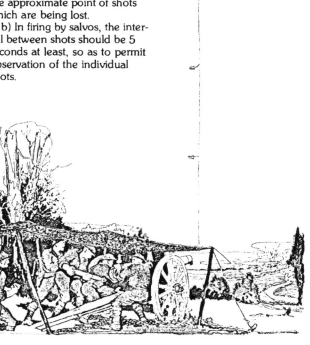

5. A visible target on which fire is adjusted immediately after adjustment on a target that is, or may become, obscured.

*In this case, the observer is not confused by the flashes of the pieces themselves or by bursts in connection with other firing.

Maj. Gen. Mason M. Patrick replaced Foulois as Chief of Air
Service, AEF, on 29 May 1918.

37. Command of the Air Service, AEF

29 May 1918

The duties of the chief aviation officers at GHQ and at army, corps, and division levels in the AEF were restated when Brig. Gen. Mason M. Patrick (soon promoted to major general) replaced Foulois as Chief of Air Service, AEF. Foulois then became Chief of Air Service, First Army. Mitchell remained with I Corps.[1]

General Orders
No. 81

General Headquarters A.E.F.
France, May 29, 1918

I. The duties of the Chief of Air Service, A.E.F., provided for in G. O. No. 31, current series, these headquarters, are as follows:

1. The Chief of Air Service is a member of the staff of the Commander in Chief, and acts as adviser on aeronautical matters.

2. He is responsible for the organization, training, materiel and equipment, methods, and all other matters affecting the efficiency of the Air Service. He will make suitable recommendations to the Chief of Staff, based on inspection and study, investigation and experience.

3. He is responsible for the preparation of all details concerning the instruction and training of air units, in accordance with the approved training policies, and he is charged with the supervision of all Army Aeronautical Schools.

4. He will supervise the training of all air units until they join the tactical units to which they are assigned, or until they are sent to the A.S., S.O.S., for final training, instruction and assignment.

5. He will prepare and submit to the Chief of Staff drafts of such manuals and other literature as may be necessary in the training and employment of all air units.

Nothing in the foregoing will be construed as in any way limiting or prescribing the powers and responsibilities of the General Staff, as defined by G.O. No. 31, current series, these headquarters.

6. General Order No. 31, current series, these headquarters, is amended in accordance with the provisions of the preceding paragraph.

II. Brigadier General Mason M. Patrick, N.A., is announced as Chief of Air Service, A.E.F.

III. The duties of the Chief of Air Service of an army are as follows:

1. In each army there will be a Chief of Air Service, who will command the army air units and who will act as adviser to the Army Commander and the Army General Staff on all aeronautical matters.

2. Under authority of the Army Commander, the Chief of the Air Service of an army, is

---

1. The Air Service and some other elements of First Army were organized before the army itself was formally organized, and Pershing took command, on 10 August 1918. Foulois and Mitchell could not get along together. After trying to have Mitchell sent home, Foulois stepped aside with a recommendation that Mitchell be placed in charge of the First Army Air Service.

charged with the instruction and inspection of all air units of the army. He will keep the Army Commander informed at all times concerning aeronautical matters, and will make such recommendations as he considers necessary concerning aeronautical personnel, materiel and methods.

3. In accordance with the general plan of operations, and in co-operation with G–3 of the army, he prepares the general plan for the employment of all air units in the army. He prepares detailed plans for the air units under his direct orders.

4. He is charged, in accordance with operation orders issued, with the apportionment of aeronautical materiel and equipment placed at the disposal of the army.

5. In addition, he is charged with the instruction and supervision of all Air Service units and personnel in the Advance Section, S.O.S., pending their assignment to tactical units.

IV. 1. Brigadier General B. D. Foulois, S.C., is announced as Chief of Air Service, 1st Army.

2. The air units now attached to the 1st Corps are detached therefrom and placed under the command of the C.A.S., 1st Army.

V. The duties of the Chief of Air Service of an army corps are as follows:

1. In each army corps there will be a Chief of Air Service, who will command the corps aeronautical units.

2. He is the adviser of the Corps Commander and the Corps General Staff in all that pertains to the Air Service. He will keep the Corps Commander informed in regard to aeronautical matters, and will make such recommendations as he considers necessary concerning aeronautical personnel, materiel and methods. In accordance with the general plan of operations, and in co-operation with G–3 of the corps, he prepares the general plans of action for all the air units of the corps. He insures the co-ordination of the aeronautical plans of divisions and supervises the employment of all air units throughout the corps in accordance with the approved plans. He prepares the detailed plans for the air units under his direct orders.

3. Under the authority of the Corps Commander, the Chief of Air Service is charged with the instruction and inspection of all air units assigned or attached to the corps; the collection, dissemination and utilization of aeronautical information within the corps, and the necessary liaison with the artillery and the Air Service of the Army and of the neighboring corps.

4. He apportions the aeronautical supplies and materiel placed at the disposal of the corps, and prepares timely requisitions for aeronautical materiel.

VI. Colonel W. A. Mitchell, S.C., is announced as Chief of Air Service 1st Corps.

VII. When aeronautical units are attached to a separate division, the senior Air Service officer on duty therewith will bear the same relation to the Division Commander and will perform duties similar to those prescribed above for the Chief of the Air Service of an Army Corps.

VIII. The 27th and 147th Aero Squadrons (pursuit) and the 96th Aero Squadron (bombardment) are assigned to the 1st Army A.E.F. These organizations will be reported by their commanding officers to the Chief of Air Service, 1st Army, A.E.F. for duty.

By Command of General Pershing:

James W. McAndrew,
Chief of Staff.

38. No Independent Air Operations

29 May 1918

Writing about his plan for strategic bombardment (Doc. 29B), Gorrell told of conversations with Trenchard late in 1917 concerning a cooperative Anglo-American bombing program. With Pershing's approval, Foulois had concluded an agreement with British officials on 26 January 1918 for organizing, equipping, and training 30 U.S. squadrons for night bombardment with Handley Page aircraft. Approving the plan and agreement in general, Pershing informed Trenchard on 6 February 1918 that he (Pershing) would instruct Foulois "to take the necessary steps towards insuring the closest possible co-operation with the British Air Service."[1] Gorrell went on to say, however, that on 18 July Pershing's Chief of Staff (Maj. Gen. James W. McAndrew) placed certain restrictions on U.S. bombing operations, and on U.S. Air Service cooperation with the British in such a bombing program. Following is McAndrew's statement, as well as an extract from the document, a memorandum from Patrick, to which McAndrew was responding.[2]

American Expeditionary Forces, Services of Supply, Office of Chief of Air Service

May 29, 1918.

MEMORANDUM for Chief of Staff, GHQ, American E.F.

SUBJECT: Approval of preliminaries for night-bombing operations.

1. In order to carry out the agreement arrived at with the British Commander-in-Chief for the joint operation of our bombardment squadrons, and approved by the Commander-in-Chief, A.E.F., February 8, 1918, and in view of the fact that:

(a) Night bombing units operate independently of other units in the Air Service (do not require the protection of Pursuit unit).

(b) The planes used are radically different from those required by day bombing and day pursuit squadrons.

(c) The final training of the personnel is along entirely different lines from that followed in the case of observation, pursuit, and day bombardment personnel, it is recommended that the development and operation of the Night Bombardment Program should be carried forward by such officers as may be designated to specialize in this Section of the Air Service.

2. Approval is requested for the Chief of Air Service to designate officers charged with the following duties:

(a) Study the development of our organization, personnel, and material in conjunction with the British officers charged with night bombardment, in order that our bombing units, when created, may properly cooperate with similar British units.

(b) Establish a center for the organization and instruction of pilots and bombers in night flying and bombing operations with required British instructors, and make special study of British training in night navigation.

---

1. Ltr, Pershing to Trenchard, 6 Feb 18, in Gorrell's History, B–6, p 33.
2. In Gorrell's History, B–6, pp 39–42.

(c) Arrange for the training of transfer pilots to fly planes from England to the American airdromes in France.

(d) Arrange for the required emergency landing fields between the Channel and the American airdromes.

(e) Arrange with the British for carrying out the present agreement of making a new and more comprehensive agreement, for doing the repair work on night bombing machines at Courban.

(f) Arrange with Ordnance Department to have officers attached to British squadrons to make study of bombs, bomb gears, etc., used on British planes.

(g) Arrange with Intelligence Department for officer or officers to make study of bombing targets with British Intelligence Officers attached to British Brigade Headquarters.

. . . .

4. It is necessary that the above points be given close study in order that our bombing operation may be properly correlated with the bombing operation of the British when the American bombing planes are received at the front.

(Sgd) Mason M. Patrick
Brigadier General, N.A.
C.A.S.

1st Ind.

G.H.Q., A.E.F., June 18, 1918.
To C.A.S., Hq S.O.S.

1. Approved subject to such limitations as are imposed by the following paragraphs.

2. While cooperating in every possible way with the Air Forces of our allies, all of our bombing forces must remain an actual integral part of the American Expeditionary Forces.

3. It is of special importance that the higher officers among our bombing personnel be impressed with the importance of the principle of the concentration of the effort to each arm, and of the coordination of all efforts, to a common tactical end. It is therefore directed that these officers be warned against any idea of independence and that they be taught from the beginning that their efforts must be closely coordinated with those of the remainder of the Air Service and with those of the ground army.

4. In making arrangements with the British it must be thoroughly understood that when our forces reach a certain importance the regions to be bombed will be designated by these headquarters and that the selection of targets will depend solely upon their importance with respect to the operations which we contemplate for our ground forces.

5. In the establishment of training schools the idea of making them purely American must govern.

6. In order to prevent interference with other projects it is necessary that all bombing projects involving matters of construction, supply or repair be taken up with the Asst. Chief of Staff, G.4 at these headquarters.

7. G.2 at these headquarters has already established the liaison requested in subparagraph (g), paragraph 2.

By direction.
(Sgd.) J. W. McAndrew,
Chief of Staff.

On 2 May 1918 the War Department informed the AEF by cable that production problems were making it impossible to meet the schedule for preparing squadrons for service at the front.[1] On 20 May Pershing replied that developments to date did not require any change in the GOP and SORP, which he had approved. Those projects, he said, "set forth our needs and desires to include June 1919." He then laid out a schedule that would put all 260 squadrons at the front by that time.[2] This new schedule reflected significant changes made in the 260-squadron plan in the SORP of 18 September 1917 (Doc. 27). The 60 bombardment squadrons of the SORP had been designated for night operations, and the 41 observation squadrons first classed as strategical aviation had become day bombardment units. Because of some confusion that had developed during the exchange of a series of cables concerning schedules, Patrick restated the schedule in the following paper,[3] to which is added a memorandum indicating Pershing's approval.[4]

American Expeditionary Forces
5 June 1918.

From: Chief of Air Service.

To: Commander-in-Chief, American E.F.

Subject: Air Service Building Program In United States

1. Cable 1224–R, dated May 3, 1918, requested our recommendations for the United States Air Plane production program, to include June 1919. Our recommendations were sent to the United States on May 21, 1918, in paragraph 1 of cable 1156–S. The United States requested further information on May 26, 1918, in paragraph 1 of Cable 1397–R, and we gave them this information on May 31, 1918, in our cable 1219–S. The building program given to the United States was based on allowing Squadrons to be efficiently operating on the front according to the following tabulation, and the United States was informed that, to accomplish this, the squadrons should reach the front 1 month prior to the time when they were expected to be operating efficiently.[5]

2. As stated in paragraphs 1 and 1–a of our cable 1156–S, the building program given to the United States conforms exactly to the General Organization Project approved by the Commander-in-Chief on July 11, 1917, as amended and completed by the Service of the Rear Project approved by the Commander-in-Chief on September 18, 1917, for an Army of 20 combat divisions.

3. It is noted that the cable 1224–R states that all we need tell America is the dates when we wish squadrons ready for service on the front and that America will then make the necessary calculations to ascertain what size building program is necessary to permit us to mobilize the squadrons on the dates when we desire. . . .

. . . .

6. It is requested that this program be reviewed and that it be returned to this office with such

---

1. Cable 1224–R, McCain (Maj. Gen. Henry P. McCain, TAG) to Pershing AMEX Forces, May 3d, in Gorrell's History, A–7, pp 89–90.

2. Cable 1156–S. Pershing to AGWAR Washington, May 21st, in Gorrell's History, A–7, pp 85–86.

3. In Gorrell's History, A–7, pp 65–68. The day of the month, missing at the top of the copy of the letter in Gorrell's History is supplied by a paper prepared by Gorrell on 29 July 1918, in Gorrell's History, A–7, p 94.

4. In Gorrell's History, A–7, p 68. It is interesting to note that the indorsement signed by McAndrew was written by Gorrell. For the date of the indorsement, which was missing, see the previous note.

5. In the table which follows, Observation and Bombardment have been abbreviated, and format for Mono- and Biplace Pursuit has been changed to save space.

additions, comments, or modifications as may be desired, and that it then be known as the "AIR SERVICE PROGRAM." It is desired to send this paper to the United States to clarify, if necessary, the cables already sent.

. . . .

Mason M. Patrick
Brigadier General, N.A.

	April 15, 1918	May 1, 1918	June 1, 1918	June 30, 1918	Sept. 1, 1918	Oct. 1, 1918	Oct. 30, 1918	Nov. 1, 1918	Nov. 30, 1918	Jan. 1, 1919	Mar. 1, 1919	June 1, 1919	Totals
Corps Obs. Sq.	3	1		6				2			3		15
Army Obs. Sq.	1	5					4		4		5	5	24
Monoplace Pursuit Sq.	3	2	3			8		8			8	8	40
Biplace Pursuit Sq.	4	3	9			16		16			16	16	80
Day Bomb Sq.				9		8		8			8	8	41
Night Bomb Sq.				12		12		12			12	12	60

ESG(G–3)

1st Ind.
G.H.Q., American E.F., France, June 5, 1918.
To: Chief of Air Service, American E.F.
    Returned.
    1. The Commander-in-Chief approves this program as a basis for production in the United States. It constitutes a program upon which it is desired the Air Service develop, provided the tonnage is available. It must be understood that the military situation will, from time to time, cause minor variations in the dates when Corps Observation and Army Observation Squadrons are needed, but this fact need not vary the building program as already furnished the United States.

(signed) J. W. McAndrew
Chief of Staff.

With emphasis on developing the aviation program, aircraft
factories, such as the Liberty Engine plant (above), worked
feverishly to meet production goals.

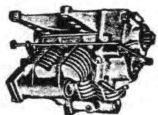

Infantrymen firing Very pistols to communicate with aviators.

40. Infantry Liaison

15 June 1918

Early in the war, failure of landline and other communications during battle caused the British and French to devise means for using aircraft to keep infantry commanders informed on the movements and locations of their various units. Although balloons were used, most operations of this type were carried out by airplanes. For such infantry liaison, or infantry contact work the Air Service, AEF, adopted procedures issued by the French in a pamphlet, "Instruction on Liaison for Troops of All Arms," dated 12 December 1916. Following are extracts from a revised edition, issued by the French on 28 December 1917 and published in translation by GHQ AEF on 15 June 1918.[1]

Liaison For All Arms

I. General Considerations.

1. The object of liaison is as follows:

To keep the commander constantly posted on the situation of the units under his orders, and to furnish him with a basis for his decisions.

To insure, between the various echelons of the command, between adjoining units and between the various arms of the service, the safe and rapid transmission of orders, questions, reports and information, and in a general way to insure all communications necessary to obtain a close co-operation, particularly between the infantry and artillery.

Consequently, to be complete, the liaison must secure the following communications:

(1) From the front to the rear.

(2) From the rear to the front.

(3) Laterally between units co-operating in the same action.

It utilizes:

(a) Means of obtaining information (liaison agents, ground observation, aerial observation, liaison with airplane, liaison with balloon).

(b) Means of transmission: Telephone and telegraphy. Radio telegraphy and earth telegraphy (T.S.F. and T.P.S.) Visual and acoustic signaling. Various signaling (by arms, by panels, by fireworks). Courier. Carrier pigeons, etc.

. . . .

Chapter IV.
Liaison by Airplanes and Balloons.

I. Airplanes.

A. Work Assigned to Airplanes.

23. In combat, besides the various duties of reconnaissance which may be assigned to them by the commander, the work of aerial observers includes:

Watching the enemy in the zone of the combat.

Liaison of the commander with subordinate echelons.

Accompanying the infantry.

In an army corps, for instance, these duties may be distributed in the following way:

(1) One or several *airplanes of command* follow the general development of the combat, watch the enemy within the assigned zone, give information as to the distribution of his forces, indications of counter-attacks, etc.

(2) *Courier airplanes* are charged with the rapid transmission of orders from the commander and of valuable information about their own situation, that of nearby units and that of the enemy.

(3) *Airplanes for accompanying the infantry* (cavalry uses the same methods as infantry for its liaison with airplanes and balloons), as a rule one per division.

They follow the assaulting troops and reserves, observe signals of the firing line and of the command posts and transmit them to the general commanding the division, and possibly to the artillery radio stations, to the command posts of brigade and regiment.

They transmit to the infantry the orders of the division commander and, generally speaking, inform the commander of everything going on in the vicinity of the first line and behind it.

24. The airplane for accompanying the infantry is provided with distinctive signs (pennants, rows of lights, etc.), and besides makes itself known by a sound signal and a signal cartridge, both determined by the plan of liaison.

Its characteristics and the signals which it uses to communicate with the infantry ought to be familiar to all men of the units for which it works.

To prevent its appearance from giving the enemy a sure indication of an impending attack, and to make all concerned familiar with their own airplanes, it is indispensable that the airplanes accompanying the infantry fly frequently over the lines during the days of artillery preparation. Outside these periods they should fly from time to time in order to practice liaison with the infantry.

The airplane for accompanying the infantry rises above the advanced units to a height which must not exceed 1,200 meters. In certain cases it may be obliged to fly over the lines at very low height, but must not come below 600 meters except in case of necessity.

It must be the constant care of the crew to assist the infantry, noting exactly its position and its needs and conveying rapidly such information to the commander and the artillery.

B. Means of Communication.

(1) *Communication From The Airplane to The Earth.*

25. Airplanes communicate with the earth by means of:

(a) *Weighted messages* (1) for important indications, sketches and photographs intended for the command posts of army corps, divisions, brigades, and in exceptional cases of regiments.

To drop a weighted message the airplane comes down to a low height (about 200 meters) above the command post concerned, calls the attention of the addressee by one or several sound signals (fixed by the plan of liaison), and drops its message so that it falls in open ground.

(The plan of liaison should prescribe, as far as possible, on what terrain weighted messages shall be dropped.)

In the course of the infantry's advance, supported by artillery fire of all calibers, it is difficult for an airplane to get through the very dense sheet of projectiles. At the moment it can drop messages on a command post located near the line of batteries only by remaining above that sheet, hence under bad conditions for carrying out its duty.

(b) *Radio telegraphy,* for urgent information (position of friendly troops, requests for artillery fire, lengthening of range, etc.), to the authorities whose receiving station is likely to hear it, i.e., to commanders of army corps, divisions, brigades, infantry regiments, artillery groups and battalions.

Such communications are made by using one of the codes of Appendix VI.[2] Only such indications as are totally useless to the enemy may be transmitted in plain language.

(c) *Visual signaling and signaling by fireworks* (conventional signals of codes in Appendix VI) after having drawn attention by a sound signal (fixed by the plan of liaison) for communications intended for such elements as have no radio stations at their disposal and whose advance position does not permit the dropping of weighted messages.

(1) The message itself is placed in a metal box provided with a white or colored pennant which increases its visibility.

(2) This appendix and the others cited have been omitted.

With the fireworks used nowadays the airplane cannot possibly indicate which element it wishes to communicate with. Such signals are consequently intended for all elements constituting the large unit for whose benefit the airplane is working. The use of projectors, on the contrary, enables the airplane to choose its correspondent. It is therefore advisable to try constantly to improve the latter method.

To be visible, visual and fireworks signals must not be used when the airplane is seen by the duties to be carried out, the better.

Signal cartridges must always be fired from a height greater than 300 meters, and as much as possible upwards, to avoid confusion with the signals made by the infantry.

(2) Watch Posts

26. In order that the airplane signals and the messages sent by them may not pass unnoticed, in case the noise of the battle drowns the sound signals, a permanent watch post service must be secured by the radio officers, or by the officers in charge of the liaison near the posts of command of army corps, division, brigade, regiment, artillery group and battalion, as soon as the post of command is established. This service is carried on by observers within the battalions and companies. (The distribution of the personnel should be such as to insure simultaneously "observation" and "watch.")

(3) Communication From The Earth to The Airplane.

27. The airplane receives communications from the firing line and from the command posts.

(a) *Firing line:* The line indicates its location:

1. *By means of position-marking panels.* All men carring panels alternately open and shut their apparatus, taking care to set it facing the airplane with that side whose color stands out better on the surrounding ground. It is better to use many panels simultaneously during a fairly short time than a smaller number of panels during a longer time; thus, the line is automatically traced very quickly and clearly and troubles caused by forgotten panels are avoided.

To reduce the enemy's chances of spotting our line, the airplane observer must endeavor to reduce to a minimum the time required to take note of the new line.

Panels are folded up again as soon as the airplane signals "understood," and in any case after ten minutes.

2. *By means of Bengal flares* of certain color (fixed by the plan of liaison). These signals constitute the surest way of indicating one's position. It is important, however, to conceal them as much as possible from hostile view, by hiding them behind a screen, at the bottom or on the front side of a shell crater, while taking care that they remain visible to friendly observers.

To avoid confusion it is forbidden to display position-marking panels or to light Bengal flares anywhere but on the line. (This interdiction applies as well to patrols sent in front of the lines as to supporting or reinforcing units).

In order to distinguish clearly the signals made by our infantry from those which might be set by the enemy to impede observation it is important to agree that panels or Bengal flares will be placed in groups of 2, 3, etc.

3. For want of marking panels and Bengal flares, the line uses all means available to indicate its location: signal cartridges of the 25 mm pistol or V.B.,[3] signal projectors sending series of alternated dots and dashes, waved handkerchiefs, pocket mirrors, etc.

The marking out of the firing line is carried out:

Either at an hour set beforehand, or on a prearranged line: for instance, the final objective or one of the successive objectives: or by order of the command transmitted by the airplane by means of the signal cartridges, "Where are you?" after having drawn the infantry's attention by a sound signal; or upon the company or platoon

---

3. Viven Bessiere; a smoke grenade.

commander's initiative, when their unit cannot advance any farther, or when, compelled to fall back, it has succeeded in securing a hold on the ground.

Orders for marking out should not be too frequent. In principle the marking out will be done by panels.

Should the observer not see the panels, or should he see them badly, he will request another marking out, which will then be executed by means of Bengal flares.

In that case the company or platoon commanders will also signal their positions by means of color signal cartridges fired with the 25 mm pistol.

The line sends its request to the airplane by means of the same fireworks and according to the same codes as for communications with the rear (see codes of Appendix VI).

The airplane transmits these requests by radio to the general commanding the division.

(b) *Command posts.* The different command posts indicate their locations by means of the identification panels described in Appendix III.

Such panels are placed, either upon initiative from the command post to draw the airplane's attention, or at a fixed hour, by order of the higher command transmitted to the command post by the airplane under the same conditions as to the firing line. Hence, as soon as the airplane sends out the signal, "Where are you?" all command posts noticing the signal should mark their respective positions. The panels are removed as soon as the airplane has answered, "Understood."

Command posts of generals commanding army corps and divisions can communicate by radio with such airplanes as have a receiving apparatus.

All command posts can communicate with airplanes either by visual signaling or by means of their rectangular panels (described in Appendix III), using the conventional signals of Appendix VI.

As a rule, visual signals are repeated and panel signals left in place until the airplane has answered, "Understood" (preferably by projector signals).

II. Balloons
A. *Duties of Balloons.*

28. The divisional balloon, whose work it is to insure liaison for the infantry, carries as a distinctive mark one or more pennants attached to the rear or to the cable of the balloon. If a night ascension is deemed necessary in order to receive signals from the infantry, the balloon indicates its presence by means of a luminous signal lit at regular intervals.

Like the airplane for accompanying the infantry, its duties consist in:

Following the progress of assaulting troops and reserves.

Observing the signals from the line of the command posts, and transmitting them to the general commanding the division.

Informing the commander of everything going on in the vicinity of the firing line, and behind it.

Sending out, if necessary, to the advanced elements conventional signals provided for in the plan of liaison.

B. *Means of Communication*

29. (1) *From the balloon to the command.* The balloon is directly connected by telephone with the divisional command post (balloon circuits) and with the army system.

It is besides provided with a radio apparatus enabling it to transmit its observations in case telephone communications should not work.

(2) *From the balloon to the firing line and to the advance command posts.* The balloon can communicate with the advance elements.

(a) In daytime by means of a cylinder which folds and unfolds at will, thus making signals corresponding to dots and dashes. These transmissions are limited to the two signals, "Understood" or "Repeat," preceded by the call of that particular post which the balloon addresses.

(b) At night by means of luminous signals, enabling it to send more complete messages, which, however, are always likely to be read by the enemy.

(3) *From the firing line and the advance command posts to the balloon.* In daytime, the firing line and the advance command posts indicate their positions to the balloon and communicate with it by means of the same methods as for communicating with the infantry airplane. However, the following should be noted:

(a) The balloon does not send out to the firing line the order to mark out the line which it occupies. Consequently it only observes the prearranged marking, or that ordered by the airplane.

(b) The balloon does not see the panels clearly.

(c) It can see the identification panels and the rectangular panels of the command posts only when they are inclined at a sufficient angle.

(d) Being far away from the lines it can hardly ever receive in daytime the signals made by the advanced elements with the 24 cm. projectors.

At night the balloon indicates its presence and position by lighting a luminous signal at regular intervals.

To this end, at an hour settled in the plan of liaison, the balloon sends out its call several times in succession and keeps its light up for five minutes.

The signalers of the different command posts take note of the direction of the balloon, orient their projector toward it, call up and then send their particular station call to the balloon until the latter sends it back. The balloon then takes them from right to left successively and receives their message, which it immediately transmits to the post of command by telephone or radio.

After these liaisons have been established the balloon observer watches the battlefield to catch any call which the different posts of command might send to him, and every 15 minutes he indicates his presence by two-minute calls.

As soon as he notices a call from a command post he starts communications with that post according to service regulations prescribed in Appendix V. Signals must be transmitted at low speed.

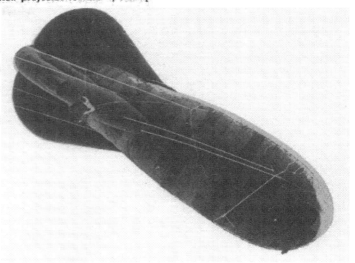

Ground panels laid out to signal aviators in flight.

41. Infantry Liaison in I Corps

June 1918

The following instructions[1] for infantry liaison apparently were written shortly before I Corps began operations early in July 1918 and before the AEF version of the French instructions of 28 December 1917 (see Doc. 40) had been received. Much attention is given to a variety of ways for aerial observers to communicate with infantry troops and headquarters. With radiotelegraphy for air-ground communications still in its infancy, and with radiotelephony even less developed, there really was no satisfactory means of communication, as these instructions indicate.

Notes on Liaison Between Aircraft and Infantry During Attack

Prepared under direction of Col. W. Mitchell, C.A.S. First Army Corps.

I. **Functions of the Infantry Airplane.** During periods of attack one infantry airplane is, in general, allotted to each Division. The functions of this plane are:—

1. To follow the advance of the attacking troops and reserves.

2. To observe signals from the

front or most advanced line and the various P.C. and to transmit them to the Division Commander and, when required, to receiving stations of the P.Cs. of the artillery, Division, Brigade, or Regiment.

3. To transmit to the infantry the orders of the Division Commander, and, in general, to keep the headquarters informed of everything that is going on in the neighborhood of the advanced line and behind it.

The Infantry Airplane, therefore, has a double mission to assure; first, to keep the staff informed of what is taking place, secondly, to act as liaison agent between the troops in the first line and Division Headquarters, or, when required, with the P.Cs. or artillery and infantry brigades or regiments. This forms a task of the highest importance and one which is extremely complex and very delicate. It can be said without exaggeration that liaison with the infantry is the most difficult mission that can be entrusted to an aerial observer. For this reason, it is indispensible, both for the infantrymen and for the aviator, that exercises should be held frequently and as closely as possible approaching the realities of active warfare. The work of liaison with infantry is extremely difficult and arduous, both for the infantry and for the aviators, that the more practice exercises held to familiarize both with the duties to be carried out, the better.

II. **Mission of the Infantry Airplane—general principles.** It is difficult to fix definite limits to the activity of Infantry Airplanes, Artillery Surveillance Airplanes, and Command Airplanes. It should not be forbidden to the observer in the Infantry Airplanes, to spot enemy batteries in action and to signal them to the artillery, or to notify the Command of points particularly swept by the fire of the enemy; nor should it be forbidden to the artillery observer to observe and report matters of interest in our front lines or trenches, but the former is solely responsible for locating the advance of our attacking infantry, whereas the latter is solely responsible for observing, adjusting and directing the fire of our artillery. The observer of the Infantry Airplane has about all he can do to see what is occurring in the neighborhood and behind the foremost lines of the infantry. Without entirely ignoring what is going on on the enemy's side, he should, in principle, only interest himself with *our own* infantry. If he fails to confine himself to this, he runs a considerable risk of failing to satisfactorily carry out his mission and obtain the best possible results. It is essential that the observer should thoroughly realize this— that what takes place beyond our foremost lines is not his concern; this latter is the mission of the Command Airplane.

III. **Mission of the Infantry Airplane**—execution. The Infantry airplane flies above our lines, slightly behind our most advanced troops at an altitude generally low, but varying with atmospheric conditions, the nature of the ground, and what the observer is looking for. This altitude, however, should never be more than 1,200 meters and only exceptionally less than 600 meters. Owing to the vulnerability of a low flying observation airplane, it should not descend below 600 meters except in cases of absolute necessity. It is, furthermore, advisable that the plane should not keep constantly to the same altitude, as by frequently changing its altitude, it is less likely to be hit by shots fired from the ground. During the course of operation, the surveillance of the battlefield should, in principle, begin before dawn and the infantry airplane should leave its field while it is still dark so as to arrive above the lines at the first moments of daylight. This is nearly always the most interesting time of day for observation. The results of reconnaissance by infantry airplanes during a light rain are often particularly valuable for the reason that at such a time the enemy takes few precautions to conceal himself, generally thinking that he is in complete security from aerial observation.

At the beginning of offensive operations, the Infantry Airplane should not arrive over the lines until a little after "H" hour, so as not to call the attention of the enemy prematurely to the point and moment of attack. When no attack is planned it is sometimes of value for an airplane to fly over the lines at dawn dropping various luminous signals in order to deceive and worry the enemy.

Fire from the ground by the infantry constitutes the principal source of danger for the low flying observation plane. The best method of contending with this and protecting himself as far as possible, is for the observer to fire with his machine gun as frequently as he can against the enemy trenches and positions. Furthermore, by machine gunning certain suspicious points, the observer often succeeds in making the enemy disclose himself by movements.

IV. **Means of communication between the airplane and the ground.**

1. *By radio.* The observer signals by radio all his observations, in general addressing himself to the Division report center. He must pay special attention to the rapidity and clearness with which he sends his messages, and he should not hesitate to repeat his message several times until the receiving station gives the signal "understood." It is advisable that the artillery receiving stations should also take any messages sent to the Division report center. Infantry airplane observer should not send by radio any information of which they are not certain. Observations of this nature should be noted on the written message to be dropped at the report center, mentioning, of course, the fact that the information is of doubtful accuracy. All radio messages should be preceded by the call letters indicating to whom the message is addressed. Coordinates, etc., must always be given in code. It is most strictly forbidden for any messages to be sent in clear.

Note: Before leaving the neighborhood of his airdrome, the infantry airplane observer will test the working of his radio with the receiving station of the group (squadron) and will not start off over the line until the latter has notified him by a prearranged signal (a Special form of panel, for example) that his radio is working properly. For this reason, the Infantry Airplane must take off from his field early enough to make this test and, if necessary, to remedy any fault in his radio and still arrive over the lines at the hour fixed.

2. *By visual signals and signal lights.* The observer carries two sorts of luminous signals:

1. The projector.
2. Signal lights of various kinds.

Up to the present time the former method has been by no means perfected, and, although it has many advantages over the light signals, the infantry is not yet sufficiently expert in reading indications sent them from an airplane by projector to allow this method to be successfully employed.

Liaison by signal lights presents several disadvantages. In the first place, such signals do not indicate the unit with whom the airplane desires to communicate (for example, they do not show that the observer wishes to call the attention of one certain battalion, rather than any other battalion that happens to be in the neighborhood). The considerable variety of signal lights which have to be employed necessitate the carrying of a large number of cartridges, with the result sometimes of overloading the airplane. The pistol, unless fixed, is long and inconvenient. It may occur, by a false movement on the part of the observer, by a violent movement on the part of the plane or by bad functioning of the pistol, that the signal light is shot-inside, or on to the fuselage or wings of the machine. To guard against the last difficulty, it is desirable that the pistol should be fastened to the edge of the cockpit. An aluminum pistol is preferable, because of the weight, to one in bronze.

Signal lights should not be fired from an Infantry Airplane at an altitude of less than 300 meters, in order to avoid confusion with similar signals fired from the ground. The pistol should be held vertically.

Before leaving his field the observer should test the working of his signal pistol. A second pistol should always be carried in case for any reason the first one fails to work, and, furthermore, in order to permit of two different signals lights being fired rapidly one after the other. The latter is of value when, as often happens, the observer is required to send successively "I am the infantry airplane of "X" Division", and "Where are you?"

3. *By sound signals.* This is another method which has not yet been completely perfected, although tests with certain instruments have given good results. Infantry airplane reconnaissance over the positions held by the first lines of our attacking troops being usually made at a predetermined hour, and the Infantry airplane flying at a lower altitude than any other plane and bearing distinctive marks and letting off identifying light signals, there is little chance that it will fail to be recognized by the many infantrymen who will be looking at it. It does not, therefore, appear necessary for a sound signal to be employed in this case. On the other hand, sound signals are practically indispensable in the case of airplanes wishing to inform the P.C. that they intend to drop a weighted message, because, particularly if the P.C. is under shell fire, the vigilance of the look-outs cannot always be relied upon. If the plane is not equipped with a Klaxon horn, or some other type of sound producing instrument, a peculiarly timed burst of machine gun fire, several times repeated, if necessary, will usually have the same effect.

4. *By weighted message.* Weighted messages are especially valuable for the purpose of confirming and completing the information already dispatched by radio or by various light signals. Weighted messages are dropped at the P.Cs. of Army Corps and Divisions, and but exceptionally to P.C. of infantry regiments. Weighted messages should never be dropped to advanced units, for orders or information addressed to the P.C. of a battalion, for example, run a considerable risk of falling into the enemy hands. It is necessary for observers to practice dropping weighted messages from a height of at least 200 meters, until they are able to drop them with the greatest precision.

Written messages, and maps showing the location of Bengal fires, P.Cs. &c., should be made in triplicate (one copy to be dropped at Division P.C. or Report Center, one copy at Army Corps Report Center, if required and one copy retained for the Squadron Commander). Before leaving the airdrome the three copies of the map, with new carbon sheets between, should be carefully affixed to an aluminum back and kept in place by gummed corners and by surgeons tape around the edges. The same is done with the message forms. The observer indicates in pencil on the map the location of our front line and P.Cs., as shown him by panels, Bengal fires &c. and any other observations of interest, noting the hour. When he has completed his mission he pulls off the tape and takes off one sheet of the map, rolls it up, and puts it in the Div. P.C. The second sheet is similarly taken off and placed in the message carrier for the Army Corps P.C., and the third is left attached to the board by means of a clip. The same is done with any messages that the observer may have written out.

V. **Means of communication between the ground and the airplane.** The Infantry Airplane observer receives signals both from the most advanced line and from the Staff (generally the Staff of the Infantry Division).

1. *Communication with the most advanced line.* Units of the most advanced line (excluding both patrols sent further out and units in support or reserve further back) signal their location by—

a) Individual panels (one for two men).

b) Bengal fires.

c) Projectors.

d) Signal lights.

e) Various make-shift methods, such as mirrors, pocket torch lights, handkerchiefs, overcoat linings, etc.

At the demand of the Infantry Airplane, or at an hour prearranged by the Staff, or at the initiative of a Company Commander or the Commander of any other unit, when this unit can no longer advance, or when after having been obliged to retire he has succeeded in holding his ground—the infantrymen lay out their individual panels. If the Infantry Airplane observer fails to see the panels, or has difficulty in distinguishing them, he repeats his signal of identification "I am the Infantry Airplane of "X" Division", and the question "Where are you", and thereupon the signals of the infantry

must be made by Bengal fires.

(a) *Panels*

In case of individual panels, because of their small dimensions, it is indispensable that they be placed together in groups of at least three or four, in order that the observer may see them clearly. Furthermore, it is necessary that they should be waved or moved about at the right moment in order to attract the observer's attention—the right moment being when the airplane has passed slightly beyond a point directly above the signalers. The observer will do his utmost to reduce to a strict minimum the time necessary for him to note the positions shown by the signals, in order not to keep the attention of the infantry for too long a time and to avoid, as far as possible, that the enemy should be able to locate our line. On the other hand, infantrymen should wave and move about their panels for a time sufficient for the Infantry Airplane observer to properly locate them. It is extremely difficult for anyone on the ground to determine the exact moment at which an airplane passes vertically over him, and it is certainly better for the panels to be shown a little too long than not long enough. However, if at the end of ten minutes the Infantry Airplane has not given the signal "understood", the panels should be rolled up.

It is necessary to insist on the very important point that the panels when laid out must be "living," that is to say, continually moved about or agitated, and not merely unrolled and left lying. If this is not done it is likely to give rise to errors of the greatest importance, for immobile panels are very apt to give erroneous, or at least uncertain indications to the observer, being easily confused with other things and not informing the observer whether or not they are the locations of the most advanced line.

Individual panels should be placed in such a way as not to be visible to the enemy, i.e., inclined on the parados of a trench, hidden in shell holes, or behind a slight rise of ground, etc. It is strictly forbidden to anyone not in the most advanced line to signal his presence by means of individual panels. This does not, of course, apply to battalion P.Cs. whose identification panels should be laid out as soon as the Infantry Airplane sends his signal "Where are you?" The laying out of the battalion identification panels is often very useful to the airplane observer, especially when he has no clear idea of the approximate location of the most advanced line. Similarly, and for the same reasons, it is desirable that regimental P.Cs. should lay out their identification panels when the Infantry Airplane sends his signal "Where are you?" (This is formally ordered in the French instructions of the 28th December, 1917. . . .)

Care must be taken to prevent the panels from becoming dirty. It is recommended that they should be carried in cloth cases or sacks to protect them from mud and dust.

(b). Bengal fires.

The panels have the serious inconvenience of being invisible, or nearly so, against light background, such as clay soil broken up by shell fire, or when they become soiled and are no longer a brilliant white—which is nearly always the case.

Bengal fires, on the contrary, are always visible against no matter what background, and constitute certainly the most satisfactory method of signaling from the ground. It is, however, important that they should be concealed from the view of the enemy, while, at the same time, being clearly visible to the observer in the airplane. For this reason they should be placed behind a screen, or at the bottom or on the forward slope of a shell hole, etc. The same way as in the case of the panels, the Bengal fires should be placed out in groups of three or four so as to be more visible to the airplane observer.

(c) *Projectors.*

Projectors can hardly be considered as a means of signaling the location of the advanced lines, but they can be very usefully employed to attract the attention of the airplane observer. They possess the advantage of being able to be employed without attracting the attention of the enemy and, furthermore, of being the more visible the worse is the visibility. Well handled they should render excellent service, but it is essential that the signalers with the infantry be very skillful in following the airplane. The present number of projectors authorized for a battalion (14) is considered to be scarcely sufficient and should be added to. Furthermore, in order to simplify the handling of a projector to as great an extent as possible, it is desirable that the signalers carry spare batteries and lamps.

(d) *Signal lights and smokes.*

Signal lights sent up from the ground give only a very vague indication of the point from which they were sent (not within 50 or 100 meters) and, therefore, are of little value to any one desiring to signal "I am here." As for smoke signals, these are practically useless during battle as it is almost impossible to distinguish them among the shell-bursts.

(e) *Make-shift methods.*

Handkerchiefs waved in the air, overcoats turned inside out, so that the lining is exposed, and waved, pocket electric torches, mirrors, etc., directed towards the airplane, etc., etc., are very ineffective and give very poor results, but they should not be forgotten in any special circumstance when other regular methods of signaling are, for any reason, not available.

(f) At present, with the apparatus available for receiving radio messages by an airplane, the results are so uncertain that it is hardly worth considering this method for signaling from the ground to the airplane in connection with liaison with infantry. For an observer to be encumbered with the radio receiving helmet and constantly obliged to look at his lamps and mess about with the handles, would seriously interfere with the efficient performance of his mission, which requires concentrated observation of what is going on below him.

2. *Communication with Staffs and Headquarters.*

The various P.Cs. indicate their locations to the airplane observer by means of the different identification panels described in Annex 4 of the instructions of 28th December 1917. These panels are laid out at the discretion of the P.C. in order to attract the attention of the airplane, or at a certain hour, arranged beforehand, or by order of the higher command,

transmitted to the P.C. by the airplane in the same manner as to the most advanced line. The panels should be taken in as soon as the airplane has given the signal "understood".

It is, of course, possible for the P.Cs. of the Corps Commander or Division Commanders to communicate by radio with any airplanes which have receiving apparatus on board, but it must be remembered that this procedure practically results in making the observer both blind and deaf to everything else during a comparatively long time when it might be more profitable for him to be employed in observing what is going on beneath him. All P.Cs. may communicate with the infantry airplanes, either by means of optical signals or with the rectangular panels of the P.Cs. as described in Annex 4, and employing the conventional signs used in Annex 8 of the instructions of December 28, 1917. In general, optical signals should be repeated and panels left in position until the airplane has given the signal "understood". To avoid enabling the enemy to locate the P.C. it is preferable, if possible that the observer should give the signal "understood" by projector.

VI. **Preparations for liaison with infantry.**

The missions of Infantry Airplanes and Command Airplanes can only be carried out effectively when the observers are thoroughly trained and have a complete knowledge of the plan

of the operations, or, as the case may be, of the defence. In case of a necessary retirement of our troops, the observer should know our own successive positions quite as well as the enemy's lines. It is, furthermore, indispensable that the observers should personally visit the Commanders of the various infantry units, down to, and including, Company Commanders at least, with whom they will have to work; that these visits should be held in the trenches; that the observers should look over the ground of operation from the first line observation posts, and that they should work out on the spot with the various Commanders the details of the missions which they will be called upon to fulfill. Delicate liaison of this nature can only be efficiently accomplished when each party thoroughly understands the other, and the only way that this can be arrived at is for each one to thoroughly know the other. No opportunity should be lost of improving the relations between the observers and the infantry officers, both when the latter are in the trenches and especially—because then they are less occupied with other duties—when they are on rest. The habit of close cooperation in working together must be encouraged to the greatest possible extent.

VII. **Practice Exercises.**

The more practice exercises of aerial liaison with infantry that can be carried out, the better. It is impossible to over do it. In the course of these exercises every one must endeavor to simulate, as far as possible, the conditions that will be met with during the actual attacks. The airplane should fly rapidly above the positions and, from time to time, fly off as if he were driven by hostile aerial attack, or forced away by clouds or other climatic conditions. The observer should strive to observe from the highest altitude possible. The infantrymen must handle their signaling apparatus exactly as they would do under the conditions of an attack and as if they were continually harassed by enemy fire, etc. The men handling the projectors must strive to follow exactly the course of the airplane until the

latter has given the signal "understood", or has repeated his call signal. (With regard to the training of the projector signalers, in addition to that carried out in exercises in cooperation with our aircraft. The signalers should, on all occasions, endeavor to follow with the projector any airplane that may pass over them, without, of course, lighting the lamp of the projector.)

If possible, during the course of the practice exercises, several airplanes should fly over the troops at the same time, only one of which acts as the Infantry Airplane and gives signals. This serves the double purpose of training several observers at the same time and of accustoming the infantrymen to pick out their

own plane from among a number of others. During the exercise the observer should precede all his radio calls by the call *e* (. . - . .), or *ex* (. - . . -). Coordinates sent by radio should be given in code, but in an obsolete code and not the one actively in use. The code signals actually in use for list No. 2 of the signals between an airplane and the infantry instructions of 28th December, 1917, should not be used for practice exercises.

In order that observers in the event of an advance should not find themselves handicapped by the lack of large scale maps (Plans Directeurs) it is advisable that in exercises of liaison with the infantry they should practice both with the Plans Directeur and with the maps of 1/80,000.

VIII. The maximum return from liaison with the infantry will only be obtained when every infantryman is thoroughly convinced of the value of the aid that can be given him by the observer in the airplane. It is indispensable to create in the infantry the spirit of the knowledge of the absolute necessity of infantry liaison and its undeniable utility.

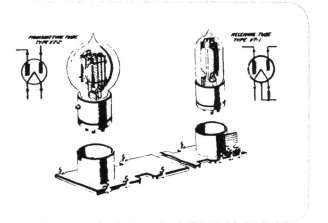

Maj. Davenport Johnson.

42. The Role of Pursuit

June 1918

The following notes,[1] which carry no indication as to date or author, evidently were written late in June 1918, at the time the 2d Pursuit Group was being organized under the command of Maj. Davenport Johnson. The group, which began operations immediately in the Toul Sector, was part of the short-lived 1st Brigade Air Service, commanded by Col. William Mitchell.

Notes on The Tactical Employment of Pursuit Aviation

Prepared under the direction of Col. W. Mitchell. C.A.S. 1st Corps.

The role of Pursuit Aviation is two-fold:

1. *Offensive*

To seek out and attack all enemy elements in the air, forcing the combat back over enemy territory, breaking up the enemy's aerial formation activity, inflicting the greatest possible casualties on his air service, and preventing his observation aviation from functioning;

To co-operate with our Day Bombardment Aviation in the attack of enemy elements on the ground, and especially enemy air elements that are forced by the bombardment of their airdromes to take to the air.

2. *Defensive*

To protect our observation aviation from interference by enemy aircraft, and to prevent incursions by enemy aircraft over our area.

Offensive.

Ascendency in the air on any given sector of the front is obtained by the attack, destruction or dispersing of the enemy air elements operating on that sector, and so completely dominating them that they are unable to carry out their missions. To accomplish this it is necessary for large forces of pursuit aviation to be concentrated under one command, so that the protection of our observation aviation may first of all be assured, and that strong, purely offensive patrols—formidable in numbers, battle formation and tactical grouping—may be thrown out to clear the air of hostile elements, inflicting great losses on the enemy's air service, breaking up his aerial defense against our aircraft and forcing his whole aviation to keep back of the zone in which it is of primary value.

At all periods during the preparation and conduct of offensive operations by our troops, it is essential to prevent the functioning of the enemy's observation aviation as it is to prevent enemy aircraft from interfering with the functioning of our own observation aviation. This is also very important when the enemy has assumed the offensive and is correspondingly difficult to accomplish as the enemy will have made a concentration of his air forces for the attack. The attack and destruction, or dispersing, of the enemy observation elements, as well as other enemy air elements back of his own lines, is the duty of the second Group of the Pursuit Wing and is most effectively carried out by offensive patrols of five to seven airplanes each, one of which may be a fast bi-place machine to cover the rear of the patrol. These offensive patrols penetrate far over the enemy's territory at an altitude of 5000 to 6000 meters, seeking combat, sweeping the air of hostile aircraft; their primary duty being to attack at once any enemy aircraft that they may sight. The patrols of our Day Bombardment should work in close co-operation with them, striking the enemy's aerial defensive organizations simultaneously with strong attacks by the Pursuit patrols, taking advantage of the breaking up of the enemy's formations and the dispersing of his offensive elements by the strong formations of the Day Bombardment aviation which are then attacked in detail by the pursuit machines of the Offensive Pursuit Patrols.

1. In Gorrell's History, C–4, pp 500–503.

Offensive patrols acting in co-operation with Day Bombardment Patrols should penetrate as far over enemy territory as the objective of the latter, in order to take advantage of opportunities for attacking the enemy air elements that may attempt to oppose them, and any enemy aircraft forced by the bombardment of their airdromes to take to the air. This does not mean that the pursuit planes should stay with them constantly, but should work in cooperation with them.

Day Bombardment patrols are frequently followed back to their lines by enemy aircraft afraid to attack the formation but waiting a chance to pick off stragglers, and our Pursuit patrols should be in readiness to take advantage of the demoralization caused by the bombing, especially the bombing of camps, hutments, parks, transport, columns of troops on the march, etc., and find special opportunities for attack with M. G. fire on the enemy personnel scattered and driven into the open by the bombs.

Such attacks at low altitude should be carried out by special patrols or special machines and not by the regular offensive patrols, which ordinarily should not attempt to descend to very low altitudes.

The Second Pursuit Group is furthermore responsible for carrying out attacks on enemy observation balloons. These also are done by machines specially detailed for the purpose and not by the regular patrols. It should be borne in mind, however, that isolated attacks for destruction of observation balloons are attended with considerable danger, as the German balloon winches can bring down their balloons very rapidly and an attacking aeroplane is therefore forced to descend very low and come under heavy machine gun fire. The results obtained are rarely in proportion to the risk run, and such isolated attacks should, therefore, be undertaken only under especially favorable

weather conditions (clouds) or when it is considered essential for some particularly annoying enemy balloon to be destroyed or forced to move further back. This does not apply to demonstrations against enemy balloons by airplanes with the object not of destroying the balloon but merely forcing it to descend temporarily and interrupting the work it is carrying out. Such demonstrations are of advantage in that they interfere with the observation or adjustment of artillery fire that the balloon observer is engaged upon, while they are not especially dangerous as the airplane does not have to descend very low. Attacks for destruction carried out on a large scale against all balloons along a considerable length of the front give valuable results, especially when carried out at the beginning of, or during, any minor operation, but these must be organized with great caution and precision.

The duties of the Surveillance Squadrons are to keep the enemy's back area under constant observation, for general activity and important movements, but especially for the activities of his air service. These machines will be bi-place or tri-place, and will carry out their missions singly or, in special cases, in pairs. They will be equipped with cameras, and with radio—by means of which they can signal the location of enemy aircraft, patrols, activity on airdromes, etc.

The most efficient and economical organization of Pursuit Aviation, it is considered, is for it to be combined with Day Bombardment and Surveillance Groups in a Combat Brigade composed of:

> The Brigade Commander and Staff;
> 2 Groups of six Pursuit Squadrons each, each with a Park and Meteorological Section;
> 1 Group of six Day Bombardment Squadrons; and
> 1 Group of two Surveillance Squadrons, with a Park, Photo Section, and Meteorological Section each.

The functions of the three types require the closest co-operation and inter-dependence. It is therefore essential that they should be grouped under one tactical command.

It is important that close liaison be constantly maintained between the Pursuit Groups and Observation Groups, and that all information of interest be interchanged between them. Observation Group Commanders should keep Pursuit Group Commanders constantly informed as to the number of observation planes they have in operation over the lines, the areas in which they are working, their altitude and the character of their missions—photographic or visual reconnaissance, artillery adjustment, liaison with infantry, etc. The Corps Air Service Commander should furthermore keep the Pursuit Group Commanders in possession of all information likely to be of value to

them, both about the enemy and about any proposed operations within the Corps.

Close liaison must be maintained between Pursuit Group Commanders and Commanders of Anti-aircraft Artillery. Anti-aircraft artillery serves as the sentinel of aviation, and the system employed by it to signal to our pursuit patrols the presence and the course of hostile aircraft, must be worked out with the greatest care and precision with the Pursuit Group Commanders.

Pursuit Group Commanders should furthermore carry out frequent liaison with troops in line and at rest, with a view to developing the mutual understanding of each other's functions and capabilities and perfecting the co-operation between them and the Air Service. In a war of movement all pursuit elements must be ready to move their airdromes, parks and all equipment at a moment's notice. At such times the liaison systems are necessarily interrupted and the closest touch by motor vehicle, radio or signaling must be kept with the necessary division, Corps and Army posts of command, and with contiguous air units.

Defensive.

The basis of an Air Service is its Observation Aviation, but the very existence of this Observation aviation depends upon a strong and well trained Pursuit Aviation, able to defend it from enemy attack, and powerful enough to assure at least a local superiority in the air in any sector selected for offensive operations. In order that our Observation aviation, carrying out photographic and visual reconnaissances, artillery adjustment, liaison with infantry, etc., may render its maximum service, it is essential that observation squadrons be enabled to accomplish their missions without interference from the enemy's aviation. This is true at all times, but especially so during periods of offensive operations.

To protect individual reconnaissance and artillery missions by individual pursuit patrols keeping continually close to the observation planes is a wasteful and inefficient method of protection, but it is sometimes necessary, especially in the case of long distance reconnaissance missions. The protection of the observation aviation is best assured by a system of defensive patrols of five airplanes each, forming a protective (lower tier) barrage. These patrols fly back and forth beyond and slightly above the line of the observation airplanes, between them and the enemy, approximately over the enemy trench line at an altitude of about 3500 meters. These defensive patrols attack any enemy aircraft that approach, but they should not attempt to penetrate far over enemy territory to seek enemy aircraft, as in so doing the successful accomplishment of their principal mission is jeopardized, the observation airplanes behind being left unprotected while the defensive patrol is away.

The duty of maintaining the Protective (lower tier) Barrage is allotted to one Group of the Pursuit Wing.

This Group is also responsible for the defense of our area against incursions by enemy long distance photographic reconnaissance planes. As such enemy planes usually cross our lines at a height of 5000 to 6000 meters and maintain this altitude throughout the course of their mission, it is rarely successful for our pursuit to start from the ground after them after they have been sighted. A method of defense against these photographic planes is for high patrols of three to five airplanes each to patrol back of our line at an altitude of 5500 to 6000 meters throughout the hours of daylight suitable for photography. The sectors covered by such patrols must be carefully selected with reference to the likely points at which enemy long distance reconnaissance planes are apt to cross our lines and the courses which they are believed to follow. The patrols must be on their beats at their altitudes as soon as or just before the light becomes sufficient for photography.

Generals Ferdinand Foch and John J. Pershing.

43. 358 Squadrons

July 1918

Two days before approving the schedule submitted by Patrick on 5 June 1918, Pershing had informed the Army Chief of Staff and the Secretary of War that the military situation was "very grave." A German offensive on the Aisne had driven back the French and seemed to be threatening Paris. The Supreme War Council was depressed. Everyone wanted more help from America. On 19 June Pershing recommended a buildup of the AEF to 3,000,000 men (66 divisions) before May 1919. After a meeting with General Foch on 23 June, Pershing endorsed a plan that would put 46 divisions in Europe by October 1918, 64 in January 1919, 80 in April 1919, and 100 in July 1919. On 23 July the War Department informed Pershing that a program for 80 divisions in France by 30 June 1919 had been recommended to the President.[1]

The job of translating the latter plan into an Air Service program fell to Gorrell, Aviation Officer, G-3, General Headquarters, AEF. Although Gorrell's plan called for only 9 additional bombardment squadrons, he was able to add 14 to the day bomber force by reducing the night bomber program by 5 squadrons. He also provided for an additional 62 squadrons of observation and 27 of pursuit, making a total of 358 squadrons for the Air Service AEF by June 1919. Following is a brief extract from the long and detailed study which Gorrell produced and which was forwarded to Patrick on 29 July 1918.[2]

ESG-G.3

EXHIBIT "A".

July 29, 1918.

1. **"Problem"**

A. Promises:—

(a) In July, 1918, the United States will have 30 Divisions in the American Expeditionary Forces in Europe.

(b) By July 1, 1919, the

1. See Cable P-1235-S, 3 June 1918, Cable P-1342-S. 19 June 1918, Cable P-1369-S, 25 June 1918, and SWC: 316: Cablegram, 23 July 1918, and related documents in Historical Division, Department of the Army, *United States Army in the World War, 1917–1919,* Vol 2 (Washington 1948), pp 449–450, 476–479, 482–483, 544, and *passim.*

2. In Gorrell's History, A-7, pp 94–101.

United States will have 80 Divisions in the American Expeditionary Forces in Europe. . . .

. . . .

B. Required to ascertain:—

(a) The size and rate of formation of tne Air Service program necessary for a balanced Army of the size indicated in paragraph 1–A. (Answer to this question is found in paragraph [and table] 5).

. . . .

. . . .

8. The above program in Table V, even with the help of our Allies, can not be met in full but should serve as a goal which the Air Service should strive to reach.

Table V.

Size and Rate of Formation Desired for the Air Service

Date	Corps Observation Sqd.	Army Observation Sqd.	Pursuit Sqd.	Day Bombardment Sqd.	Night Bombardment Sqd.	Balloon Companies
1918 July	22	12	22	8	4	52
Aug.			11	4	4	1
Sept.	3	5	11	4	4	9
Oct.	4	7	12	4	4	8
Nov.	3	5	12	4	4	7
Dec.	2	6	12	4	5	6
1919 Jan.	2	2	9	3	5	6
Feb.	2	3	9	4	5	8
Mar.	3	2	12	5	5	9
Apr.	3	3	12	5	5	10
May	3	4	12	5	5	9
June	2	3	12	5	5	8
TOTAL	49	52	147	55	55	133
GRAND TOTAL					358	133

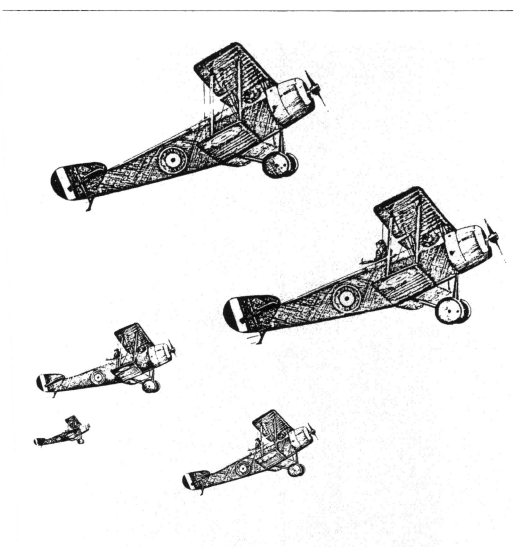

Brig. Gen. Malin Craig.

44. Liaison—A Costly Business

4 August 1918

American pilots assigned to infantry liaison found the work both dangerous and frustrating. They complained that the infantry ignored their signals, did not put out markers, and otherwise failed to cooperate. The airman's attitude is reflected in the following memorandum concerning this aspect of the employment of airpower.[1] The memorandum apparently was prepared by Maj. Lewis H. Brereton, who had succeeded Mitchell as Chief of Air Service, I Corps, or by a member of his staff, for signature by Brig. Gen. Malin Craig, Chief of Staff to Maj. Gen. Hunter Liggett, Corps Commander.

Headquarters, 1st Army Corps,
American E.F.,
August 4, 1918

Suggest Memorandum for Division Commanders:

Liaison Instructions.

1. The Chief of Air Service will be notified at the earliest possible moment of the arrival of new units in the Corps, and the date of their active operations. The Chief of Air Service will immediately have air service assigned to the unit concerned, and will notify such unit and the Corps Commander regarding dispositions made, and will cause liaison to be established and maintained immediately therewith. The attention of the unit arriving should be directed particularly to Confidential Pamphlet., No. 2, "Liaison for all Arms," dated H.A.E.F., June, 1918,[2] and Confidential Pamphlet No. 88, revised, "Aerial Observation for Artillery," dated H.A.E.F., May 1918.[3] With reference to the contents of these pamphlets, which contain the basis for all liaison and co-ordination between air service and the Corps Troops, the following should be impressed strongly upon the newly-arrived units:

(a) *Artillery:* Adjustment of fire and artillery surveillance should not be requested from aero squadrons when same can be as efficiently performed by terrestrial observation or balloons.

(b) *Infantry:* An infantry contact plane (i.e., jalennement)[4] should not be demanded from an aero squadron if desired information regarding the position of the advance units can possibly be obtained through any other source. In this connection, it is desired to point out that observation balloons can effect efficient liaison between the infantry P.C. and the advance units under ordinary circumstances.

II. When an infantry contact plane is called for, it must be realized thoroughly by the troops concerned that the infantry plane cannot remain at a low altitude over the lines for more than a very few minutes without the certainty of being shot down. It is, therefore, of the utmost importance, that watchers be designated to observe all signals from the infantry plane, and that the personnel have on hand at all times the required material to indicate the positions of the troops to the airplane, and that the signals be made immediately upon demand of the plane.

III. The cost to the Government of training a pilot and observer, coupled with the cost of an observation plane, is approximately $80,000.00. Infantry contact work is the most hazardous of all air service operations. The present state of organization of the Air Service renders replacement of planes, pilots and observers increasingly difficult. It should be realized that the expense to the Government ensuing from the loss of an observation plane properly equipped and manned, can be decreased materially by a thorough understanding on the part of the unit concerned of the necessity of having the proper material ready for instant use in indicating the location of the lines, and the utilization of such material promptly, when called upon by the observer.

Malin Craig
Chief of Staff

1. In Gorrell's History, C–12, p 35.
2. See Doc. 40.
3. See Doc. 36.
4. A marking out.

Brig. Gen. "Billy" Mitchell.

45. Command of the Air Service, First Army

6 August 1918

When the First Army was formally organized in August 1918 with Pershing as Commanding General, Mitchell was staff advisor on aeronautical matters (Chief of Air Service, First Army) and commander of the First Army's aviation units (Army Air Service Commander) (see Doc. 37). The authority to assign missions to Air Service units and the channels used in making such assignments were outlined in the following memorandum.

Headquarters, 1st Army, A. E. F.

MEMORANDUM
  Number 8

August 6th, 1918.

The following system and routine of assigning missions to the Air Service in the 1st Army is published for the information and guidance of all concerned:

MISSIONS	BY WHOM OFFERED	TO WHOM TRANSMITTED
A. *Army Observation Group:*		
1. Reconnaissance		
a. Visual	Army G–2	Group Commander through Branch Intelligence Officer
Day		
Night		
b. Photographic		
2. Command Reconnaissance	Army G–3	Army Chief of Air Service
3. Artillery Adjustment	Army Artillery Commander	Group Commander
B. *Pursuit Group:*		
1. Patrolling		
a. Offensive	Army G–3	Army Chief of Air Service
b. Defensive		
2. Protection	Air Service Commander	
C. *Bombing Group:*		
1. Tactical Bombardment	Army G–3	Army Chief of Air Service
D. *Balloon Group:*		
1. General Surveillance	Army G–3	Army Chief of Air Service
2. Artillery adjustment	Army Artillery Commander	Group Commander
E. *Corps Observation Group:*		
1. Reconnaissance		
a. Visual	Corps G–2	Group Commander through Branch Intelligence Officer
Day		
Night.		
b. Photographic		
2. Commander Reconnaissance	Corps G–3	Corps Chief of Air Service
3. Artillery Adjustment	Corps Artillery Commander	Corps Chief of Air Service
4. Liaison	Division Commander	
a. Infantry		
b. Artillery	Division Artillery Commander	Group Commander
F. *Balloon Group:*		
1. General Surveillance	Corps G–3	Corps Chief of Air Service
2. Artillery Adjustment	Corps Artillery Commander	Group Commander

Lower unit commanders should come into direct communication in arranging for the missions outlined above.

The collection, collation and dissemination of information of the enemy obtained by the Air Service is a duty of G-2 and is fully covered by the Intelligence Regulations.

By command of General Pershing

Maj. Gen. (Col. in August 1918) Fox Conner.

Believing that Gorrell's schedule for 358 squadrons could not be met (Doc. 43), Patrick prepared a different schedule,[1] printed below, for 202 squadrons by June 1919. The reduction from 358 was made by cutting pursuit and bombardment. Patrick's plan was approved, as indicated by the indorsement[2] appearing below, this being the last change in the squadron program before the Armistice.

General Headquarters
American Expeditionary
Forces Air Service.

France, 16 August, 1918.

Memorandum For: CHIEF OF STAFF G-3

Subject: Air Service Program to 30 June 1919.

1. A careful study has been made of the papers entitled "Air Service Materiel" A.E.F. Estimate of July 29, 1918, and Exhibit "A" appended thereto.

2. It was soon evident that it would be absolutely impossible to get together sufficient materiel or sufficient trained personnel to enable the Air Service to accomplish the program as laid down in Table 5 of Exhibit "A" which called for 358 Squadrons on the front by the end of June 1919, and for the same date, 133 Balloon Companies.

3. Further consideration was given to a possible program and at the last meeting of the Interallied Aviation Committee all of the Allies were asked to submit to the Committee by Monday, the 19th, August 1918, programs showing what units they expected to place at the front by end of June 1919.

4. Below is given a table in which are shown the number of Air Units we now have at the front and the number which it is

Notes

1. In Gorrell's History, A-7, p 104.

2. In Gorrell's History, p 103. The initials indicate that the indorsement was prepared or initiated by Col. Fox Conner, Assistant Chief of Staff, G-3. Having reviewed the various programs. the anonymous author of a "History of the Various Air Service Programs for the Air Service, A.E.F." (in Gorrell's History, A-7), said, "The above programs serve to illustrate two points: (a) the fact that G.H.Q., A.E.F., was at all times willing for the Air Service to expand to its maximum possible extent, and that G.H.Q. desired the largest and most efficient Air Service that could be placed on the American front; and (b) the fact that G.H.Q., A.E.F., having determined upon a policy for the Air Service did not vary in this policy but continued to allow the Air Service to expand as rapidly as possible."

	Pursuit	Obs. Corps	Obs. Army	Day Bomb	Night Bomb	Totals
Present	12	10	1	1	0	24
August	4	3	3	2		12
September	4	3	1	1		9
October	4	2	1	1		8
November	4	2	2	1	1	10
December	4	3	4	0	1	12
January	4	3	5	2	2	16
February	4	4	5	1	4	18
March	5	4	5	2	4	20
April	5	4	8	1	5	23
May	5	5	8	2	5	25
June	5	6	9	0	5	25
TOTALS	60	49	52	14	27	202

hoped may be placed at the front during each month between now and July 1, 1919. It is recommended that this be approved as the American E.F. Air Service Program for the next 11 months, including August 1918.

5. In addition to the above there are now two Pursuit Squadrons with the English which are to be released to us about the 1st. of Oct. if we so desire.

6. Also in addition to the above it is planned to place at the front by 1st. July 1919 a total of 133 Balloon Companies.

(Sgd) Mason M. Patrick
Major General, N.A.
C.A.S., A.E.F.

1st. Ind.   FC (G–3)

Chief of Staff, GHQ, AEF
France Aug. 17, 1918.
To Chief of Air Service

1. Returned. The foregoing program is approved. This program will replace all previous projects. It is desired that the Chief of Air Service prepare a cablegram informing the War Department of the new program.

(sgd) J. W. McAndrew
Major General

Maj. Gen. James W. McAndrew. (sketch by Joseph Cummings Chase)

Lt. Col. Bert M. Atkinson.

September 1918

With the successful completion of operations at St. Mihiel in mid-September 1918, the First Army, commanded by Pershing, issued battle instructions, in the form of a proposed field order, for an offensive in the area from the Meuse River to the Argonne Forest. The first objective was penetration of the Hindenburg Line for about 16 kilometers, and second being a further penetration for another 16 kilometers.

On 16 September, the Assistant Chief of Staff G-3, First Army issued instructions, written by Lt. Col. Frank P. Lahm, for employment of the Air Service in the attack. The following day, Mitchell, Chief of Air Service, First Army, submitted the Air Service plan, which became an annex to the field order that the First Army issued on 20 September. At midnight on 22 September, Pershing assumed command of allied forces that were to take part in the offensive. On 23 September, Mitchell issued a supplementary plan for the First Army Air Service, and on 25 September, Lt. Col. Bert M. Atkinson issued a plan for the 1st Pursuit Wing, which he commanded. H-hour for the attack was 0500 on 26 September.

The First Army moved three corps into the line on the front of the main assault;

I Corps was on the left, V in the middle, and III on the right. To the left of I Corps was the French Fourth Army, which was to work in coordination with the First Army. To the right of III Corps was the French XVII Corps, French II Colonial Corps, and U.S. IV Corps. For the initial operations Mitchell had under his command 54 squadrons (28 American, 23 French, and 3 Italian), with a total of 963 airplanes. In addition, his air service included 22 balloons (14 American and 8 French). The British Independent Air Force was to cooperate. Mitchell wanted the French 1st Air Division, with some 525 bombardment, pursuit, and observation aircraft, under his command, as it had been during the Battle of St. Mihiel, but the most he could get was a promise of assistance in an emergency.

Following are: A. First Army instructions for the employment of the Air Service;[1] B. Extracts from the First Army field order[2] and aviation annex;[3] C. Supplementary plan of First Army Air Service;[4] and D. Plan of 1st Pursuit Wing.[5]

A. Instructions of First Army

G-3
Headquarters First Army,
A.E.F.

September 16, 1918.

Memorandum, For: Chief of Air Service.

Subject: Employment of Aviation in Proposed Attack.

The employment of aviation in the proposed attack will be divided into four phases:

    I. Preparation.
    II. During the Artillery Preparation.
    III. During the Attack.
    IV. Exploitation.

    1. **Preparation:** Absolute secrecy must be maintained prior to the opening of the artillery preparation, consequently there will be no increase in aerial activity at this time. Sufficient patrols will be maintained to prevent the enemy's reconnaissance planes penetrating our lines; bombardment aviation will continue its normal activity (targets will be furnished from this office); reconnaissance aviation will secure the maximum information of the enemy without arousing his suspicions.

1. Historical Division, Department of the Army, *U.S. Army in the World War, 1917–1919,* Vol 9 (Washington, 1948), pp 82–88.
2. AFSHRC 248, 211–61K.
3. In Gorrell's History, N–2, pp 350–355.
4. *Ibid.,* pp 356–359.
5. *Ibid.,* C–7, pp 391–392.

2.**During The Artillery Preparation:** Pursuit aviation will attack concentrations of enemy troops, convoys, enemy aviation and balloons. Day Bombardment aviation will attack enemy concentrations, convoys, stations, command posts and dumps, in a zone between approximately 10 and 30 kilometers back of the lines. Night bombardment aviation will attack railroad centers, enemy airdromes, troop concentrations and dumps. Reconnaissance aviation will carry out its usual missions, army squadrons paying particular attention to locating the arrival of reserves.

3.**During The Attack:** The same employment as during the artillery preparation.

4.**Exploitation:** As dictated by the progress of the attack and situation at the time.

5. Four command airplanes will be held at the disposal of G–3 beginning at daylight on the day of the artillery preparation, these planes to be located as near as practicable to Army Headquarters.

6. Missions will be ordered and results reported as directed in Memo. No. 8, these headquarters, dated August 8, 1918.

7. Bombing objectives will be indicated by G–3 and detailed information concerning these objectives by G–2, 1st Army.

> R. McCleave
> Colonel, General Staff,
> A. C. of S., G–3.

FPL—P

Headquarters, Air Service, 1st Army, American Expeditionary Forces

France, September 17th, 1918. Annex No. 4, (Field Orders No. 20).

Subject: Plan of Employment of Air Service Units, 1st American Army.

I. Plan of Employment. This will consist of four stages as follows:

A. Preparation until day of attack.

B. During the Artillery preparation.

C. During the Attack.

D. Exploitation.

A. *Preparation Until Day of Attack.*

1. Surprise, being a factor in the success of operations, the utmost secrecy will be observed in movements and concentration of Air Service Units.

2. Hostile reconnaissance aviation will be prevented from entering our lines and the work of hostile balloons hindered. This will be insured by placing an absolute barrage over the front, from and including the Meuse on the east, to and including La Hazaree on the west.

3. All information necessary in the preparation of attack, especially for the Artillery preparation, will be gathered. Particular care will be taken that the suspicions of the enemy are not aroused. These missions will be accomplished by:

(a) Army Reconnaissance

Plans for the Initial
Phase of the Meuse-Argonne
Offensive

233

Col. Robert McCleave.

Aviation—Photographic and visual missions.

(b) Army Corps and Army Artillery Aviation—Photographic and visual missions, ordered by the Army Corps and Army Artillery Commanders.

(c) Night Reconnaissance Aviation—Visual reconnaissance carried out at night to obtain information of the movements and concentrations of enemy forces.

4. Bombardment Aviation, both day and night, will continue to be employed in a normal manner.

The above missions will be carried out so as to change as little as possible the usual aspect of the sector.

B. *During The Artillery Preparation.*

1. *Pursuit.*

(a) The First Pursuit Wing (4 groups) will insure an absolute barrage of the front and protect our observation aviation at every altitude from the Meuse inclusive on the east and LA HAZAREE inclusive on the west; prevent enemy aviation from attacking through the WOEVRE and will attack concentrations of enemy troops, convoys, enemy aviation and balloons.

(b) Pursuit Aviation, French Aerial Division, will be so disposed as to protect our right flank and front in case of an attack.

2. *Day Bombardment Aviation.*

Will attack concentrations of enemy troops, convoys and aviation, railroad stations, command posts and dumps.

3. *Night Bombardment Aviation.*

Will attack railroad stations and trains, troop concentrations, ammunition dumps, and enemy airdromes.

4. *Reconnaissance Aviation.*

(a) Army Reconnaissance— will carry out long distance missions, both photographic and visual.

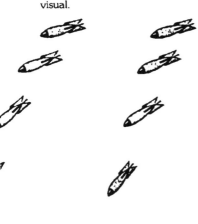

(b) Army Corps and Army Artillery—Will carry out the missions, both photographic and visual, prescribed by the Army Corps and Army Artillery Commanders, including:

The observation and results of artillery fire.

Liaison with Infantry.

Information of the enemy of benefit to the Higher Command.

(c) Night Reconnaissance— Will carry out visual reconnaissance as prescribed.

C. *During The Attack.*

The same general employment as prescribed in B. The offensive will be taken and maintained at all points and under all conditions.

D. *Exploitation.*

The offensive will be maintained, based on the progress of the attack and the situation at the time, with the particular object in view of destroying the enemy's air service, attacking his troops on the ground and protecting our own air and ground troops.

II. Four Command Airplanes will be held at the disposal of G—3, commencing at daylight on

the day of the beginning of the Artillery preparation. These planes will be located on the Souilly airdrome.

III. Appendixes.

Appendix No. 1, shows the distribution of the air forces.

Appendix No. 2, shows the plan of reconnaissance aviation.

Appendix No. 3, shows the plan of Bombardment Aviation.[6]

The plans for the utilization of Aeronautical Units with the Army Artillery and with the Army Corps conform to the general scheme and are prepared in detail by those units.

By Command of General Pershing
H. A. Drum
Chief of Staff.

Official:
*William Mitchell
Colonel, A. S., U. S. A.
Chief of Air Service, First Army.*

6. The annex has no appendix on pursuit.

Plans for the Initial
Phase of the Meuse-Argonne
Offensive

235

Col. Joseph C. Morrow.

Maj. William K. Thaw and Lt. Col. Ralph Royce.

Lt. Col. Lewis H. Brereton.

Appendix I

[The appendix is an organizational chart labeled "Air Service of the American 1st Army." Since it is not suitable for reproduction, it has been used as the basis for the following listing of units:]

First Army Air Service (Col. William Mitchell)
  1st Pursuit Wing (Maj. Bert M. Atkinson)
    2d Pursuit Group (Maj. Davenport Johnson)
      4 squadrons (13, 22, 49, 139)
    3d Pursuit Group (Maj. William K. Thaw)
      4 squadrons (28, 93, 103, 213)
    1st Day Bombardment Group (Maj. James L. Dunsworth)
      4 squadrons (11, 20, 96, 166)
    1st Pursuit Group (Maj. Harold E. Hartney)
      4 squadrons (27, 94, 95, 147)
  Army Observation Group (Maj. John N. Reynolds)
    3 squadrons (9, 24, 91)
  Army Artillery Observation Group (Capt. Bloch) (Fr.)[7]
    6 squadrons
    4 balloon companies
  Night Bombardment Wing (Commandant Villome)
    2 groups (1 French; 1 Italian)
    5 squadrons (2 French; 3 Italian)

Corps Observation Wing (Maj. Lewis H. Brereton)
  1st Corps Air Service (Maj. Melvin A. Hall)
  1st Corps Observation Group
    4 squadrons: 3 U.S. (1, 12, 50); 1 French
  Balloon Wing Co. A
    3 companies (1, 2, 5)
  3d Corps Air Service (Col. Joseph C. Morrow)
  3d Corps Observation Group
    5 squadrons: 2 U.S. (88, 90); 3 French
  Balloon Wing Co. D
    4 companies (3, 4, 9, 42)
  4th Corps Air Service (Maj. Harry B. Anderson)
  4th Corps Observation Group
    3 squadrons: 2 U.S. (8, 135); 1 French
  Balloon Wing Co. C
    3 companies (10, 16, 69)
  5th Corps Air Service (Lt. Col. Arthur R. Christie)
  5th Corps Observation Group
    4 squadrons: 2 U.S. (99, 104); 2 French
  Balloon Wing Co. B
    4 companies (6, 7, 8, 12)
  II Colonial Corps Observation Group (Fr.)
    3 squadrons
    2 balloon companies
  XVII Corps Observation Group (Fr.)
    2 squadrons
    2 balloon companies
  From Second Army Observation Group (Fr.)[8]
    3 squadrons: Pursuit, night reconnaissance, and day observation
1st Air Division (Fr.)[9]
  Day bombardment brigade
    2 bombardment wings
      7 bombardment groups
        15 bombardment squadrons
      2 protection squadrons
  Pursuit brigade
    2 wings
      6 groups
        24 squadrons

7. This group and the other French and Italian units listed here, except for the 1st Air Division, were attached to the U.S. First Army and under Mitchell's command for operations. The French organizational hierarchy was escadrille (flight)—groupe—escadre (squadron), which was comparable to the U.S. squadron—group—wing organization.

8. These units are not on the chart, but they are on the station list for the First Army Air Service for 26 September 1918.

9. Although the division appeared on the chart, it was not under Mitchell's command. See the editor's introductory note to this document.

Appendix II

September 17th, 1918.

Observation Plan—Under Battle Instructions No. 2.[10]

1. The Enemy can, in addition to reacting on the front attack, do the following:

  a. On the right bank of the Meuse he can engage reserves which he always has in the area Damvillers-Mangiennes in order to attack either on the Haute de Meuse or by debouching from the Forest of Spincourt.

  b. On the left bank of the Meuse attempt an attack as a diversion or take away reserves from this part of the front and transport them to the right bank.

  c. Bring up reserves on both sides of the river from other parts of the front.

2. In consideration of the above the following observations will be carried out:

  a. On the right bank there must be constant observation of the area north of the Forest of Spincourt.

  b. In addition, reconnaissance carried out over Montmedy—Longuyon—Spincourt—Audun-le-Roman would give notice of any arrival and unloading of reserves which might be brought from other parts of the front.

  c. On the left bank of the Meuse there must be constant observation of the area Dun—Romagne-sous-Montfaucon—Charpentry—Vilosnes in order to watch the possible movement of troops or concentration.

  d. In addition reconnaissance must be pushed along the Mouzon—Dun and Mouzon—St. Juvin railroads in order to determine if any unloading has taken place.

  e. Observation of the crossings over the Meuse are indispensable.

3. To carry out the foregoing plan the following instructions will govern:

  a. Observation Squadrons of the respective Corps will be responsible before operations for a depth of eight kilometers. Boundaries are indicated on map attached hereto.[11] During operations Corps units will not go beyond a depth of five kilometers unless they are provided with pursuit planes for protection.

  b. Enemy front lines will be photographed by Corps Machines at every opportunity. Prints of such photos will be sent to Army Dropping Ground by airplane delivery.

  c. Army Observation units will observe the area bounded on attached map by single green line, carrying out the missions indicated in paragraph #2 above.

  d. The necessary steps will be taken to secure the cooperation of the observation service of the 4th and 8th French Armies.

Approved: Willey Howell,
                          Lt. Col, G.S.
                          A.C. of S., G–2

Wm. Mitchell,
Colonel, Air Service,
Chief of Air Service.

Appendix III

September 18th, 1918.

PLAN OF BOMBARDMENT AVIATION

Four phases are to be considered.

  1. *Preparation.* Covering the period from this date until the time of artillery preparation.

  2. *During the Artillery Preparation.*

  3. *During the Attack.*

  4. *Exploitation.*

  1. *Preparation.*

Object: To hinder the arrival of enemy troops and supplies in the sector to be attacked. Destruction of enemy aviation on its airdrome and parks.

10. The proposed field order. This plan, submitted as Appendix II to Annex 4, became Annex. 9 to Field Order 20.

11. Not in Gorrell's History, N–2.

A loaded bomber awaiting takeoff.

As absolute secrecy must be observed, there will be no heavy concentration of bombing, consequently with the limited means available, the various targets indicated herewith will be bombed in turn.

2. During The Artillery Preparation.

Object: To harass the enemy by attacking his troop concentrations, convoys, stations, command posts and dumps; to hinder his movement of troops and to destroy his aviation on the ground.

Such of the following targets will be selected as are found to be the most important as shown by reconnaissance made at the time.

Preparation

OBJECTIVES	TO BE BOMBED BY	BY ORDER OF	REPORTS ON RESULTS, ETC. TO BE ADDRESSED TO
Railroad Centers:			C.G., 1st Army
Longuyon			C.S., 1st Army
Stenay			G-2
Montmedy	American	C.A.S.	G-3
Carignan	Day Bomb-	1st Army	C. of A.
Mouzon	ing		by
Vouziers	Group of		C. A. S. 1st Army
Lumes	3 Squadrons.		
Airdromes & Parks			C.G., 1st Army
Maimy	2 French	C.A.S.,	C.S., 1st Army
Mouzon	Night Bombing	1st Army	G-2,
	Groups at		G-3,
	Epiez &		C. of A.
	Chermisy		by C.A.S. 1st Army

During Artillery Preparation

Objectives	To Be Bombed By	By Order Of	Reports On Results, Etc., To Be Addressed To
Troop Concentrations, and convoys wherever found in a zone approximately 10 to 30 kilometers back of the lines.	American Day Bombing Group of 3 Squadrons	C.A.S. 1st Army	C.G., 1st Army G-2 G-3 by C.A.S., 1st Army
Dumps, Railheads, Camps & Command Posts.			
1. Brieulles S Meuse			
2. Romagne S Montfaucon			
3. Termes Grand Pre			
4. Saint Juvin			
5. Briqueney			
6. Harricourt			
7. Dun-Doulcon			
8. Saulmey			
Railroad Centers			
Stenay	2 French		
Vouziers	Night Bombing Group	C.A.S. 1st Army	
Airdromes and Park			
Mouzon			
Maimy			

3. *During The Attack*

Object: (a) To prevent the arrival of reserves.
(b) To break up counter attacks.
(c) To harass the enemy in the withdrawal of his troops & material.
(d) To destroy his aviation on the ground. Targets will be the same as those during the Artillery Preparation, selecting the ones found to be the most important as shown by visual and photographic reconnaissance made at the time. Orders for missions will be transmitted by G-3, through the C.A.S., and reports on results made as in the preceding phases.

4. *Exploitation.*
As dictated by the progress of the attack and the situation at the time.

F. P. Lahm,
Colonel, Air Service

Official:
William Mitchell.
Colonel, A.S. U.S.A.
Chief of Air Service, First Army.

Lt. Col. (later Col.) Frank P. Lahm.

B. Field Order

First Army, A.E.F.
Ligny-en-Barrois,
September 20, 1918—3 p.m.

Field Orders No. 20

. . . .
3. [Mission assignments, corps and services.]
. . . .

(K) Air Service:
(1) For plan of employment, see Annex No. 4.
(2) It will attack and defeat the hostile Air Service while screening our army front from hostile observation and attack.
(3) The army dropping ground for messages from aeroplanes will be at the Souilly aerodrome. Four command planes will be held ready to execute any mission given at the army landing field at Souilly.
(4) The Chief of Army Air Service will designate certain army balloon companies to accompany the advance. Corps commanders will designate and regulate roads for these movements.

. . . .

By command of General Pershing
H. A. Drum,
Colonel,
Chief of Staff.

C. Supplementary Plan

Headquarters, Air Service, First Army American Expeditionary Forces
France, September 23, 1918

Supplementary Plan of Employment of Air Service Units, 1st Army

1. This plan covers four phases:
(1) Preparation until day of attack.
(2) During Artillery preparation.
(3) During attack, as far as first combined army objective.
(4) Exploitation of Attack as far as second combined Army objective.
2. (1) *Preparation Until Day of Attack.*
(a) Acting vigorously over the enemy's lines between LA CHAUSSEE and the MOSELLE RIVER, on the right flank of this position and North and East of NANCY, so as to hold the enemy's attention in that direction and lead him to believe that we are to attack METZ.
(b) Stopping all hostile reconnaissance from crossing our lines and preventing observation from hostile balloons throughout the area mentioned above. In addition a Pursuit barrage to be placed between the MEUSE and the AISNE to prevent enemy reconnaissance.

(c) Gathering all information necessary for the preparation of the Attack throughout the area as far as, and including the final objectives.

(d) All missions along the new front of operations will be carried out in such a way as not to alter the usual aspect of the Sector.

3. *Special Missions For Each Branch of Aviation Under (1).*

(a) *Night Bombardment.*

Independent Royal Air Force, Night Bombardment Wing.

VILLOME, French Night Bombardment Wing.

French Squadrons of French Group of Armies of the Center.

The objectives have been pointed out in the original plan of employment covering the period of attack and are chosen so as to shut off the zone of the last operations from the present zone of attack.

(b) *Pursuit and Day Bombardment—French Air Division.*

Missions as per "a" paragraph 2, over the front between LA CHAUSSEE and CHATEAU-SALINS by means of:

1. Short distance offensive patrols across the lines, carried out by combined Bombardment and Pursuit forces.

2. Patrols covering our lines and attacking balloons. These missions should be carried out whenever any reliefs of troops are being made.

(c) *Pursuit and Day Bombardment of 1st US Army*

1st *Pursuit Wing (Atkinson).*—Barrage over front and attack of balloons between CHATILLON SOUS LES COTES—PONT SUR SEILLE. Offensive Pursuit and Day Bombardment patrols as directed in or to the East of this area.

1st *Pursuit Group (Hartney)*—Barrage patrols over the front between CHATILLON SOUS LES COTES—AISNE RIVER at MELZICOURT so as to stop hostile reconnaissance and patrols.

(d) *Army Reconnaissance Aviation.*

1. *1st Army Observation Group.* Photographic and visual reconnaissance of area included between a line from VERDUN to LONGUYON inclusive, West to the RIVER AISNE, inclusive.

2. *2nd French Army Observation Group.* Photographic and visual reconnaissance of area between a line drawn from VERDUN to LONGUYON inclusive, East to the RIVER MOSELLE inclusive.

Night Reconnaissance. 1st Army Observation Group VILLOME, Night Bombardment Group 2nd French Army Observation Group.

Visual reconnaissance to watch any movements of concentration or withdrawal of the enemy throughout the areas assigned to each aviation unit.

NOTICE: These missions have been allotted by G–2, 1st Army, in the plan of reconnaissance.

(e) *Army Artillery and Army Corps Aviation.* Visual and photographic reconnaissance— Spotting Artillery objectives and adjustments.

4. *(2) and (3) During Artillery Preparation and During Attack of First Combined Objective.*

(a) Destruction of the hostile air service at all altitudes, attack of his ground troops, and protecting our own air and ground forces.

(b) The benefit of surprise and the quick progression of the attack will give us an advantage, our Aviation therefore will be able to act very boldly. This will enable our Pursuit Aviation to fight ground troops with machine guns and bombs.

Special Missions of Each Class of Aviation.

(a) *Night Bombardment.* (During the night before D day, and during the night following D day).

Independent R.A.F.—Will attack the railway stations of METZ, SABLONS, THIONVILLE, AUDUN LE ROMAN, and the most important aviation grounds in that region. (Same general mission for Day Bombardment on D day).

Villome night Bombardment Wing—Will attack the railway stations of CONFLANS, LONGUYON, MONTMEDY, and all large gatherings of troops noticed.

(b) *Aerial Division.* Its mission will be to cover the front, up to a depth of 10 kilometers in the enemy lines, destroy enemy aircraft and balloons.

It will develop its greatest offensive power with bombs and machine guns against all enemy reserves, reinforcements and convoys, whether they are marching to the attack or retreating so as to throw them into confusion, cause a block in the road traffic and block cross roads throughout the enemy back area.

The central line of action will be on the plateau along the general axis Montfaucon—Nantillois—Romagne—Bayonville—Buzancy.

(c) *Pursuit and Day Bombardment Aviation of First Army.*

1st Pursuit Wing (Atkinson)— Barrage at medium and high altitude up to 5 kilometers on our whole front.

Enemy ground troops will be attacked by Pursuit Units with machine guns and bombs whenever ordered.

1st Day Bombardment Group, (Dunsworth)—Will attack enemy concentrations along the valley of the MEUSE—ROMAGNE—ST. JUVIN— and GRANDPRE.

1st Pursuit Group (Hartney)—Will specialize against enemy low flying airplanes, protect our infantry liaison and observation planes and attack hostile balloons on the front *Chatillon Sous Les Cotes—Melzicourt.*

(d) *Army Reconnaissance Work.*

The *1st Army Observation Group (Reynolds)*—Will cover the sector to the West of a line drawn from Verdun to Longuyon inclusive with both day and night reconnaissance.

The *2nd French Army Observation Group (De Vergnette)*—Will cover the sector east of a line drawn from *Verdun* to *Longuyon,* inclusive, with both day and night Army Reconnaissance.

The missions specified in the plan of reconnaissance will be carried out.

Four command airplanes will be located at *Souilly* ready to take off at any moment to verify or obtain precise details concerning any important piece of information that may be required by the Army Commander.

(e) *Army Artillery Aviation and Army Corps Aviation.* Their employment will be governed by the plans of employment of the Army Artillery or of the Army Corps.

These airplanes will have to protect themselves to some extent from hostile machines which have broken through our Pursuit Aviation.

Army Artillery and Army Corps airplanes should avail themselves of every favorable opportunity to attack enemy troops on the ground, when it does not interfere with their general mission.

5. *(4) Exploitation of Attack on Second Combined Army Objective (Second Operation)*

1. *General Aims.* Theoretically the same as during the preceding period. The missions will be specified according to the situation after the first attack.

2. *Special Missions of Each Branch of Aviation.*

(a) *Pursuit and Bombardment Aviation of The First Army.* Same missions as during preceding period.

(b) *French Aerial Division.* Same missions. Two principal axis along which its action will be ordered according to the situation.

    Buzancy—Stonne
    Bridges Over the
    Meuse.

(c) Night Bombardment. *Independent Force R.A.F.*—

Commandant Villome. French Air Force. (Courtesy *Attache de l'Air*, French Embassy)

Same list of objectives. *VIL-LOME Night Bombardment Wing.* —Different objectives throughout the battlefield, rail heads and bridges over the MEUSE as far as and including LUMES.

(d) Army Reconnaissance. Reconnaissance of lines where the enemy is organizing fresh centers of resistance, supply and direction of movement of reinforcement or withdrawal. (Details of these missions should be specified by G–2).

(e) Army Corps and Army Artillery Aviation. Same missions. Greater importance will be given to the Infantry Liaison work:—the airplanes should bring in direct information to the Infantry (to the Divisions, regiments and even battalions on the first line)—a greater share, too, should be given to the attack on land, (rear-guards, nests of resistance, reinforcements or reserves).

6. *Provision For A Movement Forward.*

Army Artillery and Army Corps Aviation.

Advanced airdromes for the Army Corps and Army Artillery Aviation will be selected near the post of Command of the larger units, which will be equipped for use at the earliest practicable moment in order to facilitate the liaisons. If the attack progresses normally, the advanced airdromes will become the permanent ground of the sector.

When the movement forward is sufficiently important, new advanced ground will again be selected and prepared in a similar manner.

The Equipment Section will make arrangements accordingly.

Pursuit and Bombardment Aviation.

These units will move nearer to the front as soon as terrains are freed by the Army Corps and Army Artillery.

In Special cases, these units may utilize advanced airdromes, auxiliary airdromes or the airdromes of the Army Corps and Army Artillery.

William Mitchell,
Colonel, A.S., U. S. A.
Chief of Air Service

D. Pursuit Wing Plan

Headquarters, First Pursuit Wing, Air Service, American E. F.
        September 25th, 1918.

PLAN OF EMPLOYMENT OF PURSUIT, AND DAY BOMBARDMENT UNITS FIRST PURSUIT WING

1. The operations will cover 4 phases:

   I.   Preparation until day of attack.
   II. During artillery preparation.
   III. During attack, as far as first combined army objective.
   IV. Exploitation of attack as far as second combined army objective.

While the areas and objectives will be altered from time to time the plan of employment of pursuit aviation in the last three stages of the attack will follow the same general principles.

2. (A) *Preparation until day of attack:* In order that secrecy may be obtained no airplanes from this wing will operate west of Chatillon-sous-les-Cotes until after H hour.

(B) The normal activity of the sector between Chatillon and Port-sur-Seille will be maintained and the Groups will operate over the sector of the last operations.

3. *Pursuit Aviation after H hour:*

(A) Pursuit aviation at the disposal of the First Pursuit Wing comprises the 2nd and 3rd Pursuit Groups. The sector of the 1st Pursuit Wing is from Port-sur-Seille on the east to La Harazee on the west. The sector of attack is from the Meuse River on the east to La Harazee on the west.

(B) In order to maintain a proper superiority over the enemy air service it will be necessary for our air service, not only to maintain protective patrols within the enemy's lines for the defense of our Army Corps Air Service and to attack enemy reconnaissance planes, but it will also be necessary from time to time to take the offensive with a display of dominating force sending out powerful expeditions so as to cover intermediate and high altitudes and to sweep the air clear of enemy aviation up to a depth, 10 or 12 kilometers inside his lines.

(C) One Group will protect the front, daily, from dawn to 12 h 30 and the other from 12 h 30 'till dark. In the protection of the front, patrols of one Flight will operate over the sector, Chatillon-sous-les-Cotes, Port-sur-Seille; Patrols of 2 Flights will be maintained throughout the period assigned over the sector Chatillon-sous-les-Cotes—La Harazee.

In view of the fact that it is believed that most of the enemy aviation is concentrated in the region of Metz, especial attention will be paid to the sector between the Meuse and Chatillon.

(D) *Special Missions of Pursuit Aviation:*

By requiring one Group to do its barrage work in the morning its squadrons will be available for an offensive operation in the afternoon, and vice-versa. The Group assigned to patrol in the afternoon will be on the alert in the morning to carry out an offensive mission, in which the entire Group may be called upon to participate at medium and high altitudes, penetrating about 12 kilometers beyond our advancing lines to clean the air of enemy aviation. A similar expedition may be sent out in the afternoon from the Group that has done the patrolling in the morning. The hours at which these offensive missions are carried out will be constantly various and an effort will be made to order offensive missions at hours when intelligence received from the Anti-Aircraft Artillery indicated maximum enemy activity. The strength and frequency of attacks on ground objectives will depend upon the strength of enemy aerial activity encountered.

In special circumstances pursuit reconnaissances will be ordered. While it is not anticipated that such missions will be ordered, Group Commanders will see that their pilots are familiar with infantry ground panels.

Close protection for Corps Observation photographic missions, when it is required, will be provided by the squadron assigned to barrage patrol. The Corps Observation Wing will be informed of the hours at which the different Groups will be responsible for the barrage patrol the night before. When Observation Squadrons cannot provide their own protection they will notify the Corps Observation Wing Commander who is authorized to adjust this protection directly with the Group that is responsible, at the hour in question, for the barrage patrol. The Group Operations Officer will inform the patrol leader of the squadron going out on barrage patrol that its mission has been altered from that of barrage patrol to one of close protection and the patrol leader in question will get into immediate telephonic liaison with the pilot who is responsible for the photographic mission.

4. *Day Bombardment Aviation* In the First Pursuit Wing comprises the First Day Bombardment Group. In principle this Group will be used to attack from high altitudes, large objectives such as towns and railroad stations from which traffic is radiating.

In the first stages of attack it will operate against enemy concentrations along the valley of the Meuse, Romagno, St. Juvin, Grandpre.

Special Missions of Bombardment: In emergencies when intelligence is received that specially favorable targets are presenting themselves within 6 or 8 kilometers of our front lines this Group will be ordered to attack such targets at low altitude in order to cause confusion and material damage to enemy elements arriving as reinforcements or retreating.

By order of Lieutenant Colonel Atkinson

Philip J. Roosevelt,
Captain, Air Service, U. S. A.
Operations Officer.

Col. Milling, Gen. Mitchell, and Maj. Paul Armengaud,
liaison of the French Air Service and adviser to Billy Mitchell's
Air Headquarters.

September-November 1918

Battle orders issued daily by Col. William Mitchell, Chief of Air Service, First Army, and by his successor, Col. Thomas DeW. Milling, from the beginning of the Meuse-Argonne Campaign until the Armistice, generally consisted of five major parts. These (1) described the situation at the front; (2) indicated the actions to be undertaken by the First Army on the following day; (3) provided a general statement of the Air Service mission; (4) made detailed operational assignments to the various elements of the Air Service; and (5) supplied additional instructions, information, or comment. The general mission statements for the Air Service reveal a shifting of emphasis from time to time, even from day to day, as the battle progressed. Following are extracts from some of those battle orders.[1]

Headquarters Air Service, First Army American Expeditionary Forces

France, September 25, 1918.

Battle Orders No. 7.

1. The enemy continues on the defensive at all points along the front. . . .

2. The 1st Army attacks between the MEUSE AND THE AISNE RIVERS at 5–30 H September 26th. . . .

3. *Our air service will take the offensive at all points at daylight September 26, 1918, with the object of destroying the enemy's air service, attacking his troops on the ground and protecting our own air and ground troops.*

. . . .

France, September 29, 1918.

Battle Orders No. 11.

1. The offensive of the Allied Armies continues with success. . . .

2. The 1st Army continues the attack, as do the French, British and Belgian Armies. . . .

3. *Our air service will maintain the offensive at all points, and will assist the infantry and artillery in their advance in all ways.*

. . . .

France, September 30, 1918.

Battle Orders No. 12.

1. The offensive of the Allied Armies continues with success. . . .

2. The 1st Army will remain in place on October 1st, continuing its preparations for further advance.

3. *Our air service will maintain the offensive at all points and will thoroughly cover our position from hostile air attack or reconnaissance.*

. . . .

France, October 3, 1918.

Battle Orders No. 14.

1. The offensive of the Allied Armies continues with success. . . . Our air service continues to dominate the enemy's aviation.

2. The 1st Army attacks on the front west of the RIVER MEUSE on October 4th at 5.25 H. . . .

3. *The air service will concentrate its efforts on the battlefield and will take the offensive at all points at daylight October 4th, 1918, with the object of destroying the enemy's air service, attacking his ground troops, and protecting our own air and ground troops.*

. . . .

---

1. In Gorrell's History, N–2, pp 1–96 passim.

France, October 4, 1918.

Battle Order No. 15.

1. Our Army has made substantial gains all along the line against a stubborn resistance. The Allied Armies continue to advance. The German Air Service confronting ours, after vainly attempting all day to gain control over our Air Service, was defeated everywhere.

2. Our Army continues to attack with vigor.

3. *The air service will put forward great efforts to assist the troops on the ground by close operation with them. The same orders remain in effect for October 5th.*

4. The work of all branches of the Air Service, both French and American. has been extremely severe, not only on account of the presence of the enemy in great numbers, but on account of the weather and poor visibility. In spite of these difficulties, the Air Service have [sic] shown a dash and readiness to meet every call made upon them, in a way to excite admiration from all who have witnessed the work.

. . . .

France, October 7th, 1918.

Battle Orders No. 17.

1. The offensive of the Allied armies is being maintained. The front of the 1st Army had advanced in the ARGONNE FOREST. Our Air service continues to dominate the German aviation, notwithstanding the fact that it has been largely reinforced. . . .

2. The 1st Army will seize the heights east of the MEUSE RIVER, which are occupied by about three German divisions. . . .

3. *The air service will take the offensive at all points over the front of the attack and will maintain a protective barrage west of the Meuse River to the Argonne Forest. The enemy's air service will be destroyed, his ground will be attacked, and our own air and ground troops will be protected.*

. . . .

France, October 10, 1918.

Battle Orders No. 20.

1. The Allied Armies are advancing everywhere. The enemy in front of the 1st Army has thrown his divisions into the line by regiments, in his attempts to stop our advance. . . .

2. The first Army continues its attack on October 11th. . . .

3. *The air service will support the attack and will prevent the enemy from organizing along the heights of the Bois de Barricourt. The offensive will be taken at all*

points on the Front between the Meuse River and Grandpre inclusive.

. . . .

France, October 11, 1918.

Battle Orders No. 21.

1. The offensive of the Allied Armies continues with success. . . .

2. The 1st Army continues its attack on October 12th. . . .

Our air service will maintain the offensive at all points. will support the attack from the Meuse River to Beaumont, and will thoroughly protect our positions from hostile air attack and reconnaissance.

. . . .

France, October 13, 1918.

Battle Orders No. 23.

1. The Allied Armies to our left are continuing their advance and the enemy is giving way before them. . . .

2. The 1st Army continues its attack on October 14th. . . .

. . . .

3. *The air service will concentrate its efforts on the battle field and will take the offensive at all points at daylight October 14th, 1918, with the object of destroying the enemy's air service. harassing and attacking his ground troops, and protecting our own air and ground troops.*

. . . .

France, October 18, 1918.

Battle Orders No. 28.

1. The enemy continues to fall back. . . . The 1st Army has captured 20,000 prisoners since the commencement of Operations on September 26th. . . . The German Air service opposing us, in vain, has attempted all day to gain control of the air by employing patrols of 25 to 50 machines, but has been defeated at every point.

2. The 1st Army will continue to improve its position for further attack by local operations on October 19th. . . .

3. *Our air service will maintain the offensive at all points, will protect our position from hostile air attack and reconnaissance, and will support our ground troops in their local operations.*

. . . .

France, October 20, 1918.

Battle Orders No. 30.

1. No change in enemy situation on our front. . . .

2. The 1st Army will continue to improve its position by local operations, maintaining contact with the enemy and developing his line of resistance.

3. The orders for tomorrow remain the same for all branches of the Air Service as prescribed in Battle Orders No. 28, *Special effort will be made to give information concerning the location of hostile artillery units.*

. . . .

France, November 3, 1918.

Battle Order No. 44.

1. The Allied Armies have forced the enemy into a precipitate retreat. . . . The aviation of the enemy has been destroyed or driven back wherever found, his balloons have been burned, and our airplanes continually harry and demoralize his ground troops with bombs and machine guns. . . .

2. The First American Army will take up the pursuit of the enemy west of the MEUSE and will make preparations to extend it to the east bank of the MEUSE. . . .

. . . .

3. *The air service will concentrate its efforts on the battle field, taking the offensive at all points at daylight November 4th, 1918. It will seize every opportunity to assist our troops, our corps air services will be protected, the enemy air service destroyed, and his ground troops attacked.*

. . . .

France, November 5, 1918.

Battle Orders No. 46.

1. The enemy continues to retreat with his infantry in confusion. His artillery is gradually increasing its fire. The Air Service of the enemy wherever encountered has been destroyed or forced to withdraw by our own aviation. . . .

. . . .

3. *The air service will take the offensive at all points on the morning of November 6th. The enemy air service will be destroyed and our own air and ground troops will be protected. Every opportunity will be seized to harass hostile ground troops with bombs and machine gun fire.*

. . . .

France, November 11, 1918.

Battle Orders No. 52.

1. (a) Yesterday the enemy threw into the line opposite our Third Corps his last available division on the western front.

(b) An armistice with Germany has been signed and all hostilities ceased at 11:00 H November 11th.

(c) The Allied Armies hold themselves in readiness for further advance.

. . . .

3. The Air Service will hold itself in readiness to resume operations at a moment's notice. No planes will cross the lines.

. . . .

6. Attention of all units is directed to training memoranda attached.

Aerial view of Conflans, 16 September 1918, one of the
main bomb targets of the U.S. Air Service in World War I.

49. Objectives of Day Bombardment

November 1918

The interdiction and close-support functions of day bombardment units of the AEF at the end of the war are seen in the following extract from the history that the 2d Day Bombardment Group submitted in December 1918.[1] The group, which was not organized until the beginning of November 1918, was part of the Second Army, of which Col. Frank P. Lahm was Army Air Service Commander.

Air Service—Second Army, American Expeditionary Forces, Headquarters 2nd Day Bombardment Group.

Outline of Operations

Tactical:—

I. *Aims of Bombardment Group.*
    1. Direct.
        (a) Cutting of communications lines; by bombing railroad centers, thus destroying yards, warehouses, supplies, munitions, trains, and demoralizing transportation personnel; by bombing main roads.
        (b) Destruction of enemy works; by bombing ammunition dumps, concentration camps, airdromes, supply depots, military factories, and military defenses.
        (c) Smothering of enemy attacks; by bombing concentration of troops in reserve areas or in the zone of attack, or by bombing reinforcing troops on the march.
        (d) Demoralizing an enemy retreat; by bombing retreating troops, by cutting communications, or by bombing newly established line of defense.
    2. Indirect.
        (a) Demoralize troops and lower their fighting morale.
        (b) By engaging hostile pursuit, draw them away from the zone of attack.

II. *Choice of Objectives.*
    1. Area; as in most cases this group operated with its army, 2nd American Army, its sector covering the sector of the 2nd Army and extending about 40 kilometers back of the front lines.
    2. Nature of objectives; railroad centers, airdromes, and munition dumps constituted the original objectives. These were to be bombed continually until specific and individual objectives were to be assigned in case of an attack.
    3. Choice of objectives for each mission; unless specific orders were received from A.A.S.C. this group would select the target for each mission, depending upon the following elements:
        a. Importance of the target.
        b. Number of planes available for mission.
        c. Availability of protective pursuit planes.
        d. Presence and aggressiveness of enemy planes.
        e. Weather.
    For example, if Conflans showed unusual activity, and the enemy planes were numerous and sufficient bombing and pursuit planes were available the time of bombing would depend upon the weather.

. . . .

1. In Gorrell's History, C–8, p 176.

Breguets in formation.

50. Area vs Precision Bombing

November 1918

Aerial bombardment became possible with the development of aircraft capable of getting over a target with a bomb. Then came the problem of putting the bomb on the target. The history of the Bomb Unit, Aircraft Armament Section, Ordnance Department, AEF, the organization responsible for providing bomb sights for the Air Service, stated alternatives available then, as later, to persons attempting to solve the problem.[1]

. . . .

1. Bombing from airplanes may in general be divided into two types, precision bombing and area bombing. In the first case a definite target is picked out upon which the majority of the bombs are to drop. In the latter the frank admission is made that accuracy is limited and a given area is covered in the hope that enough bombs will strike the target proper to accomplish the mission.

2. The French and British have both tended toward the latter general scheme of bombing, and the system of "sowing" bombs or releasing them in series or trail is the outgrowth of that tendency. The advantage of that system lies in the fact that the sights used in this work . . . are mounted outboard, obviating any necessity of the observer getting down inside the fuselage to sight, and therefore leaving him always ready at his guns, and offering him better protection. The disadvantage lies in the fact that admitting inaccuracy is apt to lead to carelessness in the use of sights; or their being practically ignored.

3. Bombing in general is done in formation, the leading plane of the squadron alone using a sight; and the other planes releasing their bombs when they are at what they judge to be the same point. The sighting observer is in that case protected by the other planes in the formation. His business is to sight, and his attention is not attracted elsewhere. For these reasons the general policy of the United States has been toward precision bombing; and the belief that the American Aviators would faithfully use their sights has been confirmed.

. . . .

1. In Gorrell's History, I–2, p 77.

Col. Charles DeF. Chandler.

51. Observation Balloons

November 1918

The work of the balloon observers was detailed in the following instructions which were issued by Col. Charles DeF. Chandler, Chief of the Balloon Section, AEF,[1] and republished in a bulletin of the Air Service, AEF.[2]

Instructions For Balloon Observers

Assignment of Balloons

1. When sufficient balloon companies are available they are normally assigned one to each Division, one to the artillery of each Army Corps, and others distributed to serve Army Artillery. The duties of the observer, therefore, vary somewhat, depending upon the assignment of his balloon.

2. For all balloons the observer is expected to regulate Artillery fire and conduct general surveillance of the enemy terrain within view. In addition to this, the balloons assigned to Divisions have Infantry liaison which consists in the use of preconcerted visual signals between the balloon and infantry, reporting these by telephone to the proper P.C.

3. In addition to the duties in the basket as indicated in the preceding paragraph, the observer takes his turn (usually by roster) for ground assignments such as officer in charge of chartroom and personal liaison with Division Headquarters or Artillery Brigade Headquarters.

4. When there is little movement of troops, giving time for the construction of sufficient telephone lines, the personal liaison to Artillery and Infantry Headquarters is not required to the same extent as during warfare of movement when very few telephone lines are possible; then a balloon officer assigned to Division Artillery Headquarters is expected to inform the balloon by courier, if no other means is possible, of the information desired by Division Headquarters and upon securing the information he should give personal attention that it is, without delay, made available to the officers who call for it. Likewise, the personal liaison with Artillery is expected to constantly inform the balloon of the location of batteries in their vicinity and arrange for temporary telephone of some kind from the nearest battery to the balloon position for location of fire.

General Surveillance

5. General surveillance consists in reporting all matters of military interest within view of the observer in the basket. Even while adjusting fire for Artillery the observer is expected to continue reporting events which come to his attention.

6. The military information most desired consists of the following:

Fugitive targets (troop and transport movements)
Position of enemy batteries (usually located by flashes)
Train movements, giving position of train and direction
The beginning of barrage fire, reporting its extent and changes

1. *Balloon Notes*, No. 66, 27 Nov 18.
2. *Air Service Bulletin*, Vol VII, No. 317, 7 Dec 1918. In the *Bulletin* the title was changed to "Observation."

Road transport and troop movements

Hostile balloons and airplanes

All airplanes brought down, both enemy and friendly

Fires, lights, smoke and explosions

Entrenchments or emplacements and any changes in these

Bridges of all kinds across streams and canals, particularly the construction or destruction of temporary bridges.

7. All of the general military information phoned from the basket is recorded in the chartroom log from which place it is telephoned to the various P. C.'s. according to the nature of the information. These miscellaneous reports are classified under a few general headings for the daily reports.

8. The reports of train movements are particularly important for the reason that increased railway activity is an indication that the enemy is either augmenting or reducing the movement of troops.

9. An enemy intending advance or retreat movements, usually constructs additional bridges over streams and canals. These are frequently visible from balloons and it is most important that any change in bridges, be promptly reported.

10. The observer should always be careful not to include his own deductions in reports. He should simply give facts

briefly and in case of doubt as to what he sees the report should carefully state that the information is not certain; if the information is of sufficient importance the Intelligence officers will secure confirmation from other sources such as ground observation posts and airplanes.

11. All reports from the observer should answer the four questions of WHAT (definition of what was seen), WHEN (day and hour), WHERE (indicating the place), HOW (troops in march or at a halt, Artillery active or silent, etc.).

12. General surveillance by Army balloons is ordered by Army G–3 and the information of this nature when secured is transmitted by the balloon to the Army Air Service Commander.

13. Balloons forming a part of the Army Corps Group receive instructions concerning general surveillance from Corps G–3 and transmit the information secured to the Corps Air Service Commander (Memo No. 8, Hqs. 1st Army, A.E.F. Aug. 6, 1918).

Infantry

14. The observer can easily see Infantry in column and should be able to calculate its strength from the length of the column or time required while marching to pass a given point. . . .

15. If the infantry marches not in column of four's but by two's the corresponding change in the figures should be allowed. It will be easy to determine the num-

ber of companies, battalions, etc. by the intervals between units, but note that toward the end of a long march these intervals diminish and may even disappear by reason of the lengthening inevitable in every column. The tail of every unit from the battalion up will generally be indicated by the presence of wagons, which form its combat train. If it is impossible to give with reasonable accuracy the strength of marching organizations it will be satisfactory to report "An Infantry column of such a length and having such a time of defilement is passing along the road between A to B toward B."

16. When Infantry is in line or in mass, not in motion, the estimate of the strength is much more difficult than for marching columns and it becomes a matter of experience with the observer. It should be remembered, however, that a large unit does not move over a considerable distance in other formation than in column and if it deploys, it is for the purpose of going into action and then the information of most interest would be the front along which the deployment has been made, together with a number of the lines and the density of each line.

Artillery

17. Batteries in position are located best by the flashes either early in the morning or twilight in the evening. Particular effort should be made to determine the number of guns in each battery position.

18. It has been reported that dummy battery positions within view of the balloon are occasionally made more realistic by flashing a little powder in front of them. The nature of this flash and difference in the smoke should not deceive an experienced observer.

. . . .

20. There is a serious difficulty in accurately estimating moving Artillery for the reason that frequently Infantry marches with it for defence in case of enemy attacks. At considerable distance the wagons of the Infantry transport may be confused with Artillery guns mounted.

21. During preparation for an offensive, practically all Artillery and much of the Infantry movements are made at night and without lights which would otherwise be an indication to the balloon observer, but during open warfare involving advances and retreats, there will be plenty of Artillery moving in daytime.

Cavalry

22. During the present war comparatively little cavalry has appeared in formation within view of the balloons but the table for estimating the strength is given herewith. . . .[3]

Transport

23. Motor trucks are used extensively for movements of troops and supplies. These should easily be distinguished from horse-drawn vehicles or Artillery guns by the more rapid rate of movement along the roads.

24. The railway transport of rations, forage and ammunition requires many trains of cars each day, often amounting to 25 freight cars per day for each Division when considerable ammunition is being used. Continuous balloon observation will soon determine the amount of the normal railway activity for daily replacements so that any increase in the number of trains is a reliable indication that the enemy contemplates increased activity and troop movements.

25. On French railways to move a complete Division requires approximately 35 trains and an Army Corps of two Divisions from 100 to 200 trains, considering each train as transporting one infantry battalion, one battery or a squadron of cavalry.

26. For motor truck transportation, it is assumed that each truck carries from ten to fifteen men, there being approximately fifteen to eighteen trucks per company.

Night Observation

27. Information desired and obtainable by night ascensions embraces the following:

To report the beginning of enemy attacks.

To determine the limits of the front which is attacked.

To observe and report the signals of Infantry during barrage fire.

To observe and report marker signals from front lines for enemy bombing planes.

. . . .

Infantry Liaison

29. During position warfare which may be considered as including the so-called trench warfare, all infantry positions up to the most advanced outposts are usually connected by a telephone system so complete that visual signals to and from the balloons are ordinarily not necessary. Open warfare of movement gives little time for providing telephone circuits to advanced infantry so that the development of visual communication via balloon observers becomes important. Division headquarters should know at all times

3. Table omitted.

where the advanced infantry line is located and its changes.

30. Infantry liaison consists of:

Following the progress of assaulting troops and reserves.

Observing the signals from the line of the command posts and transmitting them to the General commanding the division.

Informing the command of everything going on in the vicinity of the firing line and beyond it.

Signalling out, if prearranged, to the advanced elements conventional signals as provided in the plan of liaison.

Means of Communication For Liaison

31. From the balloon to the command—The balloon is directly connected by telephone with the divisional command post and with the army control system.

It is, besides, provided with a radio apparatus enabling it to transmit its observations in case telephone communication should be broken.

From the balloon to the firing line and to the advance command posts. —*The balloon can communicate with the advance elements:*—

In daytime by means of a cylinder which folds and unfolds at will, thus making signals corresponding to dots and dashes. These transmissions are limited to the two signals, "Understood" or "Repeat", preceded by the call of that particular post which the balloon addresses.

At night by means of luminous signals, enabling it to send more complete messages.

From the firing line and the advance command posts to the balloon:—

In the daytime by means of position-marking panels. All men carrying panels, alternately open and shut their apparatus, taking care to set it facing the balloon.

By means of Bengal flares of a determined color. These signals constitute the surest way of indicating one's position. They must be concealed as much as possible from hostile view, by hiding them behind a screen, at the bottom or on the front side of a shell crater.

By 24 cm. projectors.

At night by Bengal flares or other luminous signals or projectors. At night the balloon indicates its presence and position by lighting luminous signals at regular intervals. The signalers of the different command posts take note of the direction of the balloon, orient their projector toward it and send their particular station call to the balloon. The balloon takes these messages from right to left successively and in turn immediately transmits them to the post of command by telephone or radio.

Grenade Fighting

32. Hand grenade fighting is more readily seen by the observer than other methods of Infantry fighting; the advanced infantry line has been determined by balloon observers more often by that method than by any other.

33. Army balloons receive instructions concerning Artillery adjustments from the Army Artillery commander, communicating results to their balloon group commander.

34. Army Corps balloons receive instructions concerning Artillery adjustments from the Corps Artillery Commander and transmit data to the Balloon Group Commander (Memo No. 8 Hqs. 1st Army, A. E. F., Aug. 6, 1918).

35. To insure efficient cooperation with Artillery for the regulation of fire, balloon officers should meet with the Artillery officers each evening for the purpose of securing detailed information concerning the batteries which will fire the following day and the targets which they will engage. It is a general rule that the evening conference should arrange to divide the observation so that balloons will observe fire for all targets which can be seen from balloons. All other targets will have the fire regulated by the airplanes of an observation squadron. When personal liaison of this kind is impossible the information from the Artillery should be obtained by telephone.

36. The balloon observers should know in advance the following:

Coordinates of targets.
Batteries which will fire.
Caliber and number of pieces to fire.
Nature of fire (salvo or one piece at a time).
Type of projectiles with time of flight and type of fuse.
Interval between shots.

37. After securing information concerning the targets the observer should then procure the firing maps and photographs covering the target area.

38. Adjustments are reported on the line battery-target. Distances are reported in meters to the "right" "left" "over" and "short" stating first the deflection followed by the range, thus "25 right" "50 over".

39. Figures are given by their digits, i.e. "two five right" "five zero over".

40. The telephone communication between balloon and battery should conform to the following example:

Battery: "Battery ready to fire."
Observer: "Ready to observe."
Battery: "No. 1 on the way, etc."
"No. 2 on the way, etc."
Observer: "No. 1 two five right, etc."

41. Shots should be reported "lost" if not seen but reported as "not in position to observe" when the movement of the bas-ket a passing cloud, or other

obstacle prevents a proper view of the target. When a salvo is reported "lost" by an observer the Artillery fires the next salvo with data intermediate between that and the last salvo seen and the one lost but if the report is "not in a position to observe" the salvo is repeated with the same data.

42. In order to observe successfully for several batteries simultaneously it is necessary to have very efficient fire and telephone discipline also knowing accurately the batteries which are to fire.

Registration Points

43. All batteries need registration points for determining the error of the day thereby taking gunlaying corrections to account for changed atmospheric conditions. Balloon officers should frequently advise the batteries they serve of various clearly defined places in enemy lines which are easily visible from the balloon these being indicated on their artillery firing maps. If this is not done the battery commanders might select from their maps registration points not clearly visible from the balloon.

Army Artillery

44. If sufficient balloons are available the fire of special high power artillery can be more accurately reported by using two balloons so placed that one observes for deflection and the other for range.

Methods of Fire Affecting Balloon Observation

45. The balloon observer having continuous telephone communication with the battery firing, no system of signals is necessary such as must be employed for observation by airplane. It is therefore the fact, as a direct result, that the battery commander is not restricted in the conduct of his fire as he must necessarily be with observation by means of airplanes.

46. In the adjustment of artillery fire the balloon observer should therefore remember that his function is to OBSERVE the fall of the projectiles from the battery or batteries with which he is working. He should not attempt to prescribe to the battery commander, the methods of

fire of the battery nor the manner in which this fire is to be conducted. However, in order that the most efficient co-operation may be secured between the balloon and the battery, the battery commander should inform the balloon observer as to what methods are to be employed in making the adjustment. This is for the reason that, with observation by balloon, the method of fire adjustment will depend largely upon the ability of the observer to accurately determine the positions of the points of fall of the projectiles.

47. In general there are two methods of making this adjustment. If the observer can determine exactly the positions of the points of fall and can transpose these positions to the firing map or photographic map, the battery commander can then easily determine the distance of each point of fall from the target. The balloon observer may himself make this determination, simply informing the battery commander that such and such shot fell so many meters right (or left) and so many meters over (or short). The battery commander will then make the necessary corrections for each shot until he considers the fire adjusted.

48. In case communication between the observer and the battery is not entirely continuous it may be impractical to send the range and deflection errors after each shot. The balloon observer should then request the battery commander to fire a series of shots (6 or 8, for example). The observer observes the bursts of all shots of this series before making any report. After the last shot he calculates the center of impact of the series, with relation to an origin and system of coordinates known to the battery commander. He then informs the latter of the co-ordinates of this center of impact. The battery commander will then make the corrections necessary to bring the center of impact upon the target.

49. Through various causes, however, it is often found that the observer is unable to do more than determine the approximate errors in deflection and only the general "sense" of the shots in range (i.e., whether the shot fell short of, or beyond the target). In this case the battery commander should adopt a different method of adjusting his fire. With the elements of fire properly calculated, the deflection dispersion of any number of shots, will be slight and the battery commander will as a rule correct the deflection as a whole, basing his correction upon the total number of shots employed to adjust his fire. In case the deflection is less than four "probable errors" it will usually

not be necessary for the battery commander to make any deflection corrections.

50. The range adjustment in this case is, however more complicated and requires a preliminary fire known as Trial Fire, the object of which is to place the zone of dispersion in an area which contains the target. In observing for Trial Fire, the balloon observer simply reports, after each shot, whether the shot fell short of, or over, the target. The battery commander makes the range corrections necessary, until he has bracketed the target by two shots, each of which is less than four "probable errors" from the target. He then assumes his trial elevation, the mean range of these two shots, thereby practically assuring himself that a number of shots fired with this trial elevation, will form a zone of dispersion which will contain the target.

51. The next procedure is to place the center of impact of all shots, upon the target itself. In order to do this the battery commander must resort to what is

known as Improvement Fire. As a rule this requires that twelve shots be fired with the elevation determined from the Trial Fire. The balloon observer reports the sense of each shot, either (and this is preferable from the point of view of the observer) immediately after it has burst, or upon completion of the series. If more than six shots have fallen over, or if more than six have fallen short, the battery commander subtracts six from this number and multiplies the result by $1/12$th of 4 probable errors. This operation will give a range correction which should be added to, or subtracted from, the trial range, according as the greater number of shots were short of, or over the target. The range as deter-

mined, is known as the Adjusted Range. If time or ammunition is lacking, the Adjusted Range can be determined with less than twelve shots, by the same process. The number of shots should, however, never be less than six. After the Improvement Fire has been completed and the Adjusted Range determined, the fire is considered as adjusted.

52. When the fire of a battery has been adjusted, the battery commander may either dispense with the services of the balloon observer, or he may request the latter to observe the fire for effect, in order that the center of impact may be kept continuously on the target. This is called

Control of Fire and the observer need only give the sense of the shots or he may only give the sense of a number of shots, as for example; "Last six shots, over" or: "All shots falling short".

53. In the case of fire upon fugitive targets, or other objectives where the element of time is most essential the battery commander does not attempt to adjust his fire for precision. He simply attempts to bracket the target by quickly enclosing it between two ranges, one of which gives a majority of shots, over, and the other a majority of shots, short. The deflection is adjusted by adjusting the sheaf of fire on a certain portion of the target, and then opening the sheaf until the fire is distributed over the entire objective. The balloon observer as a rule, sends only the sense of the shot generally waiting until a salvo is fired and then communicating to the battery commander the sense of that salvo.

Telephone to a balloon.

Maj. Harold E. Hartney,
commanding 1st Pursuit Gp.

At right, Maj. James L. Dunsworth,
commanding 1st Day Bombardment
Gp. stops to chat with 1st Lt.
N. McDonald.

52. A Combat Service

11 November 1918

During the war many officers in the AEF tended to regard aviation as one of the technical services of the U.S. Army. Struggling against this attitude, members of the Air Service sought recognition for aviation as one of the combatant arms. The position taken by the Air Service is seen, for example, in the following memorandum dealing with the allocation of supplies among the various elements of the AEF.[1] For another example, see the introductory paragraph of Sherman's Tentative Manual (Doc. 55).

Headquarters Services of Supply, American Expeditionary Forces, Office Chief of Air Service

November 11, 1918. Office Memorandum No. 82.

1. The Air Service, although highly technical and specialized in character, is organized, equipped and trained for the sole purpose of taking its place on the fighting line with the other combatant services.

2. Air Service units, from the moment they arrive in France, form a part of the Expeditionary Forces and each Air Service unit is at all times a part of some distinct organization of these forces. In the S.O.S. these organizations are as a rule territorial, at the front they are tactical. At all times they are composed of units of all or several of the combatants arms as well as the purely technical services.

3. Whether in the S.O.S. or in the Armies at the front except for supplies which are peculiar to the Air Service, it receives its share of shelter and other equipment made available for the Army Organization to which it belongs and neither asks or wants more.

4. If Air Service Agencies discover supplies that are needed they should at once give notice to the proper authorities that such supplies may be made available where they are needed and ask that the Air Service share accordng to its needs in the distribution of such supplies. This is true for all classes of equipment which is used from the base ports to the fighting line. The Air Service asks for no special favors.

By direction:
H. C. Whitehead,
Colonel, A.S,
Chief of Staff.

---

1. In Gorrell's History, A–9, p 201.

Part IV:
Postwar Review

"Dead Acres" in the
St. Mihiel Sector.
(Art by Andre Smith)

53. Mitchell: Provisional Manual of Operations
23 December 1918

While commanding the Air Service of the First Army, Mitchell pulled together in one document the routine procedures of his observation, day bombardment, and pursuit units.[1] Later, after he became commander of the Air Service, Army Group, those procedures were revised and reissued as a series of operations bulletins.[2] The series contained one addition of considerable significance—a bulletin on the "Organization and Employment of Attack Squadrons."

The bulletin on attack aviation evidently was written during the last days of the Meuse-Argonne Campaign, in which bombing and strafing of German troops and positions in the battle area became an important part of U.S. Air Service operations. Those attacks, made by bombardment, pursuit, and, to a lesser degree, observation units, led to plans for organizing units to specialize in attacks of that kind. The plan, as it appeared in the bulletin, was incorporated in a "Provisional Manual of Operations of Air Service Units" which Mitchell issued on 23 December 1918. A prefatory note stated that the United States did not yet have any experience in organizing and employing attack units. In fact, the first such unit was not organized in the U.S. Air Service until the 3d Attack Group was formed in 1921.

The routine procedures for observation, day bombardment, and pursuit which had been published in bulletins of the Air Service, Army Group, were also incorporated, with revision, in the "Provisional Manual," which was issued while Mitchell was with the Army of Occupation as Army Air Service Commander, Third Army.[3]

Headquarters, Third Army
American Expeditionary Forces.
Coblenz, Germany,
December 23rd, 1918.

The following Provisional Manual of Operations for Air Service Units is approved and published for the information and guidance of all concerned.

By command of Major-General Dickman:[4]

Malin Craig,
Chief of Staff.

Official:

Wm. Mitchell, Brig. General, U.S.A., Army Air Service Commander, Third Army.

Headquarters Air Service, Third Army American Expeditionary Forces.

Coblenz, Germany, December 23rd, 1918

This manual treats of the activities of various types of units of the Air Service of the American Expeditionary Forces, and so far as subjects discussed are concerned, may be taken as a brief summary of experience of the American Squadrons gained during active operations.

For the most part, the notes deal with the routine procedure of groups and squadrons operating in the various fields of aerial activity. To these have been added articles published from time to time by these Headquarters as the need developed for a closer coordination of the work of the various units, both in their operations over the lines, and in the arrangement of a training program to satisfy their internal requirements and also to improve their liaison with other Arms:

The following subjects are discussed:—

(a) The Routine of a Corps Observation Group,
(b) The Routine of an Army Observation Group,
(c) The Routine of a Day Bombardment Group,
(d) The Routine of a Night Reconnaissance Squadron

---

1. Routine Procedure of Air Service Units, Cir No 1 CAS, 1st Army, 19 Aug 18, republished in *Air Service Bulletin*, Vol VII, No 305, 24 Dec 18.
2. In Gorrell's History, C-2, pp 232–267.
3. AFSHRC 248.211–61S.
4. Maj. Gen. Joseph T. Dickman assumed command of Third Army upon its organization on 15 November 1918, at which time Mitchell became Chief of Air Service, Third Army.

(e) The Routine of a Pursuit Unit.

(f) Organization and Employment of Attack Squadrons.

(g) Liaison of the Airplane with the Infantry.

(h) Instructions for the Improvement of Liaison between the Observation Air Service and Line Troops.

(i) Instruction of Observers and Pilots of Observation Squadrons.[5]

The notes on routine procedure are based upon actual practice of units of the types mentioned. The article dealing with the "Organization and Employment of Attack Squadrons" is based upon the experience of others in this field, as this experience has never been tested by an American attack Squadron. Active operations were suspended before the organization of a unit of this type was carried to completion.

The article on "Liaison of the Airplane with the Infantry" dealing as it does with a field in which the American airplanes operated with such conspicuous success, contains a record of the experience of our squadrons which is of the most importance.

The pamphlet entitled "Instructions for the Improvement of Liaison between the Observation Air Service and Line Troops" was issued as a guide to Observation Units in the outlining of a course of instruction for other Arms in working with the Air Service, which instruction was found to be most necessary

for the purpose of insuring proper cooperation and understanding between the Arms concerned. This is the most important and the most difficult of all Air Service activities.

In all the squadrons, but especially in the Observation Squadrons, a consistent effort has been made to maintain the efficiency of the flying personnel by constant review and practice in their own fields of work. Training programs were instituted and daily instruction carried on with energy. In order that all might profit by the experience of others, it was found desirable to compile and publish the methods of those in charge of this instruction at the different units under the title of "Instruction of Observers and Pilots of Observation Squadrons."

These articles have been assembled in the form of a manual which will serve as a valuable guide in the organization and operation of future Air Service units.

Wm. Mitchell
Brig. Gen'l. U.S.A.,
Army Air Service Commander,
Third Army,
American Expeditionary Forces.
. . . .

THE ROUTINE OF A CORPS OBSERVATION GROUP.

Instructions for daily procedure.

1. The Group Commander, Corps Observation, is charged with the administrative and tactical command of the squadrons which make up his Group, and is responsible for the carrying out of the missions called for by higher authority. He will assign specific duties to each squadron of his command, and is responsible for their performance. He exercises immediate control over the photographic section, and will assure himself that it and the Branch Intelligence Office are properly equipped and operated.

2. He is responsible for the preparation, transmission and preservation of copies of all reports, messages and orders, and that all personnel and material is in condition for effective work.

3. The immediate control of the operations of the Group is delegated by the Group Commander to a Group Operations Officer, whose selection should be based upon his ability as a executive and experience as an observer over the lines. This officer should keep in constant touch with the operations of all of the squadrons of the group, and should advise them as to the best methods of carrying out

5. Items h. and i. have been omitted.

the operations which the group is called upon to perform. He is responsible to the Group Commander for the performance of duties assigned to the various squadrons, for the preparation and forwarding of operations reports, and should keep the Group Commander constantly informed as to activities of the Group.

4. The Group Operations Officer is responsible for the proper equipment and operation of the Group Operations Room, and will supervise the training of new observers assigned to the Group. In all matters connected with operations he should act as the adviser of Squadron Operations Officers.

Assignment of duties to Squadrons.

5. One squadron of the group will normally be assigned to carry out missions of surveillance and adjustment for the Corps Artillery, as well as photographic missions as ordered from G –2 of the Corps through the office of the Corps Chief of Air Service. The Corps Artillery squadron will make such adjustments of fire of the Corps Artillery as cannot be carried out by the Corps Artillery Balloons, and will have at all times an airplane of command at the disposal of the Corps Chief of Air Service.

6. One squadron will ordinarily be assigned to each division in line. The divisional squadrons will carry out missions of reconnaissance, infantry liaison, and such artillery adjustments as cannot be done by the divisional balloon. In addition, they will carry out photographic missions ordered through the office of the Corps Chief of Air Service.

7. Squadron Commanders in addition to their administrative functions will be responsible for the carrying out of duties assigned to their squadrons by the Group Commander. The actual control of operations within the Squadron will be delegated to an Operations Officer, selected for qualifications similar to those of the Group Operations Officer.

The Day's Work.

8. In preparing the program of work for the day in each squadron the Squadron Commander and Squadron Operations Officer should meet after flying is finished for the day to frame the schedule of operations for the succeeding day. They should be provided with the following data by the officers mentioned:

Engineer Officer: Airplanes available and airplanes equipped for photographic missions listed by number.

Radio Officer: Airplanes equipped with proper radio installation.

Ordnance Officer: Airplanes equipped with proper armament.

9. This data may be conveniently posted upon a chart in the Squadron Operations Office, or on the Squadron bulletin board in the Group Operations Room. In the assignment of missions to observers and pilots the flying record of each must be kept constantly in mind. For this purpose a chart should be kept posted to date, showing the number of flying hours of each, and the character of and date of missions performed.

10. A typewritten schedule of work should be prepared showing the character of each mission, the airplane assigned, the name of the pilot and observer selected to carry it out, the time of departure, and in case of a photographic mission, the size of the camera and the number of plates to be taken.

11. One pilot, one observer, and one airplane should be designated to respond to alert calls, to be called upon in case additional work is required, or upon the failure of an airplane to perform its mission.

12. A Pilot should be designated as Officer in charge of the Field, whose duty it is to see that the airplanes assigned to duty are properly inspected and equipped, and that the missions leave the field at the time scheduled. A copy of this schedule should go to the Engineer Officer, the Radio Officer, the Ordnance Officer, the Group Photographic officer, and the Group Operations Officer. One copy shall be posted on the Squadron Bulletin Board.

13. The Engineer Officer is responsible for the proper condition of the airplane, and that it is ready for flight at the time specified.

14. The Radio Officer will see that the airplanes are equipped with proper reels, and that the radio is in proper condition before the airplane leaves the field.

15. The Ordnance Officer must see that the machine guns are mounted upon the airplane, and that the proper number of magazines and other ordnance equipment is placed in it, and that the fixed guns are in proper condition and equipped with belts of cartridges.

16. It is the duty of the Photographic Officer to see that the airplanes sent out on photographic missions are equipped with the proper cameras and plates, and to arrange for the prompt return to the photographic laboratory of these articles, upon the return of the mission, so that the plates may be developed at once. The first prints are then identified by the Branch Intelligence Officer, assisted by the observer who performed the mission. During an attack, especially, speed in distribution of the photographs is of the utmost importance, and delivery of the first urgency prints should be made by airplane.

17. Just before leaving for the field the observer should report at the Observer's Room and bring up to the minute all information which will be of assistance in the performance of his mission; he should then proceed to his airplane in time to reach it half an hour before the time of departure. He must then inspect his equipment. The pilot who is about to make a flight should also be at his airplane at least a half hour before the time set for departure and must inspect his airplane and armament and warm up his engine.

18. A daily form should be prepared and posted in the Operations Office of each squadron, upon which the observer, before leaving to carry out his mission, must enter his name and that of his pilot, the number of the airplane, character of mission and time of departure. Upon his return he must proceed without delay to the Operations Office, and enter upon the form the time of landing, with a short record of results obtained on the flight. He must then fill out a careful report of the mission, in the preparation of which the pilot can often render valuable assistance.

19. Each pilot will be assigned an airplane. He is responsible for the calibration of his own ammunition, must load his own belt, and load and unload his gun himself. He is responsible for the aligning of the sights of his own gun.

20. Each observer should be assigned two movable guns, mounted in pairs, as well as six magazines. He is responsible for the calibration of his ammunition, the loading of his magazines, and the aligning of his sights.

21. Squadron Commanders will detail to the headquarters of the unit to which their squadron is assigned, an observer to act as Liaison Officer. That all observers may benefit by this experience, it is suggested that this

detail be made for a period of one week, except during periods of intense activity, when one Liaison Officer should act throughout the period to insure continuity of the Liaison.

22. In all squadrons an Assistant Operations Officer will be appointed to act as assistant to the Squadron Operations Officer, and will familiarize himself with all his duties. He will take personal charge of the training of new observers assigned to the squadron, under the direction of the Group and Squadron Operations Officers. On account of the rapid expansion of the service, the constant training of officers who can go to newly formed squadrons fully acquainted with the duties and practical workings of an Operations Department is imperative.

Group Operations Room

23. To insure the proper functioning of the squadrons of a Corps Observation Group it is essential that the personnel be furnished with complete, accurate and up-to-date information in regard to the disposition, operations and plans of our own forces and those of the enemy. It is, therefore, of fundamental importance that each group have a conveniently located Operations Room in which all this information is assembled and placed at the disposal of the observers and pilots.

24. The Group Operations Officer is responsible for the proper upkeep of this room. He is assisted by the Branch Intelligence Officer detailed to the group by G–2. Should a squadron be operating alone, responsibility for the maintenance of an Operations Room will devolve upon the Squadron Operations Officer.

25. The information that must be available in the operations room may be classified under the following subjects:

(a) Photography
(b) Artillery
(c) Infantry
(d) Reconnaissance
(e) Miscellaneous

Photography

26. One copy of each photograph will be kept on file in the Intelligence Office and two copies placed in the Operations Room at the disposal of the observers.

27. The Intelligence Officer will keep a card index of photographs taken, showing the size of camera used, coordinates of the center, index number of the photograph, altitude and date on which taken, together with a record of the character of the photograph, whether good, fair or poor. These cards are filed according to the coordinates of the center of the photograph, each card representing a square kilometer and containing a record of all photographs whose center is within this square. Photographs will also be listed in a book

Photo finishing room.

under their index number showing the coordinates of the center,
the date when taken, the name
of the observer who carried out
the mission.

28. The photographs filed in
the Operations Room are arranged in pigeon holes according to their coordinates, each
pigeon hole representing one
square kilometer on the map
and containing the photographs
whose center is in that square.
The pigeon holes are numbered
in the same way as the Plan
Directeur; horizontally, according to the "X" coordinates and
vertically according to the "Y"
coordinates. These files are kept
up-to-date and complete by the
Intelligence Officer, replacements being made when
necessary.

29. Areas covered by photographic missions will be graphically represented upon a map,
each plate being outlined, the
index number and date at-
tached, and the area covered by
the mission colored. Each map
will show the missions performed during a week, and each
month a second map will be
prepared showing graphically in
the same manner the areas photographed during the calendar
month.

30. A panoramic view of the
sector is a valuable asset to the
operations room and should be
obtained if possible. Assemblages of photographic missions

carried out by observers of the
group tend to make the operations room attractive, and are
very valuable for study of the
sector.

31. A stereoscopic instrument
and magnifying glass must be
available for the study and interpretation of photographs.

Artillery.

32. The most important map
in the Operations Room is the
general map of the sector (1 to
10,000 or 1 to 20,000) showing
the position of all of our artillery
elements and the enemy organization in depth, particularly enemy batteries and battery em-
placement locations.

33. Friendly battery positions,
including the name of the unit
and the number and caliber of
guns should be shown by tags or
markers which can be moved as
necessary. Artillery P.C.'s and
panel stations should be similarly
marked, the markers of the latter
including information as to radio
call and type of panel used.

34. This map should be
checked daily and all information pertaining to the artillery
should be kept up-to-date and
should be accompanied by a
chart showing the daily activity
of each enemy battery.

35. Fugitive target batteries
should be shown upon a special
map, similar markers being used
to indicate their location and that
of their panel stations with radio
calls and type of panel. Upon
this map the field of fire of each
of these batteries should be
indicated.

36. A general map of artillery
objectives (1/20000) issued by
Army G–2 and showing important objectives, such as road intersections, ammunition dumps,
material depots, bridges, railroads, camps, aviation fields,
and other objectives should also
be posted.

37. A list should also be
posted showing the name and
location of the various artillery
units with which the command is
to work, the coordinates of the
P.C., the coordinates of the
panel stations, the radio calls,
the type of panels and the wave
lengths.

38. A relief map is of great
vaue in an operations room for
the study of the terrain. It is
particularly valuable in case of
adjustment of fire upon an objective upon the reverse slope,
as by a study of the contours,
the observer will be able to plan
his method of flying the mission
in advance.

39. A map should be provided
showing the position of friendly
balloons and the defiladed area
from the three general ascension
levels.

Infantry.

40. A map showing the parts of the line held by the different infantry commands, marking by tags the location of the various P.C.'s of units both in the line and in reserve, must be posted. On this map the successive objectives in case of an attack can be shown. It must show the outline of our trenches and detail of the enemy trenches, strong points, dug-outs, machine gun emplacements, etc. This map is of the utmost importance to the infantry observer in order that he may familiarize himself completely with the sector over which he must work.

Miscellaneous.

41. The Operations Room, being the information center, must contain all data obtained from various sources which bear upon the activities of the group. In it should always be found a large scale map showing the entire front line.

42. All orders or letters of interest to the personnel, daily communiques, the weather forecast and visibility report will be posted upon a bulletin board in a conspicuous place.

43. Summaries of information and bulletins from the Air Service and from the Army, Army Corps and Divisions shall at all times be available.

44. Under the supervision of the Intelligence Officer a stock of maps of all scales shall be kept on hand for the use of pilots and observers.

45. Maps showing the position of all friendly airdromes, and a map of enemy airdromes and balloon positions shall be posted. In addition, illustrations of enemy aircraft are of value. All possible information in regard to types and markings of enemy airplanes must be at the disposal of the observers and pilots.

46. The room should be equipped with a blackboard and large tables, chairs and benches, and material such as ink, pencils, drawing pens, paste, glue, elastic bands, thumb tacks; paints and pins, should be provided. Buzzers for practice in radio manipulation should be mounted. Forms for written reports of missions and a basket to file them in must be provided.

47. The Operations Room will be well lighted and always be kept clean and in an orderly condition. Every effort should be made to make it as comfortable and attractive a place as possible.

48. Owing to the fact that information of the most secret nature is constantly displayed, a rule barring all persons other than authorized personnel from the room must be rigidly enforced. Under no circumstances should other persons be admitted without special permission from the Group Commander.

THE ROUTINE OF AN ARMY OBSERVATION GROUP

49. The mission of Army Observation is the reconnaissance, in depth, both visually and by photograph, of the Army sector. The Army Observation Group is placed at the disposal of the General Staff of the Army and the missions carried out in conformity to its orders. Orders assigning missions are received by the Group Commander who transmits them to the Group Operations Officer, who is in immediate control of the operations of the group.

The Group Operations Room.

50. It is essential to the proper conduct of operations that both pilots and observers of a group have a thorough knowledge of their sector, and access to all available information in regard to enemy activity in it. For army work, it is especially necessary to

be familiar with the main lines of communication, dumps, detraining and unloading stations, and airdromes.

51. In order that this information may be conveniently assembled and placed at the disposal of the pilots and observers of the group, a Group Operations Room is maintained, equipped with large scale maps showing the location of principal enemy works, with photographs of all principal towns, dumps, railroad centers, airdromes, and anti-aircraft batteries. Bulletins and charts of special interest are posted from time to time. The Group Operations Officer is responsible for the proper upkeep of this room.

52. Pilots and observers are required to spend as much time as possible in the Operations Room, studying the sector. Instruction in reference to the work is given by means of talks, pointing out the most important features of the sector, suggesting methods of preparations for missions, and impressing upon the personnel the importance of their work, especially during an attack.

Method of assignment and execution of missions.

53. After flying for the day has ended, the Group Operations Officer will prepare a schedule dividing the work assigned for the following day between the various squadrons of the group. The division of work is based upon the number and character of the missions to be performed, and the airplanes and personnel available at the close of the day's flying, as shown by reports furnished by each of the squadrons.

54. A copy of this schedule is issued to each squadron Operations Officer, with whom a conference is held in order that the work may be clearly understood. One flight in each group will always be held on alert to carry out any special mission that may be called for.

55. The Squadron Operations Officers will assign the missions among the flights in their respective squadrons, flight leaders being given all necessary instructions covering the nature of the mission, the routes to be followed and the time of departure. In case of a photographic mission, objectives, size of camera, altitude, and number of plates to be exposed, are specified. The instruction as to the most advantageous method of carrying out a mission and the assignment of the individual pilot and observer to it is left to the discretion of the flight commanders.

56. In carrying out the various missions the flights follow accustomed routes over certain portions of the sector. As soon as a flight departs, the Squadron Operations Officer posts a tag or marker in the Group Operations Office showing the time of departure, number of airplanes, area to be covered, and the nature of the mission, this tag being taken down immediately upon the return of the mission. The Group Operations Officer is thus kept constantly informed as to the amount and character of the work as it is being carried on.

57. The alert flight remains in the vicinity of Group Headquarters to carry out special and Command missions.

58. On landing upon the field at the conclusion of a mission, the observers go immediately to the Squadron Operations Room, and make a complete report of all information obtained, plates exposed, weather conditions at the lines, and the activity of enemy aircraft and anticraft. This information is handed without delay to the Branch Intelligence Officer, who places it at the disposal of the Group Commander and the Army Intelligence Officer.

59. All the plates exposed are taken immediately to the photographic laboratory, developed and printed. Three proofs of each are sent to the Intelligence Officer. The latter distributes the proofs among the observers concerned, who identify them by indicating on each different print

the coordinates of its center, time of exposure, and the altitude at which taken.

60. All three proofs are marked, and two are sent immediately to the Army Intelligence Office, the third being sent back to the laboratory in order that plate may be permanently marked. As soon as practicable, the required number of prints are distributed according to a list on file in the Intelligence Office.

Normal Employment of the Group.

(a) During an inactive period, or before an attack.

61. During an inactive period, or the period preceding an attack, the group should dispatch daily visual reconnaissance missions, covering all important lines of communication in the sector, to include both the roads and railroads. At such times, all movements of size are carried out at night and it is therefore necessary to make observations at break of day, or at dusk in order to obtain the information. Missions should be sent out some fifteen to thirty minutes before daybreak. They can then be over the objective as soon as there is sufficient light to observe. These observations at daylight and dusk are supplemented by visual reconnaissance carried out in conjunction with the photographic missions during the day.

62. Photographs should be taken as frequently as possible of all enemy works, such as dumps, lines of defense in rear of the front lines, concentration points, aviation fields hospitals and railroad yards. As most of these will be found on or near main roads and railroads, it is advisable to make photographic assemblages of the lines of communication, and thus insure the discovery of new works, rather than to take isolated photographs of the works themselves. All photographic missions should be accompanied by at least one airplane whose duty it is to carry on visual reconnaissance which will often locate something of interest, to be photographed, either on the return trip or at some future time. During the periods mentioned, it is not necessary that Army Headquarters assign in detail the missions to be performed by the group, a general indication of what areas in the sector are considered of the greatest importance being sufficient. Under these circumstances, it is the duty of the Group Commander to so direct operations that the sector is systematically covered by both visual and photographic reconnaissances, special attention being paid to the areas referred to.

(b) During an attack, or in an active sector.

63. The general scheme of visual reconnaissance during an active period remains the same as that followed in an inactive sector, except that in such a period, enemy movements will take place in daylight, as well as night. For this reason, enemy lines of communication must be kept under constant observation. From time to time, the General Staff will require confirmation of information received from other sources, or will want the accuracy of certain deductions to be verified. It therefore becomes necessary to reserve a far larger portion of the command for the fulfillment of emergency calls.

64. The photographic work carried out during an active period will be closely supervised and directed by the Army, which will indicate, as far in advance as possible, the objectives to be photographed, together with the order of their importance.

65. A schedule is made out each day, listing the missions, both visual and photographic, to be carried out upon the following forenoon. This schedule is based upon the information received from the Army and a knowledge of the general situation. A sufficient reserve should at all times be held for special work.

66. At least one flight (6 teams with their airplanes) should be kept on alert so that when a special request is received, the mission can be dispatched with the least possible delay. While the greatest care must be exercised to be ready for an alert call, equal care should be taken that too great a portion of the command does not remain idle for lack of requests from the Army. If emergency calls do not come in, alert airplanes may be employed as deemed necessary by the Group Commander.

THE ROUTINE OF A DAY BOMBARDMENT GROUP.

67. The missions of Day Bombardment Aviation are the following:

(a) To destroy and harass the rear areas of the battlefield and to attack military and industrial objectives within and beyond the range of artillery.

(b) To cause a dispersion of enemy anti-aircraft defences (pursuit patrols, anti-aircraft batteries, etc.), throughout the zone of vulnerable bombardment objectives.

(c) To destroy in combat the enemy's air forces.

(d) To obtain information of military value by surveillance of enemy activity carried on in the course of the bombing expedition.

Preparation of a Bombing Expedition.

68. Day bombardment objectives are designated by G–3 and transmitted by the Army Chief of Air Service to the Commander of the Day Bombardment Group. Unless specifically covered in orders from higher authority, the Group Commander will issue orders specifying:

(a) The number of formations and the number of airplanes in each.

(b) The types and weight of projectiles.

(c) The route, altitude, and order of departure of each formation.

69. The method of pursuit co-operation will be explained to the Commanders of the squadrons forming the Group.

70. Unless the objective must be kept secret until the moment of departure, detailed orders should be issued in time to permit each pilot and observer to familiarize himself with all available information in regard to the main objective, the route, secondary objectives, and the region to be observed or photographed. A day bombardment expedition must be able to leave the field rapidly upon emergency order. In this case only the formation leader and deputy leader of each formation need know the exact route to be followed.

Four different types and sizes of bombs used in raids: (l. to r.) 155-mm, 115-mm, 90-mm, and 75-mm.

For the other pilots and observers a sketch of the objective and a general knowledge of the terrain, so that they may return to our lines in case of accident, will suffice.

71. Each Squadron Commander will designate the airplanes, pilots, and observers to take part in an expedition, and is charged with the responsibility for their proper preparation for the mission. He will appoint formation leaders and deputy leaders and will assign to each airplane its position in the formation.

Formations.

72. Day Bombardment Squadrons will invariably work in formation. These formations should be large, as many as eighteen airplanes being easily controlled by a leader when working at high altitudes. For low flying formations in bad weather, eight is the maximum that can be employed. All formations must have the following characteristics:

    (a) Simplicity.
    (b) No dead angles.
    (c) Concentration of fire to the rear.
    (d) Concentration of fire below the center of the formation.
    (e) Compactness.
    (f) Each airplane must be able to see the leader.

73. All formations, whatever the number, should fly in a "V" formation with the rear of the V closed. Formations of more than ten should have one airplane in the center of the V at the average altitude of the V. Airplanes in formation should be numbered as follows:

```
          1
        3   2
      5  12   4
    7           6
   9  11    10   8
```

Number 1 is the leader and flies at the lowest altitude, Numbers 2 and 3, 4 and 5, and similarly placed pairs should fly at the same altitude, number 2 and 3 about fifty meters higher than number 1, and about thirty meters to the right and left of number 1 respectively. Number 4 takes the same position relative to number 2 as number 2 with reference to number 1; and number 5 takes the same position with relation to number 3.

74. Formations should be as compact as possible, especially when dropping projectiles; and during a combat, formations should close up. Too much emphasis cannot be laid upon the training of day bombardment pilots in formation flying. If the pilots maintain a regular echelonment in height, in case of emergency they can close up quickly upon the leader, by diving. The guide should never open his throttle wide, and observers should always warn their pilots whenever their own or any other airplane appears to be get-

ting out of formation. It is fatal for an airplane to leave the formation, and the formation should not be broken up even to protect an airplane which has left it.

75. Whenever the landing field is sufficiently large, the formation is made up on the ground, the pilots having first warmed up their engines. If this procedure cannot be followed for lack of room, for example, when several squadrons are leaving at about the same time, the airplanes will take off in the order of their number in the formation, each airplane beginning to taxi when the wheels of the preceding airplane leave the ground. Number 1 throttles down when he has attained sufficient altitude to do so with safety, and flies slowly until all the airplanes are in place. He may then take up his travelling speed—never full speed. The only practicable maneuver in formation flying is an "8" upon an extremely wide curve, covering at least five kilometers.

Combat.

76. Aerial combat is not merely an incident of day bombardment, but is one of its integral phases. The normal combat of a day bombardment unit is a fight between the formation and enemy pursuit airplanes that attack it. Observers must be on constant watch for enemy aircraft and upon sighting them, the observer fires an agreed signal of warning, which signal is repeated by all the other observers. All the observers should then test their machine guns. Number 1, upon learning that enemy aircraft are in sight, should slow down and the formation should tighten up as much as possible. The pilots must make every effort to keep in formation and keep the formation compact. Under no circumstances will they be permitted to attempt an individual maneuver.

77. In the course of aerial combat it will sometimes be found that the mass of the enemy pursuit airplanes will attempt to create a demonstration by maneuvering and shooting at long range while two or three climb and then dive upon the formation, in an effort to separate one or more of the bombing airplanes from it. Observers must keep a careful lookout at all times for such attacks. The majority of attacks, however, will come from below. If the observer opens fire when the enemy is at least 300 meters distant, in most cases he will not come to close quarters. If allowed to approach nearer, the safety of a bombing airplane depends upon putting the enemy airplane out of action.

78. As there is always the likelihood of an airplane becoming separated from the formation, bombing units should be thoroughly trained in single combat against pursuit patrols. In the course of such a combat a pilot will do little shooting, but will exert his efforts to keep his observer in a favorable position. He will avoid maneuvers such as regular spirals or straight dives, but should fly an irregular course and watch his observer so as to place the latter in a position from which he can shoot to the best advantage. If the enemy gets into a position where he can shoot without being shot at, the pilot must do everything possible to spoil his aim. A climbing turn made very steeply toward the side upon which the weapons are carried is the best maneuver, as it will allow the observer to use his guns. While the pilots ordinarily attempt to place the observer in shooting position, experience has shown that at times the pilot is obliged to turn on his pursuers. The pilot should, therefore, take every opportunity to perfect his maneuvering ability and gunnery.

Bombing the Target.

79. In passing over the objective the formation will not be allowed to break up, but will tighten up as compactly as possible. Sighting errors thus produced are negligible considering the dispersion of the projectiles and the size of the usual day bombardment targets.

80. Greater accuracy is obtained by permitting the leading observer to sight for the whole formation. Accurate bombing is an art in which certain observers will excell, and these observers should be used as leaders and deputy leaders. Excitement adds to inaccuracy and if but one observer uses the sights he will know that all of the other airplanes are acting as his protection. When the leader has adjusted his sights and is approaching the target in line of sight he fires a signal "Prepare to drop bombs". When the leader's bombs start to leave the racks the other observers in the formation drop their bombs. Excellent results have been obtained by this method of bombing, which was adopted after extensive experience in active service. The greatest accuracy has been obtained when the formations reach their altitude before crossing the lines, the leader being thus given an opportunity to check his calculations before the objective is reached.

81. When several formations are directed against the same objective they should approach it at thirty second intervals, one behind the other. Upon leaving the objective they should all turn in the same direction.

82. In the performance of a day bombing expedition, it is most essential that the bombardment formation reaches the objective exactly at the time designated, in order that successful coordination between the work of the bombardment units and the pursuit units may be assured, with the object of causing the greatest possible damage to the enemy and of maintaining our ascendency in the air.

83. A Group Operations Officer will be appointed by the Group Commander of the Day Bombardment Group, and to him will be delegated the immediate supervision over the operations of the group. He will also act as the representative of G–2. It is his duty:

(a) To compile and keep available for the Group Commander and the personnel of the Group, all information of value in the preparation of a bombing mission.

(b) To keep an indexed file of photographs, and a stock of maps for use of pilots and observers. He will also post in the operations room a map (1 to 80000 or 1 to 50000) of the sector in which the group is operating, as well as a 1 to 200,-000 scale map showing the line of the entire front with its changes as they occur.

(c) To post upon a bulletin board all orders and communications of interest to pilots or observers of the group, and bulletins from the Army or its Corps or Divisions.

(d) To post a map showing the location of friendly airdromes and hospitals.

(e) To file the flight report of each crew and to interrogate personally the pilots and observers to get additional information if possible, and to transmit the information obtained to the Army Intelligence Section.

(f) To supervise the work of the Photographic Section, the developing of all plates and the printing and distribution of photographs.

84. The Group Operations Officer should receive the charts from the Army Chief of Air Service, showing bombing targets and intelligence in reference to them. He should keep duplicate copies of these, marking one of them daily with the bombardments effected. It is one of his most important functions to keep up-to-date at all times available information in reference to the locations of enemy anti-aircraft batteries, enemy airdromes, and the number and identity of the squadrons which occupy them. The photographs taken by the Bombing Group itself, will often assist in establishing the whereabouts of new airdromes and the occupation of old ones. A Day Bombardment Group may furnish information of great value from visual and photographic reconnaissance conducted during the course of the bombing expeditions, especially in regard to location of enemy airdromes and works, and the number of enemy troops.

85. The Group Operations Officer is responsible for the liaison of the group with the pursuit units in addition to the liaison with the Army Chief of Air Service, G–2, and G–3, and he should notify the pursuit group of the bombardment group's plan of operations and advise them as far in advance as possible of the hour, the altitude and return route of all expeditions.

THE ROUTINE OF A NIGHT RECONNAISSANCE SQUADRON.

86. The mission of Night Reconnaissance is to provide information to the Higher Command in regard to the trend and extent of movements behind the enemy's line made under cover of darkness. These are usually extensive if operations are impending. It is therefore imperative that the routes followed by the enemy in moving troops and material should be reconnoitered thoroughly and frequently at night, due to the fact that the most perfect day reconnaissance will often fail to disclose any abnormal activity. During active operations, the battle-field must be patrolled consistently by night reconnaissance airplanes.

87. A night reconnaissance unit is ordinarily assigned for duty with an Army, the missions of strategic reconnaissance and night surveillance·being assigned through the office of the Army Chief of Air Service.

Organization.

88. The Commanding Officer of a Night Reconnaissance ᾿ Squadron is responsible for the activity and efficiency of the unit. It is his duty to insure the proper performance of the duties assigned to the subordinate officers of the Squadron.

89. In addition to the pilots and observers, and the necessary enlisted personnel, the unit commander will be assisted by the following officers:

Operations Officer.

90. The duty of the Operations Officer attached to a night reconnaissance unit will be to advise the Commanding Officer of all tactical matters connected with the field of operations. Upon receipt by the unit of orders assigning the missions for any given night, under the authority of the Commanding Officer, he will prepare and post a schedule designating the pilots

and observers and the hours during which each of the routes of enemy movements will be reconnoitered. The Operations Officer will procure all available information of the enemy's rear areas, particularly in regard to railheads, routes, of transports, detraining points, billeting areas, camps, depots, anti-aircraft, divisions and airdromes. It is his duty to supervise the preparation of the personnel for the execution of the missions assigned to them, and he will assure himself that all information obtained by the unit in the course of a mission is passed on without delay to the Branch Intelligence Officer. The Operations Officer will have charge of the landing lights, searchlights, etc., on the ground. He will see that these are lighted at the hours specified by the Unit Commander for airplanes to leave the airdrome or whenever an airplane overhead gives the correct signal for landing. He will also make a daily report of operations to the Chief of Air Service of the Army under which he is operating, which report will cover the routes, hours of flight, and all information obtained. He must make certain that every pilot and observer is familiar with the correct landing signal for the day before leaving the ground.

Branch Intelligence Officer.

91. A Branch Intelligence Officer will be detailed by G–2 of the Army for duty with every night reconnaissance unit. This officer will see that all information obtained is transmitted to Headquarters without delay. He will make out routes covering points of concentration and the main arteries of movement in the enemy's rear areas, and he will transmit the orders for reconnaissance missions to the Unit Commander.

Supply Officer.

92. The Supply Officer will requisition and procure the supplies necessary for the unit. These will include Quartermaster and commissary supplies for which he will establish the necessary liaison with the Chief Quartermaster of the Army to which the unit is attached. In addition, he will establish the necessary channels for securing technical, Ordnance and Air Service supplies. The Supply Officer is also responsible for the squadron transportation, its proper upkeep and repair.

Engineer Officer.

93. The Engineer Officer will supervise the work of the several aero sections, and the work of the mechanics assigned thereto. He will keep on hand at all times a reserve of spare parts of electrical material, i.e., dynamo spares, searchlight spares, landing flares, etc., sufficient to meet the immediate needs of the unit and will advise the Supply Officer relative to such needs.

Adjutant.

94. The Adjutant is charged with the administrative work of the unit.

Study of Routes and Landmarks.

95. Useful and reliable reports may be expected only from observers who are perfectly familiar with the terrain, both as a result of detailed study of all maps covering the sector, and from knowledge acquired from previous flights carried out, both by day and at night. Constant effort should be made to reduce, as far as possible, the necessity for using a map by acquiring an exact knowledge of the salient features and landmarks.

96. The position of the stars and moon, (according to the hour and the phase of the moon,) should be utilized for the purpose of orientation, especially for checking the indications obtained from the compass. In order to determine with exactitude the angle of the course of the airplane, the indications given by the stars and compass must be combined with the effect of the drift resulting from the action of the wind at the altitude attained. The latest obtainable meteorological data is essential to the night flying pilot not only to enable him to judge the possibility of flying, but to permit him to correctly determine his course while he is in the air.

97. Within our own lines, there exists an organization of signal lights of the front, marking out the aerial routes which furnishes the pilot and observer with necessary indications and direction marks to enable them to take the direction of their objective and to find their field on return. Familiarity with the system of signal lights is of course essential.

98. In spite of all precautions taken within both our own and enemy lines, permanent lights will be found which form excellent landmarks. Groups of searchlights placed around important localities and objectives,

and generally lit up on the passage of any airplane are visible from very far away, and can be used as direction points and guides. The star shells fired almost continuously from the trenches, and flashes of the cannon in an active sector will permit any lost plane to find the lines again.

99. Whenever the enemy is carrying out night bombardment, their ground signal lights and direction rockets, the location of which is generally permanent, form indications of the highest value to our airplanes.

Visibility In General.

100. The closest possible study must be made of the effect of varying weather conditions upon visibility. Visibility at night is extremely variable. It depends upon two things: the clearness of the atmosphere, (absence of mist and fog) and the light afforded by the moon. The visibility of natural landmarks at night is found in general to take the following order: woods, important towns or other localities; roads, rivers and other water courses or bodies of water, (brooks, canals, lakes and ponds).

101. On clear moonlit nights the visibility is very good. At an average altitude the visibility for practical purposes of direction may extend from 10 to 15 kilometers. Woods show up as clearly defined black (or dark) blots, easily recognizable by their shape and outline. Roads appear white or grey if bordered by trees or just after rain. Water courses may be recognized by the dark strips formed by the valleys, nearly always bordered by trees or meadows, and by the reflection of the moon in the water. Canals are still more easy to identify owing to their rectilinear form.

102. On misty nights the reflections of the light on the mist interferes with observation. It is then necessary to place oneself between the moon and the point to be observed or the road to be followed.

103. On dark nights it is quite possible to see quite well, but the visibility is generally confined to the vertical. For this reason, it is not possible to fly by known direction points and landmarks, but it is necessary to follow step by step the itinerary, paying ceaseless attention to locating one's position accurately on the map. When direction signal lights are given, they may, of course, be used to fly by. On dark nights when utilizing woods as landmarks and direction points to fly by, it is better, if the woods be of large dimensions or extent, to follow along their edges than to try to fly straight across them. Large towns and localities show up in the form of grey blots with sharply defined edges. White roads, not bordered by trees, in dry weather, show up clearly, but should be followed in all their detours lest they be lost. The same may be said for water courses, which are, however, more difficult to see and are frequently only visible by the dark line of the trees and meadows bordering them, or by the bank of mist lying in the valley.

104. On bad nights when the hygrometric state of the air is pronounced, and particularly if it

is very dark and the sky is covered over, the visibility is extremely restricted. It is then very difficult to direct oneself other than by signal lights, or to find objectives except those which are lighted up. Nevertheless, it is always necessary to pay the strictest attention to watching the ground, and an experienced observer rarely fails to pick up sufficient indications to locate himself. Sorties on nights such as these should be carried out only in the event of real necessity and only over objectives close to the lines.

Visibility of Special Objectives.

105. (a) Stations: The rails are of dark color and do not show up well, but the platform, paths, etc., which practically always exist, make characteristic white patches which are easy to recognize. Sometimes red and green signal lights will be seen and often, especially when there is a great deal of activity at the station, various white lights and even arc lights are shown.

(b) Factories: When lit up they can be seen as readily as by daylight. They are usually beneath a luminous halo which can be seen from a great distance. In general, all lights are put out as soon as an alert is sounded and frequently a few will be left in order to draw the bombardment to false objectives, such as slag heaps, etc. Iron castings look like huge reddish explosions.

(c) Airdromes: From an average altitude the hangars are only visible on clear nights, but it is always possible to locate them from their relative position from the roads that feed them. Airdromes in use at night show only a very restrained amount of light—three or four red lights and occasionally a row of small searchlights lighted at the instant that an airplane is landing. Rockets and other signal lights are also used, and give useful indications as to the location and activity of the various fields.

(d) Villages: These appear as a grey blot with roads, paths and sometimes railways converging into them.

(e) Camps and Bivouacs: In open ground these are not difficult to find; the numerous paths around them make it still more easy to locate them. In woods they are rarely visible at night.

(f) Convoys and Columns: Convoys carrying lights show up that portion of the road which they occupy. Motor car headlights give characteristic white spots on the roads. Columns without lights are difficult to spot except on clear nights at a low altitude.

(g) Trains: On moonlight nights the smoke of a locomotive can be seen at a great distance, at low altitude the train itself is visible. On dark nights only the tail lights can be seen and occasionally the firebox when it is opened (especially the reflection of the fire on the smoke overhead). Only exceptionally are trains lighted up.

Execution of a Mission.

106. The altitude at which a reconnaissance is carried out depends on visibility; in order to recognize details by vertical observation, it is necessary to fly low. Good visibility is attained by flying away from the moon.

107. By allotting clearly defined reconnaissance areas to individual airplanes flying at fixed times, it will be possible to obtain reports covering practically the whole night.

108. If it is not possible to reconnoiter railway lines, roads and watercourses for movement by repeatedly flying along their whole length, one reconnaissance should be carried out between midnight and 3:00 A.M., as the beginning or end of any important movement will take place during that period. The direction of railway movement and activity at stations can be recognized by the glare from locomotives and the white smoke issuing from them. Size and nature of train movements and of entraining and detraining operations can only be observed by airplanes flying at low altitude. Increased activity at stations can be recognized by the unavoidable increase in lights on sidings and platforms.

109. Troop movements and traffic on treeless roads and over open country cannot escape an observer's attention. On roads bordered with trees, in villages, and in country affording facilities for cover, however, airplanes will have to fly low, when, as experience has shown, even the slightest movements can be detected.

110. When ordering reconnaissances for concentrations of

troops, camps, billets and airdromes, individual airplanes should not be allotted too large an area, and observers should be instructed in detail as to roads of approach of columns and assembly areas, from information gained by photographic and visual observations by day.

111. Night reconnaissance airplanes will be sent out singly in order not to attract the enemy's attention, which would cause him to extinguish lights and alarm his defences. It is recommended that Airplanes should cross the lines at great heights and then glide down. It may also be advisable to fly with the engine throttled down. Machine guns should only be used for self defense or when there is a chance of causing serious losses to the enemy. A machine which limits itself to reconnoitering may sometimes be taken by the enemy for one of his own aeroplanes.

112. Parachutes flares are most useful for night reconnaissance.

Enemy Defense Against Night Reconnaissance.

113. As regards the enemy's defensive measures against night reconnaissance airplanes, complaints received are chiefly concerned with the blinding effect of searchlights, which may render all reconnaissance impossible; on the other hand anti-aircraft and machine gun fire have not been heavy. It will be found advisable to employ night pursuit for the purpose of neutralizing enemy searchlights and anti-aircaft defense. Enemy night pursuit is a growing danger to night reconnaissance.

THE ROUTINE OF A PURSUIT UNIT.

Duties.

114. Pursuit aviation has a double mission to perform:
    (a) Offensive.
    (b) Protective.

115. *Offensive Patrols* are dispatched to cross the enemy's lines in sufficient strength to cruise over his rear area, search out enemy aircraft, and attack them with the object of causing maximum casualties and inflicting the greatest possible damage to his air service and with a further object of obtaining a definite moral superiority. Offensive patrols should cover low, intermediate, and high altitudes, and it must always be borne in mind that pursuit aviation furnishes its own protection and that the advantage of altitude will frequently outweigh the advantage of numbers in a combat so that low or intermediate patrols should invariably be accompanied by high protection.

116. *Protective Patrols,* have a double mission to carry out:

(a) To place Corps Observation Aviation in a position where it will be, and will feel, that it is protected.

(b) To protect our ground troops from the results of enemy artillery adjustment, reconnaissance, and photographic airplanes, as well as from attack by pursuit and attack airplanes.

117. Protective patrols are not to be regarded as defensive in character. All pursuit aviation is offensive in character, but the limitation of the area in which protective patrols are ordered to fly and to fight and the end which it is desired to accomplish by the utilization of protective patrols distinguishes them from offensive patrols, whose mission is to attack and destroy enemy aircraft of every sort wherever found.

118. The performance of the double role of protective patrols cannot be accomplished by the maintenance of a permanent barrage of the sector. Such a procedure is fatiguing for the pilots, expensive in material in comparison with the results obtained and renders it impossible for us to undertake offensive expeditions in force. Consequently a permanent barrage will only be resorted to at times of intense preparation for attack while it is imperative to prevent all reconnaissance of our rear areas on the part of the enemy air service.

119. It is to be noted that barrage patrols can only afford effective protection to our army corps air service when active over a limited breadth of front which, as a rule, should not exceed 15 kilometers. The size and altitude of protective patrols will depend upon the general activity of the sector, and the strength and degree of aggressiveness of enemy aviation. On special occasions a triple tier barrage may be established for short periods of time. The depth that protective patrols will penetrate into the enemy rear areas will be prescribed in orders. Patrols must not exceed this depth except in extraordinary circumstances; for them to do so leaves the Army Corps aviation unprotected. For a protective patrol to leave this area assigned to it, in order to attack enemy airplanes or for any other reason, constitutes a serious offense.

120. In order to protect effectively our Army Corps airplanes, barrage patrols should operate from 5 to 9 kilometers over the enemy lines.

121. For the rigidity of a fixed system of protective patrols there will be substituted a system which will comprise patrols especially directed against enemy army corps aviation and in addition a number of airplanes on alert, ready to take off in a few minutes, to cope with any marked increase of enemy aviation over a part of the sector of the enemy aviation in cases where ground activity makes an increase of aerial activity advisable.

122. The size of the alert or mobile reserve will be prescribed in orders. The group commanders will be responsible for its proper utilization. It is not intended to use the planes on alert to counter attack every enemy airplane reported by our A. A. A. Observation Post or the Gonio Stations. The alert will be used by group commanders as a sort of "support System" to reinforce our aviation in case of increased enemy aviation or in case of activity on the part of infantry or artillery.

123. In addition to the routine offensive protective patrols, pursuit aviation will perform 4 types of special missions:

(a) Close protection of Corps airplanes.

(b) Cooperation with Day Bombardment.

(c) Attacks on balloons.

(d) Attacks on ground troops.

124. *Close Protection of Corps Aviation* will only be arranged in special cases where the Corps Aviation has to perform particularly difficult and delicate missions. The group commander of the Corps Observation Group will request such protection from the nearest pursuit group commander and the latter will be the judge as to whether or not his missions will permit him to furnish the protection requested. It has been found that by furnishing the daily schedule of operations to the Corps Air Service in advance the Corps Air Service is generally able to arrange its missions so that they coincide with the time of a routine pursuit patrol, and this patrol after it has concluded its protection of the Corps airplanes is able to continue its patrol of the lines.

125. *Cooperation With Day Bombardment* is valuable, in that it enables pursuit patrols to obtain contact with enemy pursuit airplanes. Owing to the long range and slow speed of day bombardment airplanes, a covering protection should not be afforded. A day bombing expedition should rely upon its own strength to defend itself from attack of enemy airplanes.

126. By sending out pursuit patrols to meet day bombardment units over the objective and again at the line when returning from their raid it will often be possible to attack enemy pursuit airplanes which are following the bombers in the hopes of picking off a straggler. Under these circumstances our pursuit airplanes by knowing the altitudes and route which the day bombardment will follow, can obtain the advantage of altitude and surprise, as the enemy pursuit will have its attention directed to the bombers whom they are pursuing.

127. *Attacks on Balloons* are dangerous and difficult and should only be undertaken in order to destroy the work of some balloon which is particularly embarrassing to our troops. Very light patrols, of one or two airplanes, make the attack with a patrol overhead to protect the attacking airplanes from being surprised. Demonstrations against the entire line of enemy balloons along a considerable length of front often give valuable results by causing all the enemy balloons to be hauled down; these results are especially to be sought during the preparation of an offensive or when the attack is in progress. They must be organized with great care and precision in order that the attack may take place simultaneously along the entire front. In attacking a balloon, it must always be borne in mind that only the front part is vulnerable. At least the rear third has nothing in it but air.

128. *Attacks on Ground Objectives* often give valuable results during a major operation. The objectives of attack should, as a rule, be the enemy reserves, either in mass formation or on the march. They should be undertaken in force as the result desired is the maximum moral effect. The employment of a large number of pursuit airplanes in attacking ground objectives increases the safety of the operations by multiplying the targets at which the enemy must shoot. In a calm sector, machine gun attacks of objectives on the ground, trenches, machine gun emplacements, artillery positions, etc., produce very little effect either moral or material. They will not be attempted.

Notes on Routine Procedure.

129. *The Group Commander* will dispose tactically of his forces in order to cover the instructions or orders issued by the Army to which the Group is attached.

130. *All Tactical Work in Pursuit Units* will be performed in formation, the size of these formations varying in accordance with the situation, the mission, and the enemy's dispositions.

131. *The Formation* of five or six airplanes, i.e., the flight, will be the basis of all tactical operations, in order that the tactical efficiency of the several flights may reach maximum, it is advisable that the pilots live together on the ground as much as possible, and in addition, work together in the air at all times. Formations of five or six airplanes are extremely maneuverable and at the same time can be controlled to the best advantage by a single patrol leader. It is probable that of a flight of six airplanes and pilots, not more than five will be available for duty on any given day. Where the mission requires a greater number than five or six airplanes, two or more flights acting independently, but in liaison with one another, will be employed.

132. Either one of the following methods may be employed for the formation of flights depending upon the direction of the wind and the size of the landing field:

(a) Formation on leaving the ground—The patrol leader takes off first, flying at less than full speed, and the others follow him in order. When the patrol leader has reached the approximate altitude which he has set beforehand for formation, he will make a half circle and return over the flying field, each pilot then taking up his appointed place. Upon passing over the flying field, the patrol leader can determine the number of airplanes which have been unable to take off.

(b) Formation over a selected spot—This method of forming patrols is especially useful when several patrols are to take off at the same time. In this case, the patrol leader is the last to take off and the deputy patrol leader the next to last. The altitude of assembly is fixed beforehand and depends upon the mission, ceiling, etc. It is never greater than 2,000 meters. Otherwise, the airplanes are likely to become dispersed before the patrol is formed. The assembly point is a few kilometers from the flying field, never more than ten, over some striking landmark. Upon arrival at this point, each pilot makes left-hand turns, while he is climbing, until he has reached the designated altitude which he must maintain precisely. The patrol leader climbs to an altitude of 200 meters below the patrol and describes right-hand circles. When he considers it proper, he turns toward the lines flying extremely slowly and balancing his wings to attract attention. The other pilots then assume their places. If no airplane is seen turning to the right below the patrol, the deputy patrol leader flies to the flying field to ascertain that the patrol leader has been unable to take off. A ground sheet signal gives the indication. If the patrol leader has been unable to take off, the deputy patrol leader assumes the leadership of the patrol.

133. All formations should comprise a double echelon in depth and in altitude, the airplanes at the rear being highest up so that they can take advantage of their altitude to close in on the patrol leader by diving, in case of necessity. The usual formation is that of an inverted "V", the patrol leader at the head. Number two and number four on his left rear and number three and number five on his right rear; number two and number three should be about 200 meters apart and about 50 meters above and to the rear of number one. Number four and number five should be about 400 meters apart and about 100 meters above and to the rear of

number one. When the patrol is composed of six airplanes, number six takes position above, behind, and to the left of number four, or above, behind and to the right of number five.

134. In formations of several flights, the same principle is employed. The flight leader of the entire formation flies at the head of the leading flight. One flight behind, above and to the left of him and another flight behind, above and to his right.

135. *Single Flight Combat.* — The patrol leader determines the advisibility of combat. He will be permitted a considerable latitude in making his own disposition when the combat is joined. As a rule, airplanes number four and number five of his formation will remain above to afford protection from enemy airplanes, which may in the vicinity. The patrol leader himself will always lead the attack. In the attack teamplay leads to victory. It is, therefore, essential that all members of one flight shall talk over on the ground and practice in the air the evolutions, which the Flight Commander will use in attacking different types of enemy aircraft.

136. In case of a combat when several patrols are flying together and a large force of enemy airplanes is sighted, the leader of the forward and lower flight will determine what action to take, the leaders of the other

flights guiding on him. In such cases, it is generally preferable to attempt to attack the rear man of the enemy formation. The inability to maneuver formations of more than five airplanes, makes it possible to throw the enemy into confusion and to attack his airplanes separately. The attack by the formation leader upon the leader of the enemy's formation should, as a rule, be avoided unless the formation leader is confident of possessing superior material. The attack by the leader of the formation upon the leader of an enemy formation invariably leads to a melee in which both formations become separated, which is difficult to break off inside the enemy's lines, and which simply becomes an engagement of individuals.

137. *The Rally*—After a combat every effort should be made to regain the formation as speedily as possible. This is easy to accomplish inside our lines if conspicuous land-marks are designated beforehand within four or five kilometers of the line. Within the enemy lines, the rally is far more difficult to execute. In this case, each pilot will fly toward the fixed rally point, within our lines, but will watch at all times to give assistance to any of our pilots who appear to be in trouble. When the rally point has been reached, patrol reforms in accordance with the principles laid down in paragraph 132 (b).

138. In making disposition of his forces, the Group Commander will endeavor at all times

ing instant response should
come in to the office of the
Group Operations Officer. He
will decide whether or not the
alert is to be answered, bearing
in mind the number of airplanes
instantly available, the number,
type, and probable mission of
the enemy airplanes reported,
their altitude and direction of
flight. He will transmit the alert
to the flight or squadron which is
standing by to respond to such
calls, together with his estimate
of the situation. The Flight Commander on duty will, as a rule,
decide the number of airplanes
which will actually be used to
respond to an alert transmitted
to him, but the group Operations
Officer should be authorized to
give orders on the subject in the
name of the Group Commander
regarding the number of airplanes to respond if, in his judgment, orders are necessary.

141. After a patrol leader has
left the ground, he is responsible
for carrying out the patrol's mission. He should be permitted
complete independence of judgment in the leading of his patrol,
and in exceptional cases, may
depart from the designated route
if the situation makes it advisable. The Group Operations Officer is responsible that complete
information is given to the
Squadron Operations Officer relative to every mission, and in
exceptional cases he will explain
the objective of the mission to
the patrol leader personally. The
patrol leader will only depart
from the mission assigned to him
in such cases as this appears to
be essential.

ORGANIZATION AND EMPLOYMENT OF ATTACK SQUADRONS.

Composition of Attack Squadrons and Attack Groups.

142. An Attack squadron will normally consist of 18 airplanes, (either mono-plane or bi-plane), divided into three flights.

143. An attack group will consist of two or more attack squadrons, the normal composition being three squadrons.

144. In addition to the combat squadrons, there will also be one park squadron assigned to each battle group. Whenever practicable, all squadrons of an attack group will be located on the same airdrome.

Missions and Duties of Attack Squadrons.

145. The use of low-flying airplanes on the battle-field and their cooperation in fighting on the ground, by open gun fire, or by attacking with bombs and hand grenades, is particularly effective from the point of view of morale, both on our own and the enemy's troops.

146. The systematic and aggressive participation in the battle of flying formations against ground targets is of great importance. During offensives, attack squadrons operate over and in front of the infantry and neutralize the fire of the enemy's infantry and barrage batteries. On the defensive, the appearance of the attack airplanes affords visible proof to heavily engaged troops that Headquarters is maintaining close touch with the front, and is employing all possible auxiliaries to support the fighting troops. The morale of the troops and their confidence in a successful defense is thereby materially strengthened. The object of the attack squadrons, in addition to the losses inflicted by them, is to shatter the enemy's morale by continuous attacks in formation, and thus to exert a decisive influence on the result of the battle. Confusion to the enemy's front line troops, dispersion of his infantry and machine gun fire from their normal targets, the demoralization of traffic, the dispersion and delay of reinforcements, as well as the actual losses inflicted upon his forces, are the means by which the mission of the attack squadrons is accomplished.

147. Whenever the situation warrants, attack squadrons should operate in conjunction with bombing squadrons. The area of attack may thus be extended deeper into the enemy's lines, the bombing squadrons operating beyond the attack squadrons, and normally as far back as the rear areas of the enemy's corps, and, in some cases, to the rear areas of his army.

Employment of Attack Squadrons.

148. The successful employment of attack squadrons depends upon their concentrated, continuous, uninterrupted engagement at the decisive time and place. This condition limits their use to that particular portion of the battle front upon which the entire operations depends, and prohibits their distribution over relatively unimportant portions of the battle line.

149. The proper execution of the missions of attack squadrons makes the fullest demands on the physical and mental capabilities of the personnel. While employed on attack missions, attack squadrons must devote themselves exclusively to their particular sphere of action. Tasks

forming part of the normal duties of the observation, pursuit or bombardment squadrons must not be assigned to attack squadrons simultaneously with their attack missions. Attack squadrons, however, will report to the proper Headquarters immediately after landing, all observations made during their flights which may be of value. Their duties in connection with observation are the same as now specified for pursuit squadrons.

150. Attack squadrons are to be employed in *DECISIVE* infantry actions. At other times (when the military situation is such that there is no probability of attack missions being required), attack squadrons may be employed as protection for corps and army observation units.

151. Attack groups will normally be held under the direct command of the Chief of Air Service of an army or, (in extended operations) of the Chief of Air Service of the Army

Group. Liaison must be maintained so that the entire forces of the attack units can immediately be thrown into action at the point designated. This requires that the personnel of the attack squadrons be constantly in touch with the progress of the battle and the exact locations of the leading elements of our own and the enemy's troops. It also requires that they be thoroughly familiar with the location of the enemy's artillery, machine gun nests, bivouacing centers, his lines of communications and routes or reinforcement immediately in rear of the battle front.

152. The information outlined in the preceding paragraph will be obtained through close liaison with the Chief of Air Service of the Army and Corps, Observation Groups, Balloons, Pursuit and Bombardment Groups, Ground Observation Posts and the General Staffs.

153. During active operations, the attack units will be kept ready for immediate action, both during the day and night. Their efficient use requires that they strike at the given point at the decisive instant, and with their maximum force. Their airdromes should be located as far forward as communications and the terrain will permit. Advanced airdromes will be reconnoitered, and communications installed beforehand, and these advanced airdromes will be utilized as the military situation requires.

(a) *Offensive.*

154. In the offensive, attack squadrons will be employed in force to destroy the enemy's forward infantry lines and harass his forward artillery. They will be used to neutralize infantry and machine gun fire. They will prevent the organization of supports and their movement forward to the main line of resistance. They will prevent the sending forward of reinforcements. They will isolate and demoralize enemy concentrations. They will prevent designated routes of communications from being used. They will prevent the sending forward of ammunition, especially by horse-drawn caissons to the front lines. The above missions will be accomplished by the use of bombs, hand grenades, airplane cannon, and machine guns.

155. Accurate knowledge of the ground is the first condition for the successful action of attack squadrons. The personnel must be thoroughly familiar with their own forward battle zone, and the composition and formation of the ground troops that are to make the attack, the position and location of the forward elements of the enemy's ground troops, his centers of resistance and lines of reinforcement and withdrawal.

156. Attack squadrons must not be engaged before the attack is made by the ground troops. The proper moment for the leading elements of attack squadrons to pass over our front line is the moment when the infantry units advance to the attack. Attack squadrons should therefore be continuously engaged until a decision on the ground has been reached. They should be ready and should strike again if counter attacks are being prepared.

157. In case the advance is being successfully accomplished, the attack squadrons must utilize every possible means of turning the enemy's withdrawal into a rout.

158. Light artillery, especially that using gas to delay our advancing troops, are one of the normal targets for attack squadrons. The enemy's barrage batteries are normal targets for our attack squadrons. Special flights should be detailed to attack these batteries.

159. Special attack squadrons or flights may be detailed for harassing traffic in certain areas behind the enemy's front lines. Their missions will usually be best accomplished by rendering designated traffic centers impassable.

160. Attack airplanes should not be given missions against enemy aircraft. Their relation to enemy aircraft is normally a defensive one only.

(b) *Defensive.*

161. The use of attack squadrons on the defensive against the enemy's counter-attacks made during our offensive operations has been indicated above. When our troops are on the defensive and the enemy's preparations indicate that his infantry attack is imminent, the attack squadrons must be held in constant readiness both by day and night. Continuous liaison must be maintained during this period regarding the enemy's assembly points, troop movements and probable line of advance.

162. The enemy's leading elements become of secondary importance after the advance is actually started, and the force of attack squadrons should be concentrated upon his supports and reserves, his barrage batteries, and possibly upon certain of his interdiction and harassing batteries. Normally, the enemy's second and third assault waves will be targets of prime importance for attack squadrons after the advance has begun. If the enemy's leading elements attack by the infiltration method, our attack squadrons should concentrate upon the "follow-up" forces, and except under very unusual conditions, cannot be used against the enemy's leading elements.

163. If the enemy's infantry advance is made in connection with tanks, the isolation of the tanks from their infantry supports becomes one of the missions of attack squadrons. The

Signal Corps radio truck used to receive and transmit messages.

attack by airplanes upon tanks should be made with bombs and airplane cannon.

Transmission of Orders.

164. The commander of the attack squadron or attack group will receive detailed orders from the Headquarters to which his organization is attached. These will state the following:

(a) Exact location of our own and the enemy's front lines.

(b) Objective and sector of the attack.

(c) Nature of the preparatory phase.

(d) Method of attack.

(e) "D" Day.

(f) "H" Hour.

(g) Targets especially assigned to the attack group or squadrons.

165. Each attack squadron of the group will be given one target, one mission, or one area to cover. If the position of our front line is not exactly known, as, for instance, during rear guard actions, the enemy's batteries, routes of advance, and road centers, will normally be given as targets.

166. During active operations, especially when our troops are acting defensively, every means for the rapid transmission of information and orders must be employed. If a division intends to counter-attack, this information, giving the hour and sector, must be transmitted to the attack squadron or group assigned. Telephones, telegraph, radio, or visual signals will be used. The

attack squadron or group, will, if necessary, maintain one or two airplanes over the Division P.C., for the receiving and transmission of information concerning the time of the proposed counter-attack. Upon receipt of this information, the liaison plane will return to its airdrome and transmit its information by radio, dropped message, or by landing.

167. Selected men of the leading elements of the infantry organization should be informed of the time that attack squadrons are to operate over their sector, and particular care should be taken that the panels or flares used to mark the front line are properly displayed.

Training and Tactics.

168. The lower the altitude at which attack airplanes operate, the greater the morale and material effect. For this reason, attack airplanes will operate as low as the terrain and their weapons permit. If machine-gunning troops in the open, descents as low as ten meters are advocated. Then flying at this height, the direction of attack should be parallel to, or away from our troops. Extremely low attack is especially valuable against columns of troops or convoys, along a straight road, in cuts, and against troops massed on open hill-tops. When using bombs, the airplane should be flown just high enough to be outside the danger zone of the explosion. For the engagement of batteries in action, a height of two hundred or three hundred meters is more favorable. If the batteries are exposed in the open where the terrain permits an attack from the flank or rear, at one hundred meters, or less, (depending upon armament of the airplane), may accomplish better results.

169. Attack squadrons and groups must make use of every opportunity to carry out training behind the front for their work. The most important features of this training are simulated attacks in close formation, flight following flight, and the preparation of time schedules of departure from the airdrome, formation of flight, attack, expenditure of ammunition, and return to the airdrome, replenishment of fuel and ammunition, and repetition of attack. Particular attention should be paid to the training of flight leaders, deputy flight leaders, and the control and maneuvering of the flight as a unit. Theoretical and practical instruction and training must be given to each individual until he has completely mastered his airplane and weapons.

Relation to other Aircraft.

170. Attack squadrons are for use against the enemy's ground forces. They are not, primarily, for use against enemy aircraft, except balloons. Their use against balloons should be considered as of minor importance, except in connection with attacks against enemy artillery.

171. During the preparatory phase of an operation, they may efficiently be used as protection for low-flying infantry and artillery airplanes. These missions should be utilized for familiarizing the personnel of the attack squadrons with the sector.

172. During the operations of attack squadrons, against their normal targets, they should be protected from enemy aircraft, either by pursuit airplanes, or by one or more flights of the attack group operating as protection at a higher altitude. If the group does not contain a squadron equipped with machines of the pursuit type suitable for engaging enemy aircraft, thereby requiring that protection be furnished by one or more flights of attack airplanes, the schedule of operations should be worked out so that the protection flights be relieved by other protection flights before their fuel has been consumed, and they will then descend and expend their ammunition against ground targets before returning to their airdrome.

173. Particular attention and thought should be given by all attack personnel to the means

and methods of improving the efficiency of attack squadrons, particular attention being given to maneuvers and new weapons.

LIAISON OF THE AIRPLANE WITH THE INFANTRY.

174. The functions of the infantry airplane in its cooperation with the infantry is separated into two distinct categories, which will be specified hereafter under the titles of: THE INFANTRY COMMAND AIRPLANE. THE INFANTRY CONTACT AIRPLANE.

I. *The Infantry Command Airplane.*

Function.

175. The Infantry Command Airplane acts as the liaison agent under the direction of the division commander, between the attacking infantry and the division P.C., and as an agent of liaison for the P.C.'s of the infantry itself, of the artillery and of neighboring troops, as circumstances require and in conformance with instructions from proper authority.

176. It follows the operations of the front line troops for the purpose of obtaining the position of their lines when desired, and transmits same to the division P.C., and gathers such information as possible concerning the enemy and our own troops during the preliminary reconnaissance which is made prior to asking for the position of the front line from the infantry.

177. It transmits to the infantry the orders of the division commander; transmits to the division commander the communications of the subordinate P.C.'s made by signals; and in general keeps the division commander informed of the progress of our own front lines and as to the situation in the immediate enemy lines.

The Mission.

178. It is not feasible to limit exactly the duties of the Infantry Command Airplane where such duties may temporarily coincide with those of the artillery surveillance or counter-attack airplane. It is desirable that the Infantry Command Airplane report all activity of interest that he may see during his preliminary reconnaissance, so that his message may well include a report of enemy batteries in action; the activity of enemy and our own neighboring troops, and similar information of importance. He should always report the activity of enemy aircraft, enemy balloons, and anti-aircraft. It must be borne in mind, however, that this airplane has for its specific mission the determination of the infantry front lines, and that all other considerations are secondary. To keep the command well informed as to the situation of our front line is the first and most important duty of the Infantry Command Airplane. The difficulties that he will have to overcome to be successful do not permit those in command to expect him to give other information regularly or to have him undertake other missions. However, if, as frequently happens in the war of movement, it is not immediately possible to obtain the position of the front line, the observer may render other services in the interval which will elapse until the time when he can obtain its position.

179. He may temporarily assume the functions of a counter-battery or surveillance airplane. He may relay to the command and to the artillery the signals made by the infantry such as a request for a barrage, or for an increase of artillery range, or a request for ammunition. In the case of strong resistance by the enemy, checking our advance at any point, he may inform the command by radio or by a dropped message on the P.C., or may drop a message on a group of infantry, giving location and importance of the opposing forces.

180. The command must realize that an absolutely fixed time for obtaining the position of the line is impracticable. This is true both at the beginning of an attack, when an Infantry Command Airplane will invariably be over the lines, and later during the war of movement when circumstances may easily arise rendering it impossible to obtain the line at a specific time. At the beginning of an attack the line should not be demanded until sufficient time has elapsed for the infantry to gain some predetermined objective.

181. Infantry commanders and troops must assist the aviator so far as lies within their power. A watch must be maintained for his signals, and a prompt response made to his request for the position of the line. It must be borne in mind constantly that the success of the mission depends upon a thorough mutual understanding and cooperation between the infantry and the airplane.

The Execution of the Mission.

182. An observer, in order to render a comprehensive, valuable report must bring up to the last moment the information he obtained before leaving the airdrome. This will be done by flying over our artillery line before going to the front; locating the important P.C.'s and observing the activity of our own and the enemy's artillery, the progress of the artillery engagement, and the aerial activity; then proceeding to the lines he will note the enemy activity on the ground; the grenade and bayonet fights, and any other information of importance and interest to the command. When he has thoroughly grasped the general situation he takes advantage of a favorable opportunity and discharges his signal asking that the Infantry indicate their position.

183. The Signal used by the airplane in identifying himself, asking for the line to be indicated, sending "understood" and making other pre-arranged signals, are made by rockets of various descriptions, discharged from a Very pistol. The significance of the various rocket signals used is specified in the plan of liaison, and may be changed from time to time, if circumstances demand.

184. The infantry will at all times have specially detailed lookouts whose duty it will be to observe the movements of the Infantry Command Airplane and report to the proper officer when the airplane signals its request for the line to be shown. The responsible officer will see that panels are promptly displayed. If the signal "Where are you" is again displayed by the airplane after the panels are shown, steps will be taken to immediately indicate the line by means of Bengal flares. These should be habitually used to mark the line in wooded country, and under

other circumstances where the airplane may have difficulty in locating the lines. If the Infantry Command Airplane does not send the signal "Understood" after ten minutes have elapsed, the panel should be taken in and no more flares will be lighted.

185. After having determined the lines the Infantry Command Airplane will proceed toward the division P.C., sending by radio the information gathered, and confirming same by his written message which will be dropped at the P.C. Normally the mission of the Infantry Command Airplane is completed by this act. If it is desired to communicate with other P.C.'s, messages should be delivered after completing the mission for the division.

II. *The Infantry Contact Airplane.*

Function.

186. The Infantry Contact Airplane takes an active part in the offensive operations, and acts as the liaison agent of the front line infantry and the accompanying artillery.

The Mission.

187. It attacks the enemy on the ground with machine guns and light bombs, and by such maneuvering may easily indicate the position of enemy strong points and centers of resistance. By signals and methods pre-arranged with the infantry batteries and accompanying guns, it indicates targets which should be taken under fire, and also indicates objectives to the heavy machine guns and mortars. Its communication with the ground troops will be entirely by visual signals and dropped messages. In order that the results obtained by this airplane are commensurate with the risks undertaken, such close liaison must exist between it and the troops on the ground that prompt and unfailing advantage is taken of every signal and message given by it. Success depends upon a liaison perfected to an extent hitherto unknown, in our service; a liaison must be founded on mutual knowledge, confidence, and admiration. The Infantry Contact Airplane by its signals and dropped messages gives to the smallest party of infantry information invaluable to them in their advance.

188. Such close liaison and cooperation should exist between the infantry and the Infantry Contact Airplane that a message dropped near any group of infantry, however small, will be recovered by them and carried at once to a responsible officer and action taken without delay according to the contents of the message. In this way minor units will have information of their immediate front of greatest value to them.

189. When the information gathered warrants it, and upon the completion of its mission, the Infantry Contact Airplane communicates with the desired P.C., imparting such information as it has collected. For subordinate P.C.'s in particular this is important, as by this means information is received which will not be obtained by other means for a long period of time.

III. Liaison.

(a) *Relations of the Air Service with Ground Troops.*

190. The success of the infantry mission, command or contact, depends entirely upon the maintenance of an intimate liaison between the air service and the infantry, from the division commanders down to the soldiers in the front lines. In order to foster the spirit of cooperation necessary to success, every effort will be made to have officers of the air service units visit the infantry in the lines, for the purpose of becoming acquainted with their work, their difficulties, and the way they live. Infantry officers will also be encouraged to visit the airdromes, when circumstances warrant, to become familiar with the operations and work of an observation squadron. When possible, selected officers will be taken over the sector by airplane. Special efforts should be made to enable officers of the division and corps staffs to see the lines from the air.

(b) *Airplane to Ground Communications.*

191. Radio and visual signals furnish the most reliable and generally used means of communication between the airplane and the ground. In the American Army at the present time the dropped message is employed to a large extent.

192. The observer sends by radio all his observations, confirming his information by a dropped message at the P.C. Rocket signals, discharged from a Very pistol, and other visual signals are used for communication with the front line troops and for other special purposes, as provided in the plan of liaison.

193. The observer tests his radio set before leaving the vicinity of the airdrome, with the ground testing station there, so that no airplane ever proceeds to the front without its radio being adjusted to the stations with which it may have to communicate.

194. The dropped message is invariably used to confirm the radio message at the P.C., for which primarily intended. This is important, as the radio messages are frequently lost by the receiving station. The dropped message is used by the Infantry Contact Airplane to communicate with the advancing troops, and, by special agreement, with the infantry batteries and accompanying guns.

(c) *Ground to Airplane Communications.*

195. For the infantry airplane, these signals are all visual. They comprise panels, Bengal flares, signal lights, and rockets, and any other improvised means for attracting attention of the plane.

(d) *Panels.*

196. Marking panels are used by the front line infantry to indicate their position to the airplane, either at the demand of the airplane, at a prearranged hour, or at the initiative of the infantry commander when for some reason he wishes to indicate his position to the Infantry

Command Airplane. The Infantry Command Airplane, having seen the panels displayed without request, will immediately take the position of the line, give the signal understood, and proceed as in his regular mission. Identification panels are used to indicate the location of the P.C.'s and in case of stations equipped with radio receiving sets, the display of a panel means specifically "Here is P.C., so and so, with radio set erected, listening in, and ready to receive messages." By this means the observer locates stations with which he may wish to communicate, and all stations so adjusted may intercept his message.

(e) *Flares and Rockets.*

197. The Bengal flare is used to mark the infantry line in woods, during misty weather or fog, when it is difficult for the airplane to see the panels. If after the line has been marked by the panels, the airplane again demands the line, flares should be lit. In lighting flares, care must be taken to have airplane in a favorable position, going away from the line, as flares remain lit only about thirty seconds.

198. After the airplane has signalled "Understood," or after a period of ten minutes has elapsed, the panels should be concealed and no more flares lighted.

199. Rockets and other signals are used for special purposes, as indicated in the plan of liaison.

IV. Training.

200. The preliminary instructions of infantry must be thorough and must be continued constantly while in repose or behind the front lines, in order that the principles of close liaison and cooperation with the airplane may be kept constantly in view.

201. Instruction must be given which will impress the importance of the work done by the airplane, and the absolute necessity of complying with its demands promptly. This instruction must be aimed at all infantrymen, from the regimental commander to the private. It must be borne in mind that after the observer has asked for the line, both he and the pilot are concentrating their attention on the ground; that it is very difficult at that time to maneuver so as to avoid machine gun fire from the ground or anti-aircraft fire, and that the airplane during this interval is at the mercy of enemy

Panel markers
for communication
with airplanes.

aircraft, completely without defense. Furthermore, the longer the airplane must remain over the lines at a low altitude the heavier becomes the hostile machine gun fire. The enemy is specially trained in this type of fire, and heavy casualties invariably result to the airplane. The destruction of the infantry airplane not only means the loss of two highly trained and specialized officers, difficult to replace, but it means that a very serious delay results in the arrival of information to the command at a time when very probably other means of communication do not exist. The success or failure of an operation may easily depend on the certainty of receiving the information which it is the mission of the Infantry Command Airplane to transmit promptly.

V. *Exercises.*

202. Exercises will be held at frequent intervals for the purpose of perfecting the liaison between the infantry and the Infantry Command and Contact Airplanes. These exercises will be held at concentration points in the rear, and with troops in repose behind the lines or newly arrived in Corps areas. A course of instruction will be established in each Corps at the airdrome of the Corps Observation Group, which will have for its purpose the instruction of officers and non-commissioned officers in infantry liaison, and to give those

attending the course such a knowledge of the Air Service and its operation, possibilities, and limitations, as will establish a firm, mutual understanding and confidence. A large part of the instruction will take the form of practical exercises under conditions simulating actual service as closely as possible. Every effort will be made to make the course interesting to the students.

203. In the armies on the front, arrangements will be made whereby officers of the air service, particularly of the observation units, may visit troops in the line, for the purpose of gaining first hand knowledge of the operations of ground troops, which will aid them in aerial operations, and tend to strengthen the confidence and liaison with ground troops.

204. All commanding officers of troops having control over observation air service will take such steps as are necessary to perfect the cooperation, confidence and liaison between the infantry and the air service. It should be borne in mind in this respect, that as the most suitable place to gain a knowledge of the infantry is in the front lines, so the most suitable place to gain a knowledge of the air service is on the airdrome and in the air.

AA guns on French trucks operated by 2nd Balloon Co.,
1st Army Corps., Montrieul, France, 8 July 1918.

Brig. Gen. Mitchell and his staff, Coblenz, Germany, November,
1919: (l. to r.) Capt. I. W. Miller, Capt. R. Valois, Lt. Col. L. H.
Brereton, Gen. Mitchell, Maj. I. D. Joralemon, and
Capt. O. E. Marrell.

54. Notes of the Characteristics, Limitations, and Employment of the Air Service
1919

During the war, officers and soldiers of the infantry and artillery often expressed dissatisfaction with the way aviation was being used. Such comments were summarized and answered in a paper, "Notes on Employment of the Air Service from the General Staff View Point,"[1] prepared in February 1919 under the direction of Colonel Gorrell, Assistant Chief of Staff, Air Service, AEF. After being circulated for comments, the paper was revised in France, given a new title, "Notes on the Characteristics, Limitations, and Employment of the Air Service," and later published in Washington in an *Air Service Information Circular*.[2] The latter version is printed below.

The original paper contained sections, omitted from the published version, concerning principles of command, complaints of aviators against the infantry and artillery, the "temperament" of fliers, and the status of the Air Service as a combat arm. These paragraphs seem to be of sufficient interest to warrant their being printed as an addendum.

Principles of Air Service Operations.

1. What is the function of an Air Service? These are its chief purposes:

The Air Service aids the Infantry, helps adjust Artillery, assists in keeping the staff informed, destroys the enemy air service, by using machine guns and bombs, assists in deciding actions on the ground, and prevents the enemy air service from rendering similar assistance to the hostile forces.[3]

2. The Air Service has difficulty in keeping the staff informed because there are many things which it is hard or impossible for airmen to see because of atmospheric conditions, the speed at which airplanes travel, the blind angles on all airplanes, and the fact that from an airplane the ground appears in plan, without contours. The Air Service can not take the place of Cavalry, but the Air Service can bring back accurate, cool reports, not warped by the sights and sounds of the battlefield.

1. In Gorrell's History, D-1.
2. Vol I, No 72, 12 Jun 20.
3. The revised statement is more positive than the original: "The Air Service tries to keep the staff informed. The Air Service helps adjust artillery. The Air Service tries to destroy the enemy air service. The Air Service tries to help decide action on the ground by using machine guns and bombs." Only significant changes in content will be pointed out in these notes.

These reports can be of value only if they are quickly decoded and transmitted. The airplane secures and carries reports quickly. A well-trained staff uses them quickly.

3. Adjusting Artillery from the air in a war of movement is difficult unless all who take part in the adjustment, Artillery and airmen alike, are thoroughly trained. The first essential is a thorough understanding between the ground and air forces and a well-developed system of cooperation and of signaling or communicating information. First, the Air Service must know approximately where the Artillery posts of command are located. Second, the artillery panel crews must answer signals promptly and properly. Third, the radio must work. Fourth, the details of the shoot must be carried out smoothly, and this can be accomplished only when efficient ground communication exists. Fifth, though perhaps it should be put first, the airplane must find the target at which the Artillery is to shoot.[4]

4. Airplanes in fighting in the air must try to keep clear of enemy airplanes an area about 10,000 yards deep in front of the line of battle. If they are successful the Infantry see few air fights and therefore think our planes are not operating. Complete success is impossible. The idea of a submarine barrage by submarines against submarines is ridiculous, but no more ridiculous than the conception of a

complete aerial barrage $2^1/_2$ miles high, 5 miles deep, and as broad as the front over which the battle is raging. A perfect aerial barrage is impossible because of the difficulty a plane has, first, to see another in the air, and second, to attack it. Therefore, enemy airplanes occasionally get past the most numerous and aggressive friendly pursuit concentrations. They must be accepted by our ground troops with the same philosophy as the enemy's shelling.

5. Low-flying enemy airplanes must be fought by ground troops utilizing their machine guns and rifles. In firing from the ground on low-flying enemy aircraft remember that many a machine is hit, the pilot wounded, and the observer killed, when the airplane does not fall nor appear to be damaged. Do not become discouraged because the enemy plane which is being fired at does not fall. Many machines of our Army, disabled by enemy fire from the ground, have come home in crippled condition, with observers dead and pilots wounded. The enemy did not have the satisfaction of seeing them fall.

6. If proper understanding, cooperation, and communication exist, airplanes can enter effectively into the battle on the ground.[5] The moral damage

they do with their bombs and machine guns is to the material damage as about 20 to 1, but success in battle comes from the destruction of the enemy's morale, and not from the enemy's annihilation. The best relations based upon intimate knowledge and personal acquaintance and friendship, must exist between the Air Service and the other arms. Otherwise there will be misunderstandings and recriminations.[6]

7. The above points are illustrated and explained in the succeeding pages.

Functions of the Air Service.

8. Whatever the future development of aviation may be, up to the end of the war in 1918 its most important function had proved to be securing and transmitting information concerning the developments in and beyond the line of battle. The work of keeping the command informed was rendered difficult because what the Air Service could do and what it could not do were not sufficiently well known either to the staffs or to the troops, and

---

4. The original contained the additional statement: "This is not always easy."
5. The original began: "If good liaison exists. . . ." Similar changes were made in other places where "liaison" was used in the original.
6. The original contained an additional paragraph: "Finally, the Air Service is a combatant arm and not a staff service. It must be utilized as such."

Notes of the Characteristics,
Limitations, and Employment
of the Air Service

305

because the American Army did not have at its disposal a sufficiently large air force. The purpose of this pamphlet is to set forth simple statements of the capabilities and limitations of the Air Service.

9. As has been pointed out, the Air Service, in order to assist the Infantry, besides keeping the command informed, adjusts Artillery; fights in the air against the enemy air service; attacks ground objectives, both tactical and strategical; and prevents the enemy air service from rendering similar assistance to the hostile forces.[7]

10. The work of keeping the command informed is done by—

(a) Visual reconnaissance;

(b) Photographic reconnaissance;

(c) Thorough mutual understanding and the prompt communication of information.

Limitations of Reconnaissance.

11. Visual reconnaissances by daylight and by well-trained observers often furnish information of great value. These missions sometimes fail for reasons which are readily apparent. An airplane can not stand still to scrutinize a stretch of country. A thousand men hidden in a wood or a village can not be compelled by an airplane to expose themselves. Therefore, if they wish to remain hidden they can do so. Hence negative information, while valuable, is not always accurate. Again, the Air Service can not replace the Cavalry. If, however, the presence of concealed hostile troops is suspected, this can often be verified or disproved by airplanes dispatched on special missions, while circling at a very low altitude over the locality concerned.[8]

12. An airplane passes over the country so rapidly that troops on the ground can sometimes deceive the aerial observer; for example, a column may alter temporarily its direction of march, etc. Hence even positive information must be carefully weighed in order to determine its value.

13. No man, no matter what his flying experience, can stand on the ground and estimate the state of visibility in the air. A ground mist frequently reduces visibility from the air on days which may appear perfect for observation purposes to men on the ground.[9]

14. To the aerial observer certain things show more or less clearly, due to the fact that backgrounds and shadows affect visibility. Fields show up from the air like checkerboard squares. Soldiers standing on the line where two fields meet are hard to see, while if they are a few feet within one field or the other they show up clearly. On the line between two fields, if they are seen at all, it is generally because they are revealed by their shadows. The best cover from airplane observation is natural shadow.

15. Wheel tracks and paths are readily noted by an observer and show clearly on airplane photographs. Freshly turned earth is quite conspicuous and no amount of camouflage can conceal it completely.

7. The last clause was added in the revision.

8. The last sentence was added in the revision.

9. The original contained an additional sentence: "The only answer to the question of what is the visibility on any given day is 'Take the air and see.'"

Capabilities of Reconnaissance.

16. As the limitations of aerial observation are seldom appreciated, so also its capabilities are seldom comprehended.

17. Any staff officer who has seen war has heard tales of disaster such as are almost always brought back by the seriously wounded and by skulkers. All reports from ground observers in the front line have a tendency to be warped by the excitement, the sights, and the sounds of the battle field. It is difficult for a staff officer to avoid being influenced by these reports. A properly utilized and properly trained Air Service can discount many false reports and can clear up most of the obscure points on the line of battle.

18. To locate troops on broken ground requires flying at altitudes of 700 feet and less, at which altitudes airplanes are extremely vulnerable to machine-gun fire from the ground.[10] It is difficult to locate the lines during an attack, as our own Infantry are then too busy to show their panels; hence, though the enemy does not greatly hinder our low-flying airplanes at such a time, the airplanes do not bring back the most valuable reports. The best time for Infantry contact patrols is usually for about one hour after the capture of an objective. During enemy counter attacks, a very heavy fire against our low-flying airplanes must be expected.

19. The aerial observer, when not in action, is generally somewhat removed from the sights and sounds of the battlefield. He is not subject to the waves of emotion that can and do run through masses of men at the front.

20. The aerial observer can not do his work intelligently unless he has had proper training. To secure reports of the greatest value, the observer should be a highly trained General Staff officer. This ideal, for obvious reasons, will rarely be attained. By the proper training of Air Service officers it can be approximated. The pilot should be a young man, the observer an older man, who has received several years on General Staff training in schools established for that purpose.

The Airplane as an Instrument of Communication.[11]

21. Once the deadlock on the western front was broken, and movement—which is the essence of war—began, the staffs of large units began to experience serious difficulties in transmitting orders and in securing information. These difficulties were almost insuperable so far as ground communication with advanced elements of ground troops was concerned; the common methods failed to function with more than a small part of their former efficiency. This was not true of the Air Service. The difficulties of communication, inherent in a war movement, are present to a much smaller extent

between the staffs and the Air Service than between ground observation posts and posts of command. In future wars we may expect the Air Service to do more and more of this important work.

22. In a war of movement the Air Service will probably be the chief reliance of the G–2's of combatant units. The training for G–2 work should therefore include experience in aerial observation.

Communication.

23. To keep in touch with the front line in open warfare, only one means is reliable—the actual physical carrying of a message. Runners are slow, horses frequently impracticable, and motor cycles demand roads. Considering time and distance as important factors, the airplane is often the best carrier. Better means of communicating from the ground to the airplanes must therefore be devised. This is limited at present to a few prearranged signals which, though they may not contain all a commander desires to know, even now contain all he need know to form a sound estimate of the situation. Communication from airplanes to the ground, on the other hand, for all essential command purposes, is efficient where good training exists.[12]

10. The opening sentence of the original was dropped in the revision: "Infantry liaison flights are dangerous."

11. The original heading was: The Airplane as an Instrument of Liaison. See note 5 above.

12. In the original this is followed by a section (one paragraph) on principles of command. See addendum.

Notes of the Characteristics,
Limitations, and Employment
of the Air Service

307

Combat.

24. Aerial fighting is difficult. Its difficulties are not appreciated by the majority of those who are not aviators.

25. The greatest difficulty of the pursuit pilot is to find the enemy. The difficulty that a man in the air experiences in seeing another airplane is hard to understand. When an airplane is seen from the ground, it is generally the noise of the engine which attracts attention to it. In the air the noise of the pilot's own engine drowns all other sounds.

"Vision of the Air."

26. With no foreground or background a pilot may look directly at an airplane and not see it, because his eye is out of focus. This difficulty is hard to explain. To seafaring men it will appeal as natural. To landsmen, all that can be said is that it does exist, and aviators try all sorts of expedients in an effort to overcome it, such as looking at struts which are at different distances from their eyes and then sweeping the horizon.

27. From above it is difficult to distinguish an airplane if the camouflage on the wings blends well with the background of the earth against which it is seen.

28. An airplane seen from below can not be attacked unless the attacker is justified in accepting a serious disadvantage of position during the combat that is to follow.

29. Two airplanes on the same approximate level present to one another very small projected areas as compared with the same two airplanes as seen from the ground, for from the ground they are seen in plan.

30. For the foregoing reasons hostile airplanes often pass one another in the air without joining in combat.[13] Also observation airplanes, like ground reconnaissance patrols ordinarily avoid combat unless they are attacked.

Fighting in the Air.

31. Fighting on the ground is in two dimensions; fighting in the air is in three. When combat is joined, an airplane moving at a speed in excess of 120 miles an hour is a gun platform from which to fight a target moving at a similar speed. The difficulties involved are sufficiently obvious to explain the fact that effective range never exceeds 400 yards and that 90 percent of the machines shot down are shot down at ranges from 100 yards to 10 feet.

32. To the average soldier at the front, and to his officers, too, the sole purpose of airplanes was apt to be regarded as the driving off of enemy machines— a function which was very poorly performed in the war, to judge by the accounts of those unfamiliar with the proper employment of an air service.[14]

Tactical Employment.

33. The proper employment of pursuit airplanes includes the destruction of enemy aircraft, the protection of our own observation airplanes, and the prevention of enemy aerial attacks on our ground troops. By our success in harassing and destroying hostile two-seaters the enemy is prevented from informing his command.[15]

34. Experience has shown that maximum casualties can be inflicted on the enemy air service, and our own observation airplanes can be better protected, by adopting a vigorous offensive policy for our pursuit airplanes. This is the best defense. Maintaining our aerial front line far beyond the front line of our Infantry and clearing the enemy aircraft from the area in which our observation airplanes work, give better protection to our Infantry and to our

13. In the original the following sentence is inserted: "Probably the Infantry of both sides curse their respective representatives as 'yellow,' while the truth is that the pilots have never seen one another at all or else at least one of the planes was an observation plane, charged with the duty of getting information."

14. In the original the sentence ended: "... to judge by the accounts of those unfamiliar with the proper employment of an air service." The original then continued: "The function was ill-performed because the Air Service never attempted it for the reasons indicated in paragraph 38 [34 in revision]."

15. The last sentence was added in the revision.

observation airplanes than attempting to give close protection. The Infantry do not see combats far within the enemy's line, and consequently one hears frequent complaints and demands by the ground troops for the patrolling of our lines by our own pursuit airplanes. Such a disposition of forces would be analogous to placing all of our Infantry in the outpost zone and evenly distributing it from one end of the line to the other, while confining it to a strict defensive. Such tactics would of course inevitably result in defeat.[16]

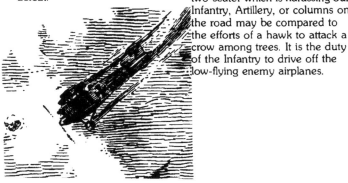

Low-Flying Enemy Airplanes.

35. As a matter of fact, the only successful way to deal with low-flying airplanes is for the Infantry to have confidence in their own weapons—rifles and machine guns—and to use them. It has been explained that it is difficult to see one airplane from another in the air. The lower an airplane is flying the harder it is to see. Once seen, a low-flying airplane is hard to attack from the air. With no room to dive or maneuver, the efforts of a pursuit airplane to attack even a two-seater which is harassing our Infantry, Artillery, or columns on the road may be compared to the efforts of a hawk to attack a crow among trees. It is the duty of the Infantry to drive off the low-flying enemy airplanes.

36. The great moral effect of low-flying airplanes results from an exaggerated notion of their capabilities. An airplane that remains over the enemy lines at an altitude of 500 feet for only five minutes may safely be assumed to cover 7 miles. It will probably be seen by all the troops of one division who are in the forward zone, and experience goes to show that, no matter with what equanimity the division withstands hostile shelling, a number of its troops will believe themselves to have been in danger from such an airplane. (One of the best American divisions in France on one occasion received 3,500 enemy shells in its sector in one day without being disturbed, and yet personal questioning by General Staff officers disclosed that almost every man in the division believed himself to have been in danger from a single low-flying enemy airplane which was over its lines for about 10 minutes.)[17]

37. All ground troops must be educated to appreciate that—

(a) Airplanes never regulate Artillery on the front lines.

(b) Airplanes seldom regulate Artillery from an altitude of less than 2,000 feet.

(c) More or less continuous observation is essential to the regulation of Artillery fire.

(d) Rifles and machine guns of ground troops are the best defense, and are a thoroughly efficient defense, against low-flying airplanes.

16. The last sentence was added in the revision.

17. The original continued: ''In addition, if, while an airplane is over the lines or during the ten minutes after it departs, shells fall near any part of the Division, as is almost certain to occur, in all probability the shelling will be attributed to the direct agency of the airplane. The attribution of such shelling to airplane artillery adjustment is invariably based upon complete, and to the aviator pathetic, ignorance of the functions, capabilities and limitations of the Air Service.''

Notes of the Characteristics,
Limitations, and Employment
of the Air Service

309

38. Infantrymen are loath to fire upon aircraft, because they fear to disclose their positions. Firing on aircraft by infantrymen does not tend to disclose the position of the Infantry, but rather by virtue of keeping the enemy at a higher altitude helps to conceal it. Many pilots and observers returning from flights have reported being fired upon by small arms, but if in any case a pilot or observer was able to locate the point from which the fire came with sufficient accuracy to demand Artillery fire against the hostile positions the case was a very rare one, probably unique.

39. If Infantry do not fire against low-flying hostile airplanes, the enemy's aviators will become bolder, descend to lower altitudes, and will remain much longer over the lines.

40. It can be stated unhesitatingly that the boldness of the German low-flying planes over the American Army on the western front was due to insufficient initiative by the Infantry, who frequently failed to engage hostile aircraft, or engaged them only in a half-hearted manner.

41. A word of caution in this regard is imperative. The Infantry must not engage our own airplanes. Before firing on any airplane its hostile intent should be established beyond a doubt.

All combatants on both sides in the late war received numerous reports of enemy pilots' flying machines captured from the other side. So far as the allied armies are concerned no German airplanes were ever flown by the Allies near the lines. No allied pilot would have dared to fly any German plane near the lines, for the one reason, if for no other, that it would have been impossible to have notified all allied pilots when and where he would be in the air, and if all allied pilots, at least within a radius of 30 miles, had not been notified, any flier in a German airplane near the allied lines would, in all human probability, have been attacked. If the low-flying airplane has not exhibited any hostile intent, the Infantry should wait to see the hostile insignia before firing upon it. To fire when it is so far away that the insignia can not be distinguished, is not productive of results.[18]

Bombing and Machine Gunning.

42. Besides its interest in the actual fighting in the air, the G-3 staff is interested in these elements of the air service which enter directly into the battle on the ground—bombers and airplanes which attack ground objectives.

43. The developments of the late war in its later months indicate that future wars will see a further strengthening of machine-gun nests as a means of defense. The airplane gave hopes, at the end of the war, of assisting materially in overcoming these obstacles. To be of assistance in the reduction of machine guns, air service units must know their location and communication must be sufficiently good so that the cooperative action between the arms at the disposal of the Infantry and Artillery can be assured.

44. The attack of ground objectives in the zone as far back of the enemy's front lines as his divisional posts of command often yields important results. For such attacks to be of maximum effect, good targets, such as columns on the road or troops in reserve, marching up to the line of battle or retreating, must be exactly and positively located before the "ground-straffers" are dispatched. Under other circumstances good results will in all probability not be achieved.

18. The last two sentences were added in the revision.

45. Bombing and its results have heretofore been little understood. The great mobility and speed of airplanes make it possible to utilize day bombardment tactically to influence an action in progress. It is considered that as compared with the material destruction wrought—which is frequently considerable—the moral effect of either bombing or machine gunning from airplanes is as 20 to 1, and victory in battle results from the destruction of the enemy's morale.

Mutual Understanding and Personal Visits.

46. The basis of the proper operation of the combined arms is mutual understanding and a spirit of camaraderie. This is best secured by the exchange of personal visits. Infantrymen, artillerymen, and staffs must visit airdromes and watch the air service work. Aviators must be sent for tours of duty with Infantry and Artillery units.[19]

**ADDENDUM
from Notes on
Employment of The Air
Service From The General
Staff View Point**

Principles of Command[20]

26. Nevertheless, in no case should Squadrons or Groups be under direct orders of G–2 and the role of Branch Intelligence Officer should be turned over to an Air Service Intelligence Officer. *Air Service units must be under the direct orders of Air Service officers, held responsible that the orders of the Commanding General, expressed (for intelligence) through G–2, are properly executed.* From a G–2 point of view the Air Service is to be regarded as any other combatant unit. The relationship between staffs of large units (Division, Corps and Armies) and the Air Service of the units should be analogous to that between, for example, G–2 of a Corps and the Divisions of the Corps. Each air service unit should have its own officer who is responsible for the collection and forwarding of all information of the enemy. He will cooperate with G–2 and maintain intimate liaison exactly as do the G–2s of divisions and

19. There were four additional paragraphs in the original. See the addendum.
20. See note 12.

Notes of the Characteristics,
Limitations, and Employment
of the Air Service

311

corps. But he is under the orders of the Air Service Officer who commands the unit.

. . . .

51. All [21] the recriminations between the Air Service and the other line troops have not been made by the Infantry and Artillery. Aviators who have fought in the war have expressed themselves quite freely when they have been called upon by ground troops for protection against enemy aircraft at a time and a place where the only airplanes in the sky were American. Frequently American airplanes have been shot at and a few have been brought down by the machine guns and rifles of our own Infantry.

52. But to be shot at by one's own friends is one of the unavoidable incidents which occasionally occur to all arms. Recriminations were more bitter when *the Air Service met with definite refusals to cooperate on the part of the line.* When *the Chief of Staff of one Division refused even to consider holding Infantry Liaison exercises* with the Air Service, when *day after day Artillery batteries changed their locations and the Air Service was not notified,* when *the Infantry took cover and hid instead of displaying their panels when an airplane signalled asking for them,* when *P.C. after P.C. was found which was without its distinctive panel,* on these occasions it was difficult for the Air Service to maintain its high spirit and morale.

Aviation Morale

53. Much ridicule has been heaped upon the so-called "temperament" of fliers. Fliers are not per se any more temperamental than other healthy young men, and are equally anxious to live up to the best traditions of the profession of arms. Nevertheless the morale of an Air Service is a sensitive thing, certainly, at least as sensitive as that of the Infantry, and subject to much the same reactions. The giving of ill-advised orders to fliers such as sending out a squadron under atmospheric conditions that render work impossible and increase the likelihood of casualties will destroy the confidence of the pilots and observers of that squadron in their superiors, with consequent loss of morale. These conditions can only be accurately appreciated by a flier. Therefore orders to Air Service units should always proceed from Air Service commanders, held responsible that the orders of commanding General expressed through their Staffs are carried out.

The Air Service Not A Staff Service

54. *Finally it is particularly desired to impress upon all staff officers that the Air Service is not a staff service but is a combatant arm and it must be considered as such to obtain success. It is susceptible to the same tactical dispositions, in accordance with the same underlying tactical principles as are all other arms of the Service.*

21. See note 19.

Lt. Col. William C. Sherman (far right) was on hand to examine
a new Vickers machine gun which fired through the propeller.
Lts. V. F. Ludden (far left), C. G. Sellers (in cockpit), and
Capt. G. C. Thomas collaborated in the briefing.

55. Sherman: Tentative Manual for The Employment of Air Service

1919

Lt. Col. William C. Sherman, who was Chief of Staff of the First Army Air Service in November 1918, and who produced a "Tactical History of the Air Service" at the end of the war,[1] also prepared a "Tentative Manual for the Employment of Air Service." Written in France in the early weeks of 1919, the manual reflected the experience gained during the war. A revised copy, entitled "Notes on Recent Operations," was sent to GHQ, AEF for publication, but GHQ apparently never gave its approval. On 11 April 1919, following a cabled request from the United States, a copy was sent to Washington. There it was mimeographed on 18 June 1919 by the Information Group, Air Service, under the title "Notes on Recent Operations." The following year it was published under the latter title as an *Air Service Information Circular*. The text printed below is from a copy of the original in Gorrell's History.[2]

Part I.

Chapter I.
General Principles

1. The name Air Service is, to some extent, a misnomer; the employment of Air Units is not an automatic thing, functioning as a service, but is an arm, subject to the same variety of a combination for differing tactical situations as are the other arms, and governed by the same tactical principles. It is proposed, therefore, to enumerate these principles, before going into a more detailed study of Air Service employment.

2. It is a fundamental of human nature for man to fear man more than the chance action of steel and lead. Therefore, in the future, as in the past, the final decision in war must be made by man on the ground, willing to come hand to hand with the enemy. When the infantry loses, the Army loses. It is, therefore,

the role of the Air Service, as well as that of the other arms, to aid the chief combatant: the infantry. That the lack of assistance from other arms would inevitably result in the defeat of our infantry does not affect the truth of the axiom. Two important corollaries therefore follow: the Air Service must know infantry and its assistants; and general officers and their staffs cannot hope to produce the most efficient knowledge, tactical combinations, unless they have a thorough knowledge, not alone of infantry, but of its assistant arms, which include the Air Service.

3. In so far as the Army is concerned, the object of war is the defeat of the enemy's armed forces in the field. This can be done only by seeking a decision in battle. It is essential to victory,

1. Published in the first volume in this series.
2. Gorrell's History, D–1, pp 167–247. See *ibid.*, C–15, for copy of version sent to GHQ. A note in D–1, p 1, states that the manual was prepared by Sherman and corrected by Gorrell. A copy of the mimeographed version that at one time was in the library of the Field Officers' School at Langley Field, is in AFSHRC 248.211–61K. The section on corps aviation was published in *Air Service Information Circular*, Vol I, No 74, 12 Jun 20, and the entire manual in another *Circular*, Vol I, No 76, 30 Jun 20.

therefore, to assume the offensive. In war, practically never does victory come as a result of the material destruction of any large portion of the enemy's forces. Often much material destruction has resulted from victory: it has never been a prerequisite to victory. The final aim sought, therefore, is not the material destruction of the enemy, which can never in practice be even nearly complete, but the destruction of the enemy's hope of victory, of his desire to continue fighting, in a word, of his morale. This fact must be particularly borne in mind, in considering the Air Service, whose moral effect on ground troops is out of all proportion to the material destruction wrought. In the line, the most certain outward sign of that superiority of morale which insures victory, is the possession of the battlefield. No other factor is so largely destructive of the enemy's morale as this. It has been truthfully said, therefore, that to advance is to conquer, and one may conquer only by advancing. These facts, seemingly trite, must nevertheless be constantly kept in mind. Whole tactical doctrines have ignored certain of these truths, with consequent disaster. Nor were there lacking men, in the recent war, who believed that the war would end in complicated systems of trenches: A failure to appreciate the very nature itself of war. In the future, therefore, as in the past, the only true expression of war is the battle, and the battle implies and necessitates movement. The long deadlock on the Western front must be regarded as exceptional and peculiar, and lessons drawn from that carefully examined, lest a rule be deduced from what was indubitably an exception.

4. It is the battle then that is sought for, and, in the battle the destruction of the enemy's morale. It is not necessary, however, at one and the same time to attack all portions of the hostile army. The morale of an army may be compared to the human body: to destroy it, it is necessary to destroy only one of several of its component parts. The battle then resolves itself into an attempt, by a crushing blow, to destroy but a limited portion of an enemy's army, while holding over the remainder the threat of impending destruction. This demands then a certain economy of forces: to the portions of the field where the blow is to be struck must be brought the superiority of force needed. For all other portions of the field, we may regard troops there employed as detachments—either to hold limited portions of the field or to ascertain the enemy's strength.

5. Before, however, the proper economy of forces can be determined, knowledge must exist of the enemy's dispositions. In former wars, this required numerous detachments of troops. The employment of these constituted the preparatory stage of the battle, which frequently absorbed a large portion of the forces available. Great tact and coolness, a careful estimate of facts, still left often no lightening of the "fog of war." It is in this phase of the battle that the relative importance of aircraft has steadily grown. Surprise exists now and always will, but air control can eliminate a very large proportion of the unknown elements, and admit of a solution based on facts.

6. The decisive blow struck, to complete the victory requires that the fleeing enemy be given no opportunity to reorganize, and that his loss of morale be communicated to the portions of his army still unstruck. The pursuit, then, is at once organized. Too frequently, in past wars, the victor, scarcely less disorganized than the vanquished, has failed to gather in the fruits of victory. Very rarely has a thoroughly organized pursuit been possible. This will be dealt with in greater detail in a later chapter, so far as the employment of aircraft is concerned.

7. The general principles briefly outlined above apply to Air Service units, not alone active cooperation with ground troops, and their attack of the enemy's ground troops, but equally in purely aerial warfare. Before, however, discussing in detail tactical use of aircraft, certain possibilities and limitations of aircraft must be considered.

8. The extraordinary development of airplanes during the great war has brought it about that practically one natural factor alone can prevent flying today: lack of visibility. A pilot travelling at rates of speed almost always in excess of one hundred miles per hour must have a fairly wide range of vision in order to know and to maintain his course. Nor can visibility be determined from ground observations, except in extreme cases. It is highly probable that with time, this handicap will be overcome to a large extent. It must, however, be accepted as a definite limitation today. A second limitation to be borne in mind is the duration of time an airplane may remain over the enemy lines. Due to the question of fuel supply, wear and tear on comparatively delicate engines, and the great physical and mental strain of flying, where every sense is keyed up to the highest, only a small average number of hours

per day per plane available can be kept up indefinitely. It is not uncommon among the uninitiated to believe that, because ten planes are available, ten may be kept over the lines all day, with short intervals for refilling fuel. Such is far from being actual service conditions.

9. From the point of view of the command, the greatest value of the Air Service to date has been in gathering information of the enemy and of our own troops. In the nature of things, this source of information should be in future wars both more nearly complete and more reliable. The observer, aloof from the battle, is less subject to its disturbing influences. He is removed from the contagion of fear and panic, so easy of transmission where men are elbow to elbow. He hears none of the reports of the wounded, nearly always breathing calamity. He receives no impressions from skulkers, "the last man left in their company," justifying their crime by reports of disaster. In short, he is physically so situated as to be able to see and report with an approach to that mathematical coolness and accuracy, that is so desirable, but so seldom secured by human beings in the thick of a fight, subject to all its disturbing reactions.

Physically, nothing is defiladed from the airplane observer's view: a situation that is rarely met with in even the best systems of terrestrial observation.

During the long period of

trench warfare, elaborate methods of liaison were established, which seldom succeeded when the war of movement—which is alone really war—began. Liaison from airplane to ground, less modified, by movement because more simple and containing fewer links to be broken, should on the contrary, always be successful in open warfare, where due care is taken. Liaison from the ground to airplane, on the other hand, is still comparatively undeveloped, and constitutes one of the problems of the immediate future.

Reports from untrained observers, whether on the ground or in the air, are generally valueless. Training is essential before one can describe even the location of the most conspicuous objects. To know what things are important, and what unimportant; to know exactly what to look for, and what negative information is of value; in short from a view to secure such information as will permit an accurate estimate of the situation, requires an officer whose knowledge and intelligence fit him to be a general staff officer. In practice, this ideal will rarely be attained. Nevertheless it will be striven for, and thereby make more full and reliable the information received in future from the Air Service.

10. An employment of the Air Service, as yet in its infancy, but capable of great results, is that of actually intervening on the battlefield, not alone by bombing

[but also] by direct attack with machine guns. In estimating the value of such attacks, we must again bear in mind that an army is defeated not by destroying it, but by destroying its morale. It has been said before that man fears man more than the chance of lead or steel. The basis of the greater fear is the knowledge that man, having both intent and intelligence, can pursue his design to a fatal conclusion, and hence is more terrible than any inanimate object, directed from a distance. Much of this feeling enters into man's fear of hostile airplanes. The latter's commanding position, rendering concealment apparently useless, induces the instinctive belief in the heart of every man on the ground that he himself is being watched by hostile eyes and being made the target for bomb or bullet; and that this hostile man can pursue him intelligently and ultimately destroy him. To this is added a feeling of utter helplessness, not justified by facts, but none the less instinctive and not to be overcome wholly by reason or training. That the moral effect of attacks from the air is, as compared with attacks from the ground, out of all proportion both to the effort expended and the material damage done, is attested by many incidents. A division of first class troops, that received with equanimity four thousand shells per day in its sector, has been known to be greatly disturbed and harassed by the efforts of one persistently active day bomber. Inquiry showed that almost every man in the division believed himself to have been in danger from this plane.

11. It is the purpose of this manual to set forth the principles governing the use of air units, and to put on record the results of experience in this war. But, two facts must be held constantly in mind: The Air Service is a combatant arm, and full training in peace can alone prevent inefficiency in war.

Chapter II. Security

1. Security in Air Service units as in all branches of the army embraces all those measures taken by a command to protect itself from observation, annoyance, or surprise by the enemy. Security of the plane in the air will be dealt with under the heading of combat, because in reality once the machines have actually left the airdrome, the general principles of combat go hand in hand and come under the province of fighting in the air. It will only be necessary, therefore, in discussing the security of Air Service Organizations to consider those measures taken by the Commanding Officer at his airdrome, that will protect him from observation, annoyance, or surprise.

2. It is essential the greatest care be exercised in selecting an airdrome, not only from the standpoint of accessibility and other general principles and shelter, but also from the standpoint of security. An airdrome, therefore, should be selected bearing these principles in mind. Airdromes, if possible, should be away from landmarks which will be visible at night; they should be away from streams; if located at the edge of a forest they should not be near a prominent portion of the forest. While it is well in selecting an airdrome to take precautions against enemy action, it is advisable to look out for natural obstacles, such as undulating ground, and high obstacles which might endanger machines landing or taking off. Every precaution should be taken that will eliminate, insofar as possible, the chances of accidents. In flying, accidents are bound to occur even at the front where pilots are supposed to be capable of flying under any conditions. After the airdrome has been located, care should be used in the location of the hangars. They should never be placed closer than 100 yards apart; in practice it has been found well to scatter them evenly around the perimeter of the field. Where there is danger of night bombing it is well to cover them with camouflage material which makes them blend with the ground, not appearing as landmarks at night. Precaution against fire must always be taken in the case of hangars, and camouflage material should not be used where airdromes are not subject to night attack, as it is always inflammable and renders the possibility of complete destruction greater. At times it is better to place hangars on good ground than to religiously distribute them evenly over the airdrome and break a lot of propellers, tail skids and machines in rough ground. After a commanding officer has located his hangars he should next look to the security of his personnel. Under normal war conditions his enlisted men and officer personnel will be scattered over the whole airdrome, but great care must be taken to keep a unit in its own area, so as to maintain proper disciplinary control. By scattering the personnel in this way danger from bombardment is minimized and protection given to the hangars and machines located at the airdrome. Often airdromes are so located that additional precautions by way of trenches and abris must be taken. If the airdrome is very close to the line great care must be taken against attack in force by enemy low flying airplanes, machine guns should be mounted and personnel properly organized for the most efficient handling of same when occasion arises. Smoke screens, if possible, should be prepared so that a dense form of smoke can be scattered over the airdrome from all directions should an attack of this nature be attempted and if under any special circumstances it is felt that the security of the airdrome is jeopardized. In this respect special guards should be maintained at all times to be ready to handle the situation.

3. Complete mobility of all units insures the safety of material when a general retreat becomes necessary. This mobility depends principally on sufficient initial transportation equipment, and its proper upkeep during the course of operation and on the maintenance of mobility in the unit at all times. Offices should be located in trailers ready to be pulled away on a moment's notice. Spare parts should be kept in trailers and in spare trucks, and movement orders should be extant at all times and revised and republished at frequent intervals.

Chapter III. Shelters

4. The maximum achievements of any Air Service organization can only be achieved when machines are properly housed against the weather and the personnel is comfortably cared for. Mobility and defense against bombardment attacks must be considered.

5. Airdrome sites should be selected on flat well drained high ground, free as far as possible from mud and dust. Good roads must lead to them and a railroad should pass in the vicinity. High grass will injure many propellers and must be removed before flying begins. Sanitation and kindred subjects will be cared for as prescribed in Field Service Regulations. See also Paragraphs 2 and 3 in Chapter 2, Part I.

Chapter IV. Orders

6. The principles laid down in Field Service Regulations for the issuance of orders apply to the issuance of orders for the Air Service.

Chapter V. Marches and Convoys

7. (a) Wings, or larger units, will move by groups.

(b) The removal of a Pursuit Group from one field to another has primarily three phases:

1. Preparation for the move.

2. The move.

3. Arrival at the new airdrome and the preparation until day of attack.

8. Preparation for the move.

(a) As accuracy is of paramount importance in any move, the Group Commanders will be given his new location and all necessary information concerning it, with instructions to make all arrangements to move—but to carry on his preparations fully with only the date, hour, and location omitted.

(b) He will, therefore, before flying to the new location immediately call a meeting of Squadron Commanders, Park Commanders, Supply, Transportation, Radio, Engineering, and any other officers who in his opinion are necessary to contribute to the working out of the operation, which must be planned with all the forethought possible. In this meeting all questions of moment will be discussed which will include:

I. Transportation.
II. Supplies—continuance of incoming.
III. Rations for at least ten days from the present railhead.
IV. Material left on the field for transport to the rear, to be placed in charge of an officer sent from the rear for that purpose.
V. Billeting to be properly adjusted with the local authorities before leaving.
VI. Pulling down of existing inter-camp lines of communication that have been installed by the group.
VII. Camp thoroughly policed before leaving, etc., etc.

(c) The Group commander will then make an aerial reconnaissance to the new airdrome with the object of returning with further particulars of importance to the move in general.

I. He will establish the route by which pilots will fly, noting the important landmarks, airdromes, gas stations, headquarters to notify if forced to land one side or the other of given points "en route."
II. He will have inspected the new field and made notes on the landing facilities.
III. The work of the construction squadron engaged in the preparation of the field and upon the construction of barracks, hangars, etc.
IV. The line of communication to outside headquarters.
V. The disposition of the hangars on the field and which squadrons will occupy them.

VI. The new Group Headquarters and the most suitable location.
VII. Men's quarters and messes.
IX. And in general an idea of the neighboring units and in which way they might be of assistance to his command in moving.

(d) Upon returning to the old field he will see that all these details are passed on to the Squadron Commanders and to those affected.

9. The Move.

(a) Moving orders will be received from the wing or the Army Air Service Commander, depending upon the tactical use to be made of the unit and will be acknowledged by notifying the Headquarters as soon as the echelons have started or are all en route.

(b) The move will be made in four echelons, by squadrons, each echelon of each squadron in charge of an officer.

I. Advance echelon.
II. Main echelon.
III. Flying echelon.
IV. Rear echelon.

10. The advance echelon will be in charge of a competent officer and will be light, consisting only of the personnel necessary to start inter-camp communication by telephone to establish squadron operations, to locate source of supply, fuel, straw, water, etc., and to set up kitchens to take care of arrivals until incoming units are settled. In regard to the above, the park commander will immediately get in touch with the Air Depot of the Army of its advanced field to insure this supply, determining at the same time the quantity of planes on hand, spare parts, etc., that may be called upon for

immediate use. Also get in touch with Parks of adjoining Armies which may be used as an auxiliary supply.

11. The main echelon will leave if possible the next day and will consist of all non-flying personnel of the Group, less the necessary personnel from squadrons and Headquarters Detachment, required to provide meals, planes, make minor repairs on those planes which may be out of commission, attend to billeting, policing, etc., etc. All material that can be taken will accompany this echelon, which will leave camp at the designated hour and will follow the route according to itinerary.

12. The following rules and regulations are to be observed on the march.

(a) All stops for meals or other reasons, other than those caused by emergency, will be regulated on schedule order issued when moving order has been received, designating time of departure and route.

(b) Speed of truck train will be between 10 and 12 miles per hour, regulated by Acting First Sergeant at head of train in side car.

(c) In towns and villages, distances between transportation will be 30 feet, every place else 200 feet.

(d) The train will never stop within a radius of one mile of any town or village.

(e) Acting First Sergeant may grant soldier permission to enter town but only for a good reason.

(f) No soldier will descend from trucks for any reason whatsoever without permission from the N.C.O. in charge of truck.

(g) Each junior N.C.O. will be in close relation with his senior N.C.O. and privates, and is directly responsible to his immediate superior for the discipline and work of his men.

(h) When train is moving, if certain trucks are lagging, put them at the head of the train.

(i) Trailers may be shifted at noon stops or at evening stops, provided that such changes will assist in maintaining schedule.

(j) Chauffeurs will work in details to which trucks are assigned and will be held responsible that their trucks have extra supply of gas each.

(k) N.C.O. in charge of each section will be responsible to the Acting First Sergeant for the loading and unloading and placing of equipment assigned to his section. He will also be responsible for the discipline of the

men assigned to his section while en route and until the squadron is settled in its new quarters.

13. The flying echelon will consist of all serviceable machines, with their pilots. This party will leave the field after the advance echelon has reached its new station to receive the planes. Flight formations will be used and each pilot leaving the gound will be given the necessary information for making the trip. On arrival at the new station each pilot will report to the commander of the advance echelon.

14. The rear echelon will consist of the necessary personnel required to provide meals, start planes, make minor repairs on these planes which may be out of commission, attend the billeting, policing material left on the field for transport to the rear, empty gas containers, etc., etc., but will terminate their work as quickly as possible, making sure that the camp is thoroughly policed and in the proper shape to be taken over by the rear units or a new organization, and leaving a proper guard for the camp, should the incoming units be de-

layed or the local authorities be unable to furnish the proper protection.

15. It is most important that these echelons be properly officered to handle any emergencies that might arise and that the move be conducted according to one prescribed route with a schedule of arriving and departing times for the main stopping points "en route."

16. Officers heading these echelons will be assisted by another officer and side car who will bring up the rear and notify the head of the convoy of any breakdowns. They will also be posted on all traffic rules for convoys, see that all rules of the road are observed and in entering congested areas will make sure that no other moving units have priority of movements.

17. All drivers will be supplied with maps and an itinerary of the move in case of breakdowns.

18. Each echelon will depart with ten (10) days' ration.

19. A medical officer will accompany each echelon.

20. Arrival at the new field and preparation until the day of the attack. As soon as the Group has arrived and a hurried inspection has shown that things are progressing nicely, the Group Commander will:

(a) Report the arrival in person to the Wing or A.A.S.C. Headquarters, as the case may be.

(b) Ascertain the locations of all units with which he will be expected to keep in liaison.

(c) Dispatch the radio and searchlight officers to establish relations with the radio and searchlight P.C.'s and to get in touch with their respective liaison officers at A.A.S.C. Headquarters.

(d) Dispatch other liaison officers, calling upon Squadron Commanders, if necessary, to establish relations with anti-aircraft batteries, balloon locations, headquarters of adjoining army units, corps observation groups, in short, developing all sources of information which will materially assist in the efficient functioning of the group as well as developing relations which will include the personal touch so essential in cooperation.

(e) See that all lines from outside sources as well as the inter-communicating telephone systems are speedily installed,

including radio and searchlight installations.

(f) Make sure that the operations office of the group is establishing itself with all scale maps necessary, information about existing line locations of allied and enemy airdromes, anti-aircraft batteries, balloon locations, searchlight locations, etc., and the proper housing of the radio and power equipment.

(g) Make arrangements for an aerial target, preferably a small lake at which the pilots may commence at once to test their guns.

(h) Visit personally the staff officers of the A.A.S.C. or Wing of the Army to which attached; Corps observation groups, either pursuit group with whom patrols will be made; C.O.'s of units working with the army operation on the right or left, etc., etc.

21. Separate squadrons will move as above, except that the aerial reconnaissance of the new station and other details of the Group Commander's duty will be performed by the Squadron Commander.

22. A separate flight will generally move in only three echelons: the advanced echelon, the flying echelon, and the rear echelon. The main body of the flight may travel with either the advance or rear parties, depending on circumstances. The Flight Commander will make the same arrangements as the Group or Squadron Commander in the moves discussed above.

Part II. Corps and Army Observation

Corps Observation
Introduction

1. The purpose of this Manual is to establish, on the basis of experience gained in the War with Germany, the general lines of technical procedure governing the operations of the air service assigned to Army Corps in the Field.

Chapter 1. General Principles

2. The Air Service of any Army Corps in the Field is an auxiliary arm. Primarily it is organized for the purpose of observing the dispositions and activities of the enemy during active hostilities. It further assists the artillery as a means of fire control. It partakes of the general nature of combatant arms in that its mission forces it from time to time into combat with enemy aerial forces. The Corps Air Service may accept but will not ordinarily seek combat.

3. The Air Service of an Army Corps is under the tactical and administrative control of the General Commanding the Army Corps. The troops of the Air Service of a Corps are Corps Troops. Corps Air Service troops assigned for tactical duty to Divisions within the Corps retain their identity as Corps Troops.

4. The basis of organization for the Air Service of an Army Corps is the Observation Aero Service Squadron. The basis of the Squadron is the two-seater airplane manned by a pilot and an observer. The Air Service of the Corps may number one or several squadrons.

5. When two or more squadrons are operating together in the same Corps they are organized into an Observation Group. The Observation Group is under the immediate command of a Group Commander.

6. The tactical and administrative control of the Corps Air Service vested in the Corps Commander is delegated to Corps Air Service Commander (C.A.S.C.). The C.A.S.C. is an officer of the Air Service. He is a member of the Corps Staff. Upon the original organization of the Corps he is designated by General Headquarters upon the

recommendation of the Chief of Air Service. Thereafter the Corps being a part of an Army, he is designated by the Commanding General of the Army upon the recommendation of the Army Air Service Commander.

7. The Corps Air Service is dependent, for technical supply and replacement of personnel, upon the Air Service Organization of the Services of Supply operating through the medium of Air Depots, Air Parks, and Replacement Squadrons of the Air Service in the Zone of Advance.

8. The details of organization, assignment and designation of personnel, amounts and kinds of transportation and technical equipment are fixed in the Tables of Organization for the Air Service of an Army Corps, Air Service of the United States Army.

Chapter II. The Squadron

9. Tactical and administrative control of the squadron is vested in the Squadron Commander. He is responsible for the tactical, technical, and administrative efficiency of his organization. He is assisted by a staff of officers in the discharge of his duties. His prime qualification is leadership. He is the rallying point of his command. The degree of success attained by the squadron will depend very largely upon the example set by the Squadron Commander. The Squadron Commander may be either a pilot or an observer. In either case he is conversant with the essential principles of the work of both.

10. A Squadron Commander in his administrative duties is assisted by a competent Adjutant.

Routine administration is supervised by the Squadron Commander but is effected by the Adjutant.

11. Routine details of squadron supply are administered by the Supply Officer. The Supply Officer will ordinarily be placed in charge of the transportation of the Squadron.

12. In the exercise of his tactical functions the Squadron Commander is assisted by an Operations Officer. This officer is ordinarily the senior observer present. A junior observer may be detailed as Operations Officer if, in the opinion of the Squadron Commander, his executive ability, practical experience, and record for devotion to duty warrant his preferment. The Operations Officer is responsible, under the Squadron Commander, for the direction of the tactical operations of the squadron. He collects, compiles, and transmits all tactical information. He assigns tactical missions to the individual pilots and observers of the squadron. He directs the establishment and maintenance of liaison. He renders, nightly, to higher authority, a detailed account of the tactical operations of the squadron for the day. He acts as tactical advisor and instructor to the pilots and observers of the squadron.

13. The Operations Officer is assisted in the discharge of his duties by an Assistant Operations Officer. The Assistant Operations Officer is an observer. The Assistant Operations Officer replaces the Operations Officer during the latter's absence.

14. The squadron is equipped with Radio Set capable of sending and receiving radio messages to and from all ground stations within a radius of fifty kilometers. The Squadron Radio Set is further equipped with an artillery spark set for receiving airplane messages on short wave-lengths. The squadron radio equipment further consists of airplane type sending sets mounted on each airplane. A detail of Radio mechanics is a part of the personnel of the squadron. The squadron Radio Section is in charge of the Radio Officer. The Radio Officer is responsible for the installation and upkeep of all radio equipment. He is further responsible for the radio liaison of the squadron. He is in personal touch with the Corps and Army Radio Officers. He is conversant with Corps and Army Radio Plans and Regulations and assures compliance with these. He assigns wave-lengths to outgoing airplanes. He is responsible for the coding and decoding of radio messages and of telegrams. He receives the test calls of airplanes leaving the airdrome unless relieved of this function by the Radio Officer of a higher unit. He investigates into the causes of airplane radio failures

and establishes liaison with radio stations of artillery and other units with which radio failures have been reported. Wherever possible he logs the messages of all airplanes of his squadron operating on the lines, with a view to determining, in case of failure, whether the faulty functioning originated aboard the airplane or elsewhere. He maintains a complete log of all radio messages received at his station. He is assisted by one or more trained radio noncommissioned officers.

15. The armament of the airplanes of the squadrons is installed, aligned, and maintained at the maximum of efficiency by the Armament Officer assisted by a staff of enlisted mechanics. The Armament Officer is responsible for the supply, calibration, and loading of machine-gun ammunition. He is further responsible for the supply of signal rockets, signal pistols, and message dropping tubes. During intensive operations he is charged with the duty of replenishing aboard each airplane, immediately the plane is announced available for flight, the stock of equipment above noted. Immediately upon taking station at an airdrome the Armament Officer establishes a machine-gun testing butt, an armament work-shop and storeroom, and erects adequate gun-racks. He assigns rear turret machine-guns to observers by number. He assures the use of rear-turret machine-guns only by the observer to whom each gun, or set of guns, is assigned.

16. The care and upkeep of airplanes and engines is the duty of the Engineer Officer. The Engineer Officer is in immediate charge of the airplane and motor mechanic personnel of the squadron. He is responsible for the instruction and efficiency of the mechanics. He is assisted by a Chief Mechanic and three Chiefs of Flight mechanics.

17. For the purpose of distribution of control the squadron is divided into three Flights. The Flight is composed of six airplanes together with the indicated proportion of pilots, observers, and mechanics. The Flight is commanded by a Flight Commander. The Flight Commander is ordinarily a senior pilot. The Flight Commander is never an observer. The Flight Commander is responsible to the Squadron Commander for mechanical and tactical efficiency of his Flight. He acts as instructor and advisor to the pilots of the Flight. When an entire Flight is detailed for a single mission the Flight Commander is the leader of the formation. The Flight Commander is ordinarily Second-in-Command of the Squadron.

18. The flight is never an administrative unit. In theory it is a tactical unit; in reality it is a technical group, furnishing a convenient sub-division for distribution of technical control. During intensive operations the operative unity of the Flight cannot be preserved. Fluctuation in the average availability of machines in the different flights, and varying qualifications of pilots, will render assignment to duty by flight roster inexpedient. Squadron Commanders will assign pilots to duty in the order of availability and according to the special qualifications of each, not Flight by Flight. During periods of comparative inactivity, however, a duty roster by Flight may be advantageously employed thus:

> One Flight, Duty.
> One Flight, Reserve.
> One Flight, Off duty.

This arrangement is desirable in that it permits pilots one day in every three of complete rest and freedom from responsibility. It has the further advantage of permitting a thorough inspection and overhaul of airplanes every third day.

19. Where a single squadron is operating separately with a division in the field the tactical organization becomes similar to that of the observation group.

Chapter III. The Corps Observation Group

20. The Corps Observation Group consists of a Headquarters, two or more observation squadrons, and a photo section. Medical ordnance, artillery, infantry, and Intelligence personnel are attached.

21. Command of the Group is vested in the Group Commander. The administrative functions of the Group Commander are similar to those of the Commanding Officer of any Army Post.

22. The Group Commander assures the efficient execution of tactical orders received from higher authority. He is responsible for the organization and efficiency of the tactical staff assisting him in his functions. In reality he is the representative, at the airdrome, of the Corps Air Service Commander. Upon his ability to visualize the specific demands of the general situation as communicated to him from higher authority depends the success of the Group.

23. The Group Commander is assisted in his administrative work by a Group Adjutant. The Adjutant is assisted in his duties by a Headquarters Detachment of enlisted clerks and orderlies.

The functions of the Adjutant are similar to those of the Adjutant of an Army Post.

24. Supplies are received by the Group for the Air Park and also the Air Park attends to certain repair of not sufficient major importance to warrant their being done at the Air Depots.

25. In the fulfillment of his tactical functions the Group Commander is assisted by an Operations Officer. The Operations Officer is an able and experienced observer. The Operations Officer is responsible, under the Group Commander, for the direction of the tactical operations of the Group. He collects, compiles, and transmits all tactical information proceeding from outside sources to the Group and all information proceeding from the Group to outside units and headquarters. He transmits orders for the execution of missions to the squadrons concerned. He actively directs and

maintains at a high point of efficiency the liaison of the Group. He organizes the Group Operations Room. He prepares the schedule of missions for each day. He renders nightly to higher authority a detailed account of the tactical operations of the Group for the day. He receives and supervises the reports of all observers. He acts as tactical advisor and instructor to the flying personnel of the Group.

26. The Operations Officer is assisted in the discharge of his duties by an Assistant Operations Officer.

27. The Radio Section of the Group is exactly similar in organization to that of the squadron. The Group Radio Officer, in addition to the duties outlined for the Squadron Radio Officer, supervises the operations of the squadron Radio Sections. Where a separate Radio Section is not detailed to the Group the Group Commander may designate a squadron Radio Section in lieu thereof. The Group Radio Section maintains operators at the receivers throughout the day and night. It constitutes one of the surest means of liaison available.

28. A complete motorized photographic laboratory constitutes a part of the technical equipment of the Group. The laboratory, together with its staff of enlisted experts, is commanded by the Group Photographic Officer. Wherever possible the Photographic Officer is responsible for the installation of a photographic barrack, with complete apparatus for developing, drying, and printing in quantity production. Airplane cameras are a part of the equipment of the Group Photo Section. The installation of cameras aboard airplanes is a function of the Photo Section.

29. The Branch Intelligence Officer is a member of the Group tactical staff. He is especially trained in the subject of intelligence of the enemy. He is assisted by a staff of clerks, draftsmen, and photo interpreters. He is responsible for the collection, compilation, and distribution of all intelligence of the enemy gathered by the observers of the Group. He provides the maps for the use of the Group. He prepares a special large scale mimeographed map for use of observers in marking the location of troops. These maps are extremely useful additions to dropped messages reporting the results of infantry contact patrols. He is responsible for the interpretation, assemblage, map and file record, and distribution of aerial photographs of enemy territory secured by observers of the Group. He maintains close liaison with G–2 of the Corps.

30. The Operations Room is the tactical heart of the Observation Group. It is the center and source, for the organizations and individuals of the Group, of all tactical information. In it are conveniently displayed detailed, large scale situation maps of the organization of the Army, Corps, and Divisional areas. Other maps show enemy situation and organizations. Charts, diagrams, tabulations, orders, bulletins, reports, photographs having a technical or tactical bearing on operations are available for immediate access. Work tables, paste-pots, colored crayons for the use of observers and pilots are provided. Maps are on file for distribution to individuals. A collection of technical works for reference of flying personnel is kept at hand. The complete Operations Room is the realization of effective liaison. Before leaving on missions observers are instructed to post themselves on the latest developments and receive final instructions from the Operations Officer or his Assistant at the Operations Room. Upon returning from missions observers invariably prepare their reports here. The Operations Room is the Headquarters of their Operations Officer.

Chapter IV. The Corps Air Service Commander

31. Technical, tactical, and administrative control of all sections, units, and groupings of the Air Service of an Army Corps is vested in the Corps Air Service Commander. The C.A.S.C. is a field officer of the Air Service. He may be either a pilot or an observer. He should be thoroughly familiar with the general principles of the procedure governing the operations of the General Staff. He is a member of the Corps Staff. In addition to his administration and tactical duties, as an Air Service Commander he is the immediate advisor to the Commanding General and the Staff in all matters pertaining to the tactical employment and operations of the Air Service as a whole. He is at all

times familiar with the tactical situation and may make such dispositions to meet it as the limitations and possibilities of the arm he directs indicate, provided that such dispositions in no way conflict with instructions emanating from superior commands. He further transmits and assures compliance with orders governing the employment of the Air Service emanating from the Staff and the C.O. He is responsible for the efficiency of Air Service liaison. He is responsible for the assurance of maximum operative efficiency of the units and staffs of his Command. He is assisted in the discharge of his duties by a staff of experienced Air Service Officers. The post of the C.A.S.C. is with the Corps Staff. The office of the C.A.S.C. is a section of Corps Headquarters.

32. The C.A.S.C. is assisted in his administrative duties by an Adjutant. The Adjutant is assisted by a Headquarters Detachment of enlisted clerks and orderlies.

33. Adequate transportation and transportation personnel must be allotted the C.A.S.C. for the carrying out of all liaison duties and establishment of courier services. Supervision of transportation is ordinarily the duty of the Adjutant.

34. The C.A.S.C. is assigned an airplane for his personal use. It is the function of one squadron of his command to assure the care and upkeep of his airplane.

35. In discharge of his tactical duties the C.A.S.C. is assisted by an Operations Officer. The Operations Officer is an Air Service Observer of wide active experience and considerable executive ability. The Operations Officer

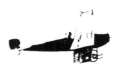

replaces the C.A.S.C. in his temporary absence. He is responsible, under the C.A.S.C., for the issuance and transmission of all tactical orders. He advises with the C.A.S.C. in all matters pertaining to the establishment of adequate liaison system by all sections, units, and groupings of the Corps Air Service. He collects, compiles, and transmits, in close liaison with the Corps and Divisional Staffs, all information, both outgoing and incoming. On the basis of the tactical situation as established by the day's information and orders he prepares, under the immediate supervision of the C.A.S.C. the general Operations Order governing the operations of the Groups for the following day.

36. The Operations Officer of the C.A.S.C. is assisted in the discharge of his duties by an Assistant Operations Officer.

37. Such personal liaison for the Office of the Corps Air Service as cannot be undertaken by the C.A.S.C. or his Operations and Assistant Operations Officers is assured by one or more Liaison Officers. These Officers are ordinarily Air Service Observers of considerable active experience. It is their duty to visit as often as may be necessary the Headquarters and Posts of Command of Divisions and Divi-sional troops and there discuss and, if possible, solve all tactical problems and collect all tactical information having a bearing on the operations of the Air Service in their relation to the commands visited. Liaison Officers render verbal and written reports on their activities to the C.A.S.C. at the close of each day.

38. It is important that all concerned recognize the Office of the Corps Air Service Commander as the sole controlling point for activities of the Corps Air Service. Ordinarily no orders emanating from Staff or Line Commanders requiring compliance by the units of the Corps Air Service will be transmitted direct to the Group or to the Squadron immediately concerned. Orders will be transmitted to the C.A.S.C. or his representative and thence will be issued to lower units. In this connection a comparison may be drawn for the tactical purposes between the regiment and the Air Service of the Corps. In the case of the regiment, orders requiring compliance by battalions or companies pass through the Regimental Commander. This practice is established by military precedent and dictated by practical considerations. In general the same precedents and considerations apply to the Air Service. Situations may and frequently do arise where it is impossible to transmit orders for the Air Service having their source in Divisions through the office of the C.A.S.C. Communications may be interrupted or extreme urgency may interfere and dictate the more direct and rapid method. In special situations of this nature it is permissible for Divisions to transmit orders direct to the Group. The C.A.S.C. in this case is informed by the Group Commander of the receipt of the order and the action taken to comply. In like manner all relations of the Group and Squadrons entered into with Line Organizations should be taken cognizance of by the

C.A.S.C. Liaison Officers proceeding to Division Headquarters and Divisional units will report in one way or another to the C.A.S.C. that visits are contemplated or have just taken place. The result of visits will likewise be reported. It is of extreme importance that the C.A.S.C. be informed up to the minute of all tactical activities of his command. Obviously, unless he is conversant with the very latest data regarding the operations of his command he cannot intelligently direct future operations nor report accurately on the accomplishment of work. Incomplete exercise of control by the C.A.S.C. will result either in duplication and the issuance of superfluous orders, or in an under estimation of the needs of the situation and a consequent failure to make adequate disposition.

Chapter V. Assignment and Functions of Squadrons

39. In assigning Squadrons the C.A.S.C., upon whom this duty devolves, will consider the tactical needs of the Corps as a unit, and the needs of the Divisions of the Corps in the line. Excepting for purposes of training, the Division in reserve will not be considered. The C.A.S.C. will ordinarily assign one Squadron to perform the missions required by the Corps as a whole and one squadron each to the Divisions on the Line.

40. The Corps Squadron has a zone of action bounded on the right and left by the Corps boundaries. The depth of the zone is ordinarily never more than ten kilometers from the enemy territory. The depth is determined in each particular case by the relative strength of enemy aerial defenses weighed against the urgency of demand for information. The Corps Squadron is charged with the duty of securing all photographs of enemy territory, whether photographs are requested by the Corps or Divisions. It is charged with such general surveillance of the course of battle across the entire Corps front as the situation may demand it. It controls and adjusts the fire of the Corps artillery and observes any preparations for enemy counter attack.

41. The Division Squadron is charged with the duty of surveillance of the Divisional Sector to the depth of flight of the Corps Squadron. It is further responsible for establishing liaison between the Divisional Commander and the troops in the front line by means of low-flying Contact Patrols. It reports the position of the enemy's advance elements and his dispositions for defense and attack. It controls and adjusts the fire of the Divisional Artillery. Observations made by Divisional planes and reported to Divisional Headquarters are repeated to Corps Headquarters.

42. All Squadrons report to headquarters of units to which they are assigned the locations of enemy batteries observed in

action and the location and density of friendly and enemy shell observed. Special reconnaissance for the location of enemy batteries in action are ordinarily carried out by airplanes of the Corps Squadrons but may be requested by Divisions of the Squadron and assigned to them.

Chapter VI. General Observation and Principles

43. The observation airplane is not designed for combat. It is charged not only with securing information *but with the duty of reporting on its observations*. Observation planes will avoid combat whenever possible, thereby increasing their chance of returning safely to report on information gained. They will avoid all danger from enemy aerial defenses whenever such action will not materially interfere with the accomplishment of the mission. In like manner the Command will carefully weigh the urgency of need for information against the risk involved in obtaining it. Where the risk overbalances the need the Air Service will not be called into action. It must be borne in mind that the Air Service is a costly, highly trained arm. Replacements of personnel and equipment are difficult and effectives must be husbanded in times of relative inactivity in order that maximum service may be counted on

when greater need arises. Airplanes must never be utilized when balloons will give the results desired. As a means of liaison between the troops and the Command the Air Service should be called upon only when all other means fail or are virtually certain to fail. Never use aerial observation when terrestrial observation is sufficiently efficient. Local actions will never be deemed sufficient reason for ordering the accomplishment of contact patrols.

Chapter VII. Information

44. With the Air Service, as with all other Arms, intelligent and successful action is based upon accurate and complete tactical and technical information of the military situation. The Corps Air Service itself is fundamentally organized with the object in view of gathering information of the enemy for communication to the commands and Services concerned. The Air Service, on the other hand, is itself dependent upon outside sources for such information as will enable it to carry out its

functions in the most efficient manner. Collection and communication of information will constitute a prime preoccupation of Commanding Officers.

45. Information may be considered under two general heads, (a) Information of the Friendly Situation, (b) Information of the Enemy Situation. Information of the Friendly Situation includes (a) Situation on the ground, (b) Situation in the air, (c) Plans for future operations (1) on the ground (2) in the air, (d) Liaison plans. Information of the enemy ordinarily available includes, (a) Situation on the ground, (b) Situation in the air, (c) Plans for future operations.

46. Sources of Information of the Friendly Situation:

1. On the Ground—
Corps and Division Staffs, Commanders of Combat Units.
Field Orders: G–3, Army Corps, Division.
Daily Operations Orders: G–3, Army, Corps, Division.
Liaison Reports: G–3, Corps, Division.
Station Lists: G–3, Army, Corps, Division.

Situation Maps:
Artillery Command, Army, Corps, Division.
G–3: Army, Corps, Division.
Plans of Employment: Artillery, Corps, Division.
Observation Post Bulletins: G–3, Corps, Division.

2. In the Air—
Army and Corps Air Service Commands.
Neighboring Air Service Units.
Station Lists: Army Air Service.
Bulletins: Army Air Service.
Operations Reports: Army and Corps Air Service.
Operations Orders, Army Air Service.

3. Plans for Future Operations—
Field Orders: G–3, Army, Corps, Division.
Operations Orders: G–3, Army, Corps, Division.
Plans of Employment: Artillery, Army, Corps, Division.
Maps to Accompany Any Above: corresponding sources.
Air Service Plans: Air Service Command and Units.

4. Liaison Plans and Data—
Road Liaison: One-way Road Maps and Orders, G–1, Army Corps, Division.
Plans of Liaison to Accompany Field Orders:
Telephone.
Telegraph.
Visual Signals.
Rockets.
Panels.
Flares.
Projectors.
Radio.
Pigeons.
M.D.S.
Runner.
Airplane Dropping Grounds.
Fixed Regulations Governing All Forms Liaison: Confidential Pamphlet No. 2 (Revised) G.H.Q., A.E.F., June 1918, "Liaison for All Arms."
Fixed Regulations Governing the employment of Aerial Observation in Liaison With Artillery: Confidential Pamphlet No. 80 (Revised) G.H.Q., A.E.F., May 1918, "Aerial Observation for Artillery."
Means of Secret Liaison:
Codes: G–2, Corps.
Airplane Codes: Plan of Liaison and Fixed Regulations as Above.
Secret letter map coordinates: G–3, Corps.
Service Code: Chief Signal Officer, Corps.
Telephone Code Name Directory: Chief Signal Officer.

47. Sources of Information of the Enemy Situation:

1. On the Ground—
Field Orders: G–3.
Operations Orders: G–3.
Liaison Reports: G–3.
Observation Post Bulletins: G–2.
Summaries of Intelligence: G–2.
Interrogation of Prisoners: G–2.
Enemy Order of Battle Maps: G–2.
Aerial Photographs: G–2 and Air Service.
Air Service Reports:
    Army Air Service.
    Corps on Right.
    Corps on Left.
    Own Corps.
Balloon Observation Reports.

2. In the Air—
Enemy Airdrome Maps: G–2, Army (Thru A.A.S.C.)
Bulletins:
    Army Air Service.
    Corps on Right, Air Service of.
    Corps on Left, Air Service of.

Operations Reports:
    Army Air Service.
    Air Service, Corps on Right & Left.
    Neighboring Air Service Units.
    Balloon Reports.
    Liaison Reports: G–3.
    O.P. Bulletins: G–2.
    Summaries of Intelligence: G–2.
    Interrogation of Prisoners: G–2.
    Interrogation of Captured Aviators: Air Service, G–2.
    Balloon Observation Reports.
    Friendly Anti-Aircraft Artillery.
    Observations of own Air Service Units.

3. Plans for Future Operations—
    Summaries of Intelligence.
    Interrogation of Prisoners.

48. Stress is laid upon the personal contact element in collecting information of every sort. Frequent conferences by Air Service Officers with other officers of the Aerial Army and with Staff and Unit Commanders of Corps and Divisions will often elicit special information, not available from other regular sources, which may be advantageously acted upon.

49. The Field Order embodies a résumé of the friendly and enemy situation and establishes the strategical and tactical plan of action which will be followed by the troops of Army, Corps, and Divisions over a considerable period. It includes annexes giving information regarding the activities of special arms and services. The general Plan for the employment of the Corps Air Service during the period of activity presumed is based upon the tactical provisions of the Field Order. The Field Order is communicated to the entire flying personnel of the Corps Air Service in order that pilots and observers may have a thorough understanding of, and take an intelligent interest in operations in which they are to participate.

50. The Daily Operations Order, G–3, embodies a résumé of the friendly and enemy situation at the close of the day and establishes the tactical plan of action for the following day. The activities of the Corps Air Service conform to the tactical demands for aerial cooperation with the troops as set forth day by day in the Corps Operations Order. The G–3 Operations Order is not necessarily, however, the sole basis for the planning of daily Air Service operations.

51. Liaison Reports, G–3, and Observation Post Bulletins, G–2, are hurried reports rushed from the forward areas by the most rapid means of liaison available. They ordinarily demand imme-

diate action, if any, by the Air Service. They form the basis for the ordering of specific missions, not for the formulation of extended plans of action. They frequently warn the Air Service of radical changes in the terrestrial or aerial situation requiring a reversal or readjustment of set plans, an intensification of general activity, or the adoption of additional precautionary measures. Their rapid transmission from the Office of the Corps Air Service Commander to the Group is at times of vital importance.

52. Station Lists and Situation Maps are the basis of personal liaison. They show the location of the units with which liaison is required.

53. The Plan of Employment of the Artillery is the basis of the plans for the accomplishment of Air Service artillery missions.

54. Accurate information of the strength and method of employment of neighboring friendly Air Service objectives, when checked against the reported aerial strength and aggressiveness of the enemy, permits an intelligent estimate of the lengths to which Corps Observation may be safely carried. Knowledge of the offensive and defensive Pursuit patrol schedule in the sector will permit the accomplishment of routine Corps Observation missions at those hours of the day when aerial support and protection is present on the lines. Dissemination of information regarding the operations of neighboring Observation Groups will promote interest and encourage emulation in the ranks of the flying and executive personnel.

55. Army Air Service Bulletins, Operations Reports, and Operations Orders contain information of enemy aerial strength, tactics, and equipment. Army Operations Orders ordinarily establish, by authority of the Army Air Service Commander, the broad tactical principles regulating the direction of Corps Air Service operations.

56. Personal liaison and courier runs are routed in accordance with one-way road regulations of Army, Corps, and Divisions, established in orders emanating from the G–1 Sections of various Staffs. Illustrative maps ordinarily accompany these orders.

57. The system of liaison established by the Corps Air Service is governed by the Corps Plan of Liaison and fixed regulations above noted. Secret messages are encoded and decoded by means of the codes and keys above noted. Headquarters are called by code name in accordance with the Code Telephone Directory prescribed by the C.S.O. Map coordinates are transmitted by a system of secret lettering prescribed by higher authority.

58. Possession of information of the enemy is a prime requisite to the intelligent direction of aerial operations, permitting concentration of observation on those points where the reaction of our own forces will be most effective, or on points whence enemy activity is apprehended and where such activity may be forestalled by appropriate dispositions based upon information furnished by the Air Service.

59. Information of our own or the enemy situation having its source in the Air Service is ordinarily communicated by the C.A.S.C. direct to the G–2 Section of the Corps Staff. G–2 is responsible for its transmission by the most rapid means of liaison available to those units concerned.

60. All information collected by officers of the Corps Air Service which has a bearing on the operations of the Air Services of neighboring or higher units is transmitted by the most rapid means of liaison available from Air Service to Air Service, without reference to G–2.

61. All tactical and technical information, whatever its nature, is of direct or indirect interest to all flying, technical, and executive commissioned personnel of the Air Service. Its rapid transmission and thorough dissemination is of prime importance.

Chapter VIII. Liaison

62. Effective Liaison involves the establishment of mutual understanding, rapid communication, and effective cooperation between the Air Service of the Corps, Air Services of other Corps, other branches of the Air Service, and other Branches and Arms of the Service to which the Corps Air Service stands in some tactical or technical relation. Information is gathered by means of Liaison.

63. Liaison cannot be carried too far. Its scope is limited only by the means possessed.

64. Liaison is carried out by the following means:

Frequent personal visits and conferences.

Permanent Air Service Liaison Officers stationed at important tactical centers of information.

Mechanical means of long-distance communication:

Telephone
Telegraph
Radio
Visual Signals
Motor Couriers
Airplane Couriers
Pigeons
Mounted Couriers
Runners

65. Liaison by personal contact, besides eliciting information, promoted mutual understanding and sympathy between the Air Service and other Branches of the Service. It is useful in acquainting other Services with the possibilities and limitations of

military aviation. It forms the basis for the laying of specific plans, prescribing of methods, and establishment of means and methods of rapid communication. Within the Corps, personal liaison will be frequently affected to include down to Infantry Brigades and Artillery Batteries.

66. The permanent Liaison Officer is ordinarily posted with Division Headquarters and Corps Air Service Headquarters of the Corps on right and left. The permanent Liaison Officer at Division Headquarters is the representative of the Divisional Squadron and of the C.A.S.C. He collects and transmits, through the C.A.S.C., to the Group and Squadron, all tactical information available. He is in close touch with the Divisional Artillery Brigade Commander. He transmits, through the C.A.S.C., all requests for missions. He is the immediate advisor on Air Service matters of the Divisional Command and Staff. He is responsible to the C.A.S.C. for the establishment of a suitable airplane message Dropping Ground at Division Headquarters. He interprets, whenever necessary, dropped message and clears up obscurities.

67. Establishment of adequate mechnical means of long-distance communication is a duty of the C.A.S.C. He must always be furnished with a direct-line telephone circuit from his office to the office of the Group Commander. The running of telephone lines is a function of the Corps Signal Officer.

68. A special Air Service Motorcycle Courier connects the office of the C.A.S.C. with the Group. Orders, reports, bulletins, and routine administrative papers are transmitted by courier.

69. Carrier Pigeons, Airplanes, and Mounted Couriers are used as a means of liaison when other means fail. Runners are employed over short distances where road communication by motor dispatch is impracticable.

70. The Air Service system of liaison includes the establishments at Corps, Division, Brigade, Regimental, and Battalion Headquarters of suitable Dropping Grounds for the receipt of airplane written messages. Signal Officers are responsible for the establishment and maintenance of Dropping Grounds. The location of Dropping Grounds is ordinarily selected by an Air Service Offficer and, wherever possible, the Radio Station is established nearby. A detail of enlisted men is on duty at the

Dropping Ground throughout the hours of daylight. The C.A.S.C. prepares a map showing locations of all Dropping Grounds in the Corps Area for the information of Pilots and observers of the Group. Distinctive panels, as prescribed in "Liaison for All Arms" (see chapter on Information) denote at the same time the locations of headquarters and the emplacements of Dropping Grounds. Dropping Ground panels are displayed by the detail on duty upon the call of the airplane. Calls are sent by signal rockets, short bursts of machine-gun fire, or radio.

71. Liaison includes the taking of any measures which serve to enlist the interest of troops in the work of the Air Service. Divisional Squadrons may display special distinctive insignia on the wings and fuselage of airplanes permitting troops to recognize planes of their own Division. The morale of troops in action is appreciably raised by the knowledge that "their own plane" is flying over them and assisting operations. Where troops constantly observe planes known to be of their own command in action a feeling of interest and camaraderie with the Air Service is developed. Cooperation of the troops during infantry contact patrols is a direct result. The dropping of newspapers and cigarettes from airplane to the troops in advance areas is likewise a means of liaison, promoting, as it

does, mutual confidence and sympathy. Visits by pilots and observers to advance positions and the front line during battle is a valuable means of promoting sympathy and understanding between the troops and the Air Service. In like manner visits from officers of combatant troops to the airdrome are encouraged. Line officers visiting the airdrome gain an intimate first-hand knowledge of the work and viewpoint of the Air Service and disseminate the information obtained upon return to their units.

72. The Corps or Division Commanders may utilize airplanes for communicating to their troops in advance areas. Orders and citations calculated to raise the morale of the forces engaged in battle may be mimeographed and dropped in quantity along the lines.

73. Airplanes communicate with the ground by radio and rocket signalling and by dropped message. Conventional rocket signals are fixed in Planes of Liaison of Armies, Corps, and Divisions. Secret Radio codes for use by airplanes are similarly prescribed. All airplane radio messages are in code.

74. Ground troops communicate with airplanes by means of signal panels, rockets, bengal flares, and electric projectors. Regulations governing the use of ground signals are published in Liaison Plans and the Pamphlet, "Liaison for All Arms."

Chapter IX. Security

75. The Chapter on Security of the Airdrome, Part I, applies in principle and detail to Corps Observation Stations.

76. During active operations over the lines, Corps Observation Planes are largely dependent for security upon the protection afforded by the Pursuit Effectives operating on the sector. Pursuit protection is of two sorts, (a) Extended Barrage, and, (b) Close Protection.

77. Pursuit barrage methods are prescribed by the Army Air Service Commander. Ordinarily formations of pursuit planes patrol the Army and Corps sectors at scheduled hours and for stated periods during each day. Certain formations are charged with the duty of clearing the air of enemy aircraft and protecting our own aircraft at low and medium altitudes. Other formations fly at higher altitudes and forbid the approaching of our lines by enemy aircraft. To assure the security of observation missions the Corps Air Service Commander prescribes the accomplishments of routine missions at those hours of the day when pursuit barrage is scheduled to operate. Close protection of Corps Observation Planes

whose mission carries them deep into enemy territory is secured by personal arrangement between the Group Commanders of Corps and Pursuit Groups.

78. Where close protection from Pursuit Units is not available Corps Observation Planes detailed for deep-flying photographic or visual reconnaissance missions assure their own security and are dispatched in formations of varying numerical strength, the number of planes depending upon the reported strength and aggressiveness of enemy pursuit aviation in the sector.

79. Security of Corps Observation Planes flying within the friendly lines is further assured by the protection afforded from enemy pursuit by the Anti-aircraft Defenses of the Sector.

80. Lacking other protection the Corps Observation Plane is dependent for security upon its own armament.

81. Security decreases in direct proportion to the increase in altitude and distance from the friendly lines. Enemy pursuit

aviation rarely ventures into the friendly lines at an altitude of less than three thousand feet. Corps Planes observing from their own lines at low altitudes are relatively secure both from enemy aircraft and enemy artillery.

82. In conducting observation the intelligent Corps Observation team seek the maximum of security. Missions are carried out at the lowest altitudes and shortest flight ranges which permit of accurate observation. The enemy lines are ordinarily penetrated by the single plane only for short periods and after careful survey of the air. Repeated short sorties over enemy territory, although they prolong the total duration of the flight, decrease the danger of attack and are therefore preferable to a single extended flight at a distance from the friendly lines. Observa-tion of Artillery fire, excepting at extreme ranges during hazy weather, can be accomplished by the experienced observer without crossing the enemy lines. Observation of artillery fire at long range is more easily accomplished from high than from low altitudes. For purposes of security it is preferable to fly high within the friendly lines than to fly low in the enemy lines, for the reason that, though the danger of encounter is increased, the plane, if attacked over its own territory, can resort to rapid manoeuvres while losing altitude and thus drop into security under cover of friendly ground machine-guns and artillery.

83. The use by observers of field-glasses is an added measure of security and is encouraged. The use of field-glasses permits accurate observation from a safe distance within the friendly lines and the rapid identification of distant airplanes. Long practice is required for the effective use of field-glasses. The ability to employ them is a rare and valuable asset among observers.

84. A sky completely overcast by even cloud strata affords added security. Sun-glare is eliminated and the area to be surveyed in watching for hostile aircraft is limited. The silhouettes of aircraft within the range of vision stand out sharply against the clouds. Broken cloud groupings decrease security. Scattered banks of clouds afford ambush to hostile pursuit. Broken cloud banks are never approached by the single plane where it is possible to avoid them.

Security from surprise attack is dependent upon the constant vigilance of pilot and observer and upon ability of airplane teams to distinguish enemy aircraft from friendly by the silhouette. Pamphlets showing the silhouettes of enemy and friendly types of planes are published by the Air Service Intelligence Section from time to time. These are made available to all flying personnel and are carefully studied and learned.

86. Security from enemy anti-aircraft artillery and machine-gun fire is afforded by effecting slight changes in course and altitude at short intervals. Where artillery fire is so dense as to assume the aspect of a barrage a long steep dive is resorted to, the dive being continued until the lowest bursts observed have passed overhead. The plane then climbs rapidly changing course at the same time.

Chapter X. Orders and Reports

87. The Corps Air Service Operations Order is based upon the tactical situation as set forth in information gathered by the C.A.S.C., through liaison channels. The Operations Order is issued by the C.A.S.C. at the close of each day and prescribes the general and specific lines of activity of the Observation Group for the following day. It contains:

    a. Friendly tactical situation and plan.

    b. Enemy tactical situation and presumed purposes.

    c. General mission of the Corps Squadron.

    d. General mission of the Divisional Squadrons.

    e. Specific missions.

    f. Special information affecting operations.

    g. Any admonitions, advice, encouragement.

88. The Operations Order is forwarded to the Group by M.D.S. If there is doubt that it will arrive at Group Headquarters in ample time it is communicated in advance by telephone.

89. In preparing the Operations Order the C.A.S.C. will advise with the Corps Chief of Staff and the Assistant Chiefs of Staff, G–2 and G–3.

90. Distribution of the Operations Order:

    Group Headquarters.
    Army Air Service Commander.
    C.A.S.C., Corps on right and left.
    Corps C. of S.
    Corps G–2 and G–3.
    Commanding Generals, Divisions of own Corps.

91. Operations Reports are prepared for the C.A.S.C. by the Group Operations Officer under the supervision of the Group Commander. They contain a narrative of the salient features of each day's aerial operations. They contain a statistical tabulation of each day's operations, by squadron, showing number and kinds of flights accomplished; number of flying hours; number of photographs secured; number of forced landings; number of planes crashed; number of combats; number of casualties; planes and personnel available for the following day's operations. Totals for the entire Group follow squadron statistics. For distribution see Par. 90.

92. A written report of each visual reconnaissance mission accomplished is furnished by each observer (a) in a dropped message to the P.C. of the Division for which the flight is made, and to the Corps P.C. in every case, and (b) in a carefully detailed narrative, prepared after landing, under the supervision of the Group Operations Officer.

93. The dropped message report is complete but concise. Skeleton phrasing is permitted. All information secured, both positive and negative, dealing with the friendly and enemy situation, is included. The tendency of the inexperienced ob-

server is to omit in the dropped message minor details of time and place. All details will be included, no matter how insignificant they may appear to the observer. Locations will be accurately described by coordinates or filled in on an attached map. The message, if dropped at the Corps P.C. by a Divisional Plane, will state in conclusion whether or not a similar message has been dropped at the Division, this in order to assure G–2 of the Corps that transmission of the information in the body of the message is or is not necessary. In preparing forms for the writing of dropped messages observers will duplicate, and thus save time, by the use of carbon paper firmly fixed between two or more message blanks, attached by means of rubber bands, thumb tacks, or tape, to a stiff backing. Photo-

graphic and artillery missions are not reported by dropped message. Their results are reported by telephone liaison from the Group.

94. The full narrative observer's report prepared at the Group tells the entire story of the mission, including information of route followed; visibility; and duration of flight; enemy road and railway activity observed; enemy aircraft observed; with description of types or silhouettes and distinctive markings; enemy balloons in ascension, giving location; enemy and friendly artillery activity, locations of enemy batteries in action; density and location of friendly and enemy shell observed; locations and activities of friendly and enemy troops; general aspect of enemy sector, carefully calling attention to any lack of activity where activity might have been expected; fires and explosions in friendly and enemy territory. Where conclusions are drawn they are carefully labelled as such and are not stated as absolute fact. Observers are encouraged to draw conclusions.

95. Inexperienced observers often omit the following essential data in reporting on missions:

Negative Information of Enemy Sector.
Exact time of observations.
Exact locations by coordinates.
Direction taken by Enemy Troops and Train movements.
Approximate strength of columns observed on roads.
Direction of flight of enemy aircraft.

An open-air P.C.

Careful supervision by Corps Air Service and Group Commanders and their Operations Officers is the sole means of training observers in the careful and complete preparation of reports.

96. Report of artillery adjustments is made by the observer at the Group. The usual flight narrative describing general conditions under which the flight was accomplished is followed by a report of number of rounds fired and number of bursts observed and by an estimate of the result obtained. Failures are carefully reported, stating reasons.

97. The photographic reconnaissance report includes the usual narrative with a statement of number of plates exposed and estimate of area covered. Failures and reasons thereof are reported.

98. Report of encounters and combats with enemy aircraft is made, by pilot and observer in conference, on a special Combat Report Form prescribed by the Army Air Service Commander. Report includes narrative of the incidents of combat; states the approximate number of rounds fired by the pilot and observer; states effect of fire on the enemy and effect of enemy fire. Time, locality, and altitude are carefully noted. Number and type of enemy planes encountered, a description of their characteristic markings, and comments on the tactics employed are embodied in the report.

99. The Observer's Report is the sum and substance of Air Service Information. Its contents are transmitted to all concerned by the most rapid means of liaison available.

100. General principles governing the composition and issuance of Orders and Reports for the Army promulgated in Field Service Regulations apply to Orders and Reports of the Air Service.

Chapter XI. Marches and Convoys

101. The principles governing the conduct and regulation of Marches and Convoys for all Air Service units and Groupings are treated in Chapter V, Part 1 of this Manual.

102. The Corps Air Service Commander and his Staff move with Corps Headquarters.

Chapter XII. Participation in Combat Observation

103. During the inactive periods in trench or stabilized warfare the Air Service of the Corps is charged with the following missions:

a. To photograph to a depth of ten kilometers the enemy's position.

b. To locate by the flash the exact emplacements of enemy batteries.

c. To adjust the fire of our own artillery on sensitive points and calibrate our guns.

d. To maintain surveillance of the enemy and assure protection of increased activity indicating preparation for hostile attack.

104. During a friendly offensive the Air Service of the Corps is charged with the following missions:

a, b, and c, as in paragraph 103.

d. To maintain surveillance of the enemy at low altitudes, reporting on concentrations of troops for local stands and reactions.

e. To observe enemy road movements for indications of the bringing up of extensive reinforcements.

f. To find and report to the Command and the artillery the location of the friendly front lines by means of low-flying infantry contact patrols.

g. To control the friendly barrage.

h. To seek and report on all indications of a general enemy retreat.

i. To seek fugitive targets, i.e. massed enemy troops, convoys on roads, and to adjust rapid zone fire on such targets.

105. During a general retreat of the enemy and pursuit by friendly forces the Air Service of the Corps is charged with the following missions:

a. To seek and report on the location of the enemy's rear guard, notifying the heads of the friendly pursuing columns as well as the Command.

b. To discover the enemy's main axes of withdrawal.

c. To report on the position of the friendly advance elements at frequent intervals.

d. To report to the heads of friendly pursuing columns any concentration of enemy troops for local stands or reactions.

e. To discover the enemy's main line of resistance.

f. To photograph the enemy's main line of resistance.

106. During an enemy offensive met by stubborn friendly resistance the Air Service of the Corps is charged with the following missions:

a, b, c, as in paragraph 103.

d. To maintain constant low-flying surveillance of the enemy and report in advance his preparation for each successive effort to break through the friendly lines.

e. To observe enemy road movement for indications of the bringing up of extensive reinforcements.

f. To locate enemy cantonments, camps, dumps, axial roads, and other suitable targets for the destructive and harrassing fire of the friendly artillery.

g. To find and report to the Command and Artillery the location of the friendly front line during and after each enemy effort to break through.

h. To control the friendly barrage.

i. To adjust rapid zone fire on fugitive targets and concentrations of enemy troops preparing for assault on the friendly positions.

106. During a general friendly retreat and pursuit by hostile forces the Air Service of the Corps is charged with the

following missions:

a. To report on the position of the friendly rear guard and the general road aspect of the friendly retreat.

b. To report to the friendly rear guard and to the Command the position of the advance guard and main body of the pursuing hostile forces.

c. To effect liaison between the Command and the right and left flanks.

107. Under all conditions the Corps Air Service holds one, two, or three airplanes at the disposal of the Corps Commander for the accomplishment of special missions demanded by developments in the tactical situation.

108. Photographic missions are requested as need arises by G−2, G−3, or the Artillery Command. During stable trench warfare tactical maps are based on data furnished by Corps and Army aerial photographs of the enemy's territory. Photographs during war of movement are of little value in studying the enemy organization but serve to acquaint the Command with details of terrain. Oblique photographs of the enemy's front-line defenses in either stable or open warfare are extremely useful. They are distributed down to include commanders of infantry platoons and serve to acquaint the Command and troops with the nature of the terrain and

defenses immediately confronting them. During stable trench warfare photographic missions are a matter of daily routine to be accomplished by the Corps Air Service upon every day of favorable weather. During open warfare photographic missions are only occasional and are requested to clear up map obscurities or most other specific demands for information. The preparation of the photographic mission involves communication to pilot and observer, by C.A.S.C., of the limits of territory to be covered. The work is carried out by formations. The usual altitude from which Corps photographs are secured is 3000 meters. It is sometimes impracticable to send formations of planes on photographic missions. In this case the mission is carried out by a single plane

flying at great altitude, 5000 to 5500 meters. The security of the plane is increased by its inconspicuousness at extreme altitudes and the rapidity with which it can cover an extended area from great heights. In the case of certain types of planes (examples of which are the French Salmson and Breguet) which retain their qualities of speed, climb, and manoeuverability at extreme altitudes, security is further afforded by the ability of the plane, relying on its qualities of speed and climb, to out-distance attacking enemy pursuit. During periods of unsettled weather photographic missions are ready to take the air from early morning. Instant advantage is taken of any break in the clouds. Under these conditions Pursuit protection will not be counted upon owing to the loss of time involved in meeting the protection at the rendezvous. During midsummer, sunlight is sufficient for the securing of photographs between 8 and 16 o'clock. Photographic missions during the spring and autumn months are ordinarily executed between 10 and 14 o'clock. In winter good photographs are secured only between 11:30 and 12:30 o'clock.

109. Location of enemy batteries in action by the flash is a routine mission of Corps Observation Units during all situations excepting that of general friendly retreat. Battery flashes are best observed just after day-break and just before night-fall. They are rarely picked up, even by the vigilant observer, in broad daylight. Where it is known or suspected that a concentration of enemy batteries has been effected within certain specific limits bounding a very restricted area a single reconnaissance plane charged with the sole mission of locating exactly the flashes of batteries in that area will ordinarily meet with success. Surveillance planes searching the sector for miscellaneous information are only moderately effective in locating batteries. The plane seeking to locate batteries in action should fly at the lowest altitude permitting observation and should remain as far behind the friendly lines as the work will permit. Once the plane's presence is detected by the enemy, batteries will ordinarily cease fire. Information of enemy batteries in action is communicated to the Divisional and Corps Commands immediately by radio and later confirmed by dropped message. Enemy batteries in action may be effectively counter-batteried by the assistance of the airplane reporting them. For this purpose the artillery assigns suitable counter-batteries. Liaison with these batteries is then effected. When

arrangements are completed between the batteries and the Air Service the counter-batteries are prepared to receive radio calls from all planes of the Corps during the hours of daylight and to adjust fire on targets reported, without delay. It is a function of the C.A.S.C. to assure wherever possible the assignment of such counter-batteries and to provide for adequate liaison in order that the minimum of failures may result. Counter-batteries thus arranged for become, during active periods, fugitive-target batteries. Theoretically, all batteries are ready to receive airplane calls and adjust at all times. Practically, better results are obtained by assigning only a few batteries for this type of work and carefully perfecting liaison arrangements. All Corps and Divisional observers are supplied with the necessary information for calling counter-batteries and conducting adjustments, in accordance with the arrangements effected.

110. Detailed instructions for adjustment of artillery fire by means of airplane observation are contained in Confidential Pamphlet No. 80 (Revised) G.H.Q., A.E.F., May 1918, "Aerial Observation for Artillery": Successful adjustment of artillery is largely dependent upon carefully accomplished liaison. The best work is achieved after a visit by the observer to the battery with which he is to conduct fire. The adjustment should be arranged by conference between the observer and the battery commander, details of method, time, panel and radio signaling, being thoroughly discussed and a complete understanding and agreement reached. Before leaving on the mission the observer notifies the battery by telephone or radio that he is about to start. In preparing the mission the observer equips himself with a large-scale map bearing coordinates in secret letters and showing the location of the target. If an aerial photograph of the target is available this will be attached to the map, properly oriented and squared off to scale. The photograph renders exact location of bursts observed extremely easy. Batteries which do not respond to the radio call of the plane may be called by dropped message. In like manner batteries whose calls are not known to the observer may be notified that an adjustment is required and all necessary data for opening fire and establishing radio liaison may be

included in the written message. The battery replies by panel signals whether or not the work requested can be undertaken and what method of fire will be used (see "Aerial Observation for Artillery"). Liaison between the airplane and artillery is at all times complex and difficult of perfection. The conditions governing its effective establishment change with the tactical situation and cannot be laid down by any rule which will cover all cases. Corps Air Service Commanders will be called upon to use great energy and ingenuity in assuring effective cooperation between the Air Service and the

Artillery. This will be particularly true during active periods in war of movement.

111. Surveillance of the enemy is a routine mission of Corps and Divisional Squadrons during all tactical situations. The Corps Squadron patrols the entire Corps Front reporting on the general activity of the entire sector to a depth varying from five to ten kilometers. The Divisional Squadron patrols within the boundaries of the Divisional Sector reporting in detail on all activity observed. Effective sector surveillance implies an accurate knowledge of the terrain by the observer. The observer should be familiar with the latest information on the tactical situation in order to concentrate his attention on those points which are of most interest to the Command. Sector reconnaissances are increased in frequency as combat activity or preparation for activity increases. During actual offensive or defensive operations they may overlap, establishing an unbroken watch on the movements of the enemy. Surveillance planes are fitted with radio equipment and are prepared to call the artillery into action whenever need arises.

112. Control of the friendly barrage may be advantageously conducted by airplane. Where the barrage extends across the entire Corps front and is participated in by both Corps and Divisional Artillery, the Corps Artillery is observed by a plane from the Corps Squadron; the Divisional Artillery is observed by planes from the Divisional Squadrons. Observers controlling barrages are provided in advance with maps showing the barrage schedule, minute by minute. Control consists in reporting by radio to the Corps and Divisional Artillery Brigade Headquarters any failure of the barrage to play accurately and on schedule time, giving approx-

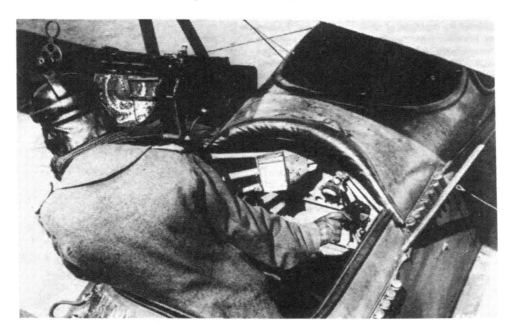

imate location, density, and caliber of bursts observed to be inaccurately placed or off schedule. Close adjustment of the barrage is not undertaken.

113. The general principles and specific regulations governing the conduct of infantry contact patrols for the purpose of staking the friendly front line are established in "Liaison for All Arms." The contact patrol is a mission of the Divisional Squadron. The contact patrol is most effectively carried out at an altitude ranging between 25 and 100 meters. Troops frequently disregard the call of the plane to display panels. From these altitudes troops can be plainly distinguished and identified by the color of the uniform. Where troops do not show panels observers will not report the location of the "front line." They

Observer watching infantry
movements below.

will report the location of the "most advanced friendly elements observed." The Infantry panel is the only guarantee of the exact location of the front line. Where troops are seen but no panels are displayed upon the call of the plane, there is room to suppose the actual front line is still further advanced. Even though the observer can locate no friendly troops beyond a certain point he will not report the location of the "front line" until panels are shown. The infantry contact plane will never proceed directly from the airdrome to the point which the advance of the friendly troops is presumed, by schedule, to have reached. It will proceed to that point where the most advanced elements were last definitely reported. Having reached this point the plane will assure itself by observation of movement of troops on the ground that the advance has continued. It will then gradually extend its observations farther and farther to the front, working back and forth across the sector, until the observer can distinguish no friendly troops beyond. The line is called at this point. If no panels are shown the plane will carry observations somewhat deeper but with extreme caution. When satisfied that the limit of the friendly advance has been reached and noted the observer will immediately report to Division and Corps Headquarters by dropped message. The contact patrol observer will bear always in mind

the possibility of enemy counter-attacks and will constantly watch for enemy troop concentrations. Where counter-attacks appear imminent the observer will drop a message to that effect to the front line elements most nearly concerned. He will then call the fugitive target battery and adjust neutralizing zone fire over the terrain where concentration has been observed. Contact patrols frequently locate enemy machine-gun nests. Where hostile machine-guns are observed the front line troops are notified of the danger by dropped message. Contact patrol planes may assist the advance of friendly troops by opening fire on enemy machine-guns, silencing them until they can be captured.

114. In directing the operations of the Air Service the C.A.S.C. maintains liaison with the Corps and Divisional Balloons. He is assisted in this function by the Corps Balloon Group Commander. The C.A.S.C. will assure himself at all times that

airplane missions do not duplicate the work accomplished, or
in course, by the Balloons. He
will establish as a principle that
work which Balloons can accomplish will not be undertaken
by airplanes. This will usually
apply to the accomplishment of
artillery missions. Certain areas
in enemy territory are obscured
to Balloon Observers by ine-
qualities in the terrain. The areas
not defiladed by the Balloons
decrease in number and extent
with the increase in altitude.
Those areas closed to Balloon
Observation at varying altitudes
will be sketched in on a map for
the use of the Corps Air Service
and Group Commanders in determining what missions properly
fall within the province of the
Balloons during varying conditions of visibility. A copy of the
Balloon defilade map is posted
for the information of flying personnel in the Group Operations
Room.

Chapter XIII. Shelter

115. The principles governing
shelter of troops in the field,
established in Army Field Service Regulations, apply to the
troops of the Corps Air Service.

Army Observation

Introduction

116. The Army Observation
units function as an organ of the
high command. They are placed
at the disposal of the General
Staff of the Army and their activities conform to the orders issued
by the General Staff. The Chief
function of the Army Observation units is to keep under constant surveillance the dispositions
and movements of enemy
forces. This consists of the reconnaissance, both visual and
photographic, in depth, of the
entire Army sector. Their prime
object being the gathering of information, it is necessary that
they operate in spite of enemy
aerial opposition. However, engaging the enemy's air forces in
combat must be avoided as far
as possible except when the nature of the mission demands and
the chances of gain are commensurate with the risk involved.

Chapter XIV. Information

117. Information of the enemy and our ground forces is
essential to the proper tactical
operation of any observation
unit whether it be an independent squadron, a group, or a
larger organization.

118. The collection, preparation, and circulation to the
smaller units of the command of
this information is the duty of the
Army Air Service Commander.
Every Commander of a large
unit, wing, or group will see that
all essential information which
he receives is circulated to the
component elements of his command. It is the duty of all Commanders at all times to act on
the principle that the collection
of information without its circulation is useless. Information properly circulated to Observation
Units has an important moral
effect upon the flying personnel.
It is to be remembered that except when actually in the air,
aviators are removed from the
sights and sounds of the battlefield and only by a thorough
information system can the various possibilities of the military
situation be brought home to
them. Unless these possibilities
are made clear it is impossible to
obtain the maximum efforts from
the personnel.

119. The Operations Officers
of the various units (separate
squadron, group, or wing) are
responsible for the supply of

their respective units with:

(a) Maps of 1/20,000 scale covering the entire sector. This map should be colored so that the prominent topographical features are easily referred to.

(b) Maps of 1/50,000 scale covering the entire sector for use by observers. It is of paramount importance that these maps be colored so as to make reference easier.

x (c) Maps of 1/20,000 scale covering the entire sector showing, by means of conventional symbols, all the important artillery objectives. These maps are printed at frequent periodic intervals by the second section of the General Staff (G–2).

(d) Maps of 1/200,000 scale covering the entire sector for use by pilots and observers.

x (e) Maps showing the organization and occupation of the sector by ground troops. This map shows the location of the different friendly divisions in line.

(f) Daily enemy Order of Battle map showing the location, both known and probable, of all enemy divisions both in line and reserve.

x (g) A map showing the location of all known enemy airdromes. This map should indicate, by conventional symbol, whether the airdrome is occupied or unoccupied.

x (h) A map showing the location of all enemy balloons.

x (i) A map showing the precise location of all the known enemy antiaircraft batteries and their calibre.

(j) A map showing the enemy areas that are defiladed from the different friendly balloons. This is valuable in that the Aeroplane observers can pay particular attention to those areas that are protected from observation by balloons.

x (k) A map showing enemy's system of railroads and the railheads.

x (l) A map showing the main roads over which traffic is heaviest. These are indispensable to observers so as to know beforehand where to look for traffic.

(m) A map showing the location of all friendly airdromes in the sector of the Army Air Service Commander. The pilots and observers should be familiar with the location of all these airdromes so that in case of a forced landing if they should become lost the breaking of a plane might be avoided.

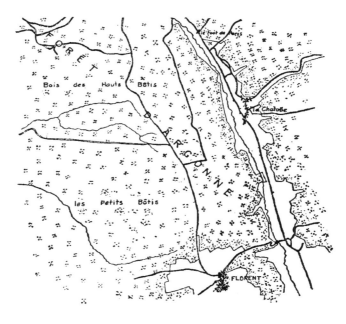

x (n) Silhouettes, photographs, and tables of performance of all known types of enemy airplanes will be prepared or secured. These are essentials and must be studied carefully by the flying personnel.

(o) Charts showing the lighting systems of enemy airdromes and signals for planes at night.

(p) All photographs available of the enemy airdromes, dumps, towns, etc. It is well to arrange these in alphabetical order in books so that easy reference can be made to them and when new photographs are taken they can be compared. Also, it is necessary that these be at all times kept at the disposal of the pilots and observers for study, as it enables them to recognize them when flying over enemy territory. Stereoscopic views of all these points should be prepared and placed at the disposal of the pilots and observers for study.

Items marked *x* are prepared and distributed at frequent periodic intervals.

120. Charts, diagrams, and maps should be supplemented by:

(a) Army Summaries of Intelligence, prepared by the second section of the General Staff (G-2). It is of paramount importance that these be supplied to the squadrons and there be at the disposal of the pilots and observers as it is difficult to prevent these officers from suffering a feeling of the other arms of the service unless these summaries are furnished to them.

(b) Air Service summaries of Intelligence will be prepared in the Headquarters of the Army Air Service Commander to supplement the Army Summaries of Intelligence. These should cover all subjects relating to the enemy Air Service and especially deal with the types of planes and of using them as learned from all different sources, such as: reports from agents, statements of prisoners and captured orders and documents of all sorts.

(c) The Army Air Service Operations Orders prepared in the Headquarters of the Army Air Service Commander, showing the activities of all Air Service Units under his command.

(d) All available documents and pamphlets concerning the enemy's forces, paying particular attention to the information concerning the enemy's aerial forces.

It is one of the duties of the Operations Officer of all observation units to attend to the details of the circulation of information within the command. It is imperative that the observations and experiences over the lines of every pilot and observer be made accessible to every other pilot and observer in the organization in the most inviting manner, without delay.

Chapter XV. Liaison

121. Owing to the absolute necessity for cooperation between the various Air Service units under the command of the Army Air Service Commander, and also the various arms of the Service, great importance must be attached to the preparation of means of communication for receiving and transmitting information and orders. A rapid and complete comprehension of the entire situation has decided influence upon the success of the operations. For mutual comprehension of plans, possibilities, and limitations nothing can be substituted for personal contact.

122. The exchange of personal visits between pilots and observers and officers of other arms stationed nearer to the front will be encouraged as much as possible. All Air Service Commanders in the field will exchange personal visits with officers of corresponding rank and will see that their subordinates of all ranks come into close personal contact with officers of corresponding rank in the divisions in the line and in reserve, in the anti-aircraft artillery, both machine-gunners and heavier gunners, in Field and Heavy Artillery, with balloon observers and all other Air Service units, both bombardment and pursuit as well as observation.

123. In order that a maximum return may be assured from the observation units, it is necessary

that the best possible means of communication be established, as follows:

(a) By direct telephonic installations to the Headquarters of the Army Air Service Commander.

(b) By telephonic liaison with all the Air Service Units under the command of the Army Air Service Commander.

(c) By liaison by radio with the station established at Headquarters, Army Air Service Commander.

(d) By dropping messages from aeroplanes on the dropping ground established near the Headquarters Army Air Service Commander.

124. Liaison by aircraft is still to be developed as a means of reporting promptly the information obtained concerning the progress of the battle but with the development of wireless telephones for communication between planes and between planes and the ground the utilization of aircraft as a means of communication will be more and more emphasized.

125. Every observation group will be equipped with sufficient supply of telephones and wire to insure the establishment of its internal liaison, the Group Operations Officer and Headquarters being directly connected with the several squadron Headquarters and Operations Offices. The establishment of telephonic liaison from the Wing Headquarters to the Group Headquarters and from the Headquarters of the Army Air Service Commander to the Wings and separate groups of his command is the duty of the Army Air Service Commander. He will arrange with the Chief Signal Officer of the Army in the field for the installation of these telephone lines before ordering those units to their new stations.

126. In order to insure close cooperation between pursuit and observation planes while in the air it is necessary for the Group Operations Officer of the Observation Group to inform the Operations Officer of the Pursuit Groups as to the time of departure of the missions, the number of planes in the formation, the altitude at which they are going to work, the probable time of crossing and recrossing the lines and the route to be covered in order that the pursuit patrols separating over the same area at the same time may be notified and pay particular attention to the safety of these formations.

127. The Operations Officers of the various units are responsible for the interrogation of all pilots and observers immediately upon their return from missions and for securing a full, accurate and intelligible report of all observations of interest to the General Staff. This report should be transmitted by him by telephone, if possible, direct to the Headquarters of the Army Air Service Commander.

Chapter XVI. Combat

General Principles

128. The object of tactics, as employed by Army Observation planes, is to avoid combat with enemy planes, to allow the observers to obtain the desired information and return to the airdrome with it. The Army Observation planes do not accept combat otherwise than as a defensive measure. Definite tactics to be employed by formations of biplace observation planes have not been adopted. It depends entirely upon the ability and initiative of the Flight Commander, the pilots comprising the flight and the conditions. Owing to the fact that the Army Observation unit operates far beyond the line of friendly pursuit patrols, it is necessary that they depend largely upon their own means of defense. However, even though formations of biplace observation planes are employed the co-operation between pursuit patrols and observation informations when the latter are operating within range of the pursuit patrols should be as close as possible. The numerical strength of a formation depends entirely upon the depth to which it must penetrate the enemy's territory and the known aggressiveness and numerical strength of the enemy's air forces. Missions must never be attempted by individual planes except when the weather conditions are such that formations flying is rendered impossible.

Formations

129. During the hours of daylight, the weather conditions permitting, the missions assigned to the Army Observations Squadrons will invariably be carried out by formations. These formations should not be too large. A formation of 4 planes, flying in diamond formation, has been found very effective as it is easily controlled by the leader and it is very flexible. All formations must have the following characteristics:

(a) Simplicity.
(b) Manoeuverability.
(c) No dead angles.
(d) Concentration of fire to the rear.
(e) Compactness.
(f) Each pilot must be able to see the leader.

130. Airplanes in formation are numbered as follows:

```
      1
   3     2
      4
```

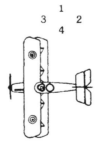

3. The copy contains a typographical error, a parenthesis for what evidently was to be a second digit. This perhaps was a zero, but *Circular* 76, p 29, gives 25, which fits with the other distances in the formation.

Number 1 is the leader and flies at the lowest altitude, numbers 2 and 3 fly at the same altitude, about 25 meters higher, 25 meters to the rear, and 25 meters to the right and left, of number 1, respectively, while number 4 closes the diamond, as it were, flying about 25 [?] meters[3] above numbers 2 and 3 and about 25 meters behind, keeping directly behind number 1.

131. In the event that the formation is attacked, the formation must be kept as compact as possible. The maximum security will

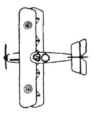

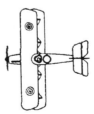

be maintained by keeping the closest possible formation—15 to 20 meters between planes. In this manner the blind angles of one plane are covered by the other planes of the formation, thereby preventing the enemy planes from closing in to short ranges without exposure to concentrations of fire from the different planes. The usual tactics employed by the enemy pursuit planes against formations of biplace planes is to remain at long ranges and firing short bursts to confuse the pilots and observers so that they will break up the formation. It is fatal for any plane to become detached from its formation as it will then be subjected to the concentrated efforts of the enemy pursuit pilots and will be easy prey for them.

132. In order that there be mutual understanding between the pilots and observers of the flight it is necessary that they know the following:

(a) The various signals for communication between planes.
(b) The mission to be accomplished.
(c) The territory to be covered.
(d) The altitude at which they will fly.
(e) Their relative positions in the formations.

133. The Flight Commander being responsible for the tactical employment of the formation while in the air must take all necessary precautions to prevent the formation from being surprised by enemy planes. He will pay particular attention to the sun and to the clouds that are above the level of the formation, behind which enemy planes may be lurking.

Single Planes

134. Missions are carried out by single planes only when the atmospheric conditions such as low hanging clouds and mist prevent the employment of formations, and the early reconnaissance, when darkness forbids the employment of formations. When single planes are operating under or above the clouds it is an easy matter for the plane to enter the clouds, which afford excellent protection, in the event of being attacked by enemy planes. However, operating at such low altitudes, far beyond the enemy lines, under and in the clouds, requires the employment of pilots and observers of exceptional ability. They must know:

(a) The terrain, thoroughly.
(b) The direction and speed of the wind at the different altitudes.
(c) How to navigate, in the clouds, by compass.

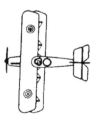

Part III. Pursuit
Introduction

1. Pursuit Aviation has for its object the destruction of the enemy air service and the protection of our own observation aviation. When opportunity offers it will take part in the battle on the ground, inflicting maximum casualties upon and weakening the morale of the enemy's ground troops. Whatever later developments may appear, up to the present time the basis of the Air Service has proved to be that portion devoted to observation. But observation aviation's very existence depends upon a powerful, well trained and aggressive pursuit aviation. That our own observation airplanes and balloons may be [protected] and may feel and see that they are protected, while the enemy's observation aviation is destroyed and driven back from the line of battle, pursuit aviation is employed.

Chapter I. Information

2. Information of the enemy and our ground forces is essential to the proper tactical operation of any pursuit unit, whether it be a separate flight, an independent squadron, a group or a larger organization.

3. The collection, preparation and circulation to the smaller units of the command of this information is the duty of the Army Air Service Commander. Every Commander of a large unit, wing or group, will see that all essential information which he receives is circulated to the component elements of his command. It is the duty of all commanders at all times to act on the principle that the collection of information without its circulation is useless. Information properly circulated to Pursuit Units has an important moral effect upon the combatant personnel. It is to be remembered that except when actually in the air aviators are removed from the sights and sounds of the battlefield and only by a thorough information system can the various possibilities of the military situation be brought home to them. Unless these possibilities are made clear it is impossible to obtain the maximum efforts from the pilots.

4. Every Wing, Group and Squadron Headquarters, including the Headquarters of the squadrons which comprise the Groups and Wings under his command, will be supplied by the Army Air Service Commander with:

(a) A map giving the location of all enemy airdromes. This map should indicate by symbols whether or not the airdromes are occupied and should bear upon its face an easily read key so that the quality and kind of enemy air service can be taken in at a glance.

(b) A map showing the precise location of all enemy anti-aircraft artillery units, showing their kind. This map and all others should be issued at frequent periodic intervals and never allowed to get out of date.

(c) A map showing the locations, both known and probable, of all enemy divisions both in line and in reserve. This map will be prepared by the Second Section of the General Staff (G–2) and its circulation down to Groups and independent squadrons is important on account of its moral effect in bringing the flying personnel into touch with the military situation.

(d) Silhouettes and photographs of all known types of enemy airplanes will be prepared or secured by the Army Air Service Commander. These should be in such form that they can be pasted or tacked on bulletin boards. They cannot be too profusely circulated and can be posted to advantage in all officer's messes and in their quarters.

(e) A map showing the location of all airdromes in the sector of the Army Air Service Commander, the Corps and Divisional sector boundaries of all units in line, the location of our antiaircraft units, balloons and other Air Service organization.

(f) A diagram or chart of telephonic liaisions within the Army area.

5. The charts, diagrams and maps should be supplemented by:

(a) Army Summaries of Intelligence, prepared by G-2. It is of the utmost importance that these be circulated down to include Groups and whenever possible should be circulated to include squadrons as it is difficult to prevent the pilots from suffering a feeling of detachment and isolation from the operations of the other combatant arms unless these summaries are furnished to them.

(b) Air Service summaries of Intelligence will be prepared in the Headquarters of the Army Air Service Commander to supplement the Army Summaries of Intelligence. These should cover all subjects relating to the enemy air service and especially deal with the types and quantities of his airplanes and his methods of using them as learned from prisoners, captured orders and documents of all sorts.

It is one of the duties of the Operations Officer of all pursuit units, under the Commanding Officer, to attend to the details of the circulation of information within the command. It is imperative that the observations and experience over the lines of every patrol leader and every pilot be made accessible to every other pilot in the organization without delay.

Chapter II. Liaison

6. Owing to the rapidity of movement of pursuit airplanes and the influence that they can exercise both in the battle for supremacy of the air and the fighting on the ground, great importance must attach to the preparation of means of communications for the transmission of information and orders. A rapid comprehension of the entire situation has a decided influence upon the success of the operations.

7. For mutual comprehension of plans, difficulties and limitations nothing can be substituted for personal contact. The exchange of personal visits between Air Service pilots and all elements stationed closer to the front will be encouraged as much as possible. All Air Service Commanders in the field will exchange personal visits and will see that their subordinates of all ranks come into close personal contact with officers of corresponding ranks in the Headquarters and the Divisions in line and in reserve, in the antiaircraft artillery, both machine-gunners and heavier gunners, with balloon observers and with all air service units, both bombardment and observation as well as pursuit.

8. In order that a maximum return may be secured from our pursuit aviation, and in order that the enemy may not throw an overmastering force of pursuit airplanes on the line at certain hours of the day, it is all important that close liaison be maintained with the front at all times. This liaison should be perfected so that every Group Commander can be informed without delay of the number, type, altitude and direction of flight of all enemy airplanes and formations approaching our front lines in the sector for which his group is responsible. This liaison may be established:

(a) By direct telephonic installations to forward observing posts established at intervals on or near the front lines, in charge of Air Service officers.

(b) By telephonic liaison with the anti-aircraft artillery observation posts. Messages relative to enemy aircraft activity from the anti-aircraft artillery to a pursuit group should have priority over the army telephone lines, because Air Service Units practically alone can be utilized to influence an action in progress.

(c) By liaison by wire with the radio-goniometric[4] stations.

(d) By liaison by radio either with forward observing posts established by the Air Service or with radio equipped forward observing posts of the anti-aircraft artillery.

9. Liaison by aircraft is still to be developed as a means of reporting promptly upon the progress of fighting in the air. With the prospective development of wireless telephones for communication between formations and between airplanes and the ground the utilization of aircraft as a means of communication will be more and more emphasized.

10. In addition to immediate reports upon the number, type, altitude and direction of flight of enemy airplanes, daily reports should be made to the Group Commander upon the size, altitude and methods of operation of all elements of the enemy air service. These reports must be prepared by Air Service officers detailed by their Group Commanders to keep watch from the ground upon the enemy air service from advance observation posts.

11. Every Pursuit Group will be equipped with a sufficient supply of telephones and wire to insure the establishment of its internal liaisons, the Group Operations office and the several squadron operations offices being directly connected. The establishment of telephonic liaison from the Wing Headquarters to the Groups and from the Headquarters of the Army Air Service Commander to the Wings and independent Groups of his command is the duty of the Army Air Service Commander. He will arrange with the Chief Signal Officer of the Army in the field for the installation of these telephone lines before ordering these several Headquarters to new stations.

12. In order that our pursuit aviation may make safe the work of our observation aviation, close liaison must be maintained with all elements of the observation air service, and the pursuit group commander should have at all times as complete a knowledge as possible of the number, altitude and route of all observation airplanes working in the sector for which his group is responsible. This liaison will also be helpful in keeping track of the movement of our advanced infantry and cavalry elements and in the selection of targets for ground straffing.

4. Direction finding.

13. While the prime duty of pursuit aviation is fighting in the air, pursuit pilots will occasionally be called upon for special reconnaissances and will make valuable observations from time to time in the course of their patrols. This will not be allowed to interfere with their combatant operations.

14. The squadron operations officers are responsible for the interrogation of all pilots upon their return from flights and for securing a full accurate and intelligible report of all observations of interest to the higher command. This report should be submitted immediately by telephone, if possible, through channels to the Army Air Service Commander, who will transmit it to the Second Section, General Staff (G–2).

Chapter III. Combat

I. *General Principles:* [5]

5. The guiding principle in Pursuit Tactics is to seek out and destroy enemy airplanes. Contact is made with the enemy by chains of formations, formations and by individual machines. Before passing on to study the tactics used by each, it is to be remembered that the primary object of the aerial force working with an Army is to keep the enemy under observation. It performs what was once the chief function of the Cavalry, and preventing the enemy observing our dispositions and maneuvers, seeks to keep him under surveillance at all times. The eyes of the Air Service are observation airplanes and balloons. But the arms and weapons are the pursuit airplanes and without the latter two-seaters would be blinded by the enemy air forces to such an extent that their missions would fail and they would have to resort to fighting tactics.

6. The pursuit elements of the Air Service have as their prime function to keep an area equal in depth to the distance over the enemy lines which is allotted to the Corps and Divisional Observation squadrons clear of enemy machines. In other words the aerial front line must be maintained, at minimum, as much in advance of the line of battle on the ground as the range of the Corps Artillery. Pursuit machines, therefore, specialize on the fighting, and of necessity have to adopt certain tactics, varying with the type of machine used, with the activity of the sector and with the altitude at which they are working, but certain principles are universally applicable.

7. The flight formation, limited in size by the number of machines that can be maneuvered by a single leader, at present five or six, is the tactical unit of pursuit aviation. When more than one flight is to be used for any given purpose, emphasis is to be laid upon the value, from the point of view of esprit, of using the flights of a squadron echeloned together in a chain of formations.

5. There was an error made in numbering the seven paragraphs which follow. The correct numbering resumes with paragraph 23.

II. *Tactics of Single Machine.*

(a) The unit of the formation.

8. A great deal of attention has to be given to the tactics of the single machine and it might be argued that this amounts to nothing more than tactics of the individual pilot. This is indeed a fact except that a great deal depends on the make of the machine in use, but there are many principles in individual aerial combat tactics that apply to all pursuit planes, which must closely be followed.

9. The individual pilot in a formation must be a disciplined subordinate officer with confidence in his leaders. A single machine must be part of the team. The team must be the unit to engage the enemy. It must be remembered that the pursuit machine has no defense after a surprise other than its maneuverability and for this reason only pilots of the longest experience and the greatest ability should be permitted to engage in individual patrols and then only on rare occasions. Up to the point where the pursuit machine is attacked its defense consists of the eyes of the pilot plus its speed. It is quite possible for a single machine to get out of very awkward predicaments provided they are seen by the pilot in time and proper tactics are employed. When once attacked the pursuit pilot depends upon his ability to shoot and maneuver for success. The only safe protection from attack the single-seater has be-

sides the eyes of the pilot is altitude, but the higher the pursuit machine gets the less likely its pilot is to see any enemy machines below him and the fewer machines will be encountered. The object of the attack of a formation is to break up the enemy group and resort to single combat without losing the chain of responsibility, so that throughout the combat the mental unity of the flight is not lost. When this stage is reached the individual pilot must close in and at close range deliver accurate and effective fire. Under no circumstances must he be drawn away from the rest of his flight, no matter what the results of his fire have been. He must carefully avoid being drifted over by the wind farther into enemy territory, or pulled away by any ruse whatsoever. If he is separated from his formation he must fight constantly, relying on being able to fly back home at low altitude if

necessary, remembering that it is fatal to dive straight away. Even in case of engine failure the aggressive spirit must be maintained until the ground is reached.

(b) When Single Machine Permissible.

10. At times opportunity presents itself for individual pilots to perform a mission. On days when the weather is very bad, for instance, it sometimes becomes necessary for individual machines to cross the lines at extremely low altitude and penetrate to certain objectives for the purpose of gaining information of great value. At other times the enemy will seize the opportunity afforded by very bad weather and use especially designed armored machines for straffing the infantry at a very low altitude. On misty days it is sometimes impossible to attack these enemy airplanes except [by] individual machines, flying as before, at an extremely low altitude and in this case all the elements of success called into

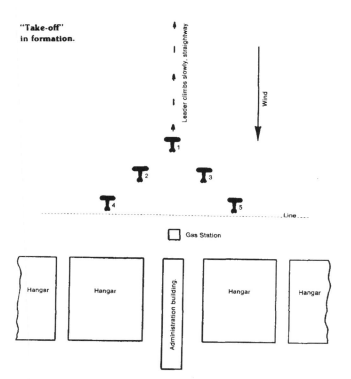

"Take-off"
in formation.

Leader climbs slowly, straightway

Wind

1

2   3

4   5

Line

☐ Gas Station

Hangar   Hangar   Administration building   Hangar   Hangar

service by formation leader must be employed. Surprise being the greatest asset, the pilot should, if possible, close in on the enemy machine by flying through the clouds a portion of the time, making allowance for speed of enemy machine and other possibilities so that the surprise will be complete and the personnel destroyed by a heavy cone of well directed fire at short range. Another occasion when it is permissible for a single machine to be sent on a mission is when a single enemy airplane penetrates far behind our lines and must be destroyed at any cost. At such a time it is well to attack the enemy with individual machines rather than wait to dispatch a formation and run the risk of the enemy machine getting back home safely with the information gained.

(Sketch by J. Andre Smith)

(c) Single-seater vs Single-seater.

11. When a single-seater attacks a single-seater, his ideal objective is to get directly behind his opponent's tail at very close range where tanks, engine and pilot are in line and where no care has to be taken as to deflection in aim. If the element of surprise has not been effected the only manner of getting this advantageous position is by making the enemy dive away. A good pilot, however, will never dive away and the fight resolves itself into a battle to gain the higher position. A pilot must never allow his machine to lose altitude or fall into a spin. This calls for perfect flying so that just the right moment of rudder is used at the proper time and so that the fight can be moved at will toward supports or away from enemy reinforcements, as the case may be. Above all, a pilot's attack must be vigorous and if he should be so unfortunate as to be outnumbered greatly, he must maneuver cooly but in a very erratic course until he can damage or destroy one of the enemy machines without himself being trapped. He must do his best to keep all enemy machines in sight and never permit an enemy pilot to align the axis of his machine in his direction. It is quite possible for one good single-seater to engage as many as three, four or even more enemy pursuit machines

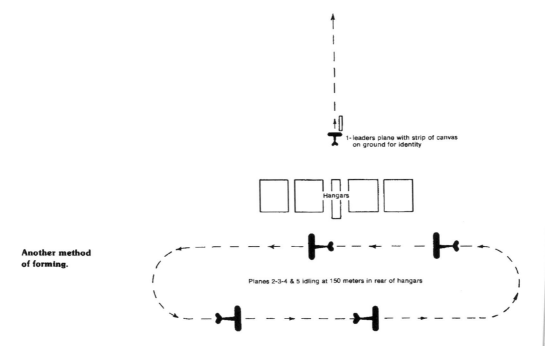

1- leaders plane with strip of canvas on ground for identity

Hangars

Another method of forming.

Planes 2-3-4 & 5 idling at 150 meters in rear of hangars

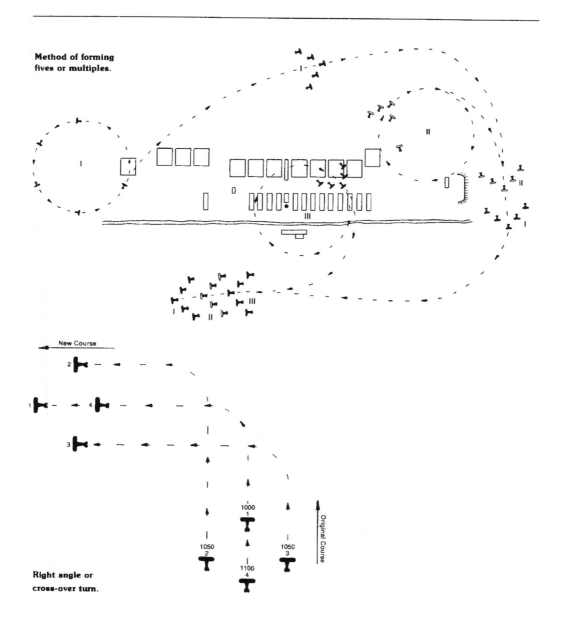

**Method of forming
fives or multiples.**

**Right angle or
cross-over turn.**

Taylor stunt.

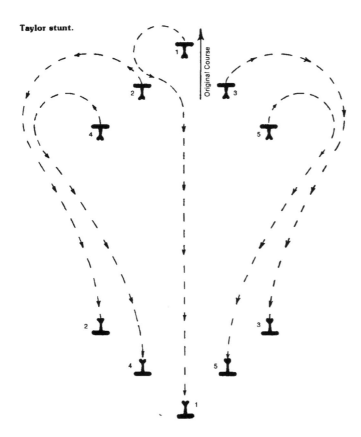

Original Course

for 20 minutes and get back safely to his lines. To a certain extent the type of airplanes will govern the particular maneuvers employed.

(d) Single-seater vs two-seater.

12. Attack by a single-seater on a two-seater machine is, of course, very much more difficult. It should be made in cooperation with another machine, but when this is not possible, the pilot should aim at closing in to short range, delivering his first burst before the observer is able to reply. When two or more machines attack a single-seater it is necessary by zigzag courses, relying on the extra speed, to close in despite the observers fire and at close range deliver hot bursts. When close in under the enemy's tail, make it a practice to turn opposite to the way he does. In this way it is practically impossible for the enemy observer to train his gun on you.

(e) Decoy work by the Single-seater.

23. There is another case when individual flying can be resorted to and this is in decoy tactics. Usually a machine goes out alone but in the sight of a larger formation. Sometimes it meets at a predetermined point at a given altitude and time, and there the formation conforms to the movements of the decoy. The best advice for a decoy machine under these circumstances is to follow an erratic

course. It should never fly straight at all. The pilots should be scouring the sky systematically and thoroughly at all times and use his head to obtain the greatest results by decoying the enemy down on him or attracting the enemy's attention from the higher friendly formation above. It is essential in decoying tactics that the utmost co-operation and confidence exist between the leader of the patrol and the decoy so that there will be no chance of them getting out of touch.

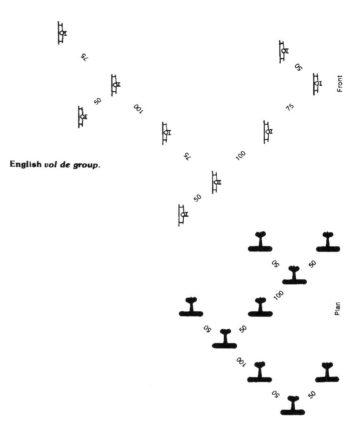

English *vol de group*.

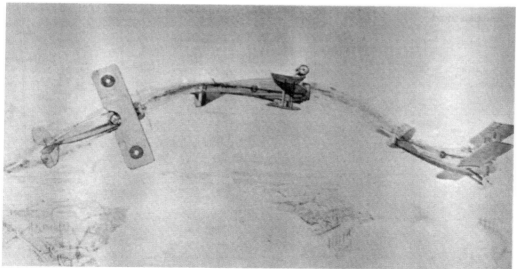

III. *The Single Formation*
(a) General.

24. Good formation flying is the greatest essential in pursuit work. The greatest results cannot be obtained by units that do not do good formation flying. A unit with this asset is certain of success and will attain the greatest point of efficiency. The first essential is to get a good leader; the second, is to maintain the relative positions of the machines; the third, is liaison and cooperation between machines of the formation and last but not least is the chain of responsibility in the flight.

25. The normal formation should comprise a double echelon in depth and in altitude, the planes at the rear being highest up so that they can take advantage of their altitude to close in on the patrol leader by diving, in case of necessity. The normal formation is that of an inverted "V", the patrol leader at the head, number two and number four on his left rear, number three and number five on his right rear. Number two and

Camouflage attack.

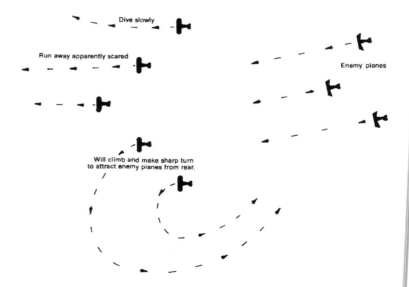

Dive slowly

Run away apparently scared

Enemy planes

Will climb and make sharp turn
to attract enemy planes from rear.

number three should be between 100 and 200 yards apart and about fifty yards above and behind number one. Number four and number five should be between two and four hundred yards apart. The shape of the inverted "V", whether the angle is to be acute or obtuse, will depend upon the visibility from the particular type of airplane in use. When several flights are used as a chain the same principle is employed. The guide for the chain of formations flies at the head of the leading flight, one flight behind, above and to his left, the other behind, above and to his right. Where chains of more than three flights are employed each echelon of three flights will use a similar formation and while guiding on the leader will also maintain its own formation.

(b) The leader and his responsibilities.

26. A successful patrol leader must possess the complete confidence of his flight, and all that that entails. While the leader is under definite orders always, a great deal depends on his ability to engage the enemy at the most opportune moment, retaining his disposition of machines and launching his attack or maneuvering his formation as occasion demands. He will be well advised to allocate certain positions to pilots and then maintain them on successive patrols insofar as possible. Communication between machines must be simple but certain, and he can obtain

this by signals with his wings or by firing Very Lights. The prospective development of the wireless telephone will be of great assistance in increasing the efficiency of patrol leading. Each machine in itself must be in a position to signal to the leader. In short there must be a chain of responsibility running from the leader through the deputy leader to each successive machine of the formation to the last man so that positions and liaison may be maintained under a competent leader, no matter what circumstances arise or what disaster befalls the unit. After much practice, that state of proficiency will be reached where a formation can be worn down to two machines but it still maintains its

unity as a formation with its leader and the second machine working in cooperation ready for combined effort.

(c) Fighting tactics.

27. The actual fighting methods of the formation are much the same as for the chain of formations, with the exception that the leader, in attacking and meeting the attacking line of machines, usually breaks off his individual attack and climbs to support the rear machines or to hold himself in readiness to get his formation together again in a hurry. It is essential to demand this of the leader in spite of the temptation he will have to close in on his adversary. He will often be under the necessity of sacrificing a personal victory to the better judgment indicated. In an attack by a formation every effort should be made to obtain unity to the last. For this purpose it is well to attack the highest and rearmost enemy machines, if attacking from above, of if from below, the straggler should be selected for concentration. Each man of the formation should be able to surmise the attentions of the leader and in this way concentrated effort is more apt to be attained. In order that a perfect understanding may prevail

Lufbery show.

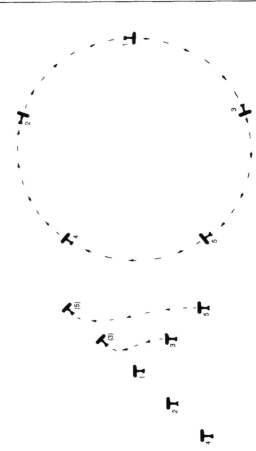

among the pilots of every flight they will live together on the ground and will be encouraged to talk over at all times the situation which have been or are likely to be encountered in the air. If it is impossible to close in on a formation owing to its superior speed or altitude, the next best alternative is to wait until the formation endeavors to make a turn and then launch the attack with great vigour. The enemy can be broken up much more easily at this point than if he is flying straight away [and] has advantage of the height and speed. Great care in the attack must be exercised by all leaders to see that the formation itself does not straggle, because on going down on the attack altitude is lost so quickly by the front line the supports often get out of touch, with disastrous results, amounting, as it does, to a split in the attacking formation. It is found in practice that it is easier to keep a formation of pursuit machines intact in a combat than larger two-seater machines provided the pilots are sufficiently well trained. This is due undoubtedly to their superior maneuverability.

(d) On the type of machine.
28. Formation flying depends so much on the machines in use that it would be unwise to pass on without calling attention to the fact that the tactics must, of necessity, alter with the type of machine employed. The ideal machine for this work of course is one that is maneuverable, and

that can be throttled down,[6] and at the same time made to fly level at any speed by means of an adjustable tail or other contrivance.[7] With a machine of this nature, formation flying is very simple, as one can fly slowly until the actual combat or until necessity arises when by opening out the throttle the necessary speed is obtained to launch the attack. Some machines, however, have motors that cannot be throttled and tails that cannot be adjusted so formation flying becomes a greater problem.

IV. *Chains of Formations.*

(a) The simple chain.

29. Aerial fighting has developed to that stage where it is necessary to send out formations and chains of formations for the accomplishment of missions. Mutual cooperation and support is essential. It has become necessary, therefore, to adopt a unit formation. The size of this unit varies and is determined by the simple fact that a flight leader cannot control more than a limited number of machines in the air at one time with the greatest efficiency. It has become necessary therefore, to send out chains of formations. Sometimes this chain consists merely of two

formations of three machines as a minimum, working in touch with one another; the front and lower formation guides and may be called the front line; the rear formation conforms its movements to the lower and supports the lower in its attack according to the requirements. They maintain their respective positions throughout the whole of an offensive patrol and are often given definite patrols when it is necessary to cover a large amount of territory with a limited supply of machines. In such cases a patrol will be ordered to cover certain points at certain altitudes and at given times and the two formations or echelons perform their mission, retaining their respective positions and relationship at all times.

30. It is interesting to compare this simple combination to a patrol on the ground. On the ground one would find advance and flank guards, but in the air these are unnecessary and the work is accomplished by a top guard. The strength of this top guard has to be considerable as this is the most vulnerable point of the formation, and great care has to be taken that it does not get too far in the rear of the main or guiding unit.

(b) Larger chains.

31. This simple chain can be augmented as circumstances require by increasing the number of each echelon or by adding

Attack on two-seater by formation of pursuit planes.

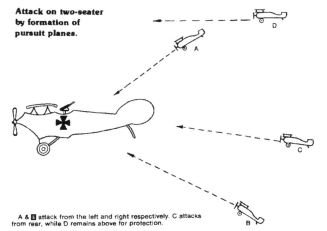

A & B attack from the left and right respectively. C attacks from rear, while D remains above for protection.

6. The rotary motors used in some planes had no throttles and were controlled mainly by turning the motor on and off by means of an ignition switch on the control stick. Some degree of regulation, however, was provided by a mixture valve.

7. The reference may be to an adjustable horizontal stabilizer such as had been incorporated in the Sopwith 1¹/₂ Strutter and some other planes, or some similar means for trimming the aircraft in flight.

one or more formations to the chain. The positions of these added formations are maintained throughout the operation and they have clearly defined functions to perform for each particular occasion that arises. For example, if three formations are patrolling, it is well to have them proceed in a triangular chain, the right rear formation serves as a support to the main body while the left rear remains above in reserve to give protection during the combat and to deal with enemy machines that detach themselves and climb with the intention of counterattacking.

(c) Chains at a distance from the airdromes.

32. This simple combination of formations is not the only kind of chain flying that has been developed. Sometimes individual formations are dispatched and they maintain their individuality and their independence until a given point is reached at an appointed time, when they take up their positions with respect to the previously designated leading flight and proceed as in the simple chain. The advantages of these tactics for use against balloons or other localities of known enemy aerial activity,

Method of assembling chain formations.

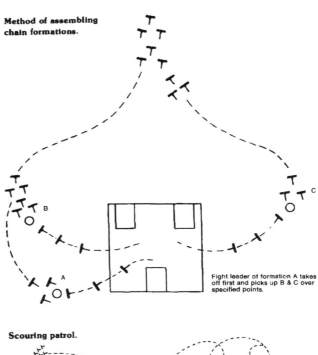

Fight leader of formation A takes off first and picks up B & C over specified points.

Scouring patrol.

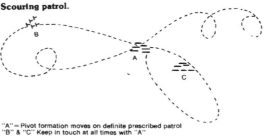

"A" = Pivot formation moves on definite prescribed patrol
"B" & "C" Keep in touch at all times with "A"

such as the rendezvous of a day bombardment formation, is obvious. It is well to point out in this particular form of tactics by chains of formations that the greatest care must be exercised by each leader of a formation. He must not give battle to any enemy aircraft before he reaches his objective and must sacrifice everything to being at his objective at the given instant. The importance of this cannot be over emphasized, as failure on the part of even one formation leader might prove extremely disastrous.

(d) Chain.

33. These tactics can be employed at any altitude but for low work prove especially valuable. These tactics have in mind at least three formations, one acting as the pivot. Each formation leaves the airdrome at a given time and proceeds over a prescribed route to a rendezvous. No time is lost in getting to the rendezvous but each formation is independent until it connects with its pivot formation at that point. On arriving there the leader of the pivotal formation flies in an erratic course but on a definite bearing offensive. The other formations, flying erratically, keep in touch but practically out of sight of the pivot in the hope that the enemy may be encountered. Should one of

these formations encounter enemy machines, a signal is given to summon the whole chain to its support. A chain of this kind is not liable to surprise as the whole sky is under observation practically all the time and it becomes impossible for enemy formations to approach without being seen by someone. On the other hand, enemy aerial activity is almost bound to be observed by someone and by signals the hostile machines can be encountered and destroyed.

Pursuit chain of formation.

Plan

Elevation

A—Leading Echelon
B—Support
C—Reserve

(e) Barrage chain.

34. These three formations of chain flying are used for offensive purposes. Pursuit aviation, however, is used a great deal for protection of reconnaissance and artillery observation machines. One of the simplest and most effective means of accomplishing this is by means of chains of formations. Each formation works individually, patrolling a given beat and connecting up at the beat with its adjacent patrol. Each patrol in itself is irregular in that it does not patrol the whole beat religiously but proceeds erratically. In this way the aerial front line is maintained in advance of the line of battle and friendly observation machines are permitted to carry out their important work of surveillance and observation unmolested. The utilization of permanent barrage chains is wearing on pilots and is opposed to the principle of economy of forces as it results in using up our available resources without permitting us to undertake those strong offensive expeditions in force which alone can cause maximum casualties to the enemy and give us a definite moral superiority. It therefore should only be undertaken at times of intense preparation for attack.

(f) Fighting tactics of the different chains.

35. The fighting tactics employed by the chains in actual combat have certain fundamental principles in common. In the attack the leaders, having done their utmost to surprise their adversary, sweep down deliberately on their opponent, relying on the support to lend necessary assistance. The latter at the same time acts as a reserve or top guard to deal with reinforcements which may arrive to assist the enemy. The primary object of the attack is to split up the enemy formation and enable the pilots of the patrol, maintaining superior altitude to destroy the enemy in single combat. So much depends on the factor of surprise that its value cannot be overestimated. Probably the best feature of a surprise attack is that the offensive formation maintains its unity or at most, if it does lose it temporarily, regains more quickly to great advantage in the ensuing combat which is bound to follow. Provision is always made for a rendezvous in case a formation is broken up. In practice it has been found that the center of the fight and the shortest line to our own side of the lines is the best rendezvous area. This not only enables a formation to get back quickly but often insures

machines supporting one another on their return journey.

(g) Fighting tactics continued.

36. Fighting tactics in the chain depend a great deal on the machine, on the direction of the wind, and on the locality, but certain principles prevail in all combats which must be adhered to at all costs. First, the leader controls the situation. Every machine must conform to his movement and support him. Second, attempts must be made to fight outwards at all times, the idea being to have your formation intact at the end of the fight, with the enemy scattered on the outskirts. Thirdly, under no circumstances must a pilot or formation attempt to dive away from a fight. It is better for a pilot when his machine is shot to keep fighting and circling and be forced down in enemy territory than to attempt to break away and dive for home. By staying with the fight he lends support to his comrades and may cause the enemy to retire and enable himself and comrades to reach safety after destroying enemy machines, whereas by diving for home he is practically certain to be shot down himself.

(h) Principles.

37. Certain principles in the fighting tactics must be forgotten in the chain of formations. First, each formation must lend sup-

port to the other. Second, if given a mission to perform, a rendezvous or patrol, it must be carried out at all costs, as the success of the chain of formation depends so much on the carrying out of the mission by each individual formation. Third, each formation is subservient to the leading formation of the chain. The successful performance of the mission assigned to the chain is of a great deal more importance than any other that might be successfully accomplished by the single formation at the cost of the greater mission.

Strafing a machine-gun battery.

Chapter IV. Attacks on Ground Targets

38. Bombing and machine gunning of ground targets can only be carried out when air supremacy is attained. This supremacy does not have to be permanent but must be temporary at least. Unless this supremacy is held at the time low flying is to be done there will be a greater loss in machines than damage done to the enemy. Ground straffs may be carried out in force by placing over the lines at a certain period sufficient number of pursuit machines to establish the line of equal safety for machines as far over as the straffing is to be done. A single pilot of experience, however, may go over the enemy lines and ground straffs when the enemy hold air supremacy, but the amount of possible damage he

may do does not equal the risk for loss taken.

39. The discussion for low bombing and machine gunning can be combined because where it is possible to accomplish one it is, as a rule, possible to accomplish the other. Low bombing, however, is more effective on troops. Bombing can be done from a greater height than effective machine gunning. Bombing is more effective on places of shelter. However, machines doing low straffing should be capable of both and in most cases a good target for low bombing is a good target for machine gunning.

40. Low straffing of ground targets is only used when large targets are available for attack. A target must be large enough to be an easy mark and important enough for its destruction to

warrant risking the loss of a machine. Only in time of great activity on the ground by either of the combatant forces are ground targets sufficiently large to warrant their being attacked from the air. In the ordinary course of war when no offensive is being launched a good target such as a staff car, or a convoy or a battery may very occassionally present itself, and the pilot of a separate machine or a patrol leader of a formation may use his judgement as to whether the situation demands that he make an attack on that target. Although ground straffing is commonly spoken of as trench straffing, the term trench straffing is a misnomer. Targets in trenches

are not large enough to straff from a height and are protected; and for a machine to go down to within 25 or 30 feet from the ground where many machine guns can be directed against it, the chance of that machine doing damage is too small to offset the chance of being brought down. When an offensive is under way large bodies of troops, cavalry and transport are being brought up to the line. These targets are large enough to spot from some distance in the air. Fire can be directed on the group and a great amount of material damage as well as

moral damage to the enemy can be done. Targets which admit of attacks from the air are any groups of men or horses or transport of the enemy large enough to be easy of mark, and materials or any sort which are of military value and which can be destroyed by aerial attack.

41. The locality of effective ground straffing varies. As troops and transports approach the front line there is a point where large movement cannot be made. Back of that point is the beginning of the effective zone of ground straffing. The farther back of the line one goes the larger are the bodies encountered. But after a certain distance the frequency of encounter will diminish. The zone for the best targets for ground straffing is that place where large enough targets to be easy of mark are found frequently. Besides the location of the target, the factor of comparative safety in distance of penetration enters the question. This factor is determined by the air superiority held, both permanent and temporary, upon weather conditions, the type of machine used, and the condition of enemy ground defenses.

42. In conducting a ground straffe the command has to consider the disposition of its forces and the method of their dispatch and orders. The disposition of forces depends upon the force available and the state of the attack. The dispatch and orders depends upon whether the target is predetermined and designated when the straffing machines leave the ground; or whether the target is to be found, the area in which targets are likely to appear being designated.

43. The problem of available force is one of the number of machines for ground straffing and the number for protective patrols. Whenever straffing is to be done there should be sufficient protective force above to make the low flying machines safe from attack by enemy aircraft. If the protective force is insufficient a ground straffing machine will be easy prey for the enemy because a pilot doing ground straffing has his attention centered on the ground and not in the air. Also formations of machines on this mission become scattered in most cases. The greater the confidence of the pilot of the low machine in the pilots protecting him, the better the job of ground straffing will be. Cooperation between the protecting machines and the straffing machines is very important. The feeling of personal relationship brings about the best

cooperation, and patrols should be arranged to take advantage of that fact whenever possible. In case the number of machines for protection is small it will be necessary to concentrate the protecting force during certain hours and send out all ground straffing machines during those hours. If the number of machines available for protection is large a barrage of machines may be kept up to serve as a protection at all times. It is more difficult to secure cooperation between the low flying machines and the protecting machines where the protecting barrage of machines is used all during the day than where forces are concentrated during limited periods. The number of machines available to do ground straffing does not affect their disposition so much as the number of the protecting force. The use of a ground straffing force, whether large or small, may be concentrated or extended according to the protective force available and the ground conditions.

44. The conditions on the ground which effect the dispatch of machines are whether the at-

tack is just beginning or is in steady slow progress. When the attack is in its first stages machines should be sent over in great numbers and force should be concentrated on that period when greatest assistance can be rendered the ground troops. When the attack has slowed in progress ground straffing may be extended for several days and a constant stream of machines kept over the enemy to harass his reserves coming up. The number over the lines at any time need not however be so great as when the attack is advancing rapidly. The reason for putting a large number of straffing machines over when an attack is in its first stages is more a moral than a destructive reason. The sight of our machines straffing ground targets strengthens the morale of the friendly troops, and weakens the morale of the enemy at a psychological moment. If an attack is slow in progress and ground straffing has been carried out day after day, the enemy must cease day movement of large bodies and transport must move in small groups with some distance between groups. If it is found that insufficient ground targets are presented it is well to concentrate on a certain period, and extend straffing farther back into enemy territory where large targets can be found. Also, the central control should know what cities and towns the enemy is using for concentration points and may designate special straffs on those centers at an unexpected time.

45. When machines are sent out for the purpose of attacking ground targets, the target may have been previously designated, and information concerning its nature and its place given. Such a target is usually one of fleeting opportunity. In such a case it is necessary for the machines which are to make the attack to arrive at the place of the target upon very short notice. For the purpose of performing missions of this sort certain squadrons should be moved to within the closest possible distance of the line previous to an attack. A certain number of pilots and machines must be kept on alert constantly, ready to leave the ground at a moment's notice after information is received concerning a target. The machine used must be one which does not require warming, such as a rotary motored machine, in order that it may leave the ground immediately. Machines for this work can not go over the line farther than their protection takes them. If a protective barrage is up the mission can be dispatched without special escort. If there is not protective force on the lines a special escort must be provided.

46. A definite target, however, may be given which is not one of fleeting opportunity, such as a town where concentration is taking place, an important railhead, etc. Machines which are to perform the mission need not be from an advanced airdrome. Targets of this nature are often given after a ground attack has been in progress for some time and when few moving targets worth while present themselves. However, the central control should know what centers are used for concentration points at all times and should direct attacks on them. These centers are usually too far over the line for a low attack from the air to be carried out unless sufficient force is sent out as an escort to provide temporary air supremacy over the target. An enemy aerodrome presents a target of almost the same nature. Any target may be straffed from a low altitude provided air superiority can be insured at the particular time and place.

47. Machines are also dispatched without particular targets being designated. The pilots may only be instructed as to the locality in which targets are likely to be found. This is particularly true during the beginning of an attack by ground troops on the enemy. In such a case the central control should know the hour of attack, the lines of halting, the final objective, and the zone of exploitation. The pilots to do ground straffing should be informed of these various lines, and orders should be issued, that up to a certain tirne targets will be attacked in a given zone; that after another definite time targets will be attacked in a definite zone farther in enemy territory. Unless this method is followed pilots will not always be certain of whether targets are enemy or their own. But even if the progress is not so rapid the central control must know the zone in which targets are likely to be found and instruct pilots to look for them in that area. The more complete the information the better will be results, for pilots should not have to spend much time looking for targets.

48. Whether machines are sent out singly, in pairs, or in a formation will depend entirely upon the situation. A small formation of three or five machines will bring best results in straffing most targets because there will be a leader of some experience to find the target and to keep a lookout for enemy aircraft. Also the formation will scatter the enemy fire from the ground. The formation cannot be large because of the danger of collision in getting at the target. Machines of a small number can take turns at attacking a target but the number cannot be large because attack must be quick and machines must not have to wait for each other any length of time. If the target is surprised fire from the ground will not be severe, but if time is given for the preparation the chance of the loss of machines will be greater. The number of machines sent to attack the same target is, therefore, limited.

49. The pilots who are to do the ground straffing must possess very definite information as to where enemy troops are located and where friendly troops are located. Uncertainty, even to a limited extent, will ruin the efficiency of the work. In case the push is rapid and the line uncertain the central control must inform the pilots of limits of the zones in which straffing is to be done. That limit should not be several miles within the enemy side of the line, for while attempting to make it safe for friendly troops, the situation is made more unsafe than necessary for the pilots. Pilots should always be informed as to the latest line reports, and, if the line is a moving one, the pilot should know the line the infantry is supposed to hold at the precise moment attack is to be made from the air. Pilots after having this information should know their maps so well that reference to them is almost unnecessary. It is impracticable for pilots to determine whether troops are enemy or their own by uniforms, etc., before the

attack from the air is made. To do this will do away with suddenness of attack, besides, in most cases, placing the pilot in unnecessary danger. There will, of course be exceptional cases where the pilot cannot tell by position whether troops are enemy, in which case they should make certain by uniforms and observation of various indicating facts before making an attack.

50. The method of actually straffing the target cannot be prescribed. The closer a machine is to the ground, down to 100 feet, the more accurate will be the bombing and shooting; also the more accurate the fire from the enemy. Effective bombing and shooting can be done from 2000 feet. The height from which work will be done will depend upon the development in types of machines, and armament, and in the effectiveness of the fire from the enemy.

51. Formations in an attack usually become very dispersed. If the nature of the target permits attack in formation, airplanes of the formation should attack one after the other. In case the formation becomes completely scattered, pilots of inexperience should not remain over enemy territory a great length of time, for they are very subject to attack. The leader should, whenever possible, prescribe when withdrawal to the line is to be

made by signal to other machines. Otherwise, the machines should not linger over enemy territory but a few moments. In case of complete dispersion each machine is to make its way back in the shortest line. If dispersion is only partial it is best to pick up the formation while withdrawing.

52. Weather conditions effect ground straffing fundamentally. Clouds may prohibit protective patrols. In this case ground straffing machines cannot work in formations far over enemy territory, the distance depending, however, upon height and nature of clouds, and visibility of atmospheres. A single machine may do effective ground straffing when clouds are under 2000 feet, going to or returning from his target in the clouds. This is best accomplished when visibility is very poor, when there can be practically no enemy machines about. The most effective ground straffing done by single machines can be accomplished in weather of this sort with very little danger of loss of the machine. The pilots must, however, be of experience.

53. The most difficult situations, however, arise when clouds exist at altitudes about 2000 feet, not rendering a protective patrol useless, but changing very greatly the cooperation between the protective patrol and the ground straffers, and rendering the [possibility of protection] against attack from enemy aircraft much more difficult than where there are no clouds. If it is possible for machines to work above the low clouds, it is necessary to have part of the protective patrol above the clouds and part directly in touch with the ground straffers beneath the clouds. [If] it is impossible for machines to work above clouds the protective patrol cannot penetrate far into enemy territory, the distance depending upon the height of the clouds. The ground straffing machines, being lower, can work a little farther into enemy territory than the protective patrol is working.

54. Machines used in ground straffing can be combatted from the ground and from the air. The greatest source of destruction, however, comes from the ground because of the greater possibilities of fire from that source, both with respect to accuracy, and as to amount and kind. Also the sources of fire on the ground are difficult to observe, and cannot easily be combatted by the low flying machine. It is necessary to perfect devices for fire from the ground and to provide machines, which are to do low flying, with a means of protection from enemy ground fire. When ground straffing is being done it must also be combatted from the air by low flying machines with overhead protection.

**Airplane
attacks captive balloon (left).
Minutes later the balloon becomes
engulfed in flames (right).**

55. The type of machine which is best adapted to ground straffing is necessarily an armoured machine. As weight is increased maneuverability, speed and climb will be decreased. The best machine will be the one with adequate armouring and with least decrease in maneuverability, speed and climb, and with greatest reliability of engine. The reliability of the engine is more important in a ground straffing machine than in other types, because that machine usually works in a place where a forced landing means the loss of a machine and pilot The least vulnerable engine to bullets is an air cooled engine. Rotary motors can be shot through and still run. It is at present considered that the best type of machine for ground straffing is a single seater, rotary motored, armoured machine with two fields of fire—one in front and one below.

Chapter V. Balloon Attacks

56. Balloon attacks may be divided into two general headings, one the individual unpremeditated attack made merely because the pilot finds himself in position for such an attack after an engagement or some special mission, and secondly the scientific attacks made with cooperation in various forms.

57. The first type is usually made with the utmost danger to the pilot as he is open to attack by enemy aircraft from above and has no efficient method of stopping attack from the ground defenses. These attacks should be discouraged save in very exceptional circumstances when they should consist only of a single dive, a long burst of machine gun fire continuing to an extremely short range, and then an immediate but cautious return to the lines. Organized balloon attacks often yield important results. They will almost always be undertaken just before or during an assault. In all balloon attacks it is most essential that the gas bag be perforated in order that the gas may mix with the atmosphere and the incendiary ammunition ignite the resulting combustible mixture. It has been found satisfactory to use ordinary ammunition for the perforation of the bag while a short burst of the incendiary fired at extremely short range, 25 to 50 yards, will in the majority of cases ignite the gas.

58. There are several methods of attacking a balloon. It should be kept clear in the mind of all pilots making such attacks that only approximately the front $2/3$rds of the bag has gas in it, the back $1/3$ being filled largely with air. Because of this, a vertical dive is not recommended. On the other hand the pilot's machine should be gotten into such position that he will be firing parallel to the fore and aft axis of the balloon. This guarantees that the bullets will puncture the bag where the gas is located.

59. In a premeditated attack one of the elemental principles is to silence ground defenses in the shape of machine guns, "flaming onions" batteries (incendiary anti-aircraft) and anti-aircraft guns of greater caliber. This may either be done by our batteries or by aircraft accompanying the pilot who is to destroy the balloon. Both of these methods have proven very satisfactory in practice. In the first case the battery commander makes arrangements for his barrage to be directed at the winch and for a considerable radius surrounding the balloon. This barrage is usually laid down two or three minutes before the attack by our aircraft.

60. In the second case the machine which is to destroy the balloon is accompanied by four or five other pursuit machines, fitted with bomb racks carrying

light bombs. These bombs are dropped on the emplacements of the anti-aircraft defenses and as close as possible to the winch. Immediately after this and at the same time that the single machine attacks the balloon, machine gun fire is also directed at these ground defenses and it has been found that the enemy in a considerable number of cases leaves his balloon up and takes cover.

61. Attacks on balloons should have as much of the element of surprise in their favor as conditions permit in order to prevent the enemy from drawing his balloons to the ground before the attack is made. In case there are clouds in the sky such cover as they afford should be utilized. On clear days great skill in maneuvering is necessary to make the balloon companies believe that the patrol has some other mission than destruction of the balloon. Very often a long, gentle glide to the enemy side of the balloon and considerably

above it, followed by a steep, rapid dive and attack, will be successful. At other times it becomes necessary to follow the balloon as it is drawn to within a very short distance of the ground.

62. When more than one balloon is to be destroyed it is much more satisfactory, whenever possible, to assign separate patrols for the destruction of each target. In this way the element of surprise is maintained to a considerable degree. It is perfectly apparent that in the case of attacking by one patrol of a number of balloons, that the successful destruction of one will warn those to be attacked later of their danger, and will give them an opportunity to draw down the balloon and prepare for an intensive defense.

63. The element of surprise may be very valuably increased by making balloon attacks just at dawn or very late in the evening. Attack at this time also removes to a very large extent the danger of interference by hostile aircraft. The effect of an evening attack on a balloon line has really very little tactical or strategical value as each balloon destroyed will be replaced in time for ascension the following morning, but there is undoubtedly a considerable effect on morale, particularly insofar as observers are concerned.

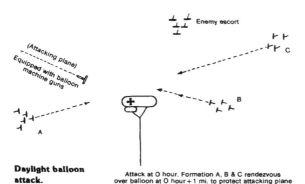

Daylight balloon attack.

Attack at O hour. Formation A, B & C rendezvous over balloon at O hour + 1 mi. to protect attacking plane

64. It is exceedingly important that observers making successful descents in parachutes should be attacked as they are extremely dangerous to our troops on the ground because of their train-ing.[8] Here again the question of morale arises and if observers are attacked as they are de-scending in their parachutes it is believed a considerable increase will be noted in the number of unnecessary descents made.

65. It has been found much more satisfactory to utilize the 11 millimeter balloon gun than the ordinary caliber machine gun. Something on the order of the one-pounder, firing a very deli-cately fused contact shell, would be even more successful for the destruction of enemy balloons. The use of bombs containing sulphur or other incendiary ma-terial did not prove satisfactory.

66. Whenever possible bal-loon attacks should be made with an escort of considerable strength, in order to allow the attacking machines to perform their mission without interruption by enemy aircraft. This protec-tion should be flying in the close vicinity of the balloon at the time of the attack, but at a higher altitude, and should be very careful not to communicate to the enemy by its actions prior to the attack information that the attack is to be made.

67. A considerable proportion of the balloon attacks made by the Allies during the recent war failed in the destruction of the balloon because the pilot did not have a true appreciation of his distance from the balloon. This realization of distance may be gained by practice with balloons behind our lines during the course of which pilots will be-come familiar with the appear-ance of the bag in the sight and will then be able to deliver their burst of incendiary ammunition at a range short enough to be efficient.

68. It should be the attempt of pursuit squadrons on any front to keep the enemy balloons in their sector down as much of the time as possible. Balloon obser-vation is extremely valuable for the regulation of artillery fire and for reconnaissance of back areas. It is even suggested that in the future night pursuit will be equipped with searchlights or other means for locating and de-stroying enemy balloons during darkness.

Chapter VI. Night Pursuit

69. With the development of the Air Service, the problem of night flying and more particularly night pursuit has to be faced and solved.

70. At first sight, it might ap-pear the limitations of night pur-suit are so great that a squadron of this kind would not justify its existence, but on more careful study one finds that the poten-tialities are great and the possi-bilities almost unlimited.

71. The main function of night pursuit at present is, of course, the defensive patrols for the pur-pose of destroying night bomb-ers. The British have already demonstrated that this is quite practical.

72. As the Air Service devel-ops, the night pursuit will be used in conjunction with patrol-ling for the purpose of surveil-lance and reconnaissance. All big movements of troops now take place by night and in time pursuit pilots will be required un-der certain circumstances to go out to predetermined objectives for the purpose of dropping a flare at a given important cross road to ascertain movements of troops or for the purpose of con-firming a suspected withdrawal or concentration. At first, night reconnaissance by pursuit ma-chines will probably be done in the late evening or in the early morning, but as time goes on and the number of squadrons of this kind increase, this kind of

8. The shooting of parachutists abandoning disabled aircraft was then, and is yet, a difficult and controversial area of international law.

work will be done in all favorable weather at night. Concentrations will be located and bombs will be carried, enabling the pursuit machines to descend and harrass same from very low altitudes with extremely great accuracy. Balloon straffing at dawn and in the dusk of evening will be almost entirely the functions of the night pursuit machine and this practice may in time blind the enemy insofar as balloons are concerned. Straffing enemy troops by machine gun fire, owing to the case with which a surprise and get away can be effected at night, will be a very safe and effective work of the night pursuit, and its possibilities are limited only by the weather conditions.

73. There are many difficult problems in connection with night pursuit that have to be faced and attempts made to solve before a squadron can hope to meet with any success. The pilots must be specially trained in navigation by night although this can be learned in a very short time by one of ordinary intelligence and can be helped greatly by increasing the number of lighthouses, mortar signals, and cooperation between the units of the Air Service, day and night forces combined. Forced landings at night

discourage pilots more than any other feature of this work, but with proper landing flares and emergency airdrome lighting sets on all fields, and cooperation of searchlights in the defended area, the dangers from this source can be reduced practically to the same as day flying.

74. Pilots find that one of the greatest problems of night pursuit is locating the enemy. They claim it is impossible to see him even with the aid of searchlights. It is difficult but it is not impossible. On moonlight nights the enemy is visible at 500 to 600 yards even when he is not in the beam of the light, and on bright starlight nights he appears as a dark shadow at a distance of 200 yards. If he happens to be picked up by a searchlight, his planes show up for a very great distance, and experience proves that sometimes machines can be held in the beam ten minutes. Sometimes he can be seen, not in the beam itself, but in the twilight formed in the air by the searchlights and fights have taken place without the beam picking him up or without the knowledge of the operators of the light.

75. As for the actual combat it is safe to say that the enemy can be engaged and brought down with slight danger of his retaliation, provided he is seen first by the pursuit pilot.

76. One of the great problems of night flying is equipment. These necessities include first-class searchlights, airplanes, airdrome lighting plants, lighthouses, motors and signals.

77. For night flying to be a success in the operations of an army it is absolutely essential that it have the proper cooperation and liaison with the neighboring arms. The searchlights are operated by the Engineers Corps. A liaison officer must be placed on the staff of the Chief of night flying who can advise and insure the proper location of searchlights and the cooperation of their personnel with the pilots. The very closest liaison must be maintained with the anti-aircraft artillery. The Chief of Air Service must have a liaison officer from

this branch on his staff, and the guns must be located and operated on his advice and with his cooperation. In addition, official observation posts are to be established in all units on the lines, each in touch with a Post of Command where there will be located a wireless transmitting station, in order that the Chief of all wireless stations in the rear will be kept familiar with indications and locations of enemy aerial activity and likewise advised of its cessation, so that he can most efficiently make his tactical decisions.

78. Defended areas—that is territory over which it is forbidden to fly at night—should be reduced to a minimum if not dispensed with entirely. Arrangements can be made whereby all machines crossing the lines could be challenged by the forward observation posts and the identity of the machine fixed at this point.

79. It is very essential to obtain the proper kind of machine for night work. In the first place the engine must be reliable, simple, and if possible, one that starts up easily and instantly. Any reliable rotary or radial motor seems best adapted for night pursuit. The machine itself must be light, maneuverable and possess great flexibility of speed, owing to the tactical necessity after overtaking a twin-engine machine for a pilot to reduce the speed to the same or less than that of the bomber. It is essential that it climb and dive rapidly and at the same time should land very slowly so that it can be safely landed in a very small area, a feature that will always be essential in night forced landing. It is well to strengthen the center section struts and take similar precautions so that in case of a turn over the pilot can be sure of getting out and it is advisable to have a machine sensitive laterally rather than fore and aft. If a machine is too sensitive fore and aft, one is apt to dive into the ground or stall on coming into the airdrome when one's attention is often diverted to landing light instruments or ground lights. With regard to fuel, it is advisable to have as much gasoline as possible. Although a patrol should not be for more than 1¼ hours, pilots frequently get lost returning and have to fly around a long time before they get their bearings.

80. Armament is an important feature. Machines should be equipped with two guns, one balloon and one ordinary. Sights should be illuminated and ordinary ammunition used with this exception, that very few tracers should be used (1 in 15). Bomb racks are essential and it is well to have a rack that can be bodily taken off with bombs and replaced on short notice as normally its employment will not be the duty of night machines.

81. The instrument board is an important feature. All instruments must be lighted and in addition luminous in themselves, and two movable [flash-lights must be provided, the whole electrical equipment being run][9] from two separate storage batteries which, in themselves, should be very accessible, yet substantially fixed. A good air speed indicator and a good altimeter are even more essential in night flying than in day, and the compass, too, must be of the very best. A machine will carry wing tip flares. A navigation light on the outer struts, and a signalling light on the bottom of the fuselage with at least one emergency parachute landing flare.

9. The words in brackets, inserted to fill an obvious omission, are from *Circular* 76, p. 44.

Normally the dangerous wing tip flares will not be used but in the case of forced landings these will be lighted, sufficiently high above the ground to insure their being burned out by the time the ground is reached. These must be examined very frequently and under no circumstances should they be used later than the date stamped thereon. There is no such word as economy in connection with the use of flares. They must not be opened until they are actually going to be placed on the machine. First-class parachute flares should be the only parachute flares carried. The signal-light beneath the fuselage must be operated by a tapper key and a permanent switch be opened interchangeably, at will and instantly.

82. Two kinds of airdrome equipment must be recognized and provided. First, that in vogue on the fields of the other night squadrons operating which must be most reliable and if necessary elaborate; secondly, the emergency landing set, which should be at hand on these fields but in addition should be placed on every airdrome in the army area so that a pilot lost in a fog may with safety call and land at any field. The arrangements of the main fields must be worked out as circumstances require, but it is essential that a good generating unit be at hand and that the bounds of the field be clearly defined. For an emergency lighting outfit, three small concentrated beam throwing lights, with power furnished by a fifteen volt storage battery placed on a trolley are recommended. These are quite inexpensive and will on every field justify their existence many times over.

83. The army area as a whole must [be] lit up with Mortars and Lighthouses, and a 36″ Sperry light at the main airdrome for purpose of defense as well as for the purpose of directing machines home is essential.

84. Certain rules must be inaugurated for landing at an airdrome at night. These must be formulated not forgetting the possibility of the enemy bombing and must consist of a signal for recognition and on the main field the use of a dummy airdrome as an adjunct. All pilots will be called upon to make circuits to the left and glide in parallel to the main line of lights. Each pilot must flash the proper code letter before landing. If a crash blocks the field, proper signals or a beam of light must be flashed to him. In this connection it will be essential to instruct and hold responsible one man at least on every field in the best methods of placing the lights, so that a pilot will never be required to come in over obstacles and so that he will be able to make a landing even if he is unfamiliar with the airdrome.

85. Probably the greatest difficulty to be encountered is the selection of pilots for this work. It is absolutely imperative that night pilots master the science of flying. It is quite possible to be a pilot in the day time and yet know very little about flying, but he who hopes to succeed at night must be capable of flying any kind of a machine intuitively and in addition must have mastered the peculiarities of the particular machine that he is to use. It is essential that he be keen about his work and the responsibility for this rests primarily with the squadron commander directly through the flight commander. He must be imbued with the spirit of determination first of all to develop this branch of aviation. He should be steady, sober, keen and industrious and so fond of flying that he sees every opportunity to get up in the air, day and night.

86. In flying a pursuit machine at night a pilot who has mastered his machine thoroughly should have no difficulty in mastering the art, whether pursuit or bomber, but it is useless for him to attempt the work until this is the case. In all armies there have been regretable accidents in this connection which have tended to bring night flying into disfavor with the pilots. It is a fact that any good day pilot will make a good night pilot provided his vision is normal. In addition to being a good pilot, the night flyer must have a thorough knowledge of the country, particularly of the landmarks. He must be skilled in the location of possible fields, airdromes, forests, rivers, bad ground, etc., and when he has first enlisted into the service of a night squadron, he should utilize every opportunity that presents itself in mastering the situation, never feeling satisfied until he knows the country thoroughly. He must be instructed in cloud flying but should be warned never to attempt it unless compelled to do so. If overtaken by a mist or clouds he must never let the ground get out of sight. If necessary he should make a forced landing rather than attempt to get home at night by flying through the mist, unless of course he is flying high and is sure of the weather.

87. After a pilot becomes competent he will practice forced landing on his own airdromes on moonlight nights, and practice combat fighting with two-seaters at night cooperating with the searchlights. Rehearsals of forced landings by means of parachute flares are practicable, the pilot using the engine if he discovers that the field sought is liable to cause him to turn over.

88. The location of instruments and the method of using them in the dark must become a matter of second nature to the night pilot, so that this will in no way distract his attention from more important things. Patrols will often be monotonous because they will cover short beats over important points. Enemy night bombers are certain to follow permanent land marks, such as rivers or forests. This means that a pilot on patrol must stay over this spot patiently and await his opportunity. He will do well to have patience and not to be distracted by neighboring lights from his particular mission. Pilots must never attempt to fly under 200 meters at night as the risk involved is too great, and on his first flights he must arise over his airdrome at a height of at least 1000 meters and take his time coming in. The morale of pilots in all branches of the Air Service must be carefully preserved, but this is even more marked in the case of night pilots. Day flying should be performed and should only be permitted between certain definite flying hours of daylight. Otherwise pilots will never feel that they are off duty and in a few weeks will become tired and disgusted with their work, and lose all their keenness.

89. The main duties in the operations of night pursuit is the defensive barrage. Patrols will be carefully planned with the object of intercepting hostile bombers at the point where they are picked up by the searchlights. Patrols will, therefore, be carried out slightly in the rear of lines and more particularly over permanent land marks. They will not last more than one and one

fourth hours and vary in altitude from 2000 to 4000 meters, according to the situation. It is inadvisable to send patrols up until enemy activity has been reported by the advanced posts and it is quite possible to determine with great accuracy when the enemy is operating by observing his mortars, lighthouses, airdromes, and so on. Balloons may be utilized for this purpose as they can render valuable assistance.

90. When a pilot is on patrol he will have his attention called to enemy aircraft by the firing of the Archie guns, by observation of the explosion of bombs on the ground and by the direction and concentration of searchlights beams. He will "cut" his motor frequently and glide as long as possible with a dead motor so that the light operators and gunners can listen for the enemy ships. In times it will be possible to institute a system of rockets and flares which will enable a pilot on patrol to follow the course of an enemy bomber and it is within the range of possibility that before long wireless telephones will come to assistance of a pilot on patrol and solve many of his difficulties.

91. When a pilot sights an enemy machine, his simple tactics will be to get under his tail, closing in to a very close range and opening up fire after throttling down, making use of the element of surprise to the utmost, for, if the enemy begins to slide-slip and maneuver, he will probably get away. Should a pilot be so unfortunate as to be seen by the enemy machine before he has effected a complete surprise, he must endeavor to keep his eye on the enemy by observing his instrument board, his exhaust or the explosive tracers from his machine guns. After a short time the enemy will steady down and probably attempt to dive for home, when it will be safe for the pursuit machine to close on him again. It is easier on a clear night to see machines above silhouetted against the sky but should he dive and get below the attacker, it is quite possible to pick up his outline once more against the lights on the ground; probably in time special illuminating lights will be provided for this purpose.

92. In addition to defensive patrols, night pursuit will be utilized in time for reconnaissance and surveillance and special machines will be dispatched to intersections and cross roads, railway stations, rivers, etc., for the purpose of locating and confirming enemy movements. In some cases parachute flares will be used and in time it will be possible to take photographs at night. The same machines will be able to carry light bombs and shutting off their motors, glide down to a very low altitude and with great precision and accuracy drop them, insuring good results.

93. Other duties, however, besides these will be required of night pursuit squadrons. They will be required to attack balloons suspended in the air or lying on their beds late in the dusk of evening after all the

enemy airplanes have landed, enabling the pilot to come back unmolested and in safety to his own lines, landing after dark. In the early dawn the same work can be accomplished and it is not without the range of possibility that the efficiency of balloons will in this way be reduced.

94. Airdrome straffing in the late evening and in the early dawn is one of the chief functions of night pursuit and airdromes may be so far back that the whole situation will be changed. Hangars probably will have to be underground and mechanics will have to live in dug-outs. On fine nights single machines will harrass enemy airdromes many times over and on [some] nights large offensive operations will be able to put machines out of action. Before and during an offensive enemy

concentrations will be straffed and machine-gunned at night from a low altitude. The Commanding Officer of a Night Pursuit unit must be ready to develop the possibilities of his command to the utmost.

95. A great deal of the success of night pursuit will depend on the location of the airdrome. The ideal place is in the center of the line of searchlights. This enables pilots to stand on their airdromes ready to take off and reduce the duration of their patrols. With an airdrome in this location, pilots are able to go up and take short flights, making many sorties per night if necessary. Many devices, such as dummy airdromes, must be used to enable the location of this advanced field to be kept secret and to prevent its being bombed. Machines will not be brought up until the night of an anticipated

raid, the actual location of the squadron being well in the rear. As a matter of general principal, it is very much better, however, to have squadron work from the field where its headquarters, hangars, machine shop, etc., are located, as advanced fields are never entirely satisfactory, and if at all practicable this should be the case. The location of this field near the searchlights, in addition to the usual advantages, keeps a possible landing ground within gliding distance of the pilot at all times and greatly increases his confidence and efficiency.

96. While it is important to have the airdrome located centrally, the proper location of the searchlights is more essential and two methods prevail. First, the concentration of searchlights around important bombing objectives from the enemy standpoint of view and, second, the location of a continuous line of lights along the whole front. There are many points in favor of both, the ideal, of course, being the adoption of both. Certainly, it is best to have as many lights as possible and in this the question of economy does not figure. Searchlights will be placed in units of three lights in triangular formation, the sides of the triangle being roughly [300 yards].[10] All the lights will be

---

10. The bracketed phrase, supplying a number that was omitted, and correcting a word that was misspelled, is from *Circular* 76, p 46.

under the control of one P.C. and where possible this will be located on the airdrome and in direct touch with the operations officer of the squadron. Another very important feature about the location of the lights and one which will go a long way to the success of the operations is that of possible "forced-landing" field. Every search light, where possible, will be placed on a possible emergency landing field and instructions given to the operators that upon a distress signal from the plane all lights so located will concentrate on their respective emergency field. In locating these searchlights and instructing the operators, care will be taken that operators understand that a plane lands best up hill and into the wind, not forgetting to point out that it is

next to impossible at night to land over high obstacles.

97. Anti-aircraft guns should be located so as to fire in zones and the best rule is to have them fire only towards enemy territory and over the enemy lines. In this way they serve as a signal for a pilot who may be in the air and at the same time there is less likelihood of a friendly pilot being hit. Enemy bombers prefer to penetrate an anti-aircraft barrage than search-lights where there are pursuit machines about. With this in view tactical distribution of the guns will be made to suit occasions and special circumstances.

Part IV. Day Bombardment

Introduction

Object of Day Bombardment

1. The primary object of bombing operations is the destruction of the material, personnel and morale of the enemy. The secondary object is reconnaissance of enemy movements in the air and on the ground. The effect of destroying the enemy's materiel and personnel is not commensurate with the effect gained by day bombardment in weakening the morale of troops and civilians in the bombed areas. The ratio of the effect and lowering the enemy's morale over that of destruction is estimated as about twenty to one.

Chapter I. Information

2. Information of the enemy and our own ground forces is essential to the proper tactical operations of a day bombardment unit. The collection and preparation of this information for distribution to the smaller units of his command is the duty of the Air Service commander. Information properly circulated to bombardment units has an important effect upon the morale of the personnel. This is the only method by which units far from the battlefield can have brought to them the actual situations at the front. Unless the possibilities of day bombardment are made

clear it is impossible to get the maximum efficiency from the pilots and observers.

3. Every unit headquarters will be supplied by the Army Air Service Commander with:

(a) A map showing the location of all enemy airdromes. This map will indicate whether or not the airdromes are occupied, and will show the quantity and kind of air forces present.

(b) A map showing the location and kind of all enemy antiaircraft artillery, which will be kept as near up to date as possible.

(c) A map showing the existing and probably locations of all enemy divisions, both in the line and reserve. The map will be prepared from information furnished by the second section of the General Staff (G-2).

(d) A map showing the location of all airdromes in the sector of the Army Air Service Commander, the corps and divisional sector boundaries of all units in line, the location of our antiaircraft artillery units, balloons and other air service units.

(e) Silhouettes and photographs of all known types of enemy airplanes. These should be posted in the operations rooms, and in the mess hall and quarters of the flying personnel.

(f) A diagram of telephonic liaison in the army area.

(g) A map showing the location of heavy and railroad artillery units and their targets.

5. The charts, diagrams, and maps will be supplemented with:

(a) Army summaries of intelligence prepared by G-2. These will be circulated to be accessible to every pilot and observer.

(b) Air Service summaries of intelligence prepared in the headquarters of the A.S.C. These will cover all subjects relating to the enemy air service, especially the quantities and types of his airplanes, and his methods of employing them in aerial warfare. It is the duty of every operations officer to make known to his flying personnel all the experiences that other pilots and observers have had over the lines.

Chapter II. Liaison

5. Success of day bombardment depends in a large measure, upon a system of well established liaison. The liaison must be such that it guarantees a rapid transmission of information and orders. A comprehension of the entire situation at the moment has a decided effect upon

the success of bombardment operations. In order that bombing raids may be made most effective, and with a minimum of losses, a close Liaison with the front must be maintained. Accurate knowledge of the enemy's aerial activity at the time is the most important factor in deciding upon the tactics to be employed in executing the raids, the route to be followed, and the altitude from which the objective will be bombed. The Liaison should be so perfected that each group commander can be informed without delay of the location, number, altitude, direction of flight and types of enemy airplanes approaching our front lines. This liaison will be established:

(a) By direct telephonic communications with anti-aircraft artillery observation posts.

(b) By wire with the radio-goniometric stations.

(c) By wire with the line of observation balloons.

6. The telephone communications from group to wing, and to the Army Air Service should be direct. The internal liaison from group headquarters to the several squadrons should be perfect. The group operations officer should be able to communicate without delay with all squadrons operations officers and with the flying field and alert tents.

7. Too much emphasis cannot be placed upon the importance of the exchange of visits between the commanding officers of the air service units. This applies especially to the day bombardment and pursuit aviation. Without these exchanges of visits it is impossible to arrive at that close cooperation so necessary between these two branches. Personal visits between officers of all branches of aviation and the officers of infantry, artillery, anti-aircraft artillery, and balloon sections are the best means of establishing a feeling of understanding and sympathy between the various arms of the service. This understanding is necessary to perfect an efficient system of liaison upon the battle field.

Chapter III. Security

8. Security embraces all measures taken by a command to protect itself from annoyance, observation, surprise and attack by the enemy. The protection of day bombardment naturally falls under combat, and will be treated under that head. Under security will be discussed only those measures taken by the commanding officer for the protection of his airdrome.

9. The selection of an airdrome depends upon several circumstances, such as accessability, distance from the front, size, security and shelter. In day bombardment it is essential to select a large field. Airplanes loaded with bombs require a long runway to take off. As they climb slowly they must have considerable distance in which to attain sufficient altitude to clear the natural obstacles which generally surround a field. The necessity, especially during an offensive, to take off on short notice, and to take up formation quickly, requires the squadrons to leave the ground together. Therefore, a large airdrome is absolutely essential for the efficiency of the group.

10. Day bombardment airdromes as a general rule are situated at 35 kilometers from the front lines that the airplanes may attain their bombing altitude without making unnecessary detours before crossing the lines. Working within the limits

above laid down the selection of an airdrome, as regards security, should be made with a consideration of the following principles:

It should be away from all landmarks which are visible at night, such as streams, intersecting highways, and large cities. An airdrome situated alongside a forest affords great security, as the hangars and buildings can be concealed among the trees. Care should be taken to place the hangars on a well defended edge of the forest. The day bombardment fields at Amanty and Maulan were good examples of forest security. On many occasions enemy night bombers could be heard circling the forest, but the airdromes were never hit by even stray bombs. These airdromes were also good examples of camouflaging material. The colors of the hangars, and buildings, blended so well with the colors of the forests that it was difficult to locate either airdrome even in daylight, especially if the clouds were low and the known landmarks in the vicinity hidden. The hangars should be spaced at least 100 meters apart so that the maximum effect of one bomb would be one hangar. All hangars and buildings should be camouflaged to blend with the surrounding color. As most night raiders carry incendiary bombs great care must be taken in choosing camouflage material and in the disposition of inflamables. The gasoline stores must be placed a safe distance from the hangars or other likely targets.

12. The distance of day bombardment airdromes from the front usually is a sufficient safeguard against daylight raids. But it is always well to organize a system of defense against low flying enemy airplanes. This defense usually consists of machine gun emplacements around the airdrome so placed that the enemy airplanes will have to pass through a barrage before reaching a bombing position over the hangars. At times the exigencies of the service make it necessary for day bombardment airdromes to be placed close to the front, as for example, when operating in a constricted area. When airdromes are close to the front, earthworks and bombproof shelters must be erected around quarters as protection for the personnel against air raids and shell fire.

13. Each group should be mobile, and should have ample transportation facilities to move all its material in case of a general advance or retreat. Lack of transportation has occasioned great losses in material. Units operating near the lines should have their supplies or spare parts packed in boxes with hinged doors, to be loaded on trucks at the first alarm. The offices should be in trailers so that all the records can be carried away. Orders covering emergencies should be prepared in advance and understood by those responsible for carrying them into effect.

Chapter VI.[11] Group Organization

16. Group Commander.
Group Operations officer.
Group Adjutant.
Group Armament Officer.
Group Supply Officer.
Group Instrument officer.
Group Radio officer.
Group Photographic Officer.
Group Officer in charge of flying field.
Group Police officer.
Group Surgeon.
Group Transportation officer.

17. The efficiency of a group depends primarily upon the organization of its commissioned personnel. The principal duties of the group officers are here designated in order of importance.

11. The index in Gorrell's History, D–1, p 165, lists Chapter IV, Orders, and Chapter V, Marches and Convoys, which are omitted from the text, D–1, p 236. Those two chapters are included in *Circular* 76 by reference to the pertinent chapters of Part I.

Group Commander

18. The group commander has all the administrative duties of a post commander. He is also responsible for the operations of his group, the orders for which he receives from the G–3 Army through the Army Air Service Commander. In compliance with these operation orders he issues orders to his squadron commanders for the execution of the designated missions. Unless specifically covered in orders from higher authority the group commander's orders cover the following essentials:

(a) The number of formations and the number of airplanes in each.

(b) The types and weights of projectiles to be used.

(c) The time of departure, the order of departure of each formation, the route, altitude, and time of arrival at objective.

The duties of the group commander should be so coordinated that the minimum amount of time will be spent in the office.

It is essential for him to keep in personal touch with all his squadron commanders, and to create a feeling of sympathy with all his flying personnel. Flight commanders and leading observers should feel at liberty to make suggestions to him regarding changes in the execution of raids, which is possible only if he adopts an attitude of sympathy toward the elements of his command. He must make frequent visits to group commanders of the other branches of aviation, especially those of pursuit groups, as such conferences are the surest means of acquiring cooperation in aviation as a whole, and of putting into effect in his group the best methods used by all the others. It is his duty to instruct his squadron commanders fully regarding the parts their respective squadrons will take in the raids. He must be a flying officer, and should participate in such raids as his duties will permit. It is absolutely essential for him to participate in enough over-the-lines duty to become familiar with the actual execution of raids. With the development of the wireless telephone he will be able to direct the execution of a bombing raid from a point of vantage impossible to a formation leader.

Operations Officer

19. The operations officer will carry out the will of the group commander much the same as an adjutant does that of a post commander. He should be chosen for his executive ability, preferably a leading observer who has had considerable experience over the lines. He will have immediate supervision of group operations. It is his duty:

(a) To compile and keep available for the group commander and flying personnel all information of value in the preparation of bombing raids.

(b) To keep an indexed file of photographs, and a supply of maps for the pilots and observers. He will post in the operations room a map of the sector (1 to 80,000, or 1 to 50,000 scales) in which the group is operating, also a map (1 to 200,000) showing the lines of the entire front with the changes as they occur. For the instruction of the flying personnel he will post maps upon which are indicated the location of all antiaircraft batteries, airdromes, artillery positions, hospitals and balloons, both our own and those of the enemy.

(c) To post on a bulletin board all orders and communications, and all bulletins of the Army, Army corps and divisions, which may be of interest to pilots and observers of the group.

(d) To transmit all information obtained from squadron operations officers to the Army Air Service Commander, and to file the raid reports of each squadron with the records of the group.

(e) To supervise the work of the group photographic officer, to see that all possible photographs of the raids are taken and proper distribution of the prints made.

(f) To supervise the work of group pilot and observer detailed to instruct new pilots and observers in the theory and practice of bombing.

(g) To instruct selected officers in the duties of the operations office, to supply operations officers to new squadrons.

(h) To post silhouettes of all types of our own and enemy airplanes in places where they can be studied by all pilots and observers.

(i) To keep in touch with the meteorological station, and to post at least twice daily the reports of weather and air conditions.

The group operations officer should keep intelligence charts showing all the bombing objectives, and mark daily on duplicate copies the bombardments effected. He should keep up to date all information of the number and types of enemy aircraft in the sector, their air tactics, and the best methods to combat them. He is responsible for the correct interpretations of the photographs taken by the group,

and for utilizing the information thus obtained. He is further responsible for the establishing and maintenance of internal liaison, liaison with G–2 Army, A.A.S.C., and all the pursuit wings and other groups.

Armament Officer.

20. The duties of the group armament officer are:

(a) To exercise general supervision over the entire armament of the group.

(b) To advise the group commander on the best types of bombs available for a particular purpose.

(c) To maintain a close liaison with the ordnance department that the squadrons may obtain, at the earliest date, any improvements in bombs, ammunition, guns or armor.

(d) To maintain a personal liaison with the armament officers of all aviation units, and to take advantage of the improvements evolved by them.

(e) To advise the supply officer of the needs of the group in armament, and see that requisitions are made out to supply them.

The duties of the armament officer are very important in the group. He is responsible for the storing and care of explosives, and for the protection of the airplanes against incendiary bullets in combat. He should be an officer of great initiative as most of the improvements in armament will be developed from suggestions made by him to the ordnance department. Nearly all real and effective improvements result from experience gained at the front.

Supply Officer

21. The main duty of the group supply officer is to keep on hand an adequate but not an over supply of spare parts. Enough spare parts is necessary to permit the group to operate at maximum efficiency; an over supply decreases the mobility of the unit when ordered to move. It requires a constant study of the spare parts used by the group to estimate the amount necessary. To prevent an over accumulation of spare parts the group supply officer must supervise the work of the squadron officers and issue spare parts to

the squadron only when actually needed for particular repairs. By personal visits to the parks one can learn what supplies are on hand, and what expected, and thus avoid submitting many useless requisitions.

Instrument Officer.

22. The duties of the instrument officer are:

(a) To keep in adjustment all delicate instruments used in bombing.

(b) To keep up to date information on the manufacture and improvement of such instruments.

(c) To recommend improvements in the instruments and requisition new and improved types.

Radio Officer.

23. The duties of the Group Radio officer are:

(a) To supervise the installation and testing of all radio equipment.

(b) To install and test all wireless telephones.

(c) To operate the radio station.

(d) To carry out orders from the group operations officer in establishing liaison with all other radio stations at the front.

Photographic Officer

24. The duties of the group photographic officer are:

(a) To command the photographic section.

(b) To supervise the care and installation in the airplanes of all the cameras.

(c) To see that all plates are properly developed and prints made.

(d) To see that all prints are properly marked.

(e) To make the correct interpretations of the photographs.

(f) To see that the observers are efficient in the manipulation of the camera.

(g) To collect all the cameras after a raid, and to assume responsibility for the plates exposed by the observers.

Officer in Charge of Flying Field.

25. The officer in charge of the flying field is responsible for discipline on the field. His duties include the following:

(a) That pilots comply strictly with the rules for taking off and landing, and for piloting while in the air.

(b) That the sleeves are properly placed and working all the time.

(c) That the landing T is always out in the day time to indicate exactly the direction of the wind.

(d) That flares and landing flights are ready and properly placed to aid airplanes landing after night has fallen.

(e) That all wrecked airplanes are removed from the airdrome without delay.

(f) To superintend the maintenance of the terrain of the airdrome that the field be in the best possible condition for airplanes to take off and land.

(g) To see that airplanes parked outside the hangars are properly aligned.

The officer in charge of the flying field has a very important bearing on the proper functioning of the group. His discipline must be very strict. Many infractions of the field rules are made by pilots returning from a raid in which the airplanes have suffered from anti-aircraft or enemy airplane attacks. The officer in charge of the flying field must report every breach of discipline to the group commander. There is a tendency for the group commander to overlook breaches of discipline when there has been a severe combat, but the field officer must enforce the flying rules to safeguard against accidents. The officer in charge of the flying field also assumes command of the ground targets for aerial gunners. He should see that the targets are properly placed, and danger flags sent up during practice.

Police Officers.

26. The police officer can be given the odd jobs which do not seem important, but which must be done for the proper maintenance of the group, when operating against the enemy. It is his duty:

(a) To see that the camp is kept clean.

(b) To see that all oil, gasoline drums and other material which cannot be sheltered are properly placed and neatly arranged.

(c) To see that necessary walks are laid out and maintained.

(d) To take proper precautions to protect the camp against fire, and to see that fire fighting facilities are maintained.

(e) To see that the enlisted personnel use the latrines ordered by the surgeon, and when a group occupies an airdrome temporarily it is difficult to make the enlisted personnel observe the above regulation.

(f) To see that an airdrome when evacuated is left in proper condition.

Surgeon.

27. The surgeon cares for the health and sanitation of the group. Close supervision of the group surgeon by the group commander is necessary. He should have a comfortable building as a hospital in which to treat flying personnel suffering from only temporary ailments. There is a tendency on the part of most group surgeons to evacuate pilots and observers for a

month or more for slight indispositions which could be cured in three days at the group hospital.

The group surgeon will see that a medical officer is on duty during flying hours, and an ambulance with a driver on the field.

Group Transportation Officer.

28. The principal duty of the group transportation officer is the care of all transportation.

(a) He will make requisition on the group supply officer for all transportation and spare parts needed.

(b) He will supervise the employment of the transportation in all marches and convoys.

(c) He will see that his chauffeurs are properly instructed in all traffic regulations.

(d) He will see that his enlisted personnel is properly instructed in the care and upkeep of all motor vehicles.

(e) He will see that no transportation is driven from the park that is not in proper condition.

(f) He will be directly under the supervision of the group commander, and will assign no transportation without his consent.

Group Adjutant.

29. The group adjutant will carry out the administrative duties of the group, and will bear the same relation to the group commander that the adjutant of a post does to the post commander.

Chapter VII. The Squadron

30. Squadron commander.
   Adjutant.
   Operations officer.
   Ordnance officer.
   Engineer officer.
   Supply officer.

31. The squadron commander is responsible for the operations of his squadron. He should be a natural leader of men. His squadron will have no more initiative than he personally shows, nor will the morale of his command be higher than his own. He must be a flying officer and must so perfect his organization as to have time to lead frequent raids. His adjutant must be capable of looking after the preparation of raids. Squadron commanders should be chosen from the best flight leaders gifted with executive ability. His more specific duties are:

(a) To issue orders necessary for the execution of missions.

(b) To give special instruction to his flight leaders on points not covered by the Operations officer.

(c) To give personal instruction to his flying personnel on the tactics employed in the execution of missions.

(d) To acquire sufficient intimacy with his flying officers to enable him to judiciously select pilots and observers for special missions.

Adjutant.

32. To the adjutant fall the administrative duties of the squadron.

Operations Officer.

33. The duties of the operations officer include:

(a) To compile and keep available for the squadron commander and flying personnel all information of value in the preparation of bombing raids.

(b) To keep an indexed file of photographs, and a supply of maps for the pilots and observers. He will post in the operations room a map of the sector (1 to 80,000, or 1 to 50,000) in which the squadron is operating, also a map (1 to 200,000) showing the lines of the entire front with the changes as they occur. For the instruction of the flying personnel he will post maps upon which are indicated the location of all anti-aircraft batteries, airdromes, artillery positions, hospitals and balloons, both our own and those of the enemy.

(c) To post on a bulletin board all orders and communications, and all bulletins of the Army, army corps or divisions, which may be of interest to pilots and observers of the squadron.

(d) To post silhouettes of all types of our own and enemy airplanes in places where they can be studied by pilots and observers.

(e) To instruct selected officers in the duties of the squadron operations officer.

(f) To make proper preparations for all the raids.

(g) To compile all information submitted by pilots and observers returning from a raid and make written report of same to group operations officer.

(h) To see that the orders of the squadron commander are transmitted to the flying personnel.

(i) To maintain an operations room similar to that of the group operations officer.

Ordnance Officer.

34. The ordnance officer is under the supervision of the group armament officer, and is responsible for the armament of the squadron. His duties are:

(a) To test and calibrate all ammunition.

(b) To supervise the care of all machine guns.

(c) To synchronize all machine guns mounted to shoot through the propeller, and to adjust all sights.

(d) To supervise placing the bombs on all airplanes scheduled for raids.

(e) To see that all bomb sights and bomb racks function properly.

(f) To test all pyrotechnics.

(g) To care for all the explosives in the squadron.

(h) To see that all machine guns mounted for a raid function properly.

Engineer Officer.

35. The engineer officer has supervision of all the airplanes, spare parts and the E. & R. shops. His duties are:

(a) To supervise the overhauling of all motors and the aligning of all airplanes, and to make all necessary repairs.

Supply Officer

36. The duties of the squadron supply officer are:

(a) To take charge of squadron stores and supplies.

(b) To make necessary requisitions to the group supply officer for supplies needed in the operations of the squadron.

Chapter VIII. Preliminary Training at the Front

37. No matter how thorough the course of training given at the instruction centers, no bombardment unit is prepared to begin actual operations against the enemy when it arrives at the front. The knowledge that the enemy is but twenty minutes away brings home to the pilots and observers the realities of war. Flying behind the lines, and a short review of the things they have learned at training schools, soon impress them with these realities, and lead to rapid and real preparation for work over the lines.

38. The pilots and observers will be given a review of their theoretical course of instruction to ascertain their fitness for further service. If their previous training is found to be sufficient they will be taught from maps the exact location of the lines, and all the topographical features of the sector. Special attention will be directed to prominent landmarks. They will acquaint themselves with the position of all our troops, anti-aircraft batteries, as well as those of the enemy. They must learn the location of all bombing objectives and be able to identify them from photographs. They must be able to identify at a glance silhouettes of all our own and enemy airplanes. They will be given instruction in the enemy methods of attack and our

tactics for defense. Formation flights will be made every day, approaching nearer to the lines. Pilots and observers who are paired off in teams will always fly together when possible. They should live together in the same quarters, and know each other intimately. On the practice flights the pilots will be given an objective, and the time will be fixed for leaving the ground and bombing the target. The formation will pass over the flying field at a given altitude for inspection by the commanding officer.

39. When the flight returns to the airdrome the signal to break formation will be given by the leading observer. The pilots will obey the rules of the flying field, landing with the T, and in rotation. This practice will be continued until the pilots and observers know the sector perfectly and can adhere to the time schedule while flying tight formation with a full load of bombs. The observers will make observations, practice signals with Very pistols, take photographs, and submit raid reports to the operations officer immediately after landing.

During this period the pilots and observers will be given instruction in aerial gunnery with shooting practice at ground targets. The Observers must become expert machine gunners to be successful in combat with hostile aircraft. This training will give the squadron commander an opportunity to select his flight leaders, and the observers who are to specialize in photography, reconnaissance and protection.

40. Leading observers will be chosen from those making the best records at the bombing schools. After operations have begun other observers will be given an opportunity to qualify in leading. Some observers make excellent records in training centers, but fail in duty over the lines, and vice versa. After this training the squadron will be ready to begin real operations. Large targets which are close to the lines and easy to hit should be chosen as objectives for the first raids.

Chapter IX. Preparation for a Raid

41. Day bombardment objectives will be designated by G–3 of the Army, and transmitted through the Army Air Service Commander to the commander of the group. Upon receipt of those orders he will decide upon the following:

(a) The number of formations and the number of airplanes in each.

(b) The types and weights of projectiles to be carried.

(c) The route, altitude, and time of departure and arrival over objective of each formation.

(d) The method of pursuit cooperation.

The pilots and observers must be allowed ample time to acquaint themselves with all available information regarding the objective, both primary and secondary, the route, and the region to be observed and photographed. The squadron commanders will designate the pilots and observers who are to participate in the raid, and are responsible for their preparation for the execution of the mission. They will designate their flight leaders, and deputy flight leaders, and will assign positions in the formation to the rest of the teams scheduled for the raid. The squadron operations officers will then prepare the operation order, a copy of which will be sent to the group operations officer.

The Formations

42. Day bombardment squadrons will invariably work in formation. The formation should be large, as many as eighteen airplanes being easily controlled by a leader when working at high altitude. For low flying formations in bad weather, eight is the maximum that can be employed. All formations must have the following characteristics:

(a) Simplicity.
(b) No dead angles.
(c) Concentration of fire to the rear.
(d) Concentration of fire below the center of the formation.
(e) Compactness.
(f) Each airplane must be able to see the leader.

All formations, whatever the number, should fly in a "V" formation with the rear of the V closed. Formations of more than ten should have one airplane in the center of the V at the average altitude of the V. Airplanes in formation should be numbered as follows:

```
        1
      3   2
    5   12   4
    7         6
    9  11  10  8
```

Number 1 is the leader and flies at the lowest altitude, Numbers 2, and 3, 4 and 5, and similarly placed pairs should fly at the same altitude, numbers 2 and 3 about fifty meters higher than number 1, and about thirty meters to the right and left of number 1, respectively. Number 4 takes the same position relative to number 2 and number 2 with reference to number 1; and number 6 takes the same position with relation to number 3.

Formations should be as compact as possible, especially when dropping projectiles; during a combat, formations should close

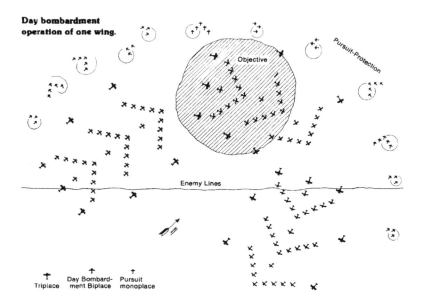

Day bombardment operation of one wing.

up. Too much emphasis cannot be laid upon the training of day bombardment pilots in formation flying. If the pilots maintain a regular echelonment in height, in case of emergency they can close up quickly upon the leader by diving. The leader should never open his throttle wide, and observers should always warn their pilots whenever their own or any other airplane appears to be getting out of formation. It is fatal for an airplane to leave the formation, and the formation should not be broken up to protect an airplane which has dropped out.

The Take Off

43. The pilots and observers should be in readiness on the field at least thirty minutes before the formation is scheduled to leave the ground, reporting to the respective operations officers. This will give the operations officers time to place any unavailable pilots or observers. The pilots will utilize this time to make a thorough inspection of their airplanes and test their motors, and the observers to arrange their maps, Very pistols, ammunition drums and to inspect their machine guns. If the flying field is sufficiently large the formation will be assembled on the ground. The flight leader and pilots 2 and 3 leave the ground simultaneously; 4 and 5 will start

as soon as the wheels of 2 and 3 are in the air, and so on until the whole formation is in flight. The leader will throttle down as soon as he has attained sufficient altitude to do so with safety. When all the airplanes are in position the flight leader may make up traveling speed in climbing, but never full speed. The only practicable formation maneuver is a figure 8 on a wide circuit of about five kilometers.

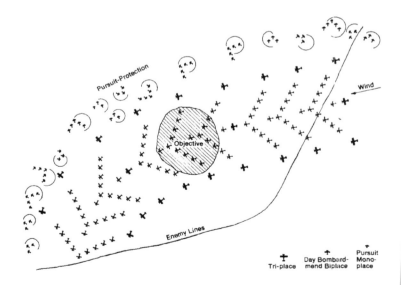

Day bombardment operation of one wing.

Flight to the Objective

44. The formation will attain an altitude of about 1000 meters in the vicinity of the airdrome, and then upon the signal of one white star from the leading airplane, follow the prescribed course to the lines. The bombing altitude, generally 4,000 meters or higher, must be attained before the formation is within five kilometers of the lines, in order that the leading observer may make the calculations necessary for the adjustments of his sight without being molested by anti-aircraft fire or enemy airplanes. The target may be approached either up or down wind. The formation should be tight upon crossing the lines. Any airplane which cannot hold its position in the formation must return to the airdrome.

Bombing the Objective

45. When nearing the objective the leading observer will steer his pilots by means of reins attached to the pilot's arms. This is necessary because the pilot has a limited visibility of objects directly under his airplane. The leading observer should recheck his calculations, and then fire the "Prepare to Bomb" signal of six green stars. When the image of the target appears at the black line in the bomb sight he will pull the bomb dropping lever. All other observers, or pilots as the case may be, will release their

**Day bombardment
operation of one group.**

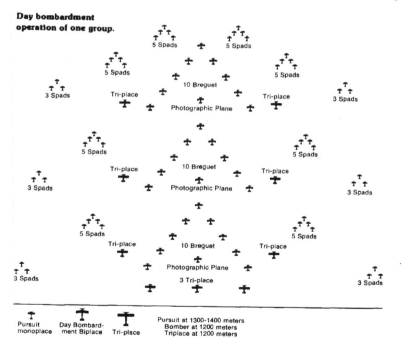

bombs the moment those of the leading airplane are seen to leave the racks. Great accuracy has been obtained by using this method of bombing. Precision bombing over the lines is an art in which only a few observers excel. Such observers should be chosen for leading or deputy positions. Bomb sighting requires cool judgment and intensive observation of the target. Excitement causes inaccuracies. If but one observer does the sighting he knows that all the others are acting as protection, and his excitement is thus lessened.

46. When several formations are sent to bomb the same objective they should bomb at thirty second intervals. Upon leaving the objective they should all turn in the same direction. In the performance of a day bombardment mission it is essential that the formations reach the objectives exactly on time in order that successful cooperation with the pursuit units designated may be assured. With successful pursuit cooperation great damage can be inflicted upon the enemy with the minimum losses to both day bombardment and pursuit.

Chart Showing Functions of Different Branches of Air Service.

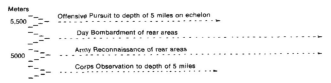

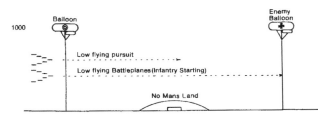

An observer and pilot demonstrate steering the pilot to the objective by reins.

During the Argonne-Meuse offensive the cooperation between day bombardment and pursuit was responsible for seventy-five per cent of the enemy airplanes brought down by the 1st Pursuit Wing.

The Return Route

47. To spend the minimum amount of time over hostile territory is the aim of every formation leader. The route from the objective back to the lines must be chosen with consideration of the direction of the wind, the position of the sun, the location of cloud banks, the most accurate enemy anti-aircraft batteries, and the probable direction of attack by enemy aircraft. If the presence of hostile aircraft does not make it inadvisable the formation leader should always take the advantage of the wind to regain the lines. It is sometimes advisable to fly toward the sun, and thus put the enemy under the disadvantage of facing the strong light. The leader should avoid passing under clouds which offer concealment to hostile airplanes. Clouds under the formation or at the same level, may be utilized for protection. Frequent changes of direction should be made, but they should be made slowly. Rapid changes of direction may cause a rear airplane to lag, which usually results in its destruction. Speed does not enter very much into the safe return of the formation. The formation should be formed to afford no vulnerable point of attack, as its safety depends upon its fire superiority.

Breaking Formation and Landing

48. Having recrossed the lines, beyond which enemy pursuit airplanes seldom venture, the formation leader begins a long glide toward the airdrome. When nearing the landing field the leading observer fires a green rocket as a signal to break formation. The airplanes circle the airdrome and land according to number in formation, Number 1 first, followed by Number 2, and so on. All airplanes land into the wind, as indicated by the T. The landing rules must be strictly observed. The observers and pilots report immediately to their respective operations officers on the field, and submit written raid reports, which include results of the bombardment, observations of enemy movements on the ground and in the air, the number of enemy airplanes brought down, and our own losses.

Low Bombing Raids

49. At the beginning of an advance, or during an offensive, by either friendly or hostile troops, there are occasions when day bombardment must resort to low bombing. Such conditions arise when the weather conditions are such that altitude cannot be attained to carry out the imperative bombardments. Other occasions are when certain bridges must be destroyed, but the topographical features around the objective make it impossible for artillery fire to accomplish that destruction. Day

bombardment must be used at low altitudes against such objectives.

50. The time element often prevents the accomplishment of such missions. The day bombardment airdromes are at considerable distance from the front lines, and time is required for transmitting the information, and for warming up the high powered engines. Often the conditions have changed before the bombers arrive at the objective. A heavily loaded bombing airplane is slow in climbing and maneuvers, and therefore unsuited for this kind of work. The best type of airplane for low bombing is one that can climb and maneuver quickly. The rotary engine, which is air cooled, and can be started very readily, and which continues to run after being hit by enemy bullets, would, therefore be better than the fixed motor for low bombing. The accuracy and volume of ground fire causes so many losses that low bombing is extremely costly, even if our forces have supremacy of the air.

51. When orders are received for a low bombing mission the group commander decides the number of airplanes to be sent in formation, never more than six. Great care should be taken in selecting the leader. He should be daring and know the terrain perfectly, and the exact location of our own troops. The pilots should be chosen for their skill and daring, as there is always danger of collisions when the bombers operate at very low altitudes. When descending to bomb the pilots should "strafe" the objective, to demoralize the enemy and prevent accurate fire from the ground. The observers use their machine guns before and after they have released the bombs.

Chapter X. Combat

52. *General Principles.* The three general tactical principles in order of their importance are:

(a) The effective bombing of the objective.

(b) The reduction of our losses to a minimum.

(c) The inflicting of the greatest losses to enemy aviation. Tactics of day bombardment in combat are, therefore, defensive.

53. Due to the size of a bombing formation, and the slow maneuvers necessary, quick changes of direction and steep dives are impracticable. The bombers must depend upon the nature of their formation, which should be such as to give them fire superiority. The formation should have symmetry, simplicity and compactness, with no dead angles, and should permit a concentration of fire to the rear and below the center. Each pilot must be able to see the leader. A formation so formed, with well trained pilots and observers, can defend itself against superior numbers of the enemy.

54. The formation is limited to the number of airplanes which can be maneuvered by a formation leader. The importance of the objective determines the number of airplanes to be employed in a particular raid. When the number required is greater than can be used in one formation the mission passes from squadron size to that of the

group. The plan of group bombing is analogous to the chain formation employed by pursuit aviation. The several flight leaders are subordinate to the leader of the leading formation, and must make their tactics correspond to his. It is a governing principle that the chain of responsibility must never be broken, from airplane to airplane in the squadron, and from formation to formation in the group. This leads to the question of formation leaders, upon whom the success or failure of operations very largely depends.

Formation Leader

55. A formation leader to be successful must have the absolute confidence of his pilots and observers. Under definite orders at all times, much depends upon his quick decisions and accurate estimates of tactical situations. The tactical situation often changes his plans. The appearance of cloud banks, a change in the direction of the wind, a sudden burst of sunlight, or new methods of attack by the enemy, make it imperative for him to think and act quickly to carry out his mission in the face of altered conditions. He must know just what reliance can be placed on each pilot. He must so arrange his pilots, and the chain of responsibility in the formation, that no matter how great the losses incurred the formation will preserve its units. He must be a model of discipline, and enforce the same from his pilots. Though tempting aircraft targets often appear he must remember that the safety of the formation depends upon its unity, and neither he nor any other pilot should break formation to attack individually. He must sacrifice chances for personal glory in combat to the object of his mission, which is to reach and bomb the objective and return without loss.

Enemy Methods of Attack

56. The deciding element in aerial combat is usually surprise. The enemy will employ all means at his disposal to conceal his approach. His most usual methods are to climb into the sun, and approach from that direction with the advantage of light and altitude. When the enemy gets between a formation and the sun he often escapes detection until he actually opens fire. He will also take advantage of cloud banks to screen his approach. Sometimes when operating as a chain one flight of enemy pursuit airplanes will follow the bombers to attract their attention, while other flights approach unnoticed. His aim is to break up the formation, or at least isolate several of the bombers, and then by concentration to destroy them. Sometimes a single enemy pursuit airplane will fly below and in front of the formation in an attempt to entice a bombing pilot to dive at him. Other enemy airplanes, at greater altitudes, will immediately dive on the bomber thus separated from the formation.

57. Having decided to attack, several of the enemy usually approach from the rear, and open fire at about 200 meters. While the observers are engaged with those at the rear other attacking airplanes will dive under the formation and attack from the dead angle under the tail. This attack is usually directed at the airplanes at the rear of the formation. Other airplanes will dive

rapidly at either side of the formation and rake the whole arm of the V with deflection fire. One, or perhaps two, will try to shoot down the leader, and thus break up the formation. Occasionally when the enemy has vastly superior numbers, he will make a determined rush at the formation. This attack, when made by experienced flights, is very hard to combat, especially if the bombers are inexperienced. An enemy formation sometimes flies parallel to the bombing formation at slightly greater altitude. In an attack of this kind the individual pilots make sudden dives at the flank of the bombers, deliver their bursts, and then sideslip to safety before regaining their positions alongside and above the formation.

Methods of Defense

58. The observer first to sight enemy airplanes fires a rocket of six red stars. The formation tightens up, and the observers fire at the nearest enemy airplanes. Fire is concentrated upon the leading airplanes until they turn back, or are brought down. When this is accomplished fire is brought to bear on the enemy airplanes which venture closest to the formation. During a combat the pilots watch the progress of the fighting by means of mirrors, and endeavor to maneuver their airplanes into the best firing positions for the observers, and at the same time keep their places in formation. The formation leader maneuvers to take advantage of the wind, clouds and sunlight. He should never increase the formation speed beyond that possible to the slowest airplane in the formation. In a group operation he will lead his formation so the guns of the other formations can be brought to bear on the enemy. The leaders of the other formations will maneuver to conform to the necessities of group protection. If an observer has his guns completely jammed, or if he is too badly wounded to operate his guns, the pilot will fly directly below the leader for protection. If a motor is put out of commission the pilot will attempt to regain the lines. The leader can sometimes maneuver a formation to protect a pilot who has been forced to drop out, but no pilot

will leave the formation for that purpose. The leader must always bear in mind the prearranged cooperation with the pursuit, and try to lead the enemy toward the rendezvous. The pursuit airplanes can inflict great losses by attacking when the enemy is engaged with the bombers.

Tactics of a Single Two-Seater

59. When a bombing airplane becomes separated from the formation the pilot and observer generally have to fight their way back to the lines. A large bombing formation attracts enemy pursuit airplanes from over a wide area. Pilots with motor trouble, or forced to drop behind because of broken control wires, are attacked by enemy airplanes from the main combat as well as those which were too late to attack the formation proper. When thus attacked the pilot must fly an irregular course. He must give his observer every chance to fire bursts at favorable targets, and try to reach the lines as quickly as possible. If the attacking airplanes are numerous, and the pilot, considering the disability of his airplane, sees no chance to cut his way through, it is well to make a tight spiral in descending. Often a pilot can risk the accuracy of ground fire if such a maneuver would throw off the attacking airplanes.

Part V. Balloons

Chapter I. Organization

1. The Mobile Army. There should be a balloon company for each division, one for each corps, and three companies as reserve balloons for each army. These companies should be completely motorized in order to assure efficient functioning with the elements of the army with which they are working.

2. Tables of Organization. The details of organization, the amounts and kinds of transportation, and the factors on which the allowance of transportation is based are fixed in the Tables of Organization, Air Service, U.S. Army.

Within a corps, a balloon company should be assigned to each division and one to the corps. These assignments should be permanent or at least continue while the divisions are with the corps, so that perfect liaison can be established.

Chapter II. Information

1. That which is collected in time of peace. This consists of a study of maps, of types of balloons and airplanes of our own and other nations, and of such other information as is available.

2. That which is gathered in time of hostilities. This consists of all information gathered during hostilities by balloon companies at the front. In general this information is only that which is seen from the basket, relative to troop movements, destructions, enemy batteries, infantry actions, information on our own artillery fire, flares, explosions, fires, etc. This information is transmitted to the Information and Operation Sections of the General Staff of the unit with which the balloon is working. The means of communication is usually the telephone, but in the event of the failure of this means, recourse is had to radio-telegraphy, radio-telephony, visual signalling, or runner.

3. The only other reconnaissance which balloon personnel is called upon to make is that by balloon observers in airplanes to make themselves more familiar

with the immediate field of operations.

4. Reports. In addition to routine administrative reports, the following reports are submitted.

(a) By balloon companies to Group Headquarters.

(1) Daily balloon company report.

(2) Observers' ascension report.

(3) Report on enemy balloons.

(4) Daily hydrogen report.

(b) By Balloon Group to Balloon Wing, and to General Staff of unit with which employed.

(1) Daily Balloon Group Report.

(c) By Balloon Wing to Army Air Service Operation Section.

(1) Daily Balloon Wing Report.

Chapter III. Security

Security embraces all those measures taken by a balloon company to protect itself from observation, annoyance, or surprise by the enemy.

(a) From observation. This consists of all the ordinary precautions taken by troops in the field to prevent observation by the enemy. It further consists of all possible efforts to conceal the position of the balloon bed. This is effected by choosing defiladed positions which are also concealed by overhead screens such as trees, vines, etc. It is further effected by the use of vari-colored camouflage balloon fabric. When the balloon is out of its bed, great care should always be taken to leave nothing in the vicinity of the bed which would disclose its position. All machine gun and automatic cannon positions should be screened from observation. When the balloon is in the air, screening should be provided for the winch, tender and personnel from aerial observation. These points cannot be too highly emphasized as they are vitally essential to uninterrupted functioning.

(b) From annoyance. This consists of an equipment of machine guns and automatic cannon on anti-aircraft mounts manned by experienced personnel. As the chief source of annoyance by the enemy is their airplanes, specialists are trained in balloon companies whose only duties are to study continuously types of airplanes and to watch the sky for them. These lookouts and the anti-aircraft armament personnel must be highly trained. Furthermore, balloon company commanders must always arrange to have at least one anti-aircraft artillery battery within protective radius.

(c) From surprise. This consists of the usual precautions against surprise as well as the proper training and functioning of lookouts.

Chapter IV. Marches

A successful march, whether in peace or war, is one that places the company at its destination at the proper moment and in the best possible condition.

In war, marches are of frequent occurrence, and success depends in a great measure upon the skill with which they are conducted.

Balloon companies, being completely motorized, move always as a motor train.

There are two types of marches undertaken by balloon companies: those with the balloon inflated, and those with the balloon packed.

Marches with the balloon packed follow the rules and regulations prescribed for motor trains.

The rate and length of marches with the balloon inflated depend on the tactical situation entirely. The rate is dependent only on the rate of travel of the winch transporting the balloon.

The most common forms of obstacles encountered during a march with balloon inflated are wires crossing the road, camouflaging crossing the road, trees bordering the road, and tall buildings on narrow streets in villages. Wires may be either insulated or high tension, and radio antennae are sometimes found stretching across roads. These latter are usually on very high poles or from the tops of tall trees. It is usually considered advisable in crossing wires to pull the wires down and when the winch has crossed them, to fasten them up immediately. This is far better than cutting the wires and splicing them together afterwards. Sometimes, however, wires must be cut and if they are, they should be immediately repaired. Often, it will be necessary to maneuver the balloon over wires rather than to cut them or let them down, but the first two methods are better if the number of wires is not too great. In maneuvering the balloon over wires, use can be made of the tender in conjunction with the winch, or by throwing the maneuvering ropes over the obstacles one by one and slowly working the balloon over in that manner.

With reference to maneuvering around trees, the height of the trees must be considered, their proximity to the road, extent to which branches reach over road, and the velocity and direction of the wind. The maneuvering spider[12] can usually be used to very good advantage in passing trees, and they may often be maneuvered around by what is known as "jockeying." This consists of taking the opportunity, when the balloon swings back and forth in the wind, of catching it at the right angle and driving quickly past the tree. Most trees, however, can be passed by running the winch on the windward side of the road and by the use of the maneuvering spider. Occasionally the balloon can be put up 100 meters higher than it is usually transported and then hauled down rapidly. This straightens out the cable and to some extent overcomes the action of the

12. The maneuvering spider consisted of several ropes—usually 4 in number, at least 1 inch in diameter to permit firm hand grasp, and usually about 25 feet long—spliced into a common eye which was fastened to the maneuvering block (pulley) through which passed the cable to the balloon. The winch to which the cable was attached was situated some distance from the block, the latter being weighted with sand bags so as to keep it down near, but not touching, the ground. The purpose of the spider was to provide a means of applying manpower to the block. By pulling on the ropes, men could haul down the balloon when the winch was out of order, or they could maneuver the block so as to bring the balloon around an obstacle.

wind on the balloon by the rapid descent. If at the same time the winch moves, the obstacle can be passed.

In passing through villages practically the same means can be used as in traveling along roads bordered with trees.

The usual maneuvering height of a balloon is about 100 meters. This, of course, varies with the wind.

Roads should be reconnoitered before the march so that the best roads can be picked.

In maneuvering with the balloon inflated, the train should be made up as follows:

(a) Light truck ahead carrying telephone material and personnel.

(b) Winch, with winch crew, maneuvering officer, and the balloon.

(c) The tender, transporting men of the maneuvering squad, and machine guns.

(d) The remainder of the trucks, in whatever order is deemed best by the company commander.

It is always more desirable to move by day than by night, but often, due to exigencies of the service, it becomes necessary to make night marches. If this becomes necessary a reconnaissance of the road by daylight is imperative. If it is possible to choose the time of marching, the early morning or the early evening are usually best as there is often a lull in the wind at those times.

Chapter V. Combat

1. Combat Principles.

(a) Duties of Company Commander. In addition to his regular administrative duties, the company commander must be responsible for the proper use of the balloon, its defence, its marches, choosing of new sites, reconnaissance of roads, liaison with units which he is working, communications, and supplies. He is assisted in the execution of these duties by the various officers within the company, but he himself is responsible for their proper accomplishment.

(b) Duties of Maneuvering Officer. The Maneuvering Officer has, under the supervision of the company commander, complete charge of the balloon and its accessories, the protection squad and the winch. He is responsible for the proper safeguarding of the balloon against attack, for the proper posting of his means of defense, for the safety of the observers, and for the housing and precautions against observations for his balloon.

(c) Protection against attack. Machine guns and automatic cannon should be so placed near the point of ascension as to give the best barrage against an attacking plane. Lookouts should be posted at most advantageous points from which they

can scan the sky. They should be close enough to the ascension point, however, to permit of a clear transmission of warning by word of mouth.

(d) Liaison. Group Commanders and Company Commanders should strive at all times to be in perfect liaison with the heavier-than-air units in their sector, the commanding officers of units with which the companies are working and the various section of the General Staff of Corps and Divisions. This is of utmost importance.

(e) Combat Orders should be issued by Group Commanders to their balloons. Those orders should conform to the combat orders of the corps and divisions. They should assign duties, and prescribe routes of movement either forward or rearward.

(f) Army Balloon Wing Commanders are responsible for the reconnaissance of all roads in their sector. Maps should be published showing all roads passable for balloons. We should confer with Signal Officers of units in the Army and arrange so that no overhead wire crosses roads marked on the map "Balloon Roads." He should see to the placing of signs, such as "Balloon Road—No Overhead Wires," on all roads in the army sector which balloons may have to pass.

Offensive Combat

1. During offensive combat, companies assigned to divisions move with the troops of the division. The liaison officer at the divisional P.C. transmits information and orders to the company commander relative to movements. In order to assure a place in the line of march in advance, the balloon company should be attached to a neighboring artillery unit, and move with it. The details of routes and positions are, of course, decided upon before the advance takes place.

2. Being in a position, with liability to move forward, in addition to the regular net of telephone lines, a forward line should be run and a forward telephone central established. The line should be run as far forward as possible, and the advance central placed so that it will be convenient to the next contemplated stop. This facilitates uninterrupted telephone communication with units with which the balloon is working.

Defensive Combat

1. In a defensive sector, all roads to the rear should be reconnoitered and routes established by each company commander. On days when the balloon cannot ascend, the personnel of the company should be utilized to construct balloon beds and positions at intervals along the line of retirement as far to the rear as time permits.

2. As in a advance, telephone lines should be run to the rear, a rear central established, and as many telephone preparations as possible made for successive rearward positions.

Night Combat

1. Balloons cannot do a great deal of work at night. They are able to see flares, signals, etc., but locations cannot ordinarily be accurately determined. By means of an electric signalling device, messages can be sent from balloons to front line positions and to the rear. Balloons can also be used as a receiving point for messages.

Chapter VI. Artillery Adjustments

1. To insure efficient cooperation with Artillery for the regulation of fire, balloon officers should meet with the artillery officers each evening for the purpose of securing detailed information concerning the batteries which will fire the following day and the targets which they will engage. It is a general rule that the evening conference should arrange to divide the observation so that balloons will observe fire for all targets which can be seen from balloons. All other targets will have the fire regulated by the airplanes of an observation squadron. When personal liaison of this kind is impossible the information from the artillery should be obtained by telephone.

2. The balloon observers should know in advance the following:

Coordinates of targets.
Batteries which will fire.
Caliber and number of pieces to fire.
Nature of fire (salvo or one piece at a time).
Type of projectiles with time of flight and type of fuse.
Interval between shots.

3. After securing information concerning the targets the observer should then procure the firing maps and photographs covering the target area.

4. Adjustments are reported on the line battery target. Distances are reported in meters to the "right," "left," "over," and "short," stating first the deflection followed by the range, thus, "25 right," "50 over."

5. Figures are given by their digits, i.e., "two five right," "five zero over."

6. The telephone communication between balloon and battery should conform to the following example:

Battery: "Battery ready to fire."
Observer: "Ready to observe."
Battery: "No. 1 on the way, etc."
"No. 2 on the way, etc."
Observer: "No. 1 two five right, etc."

7. Shots should be reported "lost" if not seen, but reported as "not in position to observe" when the movement of the basket, a passing cloud, or other obstacle prevents a proper view of the target. When a salvo is reported "lost" by an observer the artillery fires the next salvo with data intermediate between that and the last salvo seen and the one lost, but if the report is "not in a position to observe," the salvo is repeated with the same data.

8. In order to observe successfully for several batteries simultaneously, it is necessary to have very efficient fire and telephone discipline; also knowing accurately the batteries which are to fire.

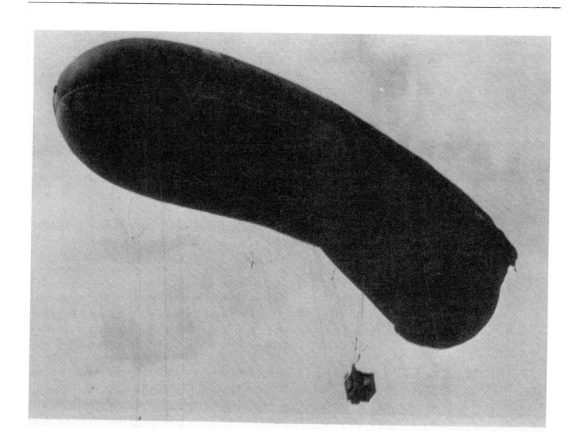

At left, Germans fire a captured French AA gun against Allied balloons.

DH–4. (art by Masami DaiJogo)

A. Funds For Military Aviation[1] 1909–1918

1 Oct 1908	Allotted by Board of Ordnance and Fortifications	25,000[2]
4 Nov 1909	Allotted by Board of Ordnance and Fortifications	5,000[2]
3 Mar 1911	Appropriated by Congress, FY 1912	125,000[3]
24 Aug 1912	Appropriation for FY 1913	100,00
2 Mar 1913	Appropriation for FY 1914	125,000
27 Apr 1914	Appropriation for FY 1915	250,000[4]
4 Mar 1915	Appropriation for FY 1916	300,000
31 Mar 1916	Emergency Appropriation	500,000
29 Aug 1916	Appropriation for FY 1917	13,881,666[5]
14 Feb 1917	Aviation Seacoast Defenses	4,800,000
12 May 1917	Appropriation for FY 1918	10,800,000
12 Jun 1917	Seacoast Defense, Panama Canal	750,000
15 Jun 1917	Emergency Appropriation	43,450,000
24 Jul 1917	Emergency Appropriation	640,000,000
6 Oct 1917	Urgent Deficiency Act	8,300,000[6]
8 Jul 1918	Aviation Stations, Seacoast Defenses	8,000,000
9 Jul 1918	Emergency Appropriation	884,304,758
4 Nov 1918	Appropriation	60,000,000

1. Adapted from chart prepared by Historical Section, Information Group, Air Service, 23 May 1919, in *History of the Bureau of Aircraft Production* (reproduced by Hist. Off., AMC, 1951). Vol I, p 104.
2. For purchase of the Wright plane.
3. $25,000 available immediately.
4. $50,000 available immediately.
5. Includes $600,000 for purchasing land for aviation sites.
6. Allocation from $40,000,000 for Signal Service.

B. Squadron Plans and Programs
1917—1918

Document	Date of Plan or Program	Observation			Pursuit	Bombardment			Total Squadrons	Date for Completion of Plan or Project
		Corps	Army	Total		Day	Night	Total		
	10 Jul 17	15	24	39	15ᵃ			5	59	Dec 18
	18 Sep 17	15	24	80ʰ	120ᶜ			60ᵈ	260	Dec 18
	1 Jan 18	(Ratio of 2 Obs to 6 Pur to 1 Bomb)							100	Dec 18
	6 Feb 18	(100 squadrons of 1 Jan 18 plus 20 bomb)							120	Dec 18
	5 Jun 18	15	24	39	120ᵉ	41	60	101	260	Jun 19
	29 Jul 18	49	52	101	147	55	55	110	358	Jun 19
	16 Aug 18	49	52	101	60	14	27	41	202	Jun 19

ᵃ Ten for corps and 5 for army aviation.
ʰ In addition to corps and army, 41 for strategical aviation.
ᶜ In addition to corps (10) and army (5), 105 for strategical aviation.
ᵈ In addition to army aviation (5), 55 for strategical aviation.
ᵉ Divided between 40 monoplace and 80 biplace.

Index*

* Photo captions indicated by *italic*.

Index

Sloane: 78
Sturtevant: 78
Thomas: 78
trainers: 69, 105
Wright: *10, 39, 68, 70–71*

Airfields
  construction and repair: 156, 171
  enemy strikes against: 146, 162, 387
  identifying: 283
  landing rules: 380
  officer in charge, duties of: 390–91
  railroads, access to: 318
  road systems, access to: 318
  safety equipment at: 380, 384
  site selection and security: 92, 148–49, 156, 184, 192, 243, 291,
      317–18, 383, 386–87
  strikes against enemy: 120, 163, 232, 234, 238–40, 251, 383

Aisne-Marne offensive: 219

Aisne River: 240–41, 247

Alerted flights: 276, 285–86, 289, 292, 372

Allen, James: 14

Altitudes, operational
  aircraft, general: 24, 29, 48, 63, 80, 87, 200, 206
  balloons: 93, 181, 406
  in bombing operations: 397
  in fire control and direction: 308, 337
  in liaison operations: 223, 345
  in pursuit operations: 213–14, 216, 285, 287, 294, 336–37, 370,
      373, 381–82
  in reconnaissance and observation: 211, 283–84, 306, 337, 342

Amanty: 386

American Expeditionary Forces
  expansion program: 219–20
  organization: 127–29
  personnel, numbers and required: 127–29, 135–37
  squadrons as elements of: 192, 263
  staff structure: 125

American Smelter & Refining Co.: 83

Index

Index

Index

Index

Index

Index

Index

Index

Index

Index

Index

Personnel
   assignment and replacement: 163, 322
   number in service and required: 1, 39, 55, 57, 59–60, 89, 96,
      101, 123, 135, 169
   safety measures for: 317
   strength in A.E.F.: 127–29, 135–37
   strength in Army: 27, 38–39, 41, 51, 53, 57, 65

Petain, Henri Philippe: 161

Philippine Islands: 4, 28, 41, 43, 60, 89, 91–92, 95, 101. *See also*
   Corregidor Island; Manila

Photographic officers, duties of: 270, 326, 389–90

Photography, aerial: 49, 63, 86, 99, 101, 117, 120, 181–83, 215,
   234, 238, 240–41, 245, 268–72, 274–75, 279, 326, 329, 340–43,
   346, 382, 388, 392

Photography, aerial, by enemy: 216

Pigeon messages: 183, 199, 334–35

Pilots
   assignments and replacements: 19, 52–53, 223, 324
   battle atmosphere, detachment from: 315, 352
   command and control by: 270
   from enlisted grades: 27, 52–53
   exchange tours: 348
   first military pilot: 17
   in French service: 98, 173
   interrogating: 349, 355
   morale: 311, 381
   number, expansion of: 55
   numbers required: 27
   qualifications, training and efficiency: 37–38, 51–52, 71, 86–87,
      98–99, 146–47, 149–50, 191, 223, 273, 277, 294, 306, 351,
      356, 373, 380–81, 389, 393–94, 400
   reports by: 399

Police officers, duties of: 391

Policing procedures: 319–21

Pont St. Vincent: 146

Port Arthur: 14

Port-sur-Seille: 241, 244

Posts of command. *See* Command posts

Index

Rastadt: 143

Rations. *See* Mess operations

Reber, Samuel: 3, 7, 27, 50, 53, 59, 62–63, 91

Reconnaissance and observation (*see also* Fire control and
   direction; Liaison operations; Photography, aerial
  by aircraft: 23–24, 30–31, 33–35, 38, 47–49, 55, 63, 99, 101,
    117, 120, 177–85, 199, 205–11, 215, 231–45, 322, 329
  alert flights: 276
  altitudes for: 211, 283–84, 306, 337, 342
  by balloons: 23–24, 43–45, 93, 121, 181–85, 202–203, 255–61,
    330, 377, 403–404
  of bridges: 256
  capabilities and limitations: 182, 184, 303–306
  by cavalry: 23, 25, 34
  combat, avoiding: 330, 346, 350
  in convoys and marches: 319
  cover and concealment from: 305 (*see also* Camouflage)
  cooperation with Allies: 238
  coordination among aircraft: 182
  crew, number in: 270
  defined: 23
  by dirigibles: 24, 45
  enemy attacks against: 242
  by enemy, preventing: 213, 231–32, 240, 244, 247–49
  of enemy elements: 341–44
  facts reported: 256, 340–41
  false reports: 306
  formations: 350–51
  of friendly elements: 341, 345
  grenade assaults, identifying: 258
  by ground forces: 34
  ground forces, estimates of: 256–57
  ground forces, support of: 35
  importance stressed: 57, 59, 216, 315, 330–31, 334
  information, scope and sources of: 331–32
  of lines of communication: 275
  logging procedures: 256, 324
  maps, value in: 272–73
  Mitchell views on: 9–12
  mission assignments and execution: 182–83, 225, 232–34, 238,
    255–56, 258, 269, 273–75, 280, 284, 295–98, 332–33, 340–46
  Motor vehicles, estimates of: 257
  of naval forces: 35, 45

Index

Index

Index

Index

Index

Index

Made in the USA
Columbia, SC
18 August 2021